Kelley Lynn Shepherd

Copyright © 2018 Kelley Lynn Shepherd

All rights reserved. No part of this publication may be reproduced, distributed, or transmitted in any for or by any means, including photocopying, recording, digital scanning, or other electronic or mechanical methods without the prior written permission of the author, except in the case of brief quotations embedded in critical reviews and certain other noncommercial uses permitted by copyright law. For permission requests, please address the author.

This book was first published on June 7, 2018 via CreateSpace independent Publishing Platform.

ISBN: 9781720670612

My Husband is Not a Rainbow:
The Brutally Awful, Hilarious Truth about Life, Love, Grief, and Loss

Kelley Lynn Shepherd

with forewords by Michele Neff Hernandez and Caitlin Kelly
with Book Cover Art and Rainbow Art by Kevenn T. Smith

*This book is dedicated to
the life, the death, and the memory
of Don Shepherd*

*I will meet you inside
the rhythms of the music*

About the Pen Name

My given name at birth was Kelley Lynn Niemi. I'm half Italian, and half Finnish. Everyone on earth pronounces or misspells my last name, ever since I was a kid. At some point during or after college, once I got really serious with the stand-up comedy, writing, and acting stuff, I decided to just use my first and middle name as my professional/stage name. I dropped the Niemi for business cards, resumes, and the like. I went by Kelley Lynn, and it stuck. When I married my husband Don in 2006, I thought about changing my last name to his: Shepherd. I tossed the idea around, and he did too. We said it out loud together, "Kelley Lynn Shepherd." I kind of liked it. His exact words were, "It sounds like some honky-tonk redneck country-western singer. Ladies and gentlemen of the Grand Ole Opry, please welcome back Kelley Lynn Shepherd!" As usual, he was right.

Some time went by after our wedding, and I got lazy. It seemed like an awful lot of hassle and process to go through legally, to change my last name. I didn't know if it would be confusing to still go by "Kelley Lynn" professionally, yet I didn't really want to change my professional name. Don didn't seem to mind one way or the other, so in the end, I just never changed my name, and life was life, and it didn't have any impact on anything whatsoever.

And then he died. Those first few sympathy cards I got in the mail from friends or family who had just assumed my name was Shepherd - it tore me to pieces seeing it written out that way, "Kelley Lynn Shepherd," and knowing it wasn't true. I started to have so much regret and sadness that I never officially became a Shepherd; that my name wasn't legally attached or connected to his. For years after his death, I cried about this and felt like nothing could make me feel any better about it. I felt like crap

Kelley Lynn Shepherd

for not taking my husband's name out of pure laziness. What kind of horrible wife is too lazy to change her name?

And then one day, I thought, "Oh my god! The book! What better place to finally be Kelley Lynn Shepherd - as the author of these pages that tell our story." And so it was, and so it is, that I am honored to bear his name, here and only here, in this sacred and special place. This book is dedicated to my beautiful, dead husband; Don Shepherd. For loving me. For choosing me. For teaching me. And for showing me, still, and all my days forward, all the many ways that love truly never dies. I love you - Until Forever.

My Husband is Not a Rainbow

Foreword Number One

Dear Reader,

In your hand, you hold a story about life-changing love, untimely death, and one woman's courageous effort to rebuild her life in the aftermath.

As I write these words, I wonder about you. Who are you, and why did you choose to read this book? Are you holding this book in your hands because you've lived through your own loss experience? Maybe you are reading these words because Don Shepherd changed your life, and you miss him. Perhaps Kelley is your daughter, sister, aunt, niece, neighbor, friend, colleague, or you may be one of her many fans. Did you know her before she met Don, before he died? Do you miss the woman she was before grief walked into her life? Maybe you never knew Don or Don and Kelley, but you've come to know Kelley Lynn in her "after" and have laid a brick in the foundation on which she is building her next amazing life. However you came to be here, I'd like to greet you one by one.

I've lived through my own loss experience: I am so sorry. Your life will never be the same again. I acknowledge this fact because so few people do. How can your life be the same when a person you love no longer walks the earth? Isn't it odd that you can live for a long time thinking of death only in the abstract? Death remains a distant reality until the day you realize that someone you love will never again walk through the door, answer your phone call, forward a funny email, or wrap you in their arms. Death sharpens your view of life in a painfully clear way, as if you are looking through a kaleidoscope pointed directly at the sun. For a time, that flash of light and color blinds you, and then slowly, day by painful day, your sight returns. But you suddenly see the world with bionic eyes. Everything will be different in your post-loss life, because surviving the death of someone you love changes you. But here is the secret; you've been changed not only by grief, but by love. Grief and love are two sides of the same coin. The good news is that love is what remains when the grief subsides. The proof of that fact will unfold page by page, I promise.

Don Shepherd changed my life: There are so many people who miss and love Don. I never met him, and yet, through Kelley Lynn's words, and yours, his kind, quirky, devoted spirit populates the world, still. Don was a gift to you, and you to him. That love lives on in you. Please do the world a favor; tell Don stories, say his name aloud, and change someone else's life in the way he changed yours. Every time you do one of these things, Don's legacy grows as you create your own. I know this book will be a gift to you, and I sincerely hope that you will share whatever unique gifts you find within these pages with the world.

Kelley Lynn was part of my life before Don died: Do you miss the person she used to be? If so, it's okay. I am sure she misses that girl, too. When someone we love dies, there are so many secondary losses to mourn. One of the most significant is the loss of innocence that accompanies grief. Once someone close to you dies, death will never again be a distant reality. A bereaved person has to adapt to the ever present possibility that someone else they love will die. The only question is when? Those days of living free from the keen awareness of the fragility of life are blissful, and fleeting.

Yes, Kelley has changed, but the person who is emerging from this loss experience is deeper, richer, braver, stronger, and more beautifully complex. I hope you take the time to get to know this version of Kelley. If you can somehow let go of your expectation that she will return to the way she was, you will be given the gift of witnessing her evolution. The pages that follow are just one step in her evolutionary process. There is much more to come, and I hope that if she invites you along for the ride, you welcome the opportunity. You won't be sorry.

You are part of Kelley Lynn's "after": I have a feeling Kelley marks time in the same adapted way many bereaved people do: BD (before death) and AD (after death). The people who have come into her life AD are a part of the world she is creating for herself while reimagining a future that was stolen by death. Many of you found Kelley because of her willingness to publicly speak her truth. She doesn't sugarcoat her experience of grief, and she doesn't shy away from using her real life as the foundation for her artistic expression. While her You Tube antics are well-documented, Kelley's generous spirit and willingness to help people in need are her most valuable gifts. Her legacy will be built on kindness, creativity, a unique ability to connect people, and a disarming, vulnerable honesty. Those of you who met her AD are the first beneficiaries of the lessons she has learned from grieving the loss of her Don. My hope is that you take courage from her courage; that you see her truth telling as permission to speak your own truth; that you allow yourself to benefit from the connections she makes so effortlessly; and that through her disarming honesty, you discover a sense of hope for your own future.

So what about me? How did I come to be writing this introduction? The road to here began in January of 2000 when I fell in love with a soft-spoken, loyal, hilarious, stunningly handsome man whose love changed the trajectory of my life. In a completely unlike myself act of lunacy, I married that man after a six month courtship. Our whirlwind romance stunned our family and friends, but somehow felt exactly right to the two of us. I will be forever grateful for the craziness that led me to walk down a dirt aisle on a beautiful June day into the arms of a man I would share my life with for a short five years. Phillip Hernandez was killed in a cycling accident 1,871 days after I married him.

Kelley Lynn Shepherd

There is a strange balance to the fact that Phil's love so greatly altered my life and that grieving his death created an equally powerful alteration. I will never forget the first time I was referred to as Phil's widow. I looked over my shoulder to see who was being introduced, because my 35-year old brain could not process the fact that the word 'widow' applied to me. That five letter word stuck in my throat whenever I tried to say it aloud. Not me. Not me. Not me. Eventually, my revulsion turned to obsession, and I researched how to be a widow, what to wear, what to do. If being a widow was unavoidable, I wanted to be the best widow possible.

Of course, at the end of my exhaustive search, I learned that there is no right way to be a widow. I was so disappointed! I desperately wanted some sort of checklist to guide me along my path and to find something or someone who would answer all of my questions. How would I know when to take off my wedding ring? When would I stop crying every five minutes? Was I supposed to clean out our closet? Did the fact that Phil's toothbrush was still sitting next to mine a year after he died mean I was crazy? The only people I could think of to ask were other widowed people, but I didn't have a clue where to find them.

Turns out, they found me. I told a few friends that I wanted to interview other widows, and a transformative journey began. Once word of mouth got moving, I met with a new widow twice a month for one year. At the completion of each interview, the answer I was seeking became more and more clear; there is no right way to be a widow. As the realization dawned that there were hundreds of thousands of ways to process the death of a spouse or partner, I came to appreciate the value of having a widowed community. Access to other widowed people's stories normalized my own. Witnessing the survival of so many people who lived through the death of the person with whom they'd planned their future became living proof that there was hope for me, too.

After coming to this life-changing realization, I felt responsible to share the community that I'd accidentally created with as many widowed people as possible. I wanted every single widowed person in the world to know that there were other folks, just like them, who were making their way through the death of their partner or spouse. I became driven by a passion I'd never before experienced to serve a specific group of people, my people, widowed people. Soaring Spirits International is an organization I founded to ensure that my people would be able to find each other, and in doing so, find a piece of themselves.

The revulsion I once felt when the word widow was first applied to me has been replaced by a fierce pride. I've met thousands and thousands of widowed people over the past ten years, and each of them has added a new dimension to my understanding of the widowed experience. I've come to believe that the word widow is an extremely powerful word. Widowed people aren't victims, we are survivors. We aren't eternally broken, we are evolving. We aren't half of a whole, we are complete in ourselves. We aren't unloved, we are eternally loved. We aren't weak, we are so much stronger than even we imagined.

I wish that reading the above words would offer some kind of magic balm to any of you who are grieving the death of a loved one, but they won't. Grieving is hard work, that's just true. But I know for sure that finding a community WILL make walking each day through the loss of your loved one a little easier to do. You will know where to turn when you need to be understood, when you want to know that you are not alone.

Kelley Lynn is providing you that very assurance, here, within the pages of her book. Her words may sound a lot like the voice in your head. On some pages you may wonder how she was able

Kelley Lynn Shepherd

to write down the very thoughts that keep you awake at night. I suspect there will be tears rolling down your cheeks now and again; for Kelley, for Don, for yourself, and for someone you love whose memory reverberates in your heart as you read her words. That's the whole point really, to connect each of us one to the other, and to remember together the ways in which love, and grief, have changed us - in many ways, for the better.

In every grief experience throughout our lives, we have the opportunity to stand mesmerized by the closed door presented by a death, or to seek out the window opened by life. My sincere hope is that Kelley's words give you permission to lean against that closed door for however long you need, and also the inspiration to seek out the window that life has cracked open just for you.

Michele Neff Hernandez
Founder and Executive Director at Soaring Spirits International
www.soaringspirits.org

Foreword Two: Electric Boogaloo

I went into the field of grief-counseling after seven years of working with adolescents in a school setting. I realized that many of the young people I was seeing simply needed someone to talk to when there was the loss of a parent, friend, grandparent, pet - the list goes on. Loss is loss, and when it's happening to you, it hurts - and often nobody wants to listen. They want the person to "move on," or in the case of younger adolescents, their friends tell a much worse story about their own loss (sort of an Olympics of who has more pain). Not very helpful.

It seemed to me that grief work was simply being present in the room and encouraging the person to remember and celebrate the life of the person (or pet, or life scenario) that they lost. I would ask to see a picture, ask them about the person's laugh, talk about some funny stories, have them write the person a letter. Sometimes, we'd walk to the river and send off a balloon with a note for the person. I would do instinctively what I felt the person needed at that time. It seemed to help, and yet, I thought, there must be more to this. Right?

That's when I decided to attend an Advanced Certificate Program to compliment my work with kids. It turned out to be a very scholarly approach for the most part. We read book after book about how people process grief as "tasks." We learned that Dr. Kulber-Ross wasn't studying people who were grieving, she was studying her own patients who were dying, so what she had to say about the "stages" was not valid in terms of helping grieving people. We learned many valuable things, and I'm glad I had the training. But when it came to working with grieving people, I found that the way I was working was just fine; that meeting someone where they are in the process is where you begin, and from there, you follow them. That's how I work. I don't lead anyone to anything. I follow and hope, here and there, to add some insight to help someone get through the really hard times.

One day my own supervisor and brilliant therapist wrote to me about a young woman whose husband had died suddenly. Because I had studied a good deal about sudden death and trauma, I guess she thought I was the person to call. My supervisor told me the young woman was an actress and comedian and writer and that she had NO money. She really needed someone who could do grief work with her now. My supervisor said: "I'm telling you - this person is YOURS. You are who she needs. I know it." I trusted her and said, "Okay. Have her call me."

That began my work with Kelley. We spoke over the phone briefly. I warned her that I cursed a lot, so I hoped that was okay, and let's not worry about the money just now. We met and started working right away. Kelley knows more about all of the details of our many sessions, because she has a phenomenal memory, but I will say that our early work ran the gamut of emotions - sometimes laughing, crying, arguing, my saying things she didn't like, her losing confidence in herself, sometimes her losing hope in ever feeling good again, and many times - my feeling absolutely powerless to help her. Sometimes her pain was almost palpable in the room.

Over the years, I began to see amazing changes that she also recognized in herself. She'd always been very astute regarding her level of self-awareness, but she was beginning to fine tune that somehow. She's worked tirelessly on knowing and loving herself. Although the inner-struggle never seems to be completely over, because that's how life works, nevertheless a strong, confident, resilient, and very caring person has come out on the other side of all her pain. It's as if she's reinvented herself.

Kelley is heroic in my eyes, because she wants to share who she is, warts and all, with everyone who has experienced loss. She is a person who was forever changed by the love of her dear husband Don and the man that he was, which I believe was ultimately his most important gift to her. I think she actually completed "task four" from my grief-counseling school days; she's found an enduring connection to Don while embarking on a continued new life. Her new insights, born of loss and hard work, are pure gold. She makes me proud every day that I know her.

Caitlin Kelly, MSEd, LMHC
Advanced Grief Counseling

Kelley Lynn Shepherd

Enough With the Introductions Already. Here's Another Introduction - MY Introduction, To MY Damn Book:

We live in a world where "Snooki" has written *four* books without even breaking a Jersey sweat; yet I had to pull together a crowdfunding campaign and beg my friends and strangers for donations on the internet just to have even the slightest chance at completing and self-publishing this very important book. (and you all came through for me, and I love you for it.)

We live in a world where some random dude online created a Kickstarter campaign called "Potato Salad," in which his entire purpose was to "make some potato salad." (Hilarious, by the way.) He had a fundraising goal of $10. He raised over $50,000 and has been featured in numerous TV shows and articles, all for doing nothing except being a smart-ass. Meanwhile, I couldn't get one lousy agent to read or publish or financially back my story. I suppose that's because my story was lacking in mayonnaise, and heavy on the uncomfortable sorrow.

We live in a world where the person you love most on earth dies, and people insist you "get over it" just weeks and months after everything you know has been shattered and thrown back into your eyeballs. People speak to you in condescending tones about the "stages" of grief, or the "journey" you are about to embark on after the death of your loved one. What a bunch of crap. Grief is not a journey. Journeys are filled with adventure and fun and wonder, and maybe you even pack up some snacks and beverages to take along the way, or a map so that you know where you might be going. Sometimes you even take along a friend or two for the ride, because it's going to be a super fun adventure.

Grief is not a journey. Grief is a fucking tsunami. It's a massive pile of shit and bones and wreckage that someone hurls into the center of your living room one day when you're watching TV and not prepared. Grief makes you claw and fight and scream, even though you can't remember how the hell to breathe anymore, and you no longer know who you even are. Grief takes every fragment of what you used to be - and the life you used to have - and hoards it away in some unreachable attic, never to be seen again. Grief is a psychotic tornado; living inside a blizzard, hiding in a dark alley.

I wrote this book for one reason; because nobody else did. Every single book about death and grief that I tried to read in those first few months of hell made me feel more alone than ever. None of the things they talked about applied to me, and everything seemed to be written in this unauthentic, plastic-coated, masking of the truth. Where was the brutal honesty about what this really actually feels like? Where was the talk of all the humiliating and terrifying emotions that one goes through? Where was the rawness, the constant shifts in mood, or the loop in your head that whispers: *this pain will never, ever go away*. Where was the talk of all the people who disappear from your life when your husband dies, or the truly embarrassing stuff like not being able to masturbate after his death for years, because your fantasies are all about a dead guy, and that's a little creepy when you're trying to get off. Where was all of that when I needed and still need a book that I can relate to? It was nowhere. And now, it is here.

Are you with me so far? Have I frightened you away? No? Good. I'm glad you decided to stay. Now, since this is the "introduction" part of the book, and since this book is probably nothing at all like any other book about death and love and grief that you've ever read, let me take a few short paragraphs of your time to explain how to go about reading it. I do this, not because I think my readers are morons, but because this book is written in several different formats, and in a rather unique way. The book follows me in real time, starting from a couple days before the sudden death of my husband, for about six full years. That part of the book, my life in the aftermath, is written in real time. Here's the general breakdown:

Facebook Posts: On the morning of my husband's sudden death, after informing immediate family and a few close friends by phone, I posted a status update to Facebook from the restroom of the hospital. It seemed like the most logical way to let everyone know what had happened all at once. That post turned into many more posts over the following days, weeks, months, and years - as Facebook became a huge part of my process. It's where I went, in the very beginning especially, to write out all my many emotions. So, I have taken many of the Facebook posts and put them directly into this book. They are unedited and untouched, and all appear in the sequential, real-time order in which they were posted. You will know you are reading a Facebook post, because underneath each one will be the number of likes and comments, to help identify it.

Blog Pieces: A few months or so after Don's death, I decided to start a blog about everything I was feeling. People were asking me to, and lots of people seemed to want to read what I had to write. The blog (www.ripthelifeiknew.com) has grown significantly in popularity over time. I have taken many of the blog posts, some untouched, and others slightly edited or shortened, and put them into this book. You will know you are reading a blog piece, because they always have titles.

"Dear Stupid Death Diary" and "Dear Dead Husband" posts: Although writing my thoughts on Facebook has been very helpful throughout this process, I also didn't want to be posting there every ten minutes and have an overkill (see what I did there?) of death posts. So, many times, I would jot down my more personal thoughts into a notebook or journal, or a letter to my dead husband, and keep it private. I want people to know the raw truth about what it's like to go through this and the types of things that go through a grieving person's mind - so I am including lots of those entries in this book. They are completely unedited, uncensored, and brutally honest.

Caitlin Sessions: My grief-counselor, Caitlin Kelly, as you read, wrote one of the two Forewords in this book. She has been a big part of my life these past few years, and our sessions have helped me greatly. She is very smart and intuitive and has a quiet brilliance to what she says and how she says it. Many times, when a particular session we had was something I felt would be helpful to others as well, I have posted our dialogue on my Facebook page. Each time I did this, the response was amazingly positive. I have come to realize that a lot of people do not have access to any sort of grief counseling, and a lot of people have mediocre or horrific support. So, if posting snippets from our sessions that may contain a message universal to others helps even one person reading this, that makes me very happy. It makes Caitlin happy too, since she is very much okay with me including some of our dialogue in this book. Please keep in mind that all of the session dialogue is written in snippets, and written completely by memory, so the conversation order or exact wording may not be exactly what was said, but what I remember. I did not record our sessions, but I do have an excellent memory, and took notes the minute I got back on the subway to go home each time. Those notes then became these pieces. I saw Caitlin professionally for about 3 years, almost every single Monday afternoon, and then slowly tapered off to seeing her less often, as needed. A lot of our sessions will remain private, between the two of us, but I've chosen to share a handful in this book that I feel the readers will get something out of. You will know you are reading a counseling session snippet because it will be written out like a conversation and will be titled *Session Snippet*.

Our Story: The story of me and Don Shepherd. How we met. Highlights from our time together. The proposal. Our wedding. The day he moved in. The little things. Big things. The exact moment in time that I knew I could trust this man with my life, and that he would be my husband. The amazing, beautiful, powerful love that existed, and exists, between two people. A lot of this will also be written in dialogue form, because Don was a hilarious motherfucker, and we had a lot of very funny and absurd conversations. In order to fully comprehend how devastating this loss was for me, you have to comprehend Don Shepherd, and who he was as a person. Hopefully, this book will help the world to do that. My idea to go back and forth in time, between the day to day in the aftermath of his death, and backwards to our love story - was an original idea, four or five years ago, when I began writing this book. This past year, a little show called *This Is Us* blew up everyone's TV screens, and as soon as I saw it, I screamed: "Hey! That's how my book is written!!!" So when you think to yourself as you are reading this - "Hey! She stole that concept from the show!" - Nope. *They* stole it from *me*. I did it first. Dammit. (I'm not mad. Just please put me on your show as an actor, and all will be forgiven.) Just know, that before there was Jack Pearson, there was Don Shepherd. And you are going to fall in love with him.

Rainbows: Those of you who are reading this who have never read my blog or followed my standup comedy and have no idea why the name of this book is what it is, will know the whole story behind the rainbow in just a few short non-chapters. Once you have read the rainbow story, you will understand about the running joke throughout this book about rainbows and rainbow pictures. There will be a few drawings/sketches of actual rainbows, seen and submitted by people from all over. The sketches will be drawn in black and white, and you or your kids can use crayons or markers to "color in your own Don rainbow" on each one. My original idea was to include the actual photos people have sent to me of real rainbows they have seen, but doing so would make this a color book, and a color book costs about 400 million dollars to publish and print and manufacture, so I'd have to sell my book at around $50 a copy just to NOT lose money. That is dumb, so I'm not doing that. Instead, you're getting a real-life rainbow coloring book inside of this great big awesome book. Later on in the book, you will find out where to go online to see the full slideshow of rainbow photos. All sketches in this book were drawn by my friend and very talented artist, Kevenn T. Smith, who also created the amazingly cartoonish and beautiful book cover art and image (Our cats, over the years, are seen pictured with Don, on the cover, under the rainbow.).

There are a few other things you will find in the reading of this book; such as love letters between me and my husband (before he was my husband), short quotes and words about grief and love and death, from some of my friends I've met through loss; and words of love from many friends and family, eulogizing and sharing stories and memories about the life of Don Shepherd.

The book begins at the very moment that this death occurred, and follows my process for just around six years' time, with higher focus during some time periods than others. Please note that, due to privacy issues, some names have been removed or slightly altered. Please also keep in mind that I had to pick and choose what was most important to include, over a six year span of life in the aftermath of loss. In order to protect the privacy and anonymity of others, some situations are mentioned in general tones without much detail. This is especially the case when it comes to speaking about situations or people that are no longer in my life.

As the reader, you have a front row seat into the mind and heart of someone who has just lost her entire world and how that mind and heart processes, changes, evolves, changes again, and transforms. You will notice, as you read, that the tone and style of writing begins to alter as time goes on in living with this loss. My hope is that this book will give you a much greater understanding into what this is really like, and that it will help others to be less judgmental when standing in witness to someone's pain. If you are reading this book, and you are one of the people who HAS been through a life-altering loss, or you are going through it now, then my hope for you is that just one thing I say in these pages can comfort you or put you in a place of peace, even for just a little while. I hope that while reading this, and for a long time afterward, you will feel less alone and you will recognize pieces of your own tsunami in these writings. As Red stated in the last line of my very favorite movie, *The Shawshank Redemption,* "I hope."

We begin our tsunami in the most logical of places;

The end.

My Husband is Not a Rainbow

FB Post: (July 3rd, 2011): Hubby and I had a great, fun day with our friends John and Jessica. Thank you so much for coming over and hanging out with us, and for bringing me my favorite thing in the world - cupcakes from Magnolia Bakery in NYC! John, I'm sorry that your Mets continue to suck and lose to the Yankees. Wait, no I'm not. BAHAHAHAHA!!! I love my weird, awesome friends.
LIKES: 28   COMMENTS: 9

FB Post: (July 8th, 2011): The 'Opie and Anthony Show' today was talking about the saddest songs ever. I'd love to know the ones on your list that make you cry or sad. Mine are: The Diary by Bread, Bring Him Home from Les Miserables, Hurt by Johnny Cash, Don't Cry Daddy by Elvis, In the Ghetto by Elvis, and My Beloved Wife by Natalie Merchant. There are more, but these come to mind. What are yours?
LIKES: 34   COMMENTS: 25

FB Post: (July 11, 2011): I seriously might have a heart attack from laughing after watching the season premiere of 'Curb Your Enthusiasm.' The scene with Larry David instructing a pre-teen Girl Scout through the bathroom door how to insert a tampon was SO wrong, so inappropriate, and so brilliantly funny. I'm so happy this show is finally back.
LIKES: 17   COMMENTS: 6

FB Post: (July 13, 2011): This is the worst and saddest day of my life. My husband Don went into cardiac arrest and died this morning. He was at his 2nd job and they found him on the floor. He was only 46 and he was my everything. I dont know how else to tell people except this way. Im at Palisades Hospital. I dont even know what to do next
LIKES: 30   COMMENTS: 268

Kelley Lynn Shepherd

The End

On July 13, 2011, everything disappeared, and I got a brand new life. It was not a life I asked for or wanted. It was not a life I understood. It was the life that was handed to me without warning. This life hit me smack in the face at about 6:30 AM, when I was jarred awake by a phone ringing over and over and over again. My husband had gone to work at 4:30 AM or so that morning, and because it was insanely early, he never liked to wake me up to say good morning or goodbye. He always wanted me to get my sleep, because he knew how hard it was for me to sleep. He had picked up a second job at the local Petsmart, stocking dog and cat food and pricing things, to pay off his recent and very expensive dental bill, so that we could save up and eventually afford a new car, and then maybe move into a better apartment together. That was the plan, to finally let go of his '97 Grand Prix Pontiac that had been giving us issues for a while and finally get a new car. He was going to quit the second job as soon as the bill was paid down. He was trying to support his family. Me. Us. He was really tired, but he never once complained. Never. He even somehow found the time to volunteer once a week, on his day off, at that same Petsmart - helping at the rescue and adoption center for cats and dogs. My husband always took care of everyone. Especially me.

I rolled out of bed, half asleep still, and dialed into my voicemail to see who was calling me over and over so early. "This is Palisades Hospital with an urgent call for Kelley Niemi. Please call us back immediately." My hands shook as I called the number listed on my caller I.D. The voice on the phone sounded far away and cold. "You need to get here right away. We have your husband." My voice was barely audible. "What do you mean you have him? He just left for work an hour ago. Is he okay? Are you at his work? What's going on?" The woman on the other end remained calm. "We have your husband here," she repeated. "Can you get here? Do you have a car? We can send

My Husband is Not a Rainbow

someone to come for you if you don't have..." I cut her off. "My husband took the car to work." I hung up. I don't know why I hung up. I couldn't think logically, all of a sudden. Something inside me knew this was awful and terrifying news, but I didn't know what. But I did know, because I'm married to a man in EMS, and I remembered him telling me how if someone dies or there's a sudden accident or something traumatic, the hospital never tells you over the phone. They aren't allowed to. They have to do it in person. Something about the shock of the news, is what he told me. I paced back and forth across the floors of our apartment, saying out loud to nobody and to the universe: "No. This isn't happening. This isn't happening. This isn't happening." But it was happening. And it couldn't be stopped. The tsunami had busted through and into my life.

I must have called a taxi service, although I don't recall that taking place. Somehow though, minutes later, I was in a cab that was going to the ER. I was completely alone, and everything was spinning and cloudy. The hospital is only about a three minute drive from our apartment, but this man hit every traffic light, and time seemed to freeze on this literal ride to my brand new life. When we finally arrived, money somehow appeared in my hand that I tossed at him, and I sprinted out of the cab and into the ER waiting room doors.

Everything that happened next and since then is a blur, and yet, very specific. It's in slow motion, yet seemed to go by in sixty seconds. As I stood at the front desk in the waiting room, the woman on the phone said under her breath to someone, "She's here," and then hung up. Seconds later, a gaggle of nurses and one important-looking doctor all came walking toward me very slowly. They looked like a medical mafia of some kind, and it reminded me of Michael Jackson's "Beat It" video. Why is everyone paying so much attention to me? Surely there are other, much more important emergencies happening in this ER than whatever it is that happened to my husband.

Kelley Lynn Shepherd

You know on TV when they take the person's wife or husband into a special room off to the side, close the door, ask them to "please sit down," and then say a whole bunch of scrambled words that end with, "cardiac arrest... we tried to get him back... we did all we could... he is one of us, this is a tough one for all of us here... he didn't make it... I'm so very sorry." Yeah. That is exactly what happened. Except it wasn't a TV show. It was me. I was the one sitting there, trying not to faint. Trying not to suffocate. It is a good thing they tell you to sit down. The animalistic cry that came out of me upon hearing the words, "he didn't make it," was a sound I had never heard before, and it scared me. I frightened myself with my own cries of terror. I flew forward in my chair, my knees violently knocking against the hardwood floor with a crack. I wanted to throw up or run away or both, but nothing in my body would let me move off the floor. One of the nurses held onto me as I thrashed at her and screamed into her arm over and over and over, "NOOOOOOO!!!!!" It was as if someone else was screaming that. Someone else was pounding their fists on the cold hard floor in front of them. Someone else was yelling the word NO over and over into a long, dark tunnel. Someone else was dry-heaving and thinking of ways to escape and hitting every single thing in sight, even the air. That had to be someone else. But it wasn't. It was me.

Someone gave me bottled water. Someone else gave me a washcloth of some kind to put on my face, as if luke-warm wetness on my cheekbones was going to be so soothing, that I would say with delight, "My husband is dead, but boy oh boy is that water refreshing!"

My hands and arms were shaking. My eyebrows were sweating. Everything was sweating. The cheap fluorescent light on the ceiling made my head ache, and looking at the floor made me feel dizzy. I didn't know where to go or what to do next.

My Husband is Not a Rainbow

Everything felt uncomfortable, like I had suddenly forgotten how to sit in a chair properly. A woman asked me to sip water again, but I couldn't. I physically couldn't. The lukewarm water made me want to vomit. She asked who could she call for me, or did I want to call them myself. Oh my god. People. Calling people. I have to call people and actually tell them *this*. I took my phone from my purse and tried finding numbers for Don's sisters, but didn't have either of them in my contact list. This panicked me, and I started crying. My fingers were sweating, and I couldn't grip the phone. Still shaking. Another nurse came into the room with a large manila envelope. I've seen this before on cop shows. It had Don's things in it. His keys. Wallet. Phone. I had no idea how to use his phone. It kept beeping and making noises as I tried to find his contact list and his sisters' numbers. The only number I could recall in that moment was my husband's cell number, which was useless, and my parents' home number in Massachusetts. I don't know how we finally figured out the numbers, but we did, I guess. It all became a blur. My life is now a blur.

As we figured out the numbers, I stood in a tiny hallway next to the tiny room they brought me into, because my cellphone was starting to lose signal in the tiny room, and it desperately needed to be charged. I called my good friend John. No answer. Holy shit. I have to leave this AS A VOICEMAIL??? I had no choice. I think I said something like, "I'm at the hospital, and Don is dead. Can you please get our friends together and come be with me or get me or something? My phone is dying. Thanks." These are the kinds of things you say, when in absolute shock.

A slew of calls were made by the nurses, from a landline phone inside the tiny room. Don's sisters. My parents. I thought to myself: "Thank god Don's mother is already dead, because this might have killed her." The nurse put me on the line with my mom, who was too shocked for words, and mentioned that my dad wouldn't be able to get out of his work shift in time to make the four hour trip to New Jersey with her, but that she was on her way. When I first told her that Don had a heart attack and was dead, she screamed, "Whaaaaattt????" into the phone really loudly. It was actually comical. Nurses kept walking in and out of the room and trying to feed me water.

A few minutes went by. I guess. A doctor came in and sat across from me. He looked like Anthony Edwards from the show "E.R.," but he had really hairy knuckles and fingers. His glasses were all steamed up, and he looked like a huge nerd as he said words to me that sounded a lot like: "Mmmyyhpgbyhuggh nnnnbh ytukerptt." It was like the teacher from the Peanuts comic strips. "Waah waah waah waah." I don't know what he said. Something about how my husband was "one of them," because he was a local EMT, and how they did everything they could to save him, and how they were able to "bring him back" a couple of times, but then he was gone again. He mentioned something about organ donation and seemed to be asking me a question, but I couldn't focus and kept staring at his hairy knuckles. The hair was so thick, it looked like it was dancing on top of his fingers.

Some more time went by. I think. A lot of time. Do I really have to go back home at some point? I wonder if I can just put a futon bed in here and live inside this tiny room from now on. If I don't leave this room, then I don't have to deal with anything outside of it, right? Yeah.

A few of Don's EMS brothers and supervisors showed up a bit after that, and we went into a different, slightly less tiny room, where they sat with me and cried with me and helped me to make some decisions that I really had no idea how the hell to make. They helped me decide whether or not to donate my husband's organs and tissues and eyes. For some reason, maybe because he was in a rush when he moved here from Florida to New Jersey back in 2005, he never put that he wanted to be a donor on the back of his license. However, I felt in my heart somewhere, that it would be something he would want to do. I just kept thinking about driving Ginger, our three year old kitty, to the vet ER in the middle of the night in 2010. She had thrown a blood clot while chasing her sister, Autumn, around the apartment, and the news wasn't good. When the doctor came into the little tiny room they had put us in where bad news happened, and showed us the x-rays, Don started to cry. He knew she wasn't going to make it. He took my hand and traced it along the x-ray, showing me and explaining to me her fate. "See, Boo? Her heart was too big, and it was cutting off the oxygen to her lungs. My poor sweet girl was dying this whole time and didn't even know. She was totally fucked."

Later, when the doctor left us alone in the tiny room after they had put Ginger to sleep, Don cried hard into my arms and said with all seriousness, "I wish I could have given her a piece of my heart, Boo. I wish my heart could have saved her. I would have done it in a second to save my sweet girl." Knowing who Don was, recalling that memory, and with the support of his EMS supervisors, I decided to donate. The people from the Organ Donation place had called twice already during the time I was at the hospital and said they would call again in a few hours for my decision. I felt like my soul had been ripped out, and I was so damn tired. But my hell was only just beginning. As the EMS guys left, I waited for my friends to show up, so that we could actually get the hell out of this place and figure out what to do now.

But before all of that happened, I was there alone. Waiting. Pacing. Dazed. I kept walking back and forth across the floor and hallways, as if that might somehow change what they had told me. Maybe if I kept moving, none of this would be true. Just keep moving. I have to call Don. He won't believe all of this. No logic to my brain or thoughts. I don't know how I was standing up or breathing. I kept sweating and sweating and staring at his phone. I kept trying to figure out his phone and how it worked. I tried to find a text message from him to somehow comfort me, but I couldn't figure out how to find any of his texts. I kept getting frustrated with myself, thinking "Well, if he's really dead, then I'd better damn well learn how to use this stupid phone of his, because he can't show me!"

My own phone was almost completely dead at this point, and I had left the apartment in such a hurry, that I didn't think to bring a charger. Hell, I wasn't even dressed. I was in the tank top and shorts I had slept in the night before, with no bra and holes in my shoes. I would have made a great feature on that website: "People of WalMart." They should start a new one: "People Who Were Jarred Awake By their Spouse's Sudden Death."

And then it happened. The saddest and most surreal of things. They asked me if I wanted to "see him." I had to see him. My heart skipped and fell and thumped. I was so scared. I had to see him. He is my husband. My life. My love. My everything. Yes. Bring me to him, please.

The nurse brought me to yet another tiny room, which seemed even tinier than the last tiny room, and said, "I will give you some time with him." She then left, and I walked into the tiny room and looked at the stretcher type bed he was lying on. I creeped over to him slowly, as if afraid to wake him up. I felt like I wasn't me, or it wasn't really me doing these things, and it wasn't really him lying there. I felt like at any moment, a director would yell, "Cut! Try that scene again, where you're walking up to him. That wasn't believable the first time." But nobody yelled anything, and the silence was so terrifying. I sat next to him, held his hand, his face, his hair, said words to him. I hugged him tightly a few times. I felt empty. All of it felt empty. I stared at him. He looked like he was taking another one of his famous naps. It didn't seem real, except for the tubes coming out of his nose. I couldn't breathe suddenly, and I didn't want to leave the room ever. Leaving that room meant that I had to do the next thing, and that I had to continue to hear people saying that he was dead. Please stop saying that. Please. He just left for work a few hours ago. How can he possibly be dead? We were just sleeping in the same bed together, right next to each other, and he was perfectly fine. There is no way he is dead. How do you go from perfectly fine, to dead? I felt sick to my stomach. I leaned into him and kissed his forehead as I touched his hair again. "I love you, Boo. I love you so much. I'm here. Please don't be gone. Please don't be gone. I'm so sorry. I'm so, so sorry." I don't know why I was apologizing, it is just what came out. I slowly took his hand and then put it in mine, and then I moved his body so that his arm was wrapped around me, and I lied down next to him that way. I faced him, and I just cried and cried. Why was this happening? How can this really, actually be happening? I started to half-ass sing the silly song I always sang to him that I made up, "The Shmoopie Doodle Song." I wanted to make him laugh. I waited for his adorable, usual participation and reaction to the song, and then I just sat on the edge of the small, weird bed, awkwardly.

I didn't know what to do or what to say. I felt like a failure, like I was terrible at this "saying goodbye" thing. Is that what was supposed to be happening here? Because I refused to say goodbye to my husband. Ever. I was so exhausted and confused and felt as if knives were stuck in my abdomen. What do you say to your dead husband who looks like he is napping in his white socks and pants and Petsmart t-shirt? So I went with, "I love you so much" again. I think I said it to him at least twelve more times. Maybe thirty. I couldn't stop saying it, and I didn't know when to stop saying it, and I didn't want to stop saying it. Then I thought to myself, out of nowhere, that I had taken turkey burgers out of the freezer the day before, so I could make them and we could try them tonight for dinner. And I wanted to ask him about the turkey burgers, or tell him that I could still make them if he wanted. I could still make them.

Kelley Lynn Shepherd

And then, at some random and nonspecific moment, I got up and walked out of that room. It was impossible leaving that room, and I didn't really walk out. I floated or glided out, like I was unconscious or a zombie of some kind, sleepwalking. I wanted to stay with him forever, but there was a larger part of me that still didn't really comprehend what was happening. "I'll just see him later," I kept thinking. Later. Maybe he will come back to life, just like on my favorite ridiculous soap opera that he always made fun of: "General Hospital." Nobody who dies on that show ever actually dies. They always come back to life months or years later. Or maybe it was his evil twin that died, and not really him at all. There had to be some explanation. Whatever it is, he can't really be dead.

In my confusion and dazed existence, I waited in the halls of the hospital E.R. Nobody bothered me. Life went on. Doctors treated other patients, and I disappeared into the crowd of people. At some point, I saw another stretcher go by, and my heart skipped or stopped or something. That familiar uniform that my husband wore to work everyday, the one he looked so sexy and cute in. I kept thinking, "This is what he does everyday. Brings in people who might die minutes later." And now he was one of them.

"Where will you take him now?" I asked someone that was suddenly near me. "To the coroner's office for an autopsy. Someone that young doesn't just collapse and die like that. Hopefully we can determine more details as to why he went into cardiac arrest. He will be going over to Newark." Newark? NEWARK??? He fucking hated Newark! "That shithole?" he used to say. Wonderful. I'm leaving my husband with a bunch of people who are taking him to Newark.

Suddenly, I realized I hadn't used the restroom since waking up. I walked over to a small bathroom and sat down on the toilet. I took out my phone, which had about a four percent charge on it, and I posted a status update to Facebook, similar to those I had seen many times about other people dying. Someone's mom or grandmother or a good friend. But this time, it was me, posting a death message about my own husband. I was letting everyone know that he had died. I clicked SEND, then I turned around and shoved my face in the toilet and threw up. I couldn't stop. It was just like in the movies, where someone gets tragic news, and their reaction is to throw up. I never understood that in the movies, and now here I was doing it. Throwing up and crying and posting on Facebook from the toilet of an E.R. restroom. I had zero control over what was happening or why.

As I walked out of the restroom and back down the hall, my Blackberry immediately started buzzing with emails, texts, messages. Modern technology and social media had gotten the word out in seconds about Don. I thought about how the last time my phone beeped that furiously over and over again, it was because a comedy YouTube video I did was going viral. Don and I were celebrating and laughing like hell each time my phone vibrated. "You're famous, Boo! Finally! Now we can get out of this shitbox called New Jersey!" He laughed and laughed at his hatred of all things New Jersey.

I sat down in the doorway area leading to the outside world as I waited for my friends to come and pick me up. They were all coming from various jobs, since it was a Wednesday morning, and so it had taken them a good couple hours to arrive at the hospital. I sat on a folding chair by the door and started to cry. I thought about how I never wanted to go home ever again, because it was not home now. Thoughts of what to do next overwhelmed me. Endless calls started pouring into my phone, but for whatever reason, I only picked up two of them. I had no idea how long my phone would last, and I couldn't get out words anyway. Meg, one of Don's dearest friends and long-time EMS partner on the ambulance, called me. The only thing I recall is both of us crying as she said in a shaky voice, "Oh, Kelley! Oh no. Is it true? It's not true, right?" I could feel her heart breaking over the phone from the shocking loss of her friend. Dianne called too, my childhood next door neighbor and friend. I don't recall one word I said on that call. I just needed to hear another human being speak that wasn't a nurse or stranger. I was so numb. My phone kept ringing, buzzing, making noise. It was the noise of something life-changing. It was the noise of death.

Minutes or hours later, I can't recall, my friends car pulled up. John, Jessica, and Kevin. I was standing outside the ER entrance, and it was so ungodly hot outside. My hands were sticky and sweaty, and I felt so weak. Kevin got out first. Just a few nights before, we had gotten into an argument over email. He had wanted some space from all of us, to figure out some things he was going through, and I didn't understand. Reading his email with me, Don understood. He said, "We have no idea what he's going through, Boo. If he needs some space, then we should respect that and give him some space. Sometimes, people just need to be alone for a while, ya know? He's our friend. We can do that for him, and when he's ready, he will come back to us."

Kevin got out of the car, and none of that mattered anymore. It just didn't matter. The three of them walked toward me so slowly. It felt like three weeks before they finally reached where I was standing. I could hear their shoes touching the dirt in the parking lot and making a swishing noise. I felt like I was in the Old West, and there was about to be a duel. Instead, there were hugs, and words, and awkwardness, and everything was different. Our little group of friends was altered. The puzzle had a missing piece. For no reason, I suddenly remembered that someone, me, had to call Rob in Florida, and tell him what had happened. Rob was Don's very best friend back in Pinellas County, and they were partners on the ambulance at SunStar for a long time before Don moved up here to be with me. His wife,

My Husband is Not a Rainbow

Mindy, answered when I called, and there was a long pause when I told her, and then, "No. No. No! He is at work. How am I going to tell him this? No! Kelley, I just can't understand this." It was heart-wrenching. I hated having to call other people and repeat the words that Don was dead. I hated it. It was the most awful feeling in the world.

As we drove John's car to the Petsmart where Don was working when he collapsed, there were lots of silent tears. We were all collectively stunned, and nobody knew what to do. About five minutes after pulling out of the hospital parking lot, my heart suddenly felt like it would fall out of me and die. I felt panic and dread, and I forgot how to breathe. My mind raced over and over again with this thought: *How can I just leave my husband there, all alone, in that tiny room, dead? How can I do that to him? He is all alone in there. What if he is cold, or hot? What if he wakes up? What if he isn't really dead? He is all alone. I should have stayed with him longer. I shouldn't have left him that way. How could I betray him like that? He is dead and alone. Alone and dead. And they are bringing him to NEWARK!!!*

I had to force myself to stop thinking about it, but I'm not sure how I did that. At one point, I had grabbed hold of the door handle to the backseat, just like Meryl Streep did in that scene in *The Bridges of Madison County.* Like her, I contemplated my escape. I would run out of that car, back to the hospital, and see if I could sit with my husband for just a little bit longer before they took him away to Newark forever.

We arrived at Petsmart, where I talked with some of the employees that were there when it happened. Everyone was solemn and speaking in hushed tones. I was directed to the back of the store, where I spoke with someone in management inside of another tiny room, which I guess was his office or something. He told me how the other manager was so distraught over Don's death, that he was sent home for the day. I couldn't focus on anything. I couldn't cope with being inside the store where he collapsed. I didn't want to see any of it. I didn't know any of these people, and the words they were saying to me were just more Peanuts cartoon teacher. I just wanted to run far away to somewhere, anywhere, where my husband wouldn't be dead anymore. But I had to take care of things. I had to go there and pick up his car. Our car. Don's precious baby that he had driven to work, just hours before. Oh, how he loved this car. I got in, with Kevin sitting in the passenger's seat, and just hoped like hell that it would start. "Please just get me home one more time," I begged the car. The car was always breaking down, always in the shop or always Don fixing it. Kevin asked if I wanted him to drive, but the car had no power-steering, so I wanted to be the one behind the wheel. At that very moment, driving that car felt like being a part of Don somehow, and I wasn't about to let that go.

We got back to our apartment, and we sat. I couldn't stop thinking about how wrong it felt to just be sitting in our apartment while Don was still lying there alone and dead. Couldn't I do something? Couldn't I help somehow? Maybe this whole thing was just one big misunderstanding, some sort of mistake. A couple hours later, my mom arrived from Massachusetts. By that time, the apartment was filled with lots of friends and tons of food. I felt so loved, so tired, so overwhelmed. People just figured things out, got themselves to my apartment, and took care of me instantly. My doorbell kept ringing with more people. There was panic and confusion inside my head, and my heart wanted to shatter into a million pieces right there on the floor. My head started to pound, and I couldn't move. I didn't understand what was happening. I heard the voices of my friends around me - talking, laughing uncomfortably, trying to find something to say, trying to make things okay with bagels and potato salad and fruit and baked ziti.

Rodney, Andrew, Vanessa, John, Jessica, Kevin, Marina, my mom - and then later that night, Shawn. Other friends called all day long. The phone was passed to my mom, who spoke with Don's sisters Marsha and Karen, and others, for me. My brother called. My dad. My best friend, Sarah. It was all too much, and I remember it in pieces. I remember telling Don's sister, Karen, that I had decided to donate his organs. I think I wanted her permission or her confirmation that it was a good decision. I also remember asking her if Don had ever mentioned anything to her about being cremated or not. She told me that I should do whatever I felt was best, whatever I felt he would have wanted. I didn't have a fucking clue what he wanted, and I had a migraine thinking about it. I didn't want to talk about ashes anymore, or caskets, or taking organs out of my husband's body and giving them to other people who got to still be alive. I wanted to throw up again.

Everyone was offering me sandwiches and water. At some point, I pretended to have to use the bathroom and sat on the side of the bathtub and cried. I had to get away. I had to be alone. Our cat, Autumn, was sitting inside the bathtub, and she looked up at me sadly, searching desperately for answers. We stared at each other, knowing there were no answers to be had and knowing that the life we knew was gone forever.

Words About Don

"My name is Dave, and I'm Kelley's brother. The first time I met Don, I knew right away that he was a man's man. He didn't hold anything back. He liked talking about cars and sports and was just an interesting person in general. He was very smart, about many different topics, and he had lots of things that he was interested in, lots of hobbies and activities. I almost felt a little bit smarter after visiting with him, like in a way, he had taught me something without even knowing it.

Kelley Lynn Shepherd

Kelley and Don would travel to Massachusetts to see my parents and us as often as they could. Everytime I would see Don, you could tell that he was truly happy to be there, which meant a lot. He was definitely family, and the only brother I ever had. My parents loved him like a son. I honestly looked forward to seeing Kelley and Don anytime that I could. I will miss playing catch with him in my parent's yard, as we did every time he came here. I will miss watching him play with my son, which I knew they both loved. I will miss busting his balls about being a Yankees fan and about how much better the Red Sox are than the Yankees. I actually taught my two year old son, Brian, how to say, "Yankees Suck!" just for Don. Watching Don's face when we sprung that one on him was classic. Most of all though, I will miss seeing Don walk through that door with my sister, next time I see her. He made her so happy, and you could just see that, every time they were together. As Kelley's brother, I couldn't have been any happier that she married Don. You did really good, sis. Don will be missed by everyone that knew him, and I will never forget him. At least the memories will last a lifetime. Love you, sis." - David Niemi

The Beginning

It was February 25, 1998. I was living in an apartment with my oldest childhood friend Sarah, in Forest Hills, New York. Our entire childhood growing up in small town Groton, Massachusetts, we both had the dream of moving to NYC and becoming performers of some kind. Now we were roommates and on our way. Sort of. I was a Tour Guide at Radio City Music Hall, a waitress at a hole in the wall Irish pub in the city, and I was auditioning now and then for acting work. I hadn't yet begun my stand-up comedy pursuit, and my personal life was on a downward spiral. A while before, I had been through a hugely traumatic event that I had shared with absolutely nobody, except for a very rude and unhelpful "counselor" on an anonymous hotline one evening. I was no longer trusting of men, and I had become very insecure and unsure of myself as a person. As a result of my trauma, I had gained a whole bunch of weight over time. I went from being a little bit overweight - to "Precious" (based on the novel PUSH by Sapphire). Somewhere subconsciously, I must have told myself that if I was fat and unattractive, that nobody could ever hurt me again. No man would want to touch me. I built a shield of flesh for myself and then lived inside it for a long time. Like a whale, comfortable in my blubber. It was oddly peaceful to shut people out. I was unhappy and unfulfilled, and I didn't feel like myself at all. I wasn't really sure where my self had gone or if she would ever come back. I was stuck.

Sarah had recently bought a new desktop computer, and she put it in our living room entranceway for both of us to use. It was the very first computer that either of us had ever really owned, so it was kind of a big deal. This was during the time when AOL (America Online) was still what most people used and also during the time when dial-up was pretty much the only option for getting onto the internet. So it often took forever to get online, and there were lots of weird noises in doing so. It sounded like a car engine was breaking down inside of a cat's stomach, or like a fax machine was having a loud seizure inside of a tunnel. It was a horrible, awful racket. It was also completely normal, and we didn't have anything better at the time. When you finally got to your AOL home screen, and that annoying voice spoke, "Welcome! You've Got Mail!" that was just about the most exciting thing anyone could ever imagine in life. Receiving an email from someone was like a small victory. It was evidence that you were cool. "You've Got Mail!" meant "You've Got Friends!"

Lots of times, if Sarah was out or had gone to bed, I would log onto AOL and just sort of browse around. At that time in my life, the last few guys I had dated, I had met them all online. This was because I felt so badly about myself, that I just wanted to hide behind my keyboard and talk. I wanted to feel close to someone without getting too close to someone. The computer monitor was just another shield, protecting me from getting hurt or rejected. In real life, I was Kelley. On the internet, I could be nameless. I was a mystery called "Camelsocks."

Usually, if I began talking with someone online, it was in some sort of Music or Comedy Chat Room. Chat Rooms were all the rage back then on AOL. You would choose a topic, something that interested you, like baseball. Then you could go into a chat room, for free, with lots of other people who wanted to talk about baseball with you. It was amazing, especially for insomniacs with trauma issues.

There was one room in particular that I liked popping into. It was called "Guess That 80s Song!" and it was a Trivia Game someone had made up. One person would type out a lyric to 1980s pop or rock song, and everyone else would have to guess the song and artist. The trick was to type your answer faster than everyone else in the room, because that made you the winner. I would sit there, fingers at the ready, waiting to receive my one-hit wonder, obscure song lyric. I was a master at this game, because I have always been obsessed with the 80s. It was my childhood, my teen years, and just an overall hilarious decade. The clothing, the music, the films, the Valley Girl voices - endlessly entertaining. I looked forward to playing this silly lyric game as a sort of wind down period after a long day at work. It was fun.

Normally, there would be anywhere from ten to about sixty people in this Chat Room. Sometimes more. On February 25, 1998, there were only two; Camelsocks, and Wayabovepar. What follows is a shortened version of the five hour long chat conversation between these two screen names. It is written completely from memory, all these years later. So, although it is definitely paraphrased, it is not too far off from our actual dialogue. (I really do remember things this vividly) Here is the very first conversation I ever had with Don Shepherd:

Wayabovepar: Um... are we in the right place? (crickets)
Camelsocks: lol I guess it's just you and me in here. Was it something I said?
Wayabovepar: It was probably your weird-ass name. Camelsocks? What the hell is a camelsocks? Lol
Camelsocks: It's nothing. It's just random.
Wayabovepar: Yeah, that's one word for it.
Camelsocks: Well what the hell does your name mean?
Wayabovepar: It's a golf reference. You know... golf? Par? Caddyshack? Hello?
Camelsocks: How old are you, 90? You have a golf reference as your screen name? Am I talking to a senior citizen?
Wayabovepar: No lol. I just love to play golf, but I'm not that good. Hence the screen name. You know what? If I have to explain the joke, it's not funny anymore.
Camelsocks: Either that or it's just not that funny.
Wayabovepar: Wow. Rough crowd. Seriously, where is everyone? I'm stuck in here with someone named Camelsocks who has known me all of 3 minutes and is already mocking me?
Camelsocks: It's a gift. I love to mock.
Wayabovepar: Great. And I'm your new target.
Camelsocks: Well it's either that or we play the lyrics game.
Wayabovepar: Go ahead. Give me a lyric.
Camelsocks: Jumbo me said oh you jumbo. OH jumbo jumbo. Jumbo me ta said you won ah. Yeah. Jumbo jumbo!!!!
Wayabovepar: LOL What the hell was THAT???
Camelsocks: You don't know it?
Wayabovepar: Oh, I know it. It's freakin Lionel Richie. "All Night Long."
Camelsocks: Yup. Very impressive!

Wayabovepar: But those aren't the lyrics. Not even close! Jumbo jumbo? Really? LOL.
Camelsocks: Well what does he say then? That's what it sounds like lol.
Wayabovepar: I don't know what the hell he says, but I know it's not "Jumbo jumbo." You're not right in the head lol.
Camelsocks: Hey, I could have given you the lame "Hello, is it me you're lookin' for?"
Wayabovepar: What is this, the Lionel Richie hour? There are other artists, you know.
Camesocks: True.
Wayabovepar: Spandau Ballet!!!
Camelsocks: Oh, you're good! So you're obsessed with the 80s as much as I am, I see.
Wayabovepar: Yeah, what's not to love.
Camelsocks: Have you played the lyric game in here before?
Wayabovepar: Nope. First time. And it's just you. I'm starting to think I was set up.
Camelsocks: Yes. This is how I trap men. I lure them into 1980s chat rooms, then I feed them with Jumbo Jumbo lyrics. You ARE a man, aren't you?
Wayabovepar: Yes. lol I knew it. I'm doomed.
Camelsocks: Good Grief!
Wayabovepar: This is too weird. You love The Peanuts too?
Camelsocks: Yup. My friends called me Lucy in college. I guess that meant I was bitchy.
Wayabovepar: At least they didn't call you Pig Pen. That would mean you smelled.
Camelsocks: I smell of perfection.
Wayabovepar: Oh boy. I can see why they called you Lucy :)
Camelsocks: There are normally a ton of people in this group playing this game. I don't know what's going on tonight. It's usually really fun.
Wayabovepar: Am I boring you? Lol
Camelsocks: No. You are fun to mock. I enjoy mocking you.
Wayabovepar: Glad to be of service, Camelsocks.

My Husband is Not a Rainbow

Camelsocks: So where do you live anyway?
Wayabovepar: In the Largo area.
Camelsocks: Where's that? Mars?
Wayabovepar: Close. Florida lol.
Camelsocks: Florida? Who lives in Florida?
Wayabovepar: I do. I just told you that lol.
Camelsocks: You really like that "lol" button don't you?
Wayabovepar: Apparently I also like being abused by total strangers online. You have a problem with my lol?
Camelsocks: I just feel you overuse it. I don't feel that you are actually laughing out loud.
Wayabovepar: Well, no shit. Nobody is actually laughing out loud each time they type that. You're kind of a smart ass. Where do you live? Wait, let me guess. New York!
Camelsocks: Correct.
Wayabovepar: I knew it!!! Lol
Camelsocks: There's that lol again…
Wayabovepar: lol You're a piece of work…
Camelsocks: We could go back to talking about Lionel Richie. His love songs are rather lovely, don't you think?
Wayabovepar: He's a dork lol.
Camelsocks: Have you ever been to NYC?
Wayabovepar: Nope. Would love to though. What's it like?
Camelsocks: It's pretty amazing. Nowhere like it in the world.
Wayabovepar: I'll bet.
Camelsocks: Holy crap! Look at what time it is!
Wayabovepar: Yeah. 3am. I was just fixin to go to bed.
Camelsocks: OH, wait a minute now. FIXIN? You were FIXIN to go to bed? Well, I'm talkin to a true redneck here. Yeeehaw!!! Let's go meet Bo and Luke Duke down at the Boars Nest!!!
Wayabovepar: Oh Christ lol. I'm not even from the South, actually. Grew up in Whittier, California, but picked up some of these southern phrases from living down here I guess.
Camelsocks: Yeah, well I wasn't about to let that one slide. Fixin. Anyway, I had no idea it was so late.

Wayabovepar: Well I am pretty awesome. It's easy to lose track of time when speaking to someone of my high caliber of awesomeness.
Camelsocks: Smart ass.
Wayabovepar: We have been talking for 5 hours on here, and I just realized I don't even know your name. I refuse to go to sleep with the reality that I just spent the past FIVE hours talking with someone named Camelsocks lol.
Camelsocks: Okay, it's only fair. My name is Kelley.
Wayabovepar: Really? I love that name. It's pretty.
Camelsocks: Well thank you. I had absolutely nothing to do with it.
Wayabovepar: Well it's nice to meet you Kelley. I'm Don.
Camelsocks: Hi Don. Nice to meet you too. I normally pop in here at night after work, if you feel like giving the room another shot.
Wayabovepar: Yeah. That sounds good. I should be around tonight. I'll come in and see if you're here.
Camelsocks: I'm fixin to log-in again tomorrow night.
Wayabovepar: Good. I'm fixin to spend more time taking your abuse.
Camelsocks: I'm fixin to mock you silly, Florida boy.
Wayabovepar: Florida boy lol. Is this your way of flirting with me?
Camelsocks: Absolutely.
Wayabovepar: Good to know. I was hoping. Good night, sweet Kelley.
Camelsocks: Goodnight Florida boy.

I couldn't stop smiling when I went to bed that night. A five hour dialogue felt like five minutes, because it felt as if I had known him forever. I remember not being worried that he wouldn't show up to talk some more the next night. I wasn't sure why exactly, but I felt as if my life had just changed in that moment. February 25, 1998, was the day that my life began. It was the day that I met my husband.

My Husband is Not a Rainbow

"Grief is about as useful as a bag of hair."
– Wade Winfrey

Dear Stupid Death Diary:

It's about five am in the morning, and my mom slept over last night, and I'm writing this on some notebook paper because I can't sleep, and I need to scream or murder someone or something, but I can't, so I guess I will just write. My mom is sleeping on our couch. I'm sitting in our bedroom at my desk. Usually, about an hour from now, is when Don would be coming home from his overnight shift working EMS. Instead, he is lying in Newark somewhere, dead. Is this real? I don't understand how this is real. My friends were at our apartment most of the day yesterday, and it was so weird. Nobody knew how to act or what to do. I felt like an alien. Then after they left, my mom called my brother so I could talk to him and then my dad. It hurt too much just hearing the cracks in their voices, knowing they didn't understand any of this either. My friend Shawn showed up late last night on a whim, because he didn't know what else to do except take the bus over here and be with me. Very sweet. The buzzer went off, and we had no idea who it could be. He made me eat half a turkey sandwich, which tasted like nothing. I feel sick.

There is so much stuff in this apartment. Piles of stuff. We have no space. I don't know how to process seeing his stuff here and knowing that he won't be using any of it again. I think we are going to stay here another day, then drive back to Massachusetts and stay there until we find out the date for the funeral and services and then come back. I don't know why the hell I'm writing about this. I feel the weird need to document everything. Maybe I need evidence that this actually happened. My main thought, over and over, is that I really need to tell Don about all of this. He won't believe it. I need to call him up and tell him that the craziest thing happened - he died.

The organ donation people called again to get my final decision and then ask me about twelve billion very personal questions about my husband, to make sure he was in the position to donate, I guess. Seriously, one of the worst, most horrifying phone calls I've ever been on in my life. It was over an hour of horrific questions. Very graphic. The condition of his body, details about his eyes, skin, things I can't even repeat. I started crying halfway through the call and then couldn't stop. How can they talk about him that way? Such clinical terms. I don't know how to do any of this.

"My heart reaches for hers the way your foot might move forward for the next step on a staircase only to find the ground gone beneath you. So much of grief is turning to share something with her, and falling into the abyss." – Michelle Wirth

FB Post: Today was another terrible day. Setting up funeral arrangements. I just want this day to be over. I will be posting about services later tonight. Still waiting on a few details. It's going to be a beautiful military/EMS style memorial (Don was an Air Force vet), and none of it should be happening. Look for details in a few hours. Thanks.
LIKES: 87   COMMENTS: 142

My Husband is Not a Rainbow

Dear Stupid Death Diary:

I hate you. I hate that I need to write in you because my husband died, and there's nobody I can talk to that would even remotely understand. Mom and I are going to Massachusetts tonight and then driving back early on the 17th to Hackensack, New Jersey for the services. Don's EMS managers and supervisors offered to cover all the funeral expenses and walk us through everything. I am speechless about that. I have no money. None. I feel like a failure wife because I can't throw my husband a nice funeral. But now I can, because they are taking care of it. Mom and me met with them today at the Hackensack Medical Center and Vanguard offices, where we talked about funeral specifics. The funeral director met us there. I looked through books of urns and caskets and was asked multiple questions about my forty six year old husband who shouldn't be dead. Don's coworkers all have the same twisted humor he had, because you have to have dark humor to get through the trauma you see on that job. While we were picking out caskets, we turned to one page of this huge book, and the funeral director said, "How about this one right here? This is top of the line." Suddenly, all the lights in the room flickered off and on. Everyone looked up, and his Supervisor Joe said, "Okay Don. Calm down. You don't like that one. We'll go with something else." Since I had decided to have Don cremated immediately after the services, (the military wanted half-open casket for service so they could drape the American flag over it, which is customary), it seemed silly to buy an expensive casket if he wasn't going to be "residing" there. The funeral director then told me that renting a casket was an option. Really? Something about renting a casket struck me as funny. Don would probably say something like, "Even when I'm dead, I still can't afford to buy my own place. " So we rented.

Then we chose funeral cards. Most of them were boring or too religious or just lame. I could hear Don in my head mocking these funeral cards. The funeral director told me that we could write our own words or message, if we wanted, to be printed on the cards. So we came up with a poem that we all felt Don would have greatly appreciated. We could all picture him saying this, "Hi, I'm Don. I was here. Now I'm gone." I couldn't believe they were actually letting us print these up. Seriously? This was hilarious. So we printed up some of those to give cool people and normal boring ones to give the people who wouldn't get the humor. Then the funeral director asked if I wanted music over the speakers during the visiting hours for the wake. I said, "Can I have Aerosmith and The Beatles and The Who and Steely Dan?" He said, "You can have anything you want." "Well, that's what I want. That's what Don wants." I then made it known that it was very important to me that this funeral be a memorial focused on the life of Don, and not some religious pushing ceremony or a commercial for The Lord. I wanted it one hundred percent about Don and his life. People getting up and telling stories, talking about him, and ending with me delivering the final Eulogy. He told me again that this was a funeral home and not a church, so we can do whatever I want. Since Don was both Air Force Vet and EMS, the service would be a combination of both. The Air Force would be there and lining the walls with flags, TAPS would be played, and hospital staff would all come in their uniforms - doctors and nurses and paramedics/EMS alike - as a sign of respect, leaving their shifts to attend.

One of the funniest things that happened while sitting around this long table planning the services, was when the funeral director started asking us about what information we would like to put on the announcement in the local paper and bulletin about service details. He was talking about the part where you let people know where to deliver flower arrangements, or you say "in lieu of flowers, donations can be made to blah blah blah." He asked if Don had any favorite charities or things he felt passionate about. So I told him that Don loved animals, and that he volunteered his time at Petsmart's program for adoptions. That's where he collapsed. So we decided to call up Petsmart to find out the name of the organization they work with for pet adoptions. We asked to speak with the manager that knew Don, and we were put on hold to wait for him. While the funeral director was on hold, the following dialogue took place between those of us in the room, as soft "elevator music" played on speaker phone in the background.

Mom: So, in this announcement, we can request that people give flower arrangements, or we can request that people give to a charity in honor of our son-in-law instead, right?

Funeral Director: Mmmhmm. Yes, that is correct.

Mom: Well, is there a third option?

Director: What do you mean?

Mom: What I mean is; yes, Don loved animals a lot, but he loved my daughter more than anything in this world, and I know for sure he would want her to be helped and taken care of. This death was so sudden, and they really had nothing. I mean, nothing. There is no life insurance, she is going to lose her health insurance, they have no savings, and she somehow has to figure out how to remain in their apartment with his car and pay the bills, all by herself, on her very small adjunct professor salary.

Director: Ah, okay. I see. Well, there is always the option of letting people know that in lieu of flowers, you'd like donations to go directly to The Shepherd Family, meaning Kelley.

Mom: We can do that?

Director: Of course we can. We can do anything you want.

Mom: Well then, that is what we are doing. Never mind this charity stuff. My daughter needs to get by somehow. I'm sorry, but I had to say something. I can't sit here and watch all this money that my daughter very much needs go to a bunch of cats!

Don's Supervisor: Yeah, screw the cats. This is way more important. We will help the kitties later on. We promise, Don. Right now, we need to help your wife.

(hold music stops and Petsmart person comes to phone.)

Petsmart: Hello, I understand you were interested in finding out more about our cat adoption program and how to make a donation?

Director: Uhhh... Yeah... Sorry... Wrong number...

"What do you call the Seven Dwarfs when they pass away?
Dead, dead, dead, dead, dead, dead, and dead."
– Gabe Easter

Dear Stupid Death Diary:

I'm so tired. I want to go back to how my life used to be. I hate this one. It's July 16th. Mom and me drove "home" today to stay two nights and pick up my dad, then come back to Jersey on Sunday for the funeral. The word home is in sarcastic quotes because it's not the same home I've been coming back to my entire life. It's not my parents' home in Groton Mass, on Taylor Road, where they lived their whole marriage and my whole childhood. Instead, we pulled up to a very modern "over 55" condo community in Lunenburg, and to a really nice condo rental. My parents lost their home to foreclosure, after being victims of the economy, and everything came to a head this month. They have to be out just days after Don's funeral, and I can't believe any of this is happening to us. I think I'm in denial about my childhood home right now. This new place is nice as hell, but it isn't my home. It felt so weird walking in here, almost like it was some vacation we were on, and maybe Don couldn't make it because he had to work. That fantasy soon left my brain though, as soon as mom pulled into the driveway, and I saw my dad's silhouette standing in the garage, waiting for us. He was pacing back and forth, holding the cigarette in his hand nervously. When I got out of the car to hug him, he was crying, and I was too. What the hell do you say to your daughter whose husband just randomly died? I don't know, and neither did he. He started asking me all kinds of "dad" type questions, like how our car was running and if I had enough gas and oil and things like that. There is just so much sadness here. Everywhere. There is literally nowhere to go ever again to escape the extreme sadness. I carry it around in me, like a plague.

"I'm grateful I do not consider myself to be anywhere near above the primal stages of rage, frustration, indignation, sorrow, angst, and hurt. All those feelings make a person, in the end, a mere participant in the human experience." – Sarah Chamberlin

Dear Stupid Death Diary,

Lots of visitors today at mom and dad's house. My brother and Jen came over. They left my nephew Brian home with their parents, since he is two and a half and doesn't really understand what is going on or what "your Uncle Don is dead" means. My brother looked so shaken, and much like my dad, had no words except that he is so sorry and can't believe this happened. We have all become masters of awkward silence at this point. It is so hard to be inside of this heavy grief-filled air. My sister-in-law, Jen, started crying the minute she saw me. We went back and forth between the two locations of Groton and Lunenburg, packing up my parent's lives into box after box and bringing everything over in slow trips. They have until August first to be out of the house, but they are already living here in the condo. We went over to the old house later in the evening, where more friends and family stopped by, and we ate cake off paper plates, since half the house is packed up. My cousins, Tabatha and Laura, and my Aunt Ginny came by, and my cousins gave me a beautiful memory light lamp that looks like an Angel when lit. Our friends, Nancy and Ron came by, our neighbor Eve, Norma and Mike, so many people. Everyone in shock, and lots of them planning on making the five hour trip to New Jersey for the services. It is all so overwhelming. I don't know how to be or what to say to anyone, and they don't know what to say to me. I only know how to write stuff here, in this stupid death diary that I hate.

FB Post: There are things that need to be said publicly about the amazing man my husband was. I am going to write something up and do my best to say them tomorrow at his funeral. I don't know how I will do this, but I'm determined, because it's what he deserves. I may need to lean on some of you to get through it. Literally.
LIKES: 122   COMMENTS: 76

FB Post: Today's the day. Had 45 minutes of sleep, after finally finishing writing my husband's Eulogy for the service. My sweet Don, get me through this, please.
LIKES: 99   COMMENTS: 154

***"Oh, take me back to that quiet place,
where we were last together." – Diane Fisler***

Dear Stupid Death Diary,

I'm in the backseat of the car, driving from Massachusetts to New Jersey with my parents to attend my husband's funeral. Every single thing about that sentence is so completely sick and wrong and unfair. How can I be going to my husband's funeral? How? We haven't even bought a house yet, or had our family, or retired, or had kids or grandkids. This makes no sense. The car ride is pretty silent. We are driving directly to the funeral home without stopping at my apartment first for anything. We all have our dress clothes inside the car on hangers, and we will change when we get there. The man that runs the funeral home, Joseph, is so nice. A very sweet man, and very funny too. Don would like him. I am texting back and forth in the car with my friend Gregg (Opie from the Opie and Anthony Show on XM radio) Hughes. I just told him that I'm on the way to the funeral, and that I'm giving eulogy. He said, "You got this. You will honor your husband today. You will be great." Then he posted on his Twitter page, asking all the fans of the radio show to please show me some love and support today, because I truly need it. I thought that was so nice of him. Don would think it is SO cool that Opie gives a shit that he died.

***"There will never be a day that I won't think of you."
– Kathryn Monaco-Douglas***

Dear Stupid Death Diary,

We are back at my apartment after the services and the food reception and the family and friends and everything else.

Kelley Lynn Shepherd

Something inside me is saying that it's important to write down the details about today, and I will, but not today. I sort of feel like I've already forgotten them, even though the vision of my love in a casket will stay in my mind forever. Everything is a blur. People said I was "so brave" for doing the eulogy and for being so strong, and for I don't know what else. I don't know, for breathing? I don't feel brave or strong. I feel like I'm suffocating and want to die. I feel like I am under a microscope. Like everyone is watching me. Sammy and Autumn are so confused and sad. Autumn hasn't lifted her head up in days. She just lies down with droopy eyes and barely blinks. Sammy sits by the front door of our apartment, waiting for Don to come home from work. Every few minutes, he meows, but it's like a cry. I can't listen to it anymore. It's too heart-wrenching. I don't know how to make it better. I am not Don. Don was a better kitty parent than me. I don't know how to exist right now. I feel sick again. I'm not really sure whether or not I've eaten anything since some watermelon cubes early this morning. Every single part of me feels dizzy and hot, and the air is sticky and suffocating. I just want to lie under my blankets forever.

***"I wasn't ready to let you go. I wasn't ready for you to die. I wanted a chance to do it better. I wasn't done loving you."* – Kerry McKim**

Dear Stupid Death Diary,

It's been five days since my life ended, when my husband's life ended. Today, my parents went back home to Massachusetts, and now I'm truly here in this apartment alone. Alone. Maybe its punishment for leaving Don dead and alone in Newark. My parents really didn't want to leave, but I need to take care of some things here before I head back to their place for a while,

My Husband is Not a Rainbow

and I just really needed to have some time by myself to scream and cry and yell and sit and stare at the walls. Friends have been everywhere since this happened, and it is amazing. There is so much love. Everyone wants to help. People are stopping by all the time making sure I'm not alone for too long. Taking me to lunch, dinner. Bringing over food at all hours of the day. I've felt sick to my stomach since Wednesday. What day is it? I think I just sat here on our couch for three hours straight, without moving or knowing I was sitting here. I might be losing my mind. My parents call over and over. They are worried, but I asked them to please go home for a week or so, and then I will follow. I just need to think. How can I make all of this go away? How?

(later that night)

My first full night completely alone in our apartment. Tried sleeping in our bed. Not happening. I keep staring at his pillow, hoping his head will magically appear there, where it used to be. I just keep crying into my pillow. Is this it? Is this my life now? I ran my hands over his pillow and his side of the bed a few times. I don't know why. Maybe I want to smell him there. The kitties are now wondering where their Papa is. They are so depressed, it's making things even worse for me. I am not sure if I will ever sleep again. How can I sleep when my husband is dead forever?

FB Post: Today is one week since my husband died. I know people are trying to help, but please, if you like me at all, do not tell me that God has a plan, or that it was his time. Really? He was 46 yrs old, and we didn't even get 5 years together of marriage. His time, my ass. And if he were here, with his twisted humor, he would tell me to tell those people to kindly fuck off and have a nice day.
LIKES: 87   COMMENTS: 64

Dear Stupid Death Diary,

Wrote on my Facebook page earlier, asking people to stop saying his death was God's plan. I wanted to say a lot more things, but I don't want everyone to hate me either. I cannot believe the shit people have said to me already. Even at the funeral. Who does that? A woman that worked with Don, that I barely know, told me that I'm young, and I will find someone else soon. I wanted to slap her. This wasn't some silly high school crush. This was my HUSBAND. That is so insulting, that anyone would think he is just disposable like that. It makes me cry just thinking about it. Lots of people have written on my FB page or sent me messages about trusting in the Lord and "He's in a better place," all sorts of other non-comforting rude crap. This is incredibly upsetting. My stomach is in knots, and my eyes hurt and burn from crying and not sleeping. How the hell do people DO this?

"Alone. Judged. Alone.
In a room filled with people,
Never have I felt more alone." – Jackie Lumar

ELEVEN - a Dream / Visitation from Don

I had a dream. Or a visit from my husband. Whatever it was, here it is: I am inside of a Best Buy, in the movie section, and I pick up a copy of "This Is Spinal Tap," and slowly start sobbing; because that was Don's absolute favorite movie. As I was sobbing, a large hand touches me on my shoulder, and I turn around. It's Don. He is in one of his favorite shirts; a t-shirt we had bought the very first time I took him to the U.S. Open tennis tournament. It says, "You call that a serve? Take that back to New Jersey!" I didn't think it was all that funny, but he found it hilarious and wore it all the time while playing tennis. Anyway, in the dream, I turn around and look into his beautiful blue eyes and sob even harder.

"I miss you so much." I cry into his chest.

"I know, Boo," he says, as he lightly runs his fingers through the back of my hair, sort of scratching it the way he used to do.

"Why are you here? Are you back now? You didn't really die, right?"

"Yes, I did. I'm sorry, honey. I didn't want to. It just happened."

"But it's not fair. You were always outside exercising, trying to stay in shape. You played tennis two days before, in ninety five degree heat!"

"I know, and I left this in my tennis bag by mistake. If only I would have moved it into my wallet, they would have been able to call you a lot sooner while I was still alive. You couldn't have done anything to save me, but maybe we could have said 'I love you.'"

He pulls out his driver's license and Emergency Hospital Card. The one where they ask your blood type and to name someone to call in case of an emergency. It says "Kelley Lynn Niemi - Wife" and my phone number.

I look at the card and keep crying. "When the hospital called me and woke me up, you were already dead."

"I know, Boo. It wasn't supposed to happen there. I kept those things in my tennis bag whenever I played tennis, just in case. People usually have heart attacks while running, or playing tennis, or doing something strenuous. It just made more sense to have the information in that bag. I forgot to take it out before work that morning. I feel so badly that the paramedics or Petsmart staff didn't know your number or to call you. You know, my dad had his heart attack on his golf course."

"Yeah - in his late 80s!"

"I guess I didn't get that lucky. I had to die in a freakin' Petsmart in New Jersey!" He laughs and kisses my forehead.

"You made me so happy. I'm not happy anymore. All I do is cry and try not to cry."

"It's going to take a very long time, Boo. I was pretty awesome."

We both laugh.

"Are we really standing here, holding each other in the middle of a Best Buy?" I ask him.

"It's just a dream," he says matter of factly, lightly smiling at me. "It's not real. You're heart wants so badly to talk to me again, to hold me again, so your mind is letting you in your dreams."

"But I have nightmares. And even these dreams that seem nice now', are awful, because when I wake up, I realize none of it was real, and you're still gone. And then I feel like shit."

"I know, Boo. It's all part of the grieving process. You're going to feel like shit for a long time, and I hate that. That's the crappy thing about dying. It's the people you leave behind that suffer."

"But you got screwed, just like Ginger. Why didn't you get more time? You deserved so much more time!" I sob intensely now.

My Husband is Not a Rainbow

"I wish there was an answer to that question that would comfort you. But there isn't. It makes no sense." It feels like his hug isn't as tight anymore.

"Please, please don't go. You just got here." I pause, then ask "Will I see you again?"

"Yeah. Probably for a while. And then not. And then yes again. Eventually, you won't need to." He wipes away my tears.

"I can't imagine a day where I won't need to see you. I love you."

"I love you too, Boo." He starts to walk away, then turns back. "Oh, I noticed last night that you did some laundry. I never thought I'd see the day… Boo doing laundry. " He laughs his awesome laugh.

"They just put in brand new washers and dryers downstairs. They aren't like the old ones. I had no idea what I was doing. The settings were all different. Too many numbers."

"Stop being so overdramatic," he says as he laughs at me. "You'll figure it out. Here's a hint. The liquidy stuff… that's called detergent. It goes inside the machine." He always loved mocking me.

"I'll try and remember that," I said, still sobbing.

He turns around one last time. "Oh, and one more thing." I reach out to take his hand while he talks, but he is too far away now. "The old washers had settings that went to ten. These new ones go higher. These go to eleven." He gives me a wink and a smile, knowing that I will catch the "Spinal Tap" reference. And then he is gone.

Kelley Lynn Shepherd

I wake up with a massive headache, and my pillow is soaking wet from tears. I look over to his side of the bed, and it's still empty. I sob and sob for what seems like half hour, but probably isn't. Sammy runs up onto the bed and purrs, rubbing his face against mine. "It's okay, mommy," he seems to be saying. Then he throws up on my arm.

"Today I found a picture of us. You were holding my hand. I was touching your arm. And I've already forgotten how it felt to smile that way..."
– Gin Hayden

Dear Stupid Death Diary,

I still hate you. No sleep again. Sat in bed with the TV on. Tried convincing myself he is just at work on his overnight shift. He will be home soon. I just don't understand this. He was FINE. He was perfectly fine and healthy. How does someone go from perfectly fine to collapsing and dying? The super of our building, Ruben, came over to check on me earlier today. That was so nice. I had no idea what to say to him. Him and Don would talk guy stuff sometimes outside the building, laughing and chatting it up. Him and his wife even came to the funeral. Such a nice thing. My mind is so scattered. My thoughts make no sense. I want to hug my husband. I can't shake the image of him inside that casket. I close my eyes, and I see it over and over again. I look like death because I don't sleep, or I wake up thinking it's that morning again, when he was randomly dead. Taking a shower feels like running a marathon. I broke out in hives all over my arms and legs, and I have thrown up a few times. I googled it, and it said stress-induced hives, puking, can be caused from grief. I can't afford a doctor. I have no health insurance and no money. Don would hate this for me. He would hate that he can't just take care of this for me and make me feel better. I feel unsafe and alone. I can't sleep. I'm so scared.

Dear Stupid Death Diary,

Went to lunch today with my best childhood friend, Sarah. We went to PF Changs, about five minutes from my apartment. It was the only place I could think of in this neighborhood that wouldn't remind me of going there to eat with Don. He hated Chinese food, so we never went there together. Not even once. Perfect. We sat there together, and Sarah kept tearing up and crying. I was more stone faced. I don't know what's wrong with me. I can't seem to cry in front of my friends, or something inside me doesn't want to. Then, I get back to this stupid apartment, and it all comes out like a tidal wave. She said the perfect thing to me today. She probably doesn't know it was the perfect thing, but it was. She said, "When we were growing up together as kids, and I would think about our futures and what might become of us, this is not what I saw for you. This was not supposed to happen. This was not what I had dreamed or envisioned for you." Then she told me that she has no idea what she's doing, and that she will probably be a terrible friend and say all the wrong things. But so far, it's just the opposite. She is one of the few people who has said the exact right thing. She kept crying, and finally, I said to her, "Are you going to be okay?" We both laughed, and she yelled defiantly, "NO!"

(later) Wide awake again at four AM. Went on Facebook and did a search for private, closed groups for widowed people. My stomach felt sick just typing that word. Widowed. But I NEED to talk to someone, just one fucking person who isnt eighty years old, who is going through this and who won't feed me a bunch of cliches or just say how sorry they are over and over. I can't take this anymore. I'm going insane. Found a few groups that look like they might be okay. Going to create a post and tell my story, I guess. Welcome to my weird new life. I hate it.

"We don't survive it. We let it kill the old us, and then we rebuild." – Michelle Miller

FB Post: I'm on the Jersey bus headed into the city to meet a friend. It's my first venture into Manhattan since he died, and I'm on this bus crying loudly and hyperventilating hysterically like a lunatic (remembering all our trips into the city together.) But - because it's NYC, nobody gives a shit. Just another ordinary day here. It's a bit liberating.
LIKES: 45   COMMENTS: 34

FB Post: Laughed really hard today with my friend, Bobby. We walked around Manhattan and went into Borders to make fun of the "grief book" section and how lame and off-base it is. There was one called "A Cup of Comfort". I said to Bobby, "this gives me no comfort." Another was titled "God Called You Home." I almost puked right there in the store. I know Don was laughing too.
LIKES: 19   COMMENTS: 5

FB Post: Today, I had my very first panic attack. I literally thought I was dying or having a heart attack, one week after my husband had one, and I thought I would be found collapsed on my apartment floor with cats eating at my face. Thank you to my brother, who has had anxiety attacks before, and who talked me down over the phone and told me what it was and to breathe and talk myself down from it. Thank you to John and Jessica for coming over here, sitting with me, making sure I was okay. Holy

crap that was scary. I'm really not a fan of this widow thing. I had no idea it would be so scary.
LIKES: 44   COMMENTS: 67

"Each and every thing is now a source of fear
Each and every thing is now something that can kill you
Or bring you a new source of grief if it takes another one that you love"
-Shantelle Buethe

Dear Stupid Death Diary:

I can only say this here in my private place, because I'm afraid if I say it anywhere else, people will tell me to get help, or want to put me on meds immediately, or whatever else. But there's nothing wrong with me. My husband is dead, and my heart hurts so much, that I can't function or breathe right or even think of one reason that I should not die. I really don't want to be here anymore. The panic attack scared me so much. I don't want more of those, and I know there will be more. It came out of nowhere, and I couldn't calm it down for the longest time. Sammy and Autumn are here, and they need me to feed them and hold them and give them love. Their Papa is gone, and they are stuck with me instead. I'm so sorry I am not him. I really suck at being a cat mom. I will try not to kill myself, but there is a big part of me that truly hopes that if I ever do fall asleep, that I don't ever wake up. I just don't know how to exist with this level of sadness. It was suggested to me by a few that I should start taking meds to cope, that I am "depressed" and other things. My fucking husband just died. A goddamn week ago! And people are already treating me like there is something wrong with me for being sad and devastated, when every single thing in my life is now gone and different. I don't want medication. I don't want to numb myself. One thing I know is that I NEED to feel this. I don't know HOW, but I know I need to. No judgment at all for anyone who takes meds, but it's not for me. There is too much addiction in my family to go down that route, and I don't want to be so numb to my own emotions and then one day have to face them all at once. That would be hell. But so is this. I'm crawling out of my skin.

Dear Dead Husband,

Hi Boo. I've been talking to you out loud in our apartment, but I always feel like such a jackass when you don't respond. Today I had to tell your new tennis friend / partner Maurice that you died. He was so nice on the phone. He said he only knew you for a few months, but that he will cherish the tennis racket that you gave him forever and remember you forever. He said you taught him a lot about tennis and that we lost an incredible soul. Me, him, and his girlfriend Julie are going to go stand down at the tennis courts on our street where you played and remember and celebrate you, have a moment to honor you there. I promise to honor you forever. I love you.

"If anything perpetuates my grief, it will be that life goes on.
If anything heals my heart, it will be that life goes on." – Kim Kinney

Dear Stupid Death Diary,

Just got back from having brunch in the city at this new place owned by Justin Timberlake called Southern Hospitality.

My Husband is Not a Rainbow

Comfort food. Met Andrew and Rodney there. Took the bus in, and once again felt another panic attack coming on while sitting on the bus. I felt like there was a knife in my side, and I couldn't stop sweating or crying. I got so dizzy and filled with fear. I walked into the restaurant and immediately had to go into the restroom to talk myself down again, breathe my way out of it, and threw up again. Why do I keep getting sick to my stomach? I remember seeing that in movies and thinking it was bullshit. People throwing up because they were so upset. But it's happening. The hives were all up and down my arms. And I was so dizzy and hot. It's like my body couldn't physically cope with him being dead, so I'm just forever nauseous now. Like my body now needs to "prepare" before being with other humans. It's so exhausting to just NOT FALL APART when around people. Every time I speak, I want to cry instead.

While there, we talked about the idea of some of my comedian friends putting on a comedy benefit show to honor Don and to help me with some of my bills in this new life with no husband and no secure future. Andrew is going to produce the show, and we will do it at The Met Room, the sister club to Gotham Comedy Club. My friend and legendary comedian, Elayne Boosler, has already agreed to headline the show. She told me that a couple nights ago while we were talking on the phone. I couldn't stop crying, I was so moved by her generosity. I will also get up onstage for the first time since he died and do some stand-up about death and grief. I never thought I'd type THAT sentence. A lot of people will be involved in this show, and we will make him proud. So I guess I have to not die just yet. I need to honor him. This will be my reason to keep not dying. To honor him. I love you, Boo.

Kelley Lynn Shepherd

"Grief is an ocean filled with dirt. Music that pierces your eardrum. Grief is the sky inside of your throat. Trapped. Scared. Waiting to be free." – Me

Dear Stupid Death Diary:

The word widow really bothers me. I hate the sound of it, hate what it means. In my heart, mind and soul, I am still married. Don is my husband. He is not physically here, but he is my husband. I can't just wipe that away like it didn't exist. I don't want to. I won't. I loved being married to him. I love being his wife, and it makes me feel sick to say anything different. I keep rubbing my thumb over my wedding ring and asking him to please come home. How is this a real thing that is happening? This sucks.

Dear Dead Husband,

I like writing to you more than I like writing to "stupid death." There are so many things that I ache to tell you. I have a constant migraine since the day you died, from all the crying and stress and weird eating and lack of water. I suck at drinking enough water, apparently. Had to close some accounts today and deal with some other logistical stuff that was horrible. Got in your car to do errands and realized I didn't have to move the seat from your position to mine, and broke down crying. I was in the grocery store today and saw an older married couple. They were arguing about which brand of toothpaste to get. I thought about how we got robbed of our lifetime together. I can't stop missing you for one second. I'm so damn sad. We have so many amazing friends, family, so much support - and yet - I have never felt more alone or lonely, ever. I didn't know I could miss someone this much. Everyone keeps hugging me. I want to hug you. I hate when people touch me. It feels weird and it itches all over. I feel un-human somehow. Like your death made me so that I'm no longer a person.

Nights are the worst. I look over, and you're not there. Sammy and Autumn aren't doing well. Sammy lays by the door all day long crying and waiting for you to walk through. I don't know how to comfort him, because watching him look for you just makes me sob even harder. I just can't understand why this happened. You were such a force of life and goodness. Why was that taken away? I love you so much.

"I miss you. And I miss the me that you took with you." – Amber Parker

Dear Dead Husband,

It's the last day of July today. I think. Who cares anyway. It's been over two weeks without you here. I just watched my first Yankee game (only the last two innings) without you. It gave me no joy. I missed your commentary too much. The silence was horrible.

I met Maurice and Julie today, your tennis friends. We went to the courts to remember you and tell stories, and they brought me flowers inside a tennis ball can with your name written on a tennis ball inside. So adorable, it made me cry so hard. Everything does now. Apparently, I cry a lot now. They are really great people, and live only two buildings over. This whole time, we had these awesome neighbors we could have been friends with, and we didn't even know. Maurice and I are going to make sure that we do something meaningful with your tennis rackets. We will make you proud. I promise not to kill myself for a while, so that I can keep honoring you. I know you wouldn't want me to die also, but it's honestly so incredibly hard to be alive right now. I love you.

Dear Dead Husband,

Still not sleeping. Last night, I slept one hour. I lie there, and I can't focus or sleep or blink or do anything. I keep the TV on all night long. The silence of where your breathing or snoring used to be is deafening. I ate popcorn for dinner last night, and a rice krispie treat for breakfast. Your coworker and friend, Mary, from the Petsmart adoption center came over today to help me out with the cats and to see if they needed a vet visit. She is going to feed them if/when I need to get out of here and go visit home often. She is so nice. She told me a story that she meant to be as a comfort to me, but I was trying so hard not to laugh out loud because it struck me as so ridiculous. She told me that you are a rainbow. I know. Stop laughing. I think she just gave me some comedy gold. I will have to write it up as a blog somehow and then tell the story at the comedy benefit. A rainbow? You? Not ever.

My Husband is Not a Rainbow

There is this very sweet woman who runs the pet adoption volunteer section of Petsmart, where my husband volunteered and worked with the animals. Her name is Mary, and she was a wonderful friend to my husband. They worked together and shared a love of animals. A couple days ago, Mary was at our apartment helping me with the kitties. As we sat there, she got very serious suddenly, and she told me this story, "Kelley, the most amazing thing happened to me while I was driving to Don's funeral that morning. It was a miracle. I just have to tell you about it." Her eyes widened with anxious pleasure as she anticipated the wonder of her own tale. She leaned forward:

My Husband is Not a Rainbow

"I was in Jersey, heading to Hasbrook Heights for the services, and I was driving along Tonnelle Avenue, and I started thinking about Don and how I just couldn't believe he was really gone. I started crying really hard, and I couldn't stop. And then, it was raining while I was crying, and then it stopped, and it got a little sunny. And then, out of nowhere, I saw something incredible."

As she continued talking, I noticed that she had tears in her eyes. I, on the other hand, sat there and listened like a robot. She delivered this next part of the story as if she had never been more sure of anything in her entire life. Meanwhile, I was attempting to suppress my laughter at the sheer ridiculousness of what she was about to tell me.

"Do you know what I saw, Kelley?" she said dramatically and with purpose. "It was a rainbow. I saw a rainbow, Kelley. And it was Don. I know it was. Don was a rainbow, and he was there in front of me. Telling me not to cry, and that everything would be just fine. And then I felt better, because Don came to me as a rainbow and made everything okay. Your husband is a rainbow, Kelley. Isn't that amazing?" "Sure. Yes. Amazing", I lied. But inside my head, this is some of what I was thinking:

Seriously? A rainbow? Where do I even begin with how hilarious this concept is to me. I know my husband pretty well, and he would NEVER, ever come back as a fucking rainbow! ESPECIALLY in New Jersey!!! He hated New Jersey! So, if he ever did come back as a rainbow, which he wouldn't, it would NOT be on Tonnelle Avenue in New Jersey. He wouldn't give New Jersey the satisfaction of his beauty. Just wouldn't happen. Secondly, if he WAS a rainbow, which he wouldn't be ever, don't you think he would make damn sure that that his WIFE saw him? You think he's gonna waste his one cameo appearance on a co-worker, and not ME? And if that was Don, then explain all the other people driving along that day, who saw the same rainbow. They don't even know Don. To them, it's just a

Kelley Lynn Shepherd

rainbow. They happen sometimes, usually right after it rains, and then the sun comes out. Boom! Rainbow. My husband would never be a rainbow. Maybe someone else's husband would show up that way, but not Don. Not his style. No. Don would come back as a kick-ass guitar solo in an old, classic Aerosmith song. THAT is my husband. Not a stupid rainbow.

A couple days later, my mom had driven back up to our apartment again to stay with me for a couple of days and help me out with some of the endless, annoying new "widow chores" that had to be done. This involved closing accounts, opening new ones, figuring out passwords, copying death certificates, and making a whole slew of phone calls to a whole slew of people I did not want to talk to. One of those calls was to AT&T. I was attempting to change our "family plan" on our cell phones over to a "my whole family is now dead, so I need a single person" plan. At first, my mom tried making this call for me, but they insisted on speaking with me, so I got on the phone. This was my conversation with customer service:

Me: Hi, my husband recently passed away, and I'm calling to switch our family plan over to just my name.

Her: Okay ma'am. We can certainly help you with that. What is the name on the account please?

Me: The account is under my husband's name, Don Shepherd, but this is his wife, and I need to switch it over to my name.

Her: I do understand that. However, I am going to need to speak with the person whose name is on the account, Mr. Don Shepherd...

Me: Riiiight. Believe me, I would love to speak with him too. But I can't. And you can't. Because he's dead. So, he can't come to the phone right now...

My Husband is Not a Rainbow

Her: We do understand, and we are so sorry for your loss. However, we are not authorized to switch over that account without speaking to the account holder, and that would be Mr. Don Shepherd...

Me: Right. I'm aware of what his name is, but saying it over and over doesn't make him any less dead. I'd love to make a conversation happen for you, but it's just not possible, and you're gonna have to talk to ME!

Her: We here at AT&T are so sorry for your loss and send our condolences (long pause), but I do need to speak with the account holder in order to move forward.

Me: (losing it at this point) Okay. Please hold. (calling out to next room) Honey? Don? Boo? You've got a call! (back into phone) Nope. Still dead. Still can't come to the phone. You know, because he's dead and all...

Her: Ma'am, you can also utilize our services online at our website, but you would need the account holders password or authorization to make any changes. Perhaps that would be easier for you at this juncture...

Me: Okay. What part of dead aren't you comprehending? My husband is dead. He DIED! He no longer breathes air. (no response) You know what? Let me try putting this in terms you can understand. Here we go, You ready? My husband is a fuckin' RAINBOW, okay? He's a rainbow on Tonnelle Ave in New Jersey. So, if you'd like, you can hop on over there yourself and talk to him and get the authorization to switch the account over to my name. He usually appears over there right after it's rained and then it's kind of sunny...

Actually, that is not what happened. Well, not exactly. The entire phone call went down the way I just told it, except for the ending. That thing about me yelling at the woman and telling her that my husband is a fuckin' rainbow - that is how I envisioned the phone call ending, because it's funny, and it's a great story, and a great comeback, and a great bit for standup comedy. In real life, though, the ending was much less dramatic and much more real.

What actually happened is that this woman on the phone frustrated me so much, and I was in such pain and grief and exhaustion, that I started crying right there on the phone out of sheer stress. My mom, who had been sitting nearby the whole time listening, grabbed the phone out of my hand and went into classic bitch-mom protective mode. "Now you listen here," she said defiantly to the AT&T robot-fool. "My daughter just lost her husband a couple weeks ago, and she doesn't have time for this nonsense. I don't care how you do it or what you have to do, but we are not hanging up this phone until she gets that cell phone account in her name! Just do it, and do it now please!" And just like that, it was done. There is nothing quite like a pissed-off mom trying to protect her grieving daughter.

Following Page Rainbow illustration: Leah McInnes was with Don in Saskatchewan, Canada. Really, Don? Who goes to Saskatchewan?

My Husband is Not a Rainbow

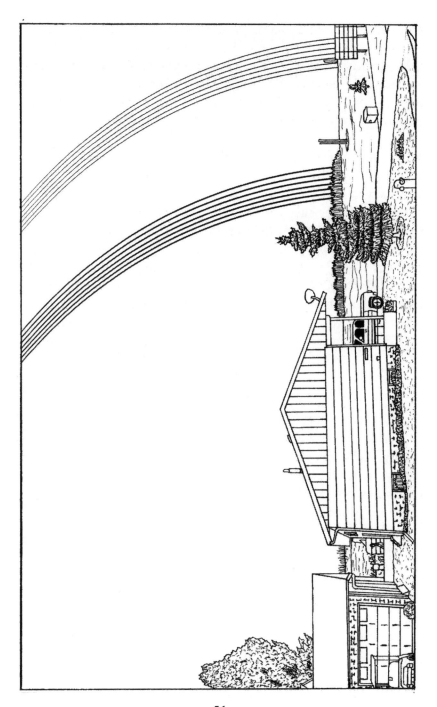

Kelley Lynn Shepherd

Dear Stupid Death Diary:

So it's now August, and it's a new month without my Boo-Bear. Today was awkward. Spent the day out at Long Beach, because my awesome friends thought it might be a good little get away, going somewhere I have never been before and wouldn't have Don triggers or pain. It was me, John, Jessica, and Kevin. John drove, and we sat in awful traffic for a very long time. The conversation was strained, weird, uncomfortable. It was like everyone in that car knew that Don was dead and that our little group of friends was falling apart, but nobody was saying it. I did a lot of staring out the car window. When we got there, we walked along the beach, got ice cream, had lunch, and dipped our toes into the cold water. I love my friends. I love that they did this for me. But something about it, it felt like the beginning of the end of us. The "us" that we knew, is no more. It has been forever altered by death and pain. My husband is gone, and nothing will ever be the same again.

Words About Don

"Without thinking about it much, it was obvious that my friend Kelley had unconditional love, a true supporter. We all deserve to get to spend our lives with our biggest fan, and when you know a friend has this, it brings a subtle secure feeling that helps you sleep just a little bit easier at night. Don gave this to Kelley, and she to him - and it was my husband who said that when they married: 'You didn't even question it, or have even one ounce of hesitation.' Sure, I will miss his crazy sense of humor and his content and laid-back way of being. And, of course, I have awesome sweet memories of all of us skating together at Rockefeller Center in celebration of my birthday. But the most important thing to me is that my friend is now missing her soul mate. I'm sad and angry that Don is now gone from this earth,

My Husband is Not a Rainbow

but I honor him for the husband he was, while he was here." - Sarah Chamberlin, my childhood friend

Dear Stupid Death Diary:

Tomorrow, I'm going home to mom and dad's place in Massachusetts, for a couple of weeks or so. I have to start teaching again the last week in August for fall semester, so I still have some time off before fully dealing with life and work and all that comes with it, without Don. I will be driving his car the five hours to Lunenburg, to their new condo rental. I have to hope the car will survive the trip for me and not break down or have the service engine light come on, like I'm so used to seeing. We still have so many things to figure out: Where I'm going to live. Will I stay here in this apartment? Will I go somewhere else? Where? Will we sell the car? How will I get around if I sell it? I know my parents want me to pack up my life and leave NY and just come live with them, but I can't. I just can't. I don't know much right now, but I do know I can't do that. (Sounds like a Meatloaf song.) Let's hope me and my car make it back okay. I can't wait to leave these walls of depression for a while.

"It's Sunday. It's Thursday. Means nothing to me. Time is an asshole. I'll never be free." – Me

Dear Stupid Death Diary:

This shit sucks. I don't know how anybody does this. I thought coming home would help things a little. It didn't. It hasn't. Nothing has any meaning or purpose for me. Total number of times today that I've burst into tears or had to leave the room to burst into tears? Five. I didn't think it was possible to ache this much. Earlier, I was sitting on the couch in the living room, which really isn't their living room, because it's in a condo I've never seen before, and I just started crying really hard. My mom jumped over to me and put her arms around me, and she cried some too. It's been three weeks today, and I still don't want to be here. I don't want to be anywhere.

"I can't tell if I forgot you,
Or if I injected that part of me
with novocaine.
I can't tell whether I'm burying you,
Or if I'm just trying not to
be buried myself." – Caitlin Belforti

Dear Dead Husband:

We made some huge decisions today. Me and my family. Our family. Tomorrow is the official moving day into the condo house, and the last day we can bring more boxes over from the Groton house I knew my whole life, and the only one you knew in yours. Tomorrow, I will have to say goodbye to yet one more thing. And then, there's your car. My brother is going to buy me a used car that his best friend is selling to him, and he is going to take your car and see if he can sell it to some deserving person who can use it to drive locally. It's going to be so sad letting that car go. Today, we all sat around the dining room table and talked about "what now." We decided our car is just too old and unsafe for me to keep. They started asking a million questions about how will I get to work, how will I make it on one paycheck, what will I do. It all became too much, and I just lost it crying. My brother looked at my dad, and they both walked outside and talked. About fifteen minutes later, they came back in with a plan. My brother's best friend Brenden is selling his used 2002 Bonneville Pontiac. Your car is a '97 Pontiac, so this would be much safer. My brother is going to try and get it for a couple thousand. Then my brother is going to try and sell your car and then give me the money. Everything my family is doing for me is so sweet. I can't get over that my brother is actually buying me a car. Isn't that the nicest thing you've ever heard? I love them so much, and this is so sad. Too many things to let go of all at once. I'm heartbroken. I wish I could kiss you goodnight. I love you forever.

FB Post: Tonight my 2 and a half year old nephew was trying to reach a movie high up on a shelf, and kept asking for tall people, like me, grandpa, and Uncle Don to help him. "Uncle Don's not here," I said. "Where'd he go?" Brian asked me. It took everything inside of me to not break down into hysterical tears right in front of the poor kid. And also, I had absolutely no idea how to answer his question. I don't know where the hell he went. I wish somebody would tell me.
LIKES: 31   COMMENTS: 11

Country Music Hell

Today, we were in my parent's car, going somewhere, and my dad put on some horrific country music station. Not only did he put it on, but for some reason, we couldn't shut the speakers off in the backseat, which is where I was sitting. So the sounds of Travis Tritt or Randy Travis or whoever the fuck it was, was blaring in my eardrum. I started listening to the annoying twang of the "geeee-tar" and all the praising of Jesus and America and beer, and I felt myself starting to get nauseous. This was, of course, one of the few times in the past month that I actually WASN'T already feeling nauseous to begin with, so the fact that country music made me feel nauseous just got me angry. Which made me more nauseous. You see the pattern forming here?

Then I started thinking about how much Don hated country music, even more than I hated it, and all the times that we would mock how every country song sounds exactly the same, has the same topics, similar sounding voices, and the same 3 chords. And how every country singer's name even sounds the same. I used to joke that when you become a country singer, they hand you a big book of names to choose from, and there are only about forty names total in that book. It's true. They are all parts of the same name, just switched around or in different order:

Brooks and Dunne. Garth Brooks. Toby Keith. Keith Urban. Trace Adkins. Rhett Akins. Alan Jackson. Jackson Montgomery. Montgomery Gentry. Leanne Womack. Leanne Rhimes. I could do this all day…

Don and I used to laugh about this for hours. He would get out his guitar and start strumming up a country sounding tune, and I would start singing to it in this obnoxious twangy voice and make up lyrics on the spot. We would write instant country songs, just to show how easy it was and how bad most of them are. We did this mostly to amuse ourselves when we were bored, broke, and inspired - but one time, we did this for my mom, and we got her laughing pretty hard.

So I'm in the car, and now I start thinking about how Don and I both couldn't stand "American Idol" winner Scotty McCreery (I called him "Scotty 'Baby Lock Them Doors' McDreary, or the 'Tool on the Stool'), and how we both predicted from day one that he would win the whole show, because America loves a boring white guy who sits on a stool and sings about trucks and Jesus in a low voice. Don did the funniest impression of him. It was hysterical, and I would laugh every single time he did it. I would actually make him do it for me. I would request it often.

My Husband is Not a Rainbow

"Boo! Do Scotty!" The impression was of him singing that stupid song that he sang on "Idol", and he would sing the lyrics: "Baby lock them doors and turn the lights down low!" He would sing it and make these faces that Scotty made, where his mouth went over to one side, and it made me laugh so hard.

And so the stupid country song is getting louder and louder, or it seemed that way in my head, and then it goes from Travis Tritt to that obnoxious Carrie Underwood "Jesus Take the Wheel" song. I started to breathe really fast, the tears started coming again, and I felt another panic attack coming on. It wasn't anything about the lyrics or the songs themselves that was making me emotional. It was the idea that the music was so lame, and that it was making me think of Don and I mocking it, and that we would never laugh that way together, ever again. And for some reason, being in the backseat of a car, seatbelt on, nowhere to run or escape to, is usually what makes me get that trapped, claustrophobic feeling that I've become so familiar with in the past month. I started to focus on my breathing and try to slow it down, until I finally felt as if my heart was beating correctly again. At that moment, my mom was looking at me concerned and asked if I was okay. "Do you want the music off?" she asked. All I could do was shake my head yes, but what I really wanted was for Jesus to take the wheel and drive us straight into the nearest lake somewhere, just so I could get out of this hellish prison of a car.

Tonight, my parents are inviting Aunty Eve over to watch The Country Music Awards. Wonderful. I'm stuck in a condo where the huge TV will be blaring song after horrible song for three mind-numbing hours, watching men in ridiculous hats parade around and sing about whiskey and cheatin' wives. I must find a method of escape. Don is so damn lucky to be dead.

Kelley Lynn Shepherd

"When I die, I think my version of Hell would be sitting at the bar in some awful country-western club on Karaoke night, listening to some off-pitch dork twang away on some terrible country tune about cheatin' wives and Jesus." – Don Shepherd

FB Post: Wish I could hear you playing your guitar in the next room, excited to call me in to sit on the couch next to you, so you could play me the last few chords you just learned while I was at work. No more new chords. My world is silent without you in it.
LIKES: 14   COMMENTS: 3

*"Can you please tell me how to go on.
I'm tired and hopeless and life feels so long.
What are the words to this horrible song?"* – Me

Dear Stupid Death Diary:

Someone, a family friend, actually said to me today, "It's become clear that you need to move on." He's a friend of my parents who said it, has been a friend of our family for years. He said it to me in an email, as his response to a blog post I had written about missing my husband. This hurts and angers me on so many levels. Move on? Really? It JUST happened! I thought I was doing an okay job with coping so far, but apparently I should have forgotten all about my husband by now. My parents were comforting me because I was crying over the fact that this person said this. I just don't understand all the judgments from people who have NO idea and who have not been through this hell. It makes no sense to me. They have no clue what they are talking about. Some people just shouldn't speak. Ever.

FB Post: So I've decided to write a book. I don't know when I'll start or when I'll finish, I just know I want to do it at some point. I will start with a blog, and then eventually, take some of the blog posts and turn them into a book of some kind. I don't know the first thing about publishing, but I'm a writer, and it's the only thing that has helped me so far. It's my mission that Don's life and death are never forgotten and that his enormous heart and story is told to as many people as possible, so that he will live forever.
LIKES: 145   COMMENTS: 93

"In death, we are all equal.
In grief, we are all unique.
In love, we are all survivors." – Dianna Walker

FB Post: So, it's August 13th, and it's officially been one month since you died. I still can't believe it's true. Tonight, I am wishing that I told you way more often how much I loved you. I'm wishing that I had said THANK YOU for all the things you gave me, especially the pure joy and love. The one thing that keeps me going is that I finally found a way to make sure you are never forgotten. I'm writing a book, honey. And YOU are the star. I love you so much. Xoxo …
LIKES: 14   COMMENTS: 7

FB Post: Can't sleep. Can't stop crying. Can't stop missing. Can't breathe. Can't move. It's been one month and one day

since he died, and the pain is so unbearable, especially in the middle of the night.
LIKES: 7   COMMENTS: 1

"Don't want to move forward, can't stand to look back.
Just leave me on the railroad track." – Me

Alien

This morning, my brother, Dave, dropped off his son, Brian, on his way to work so that mom, dad, and I could babysit him for the day. My mom usually has him one day per week, and today is that day. It is also somehow suddenly August, and my parents' sixty sixth birthdays were both in July. Because Don died two days after my dad's birthday and a week before my mom's, we never really acknowledged it. Nobody was much in the mood for celebrating. David thought that tomorrow we could hang out as a family and just get take-out or do something nice for mom and dad together. He is talking to mom about this in the bathroom, as if I am not here. They are planning the day out for tomorrow and trying to make decisions about food and details. I take my brother into the other room and insist on giving him some money for our parents' birthdays, because I want to chip in. I want this to be from both of us. I give him sixty dollars, and I practically have to force it into his hands. He won't take it. He keeps saying, "No, no, that's too much. No, you don't need to help. It's okay."

What he doesn't understand is that I NEED to help. I need to feel like a contributing member of society again. Ever since Don died, nobody has let me pay for anything. People keep buying my food, gas, clothes, everything. I understand why they are doing it, and I appreciate all of it greatly, but I feel like a child who can't help her own brother get a small gift for our parents. I feel invisible lately and like people think I am made of glass. Like I will break in half or something right in front of their eyes. All the whispering and all the NOT mentioning of Don around me. As if I'm unaware that he is dead. I wish that someone would just TALK ABOUT HIM and say how much they loved him and what he meant to them. Or say that they miss him too. I know they are feeling it, but nobody talks about it ever. They don't say anything, and when they don't say anything, it makes me question whether or not they feel anything. Do they even miss him? They have to. Why aren't they saying so? It's the great big elephant in the room. Kelley's husband died, but let's not discuss it. It might upset her. I wish people understood that every moment of living in this world without him is "upsetting," and that I am never NOT thinking about him, and that talking about him is thousands of times better than not talking about him. But for the most part, people don't see this and continue to talk around me or in whispers. They whisper about me and about what happened, as if I can't hear everything they are saying. I hear you, and I want you to talk to me, instead of around me and through me and behind me. I give my brother the money, and for a tiny second, I feel human again.

Dear Stupid Death Diary:

My heart feels like it is going to explode. I think my heart might actually fall out and land on the floor. Jen and Dave had some news for us today. She is pregnant with their second child. They actually knew that she was pregnant when they drove to New Jersey for Don's funeral last month, but out of respect for me and the timing of things, they decided that was not the time to let us know. I am so happy for my brother and sister-in-law. Really. Truly. But here on these private pages, I can say that I am currently locked in the bathroom, quietly sobbing my head off. I don't want to feel this way. It's the grief, and I feel ashamed about it. My brother is having another child, more family, and my husband is dead forever. He is dead. He will never be a dad. He will never get to play with little Brian ever again. And now, he will never get to meet his little niece or nephew. I feel like someone keeps stabbing me over and over, and I have a migraine from the pain. We talked about having a family. Kids of our own. We talked about natural vs. adoption, and how much Don loved the idea of helping a child who is already here and needs a forever home. We talked about this often. These ideas about our family in the near future. The world was open to us and our dreams. We thought we had lots of time to decide and prepare and keep talking. And now he is just dead, and everything means nothing, and everything hurts. I hate feeling like this about my own brother. I hate my own jealousy of his life. He has everything that was taken from me. I hate that he is being so damn sweet to me and has done so much already to help me, and here I am, bitter and jealous. I hate my life, and I hate who I am becoming.

"All the things we will never do,
I miss them more,
When I miss you." – Mark Teo

The Friendship

It was February of 1998, and after our very first online five hour chat in that music trivia room, Wayabovepar and Camelsocks (otherwise known and Don and myself) found themselves talking to one another almost every single day.

At first, we would both log into the Music Chat Room on AOL, maybe play the lyric game for a while with whomever else showed up in there, and then eventually pair off into a private Instant-Message box, where we would have multi-hour long talks into the night. At the time, we both had day jobs, so this became our nightly routine. We would sign on sometime around nine PM, and talk for a couple hours or more. I would try and wait until my roommate, Sarah, went to bed, so that I didn't disturb her. Don was living in a house in Florida with someone he had dated for a number of years and her two children. The romantic part of the relationship had been petering out for some time now, and he was making plans in his head to find the right time to move out and get his own place. He wasn't ready yet, though, and not ready to leave the kids, whom he had helped raise and had become quite close with. Meanwhile, I was in the midst of perhaps my second or third unhealthy, casual, no-commitment relationship - with a guy that wasn't right for me. Over time, I would end that relationship, only to date someone else for a few short months, who also was not right for me. I didn't know it back then, but I was in a desperate search for self-worth and validation. I had been through an unspeakable trauma, and ever since, my choices in the opposite sex made little to no sense. I had also gained a lot of weight because of this trauma, and I felt like some sort of fraud who was living in someone else's body. So, the fact that neither Don nor myself were technically "available" in the beginning was actually a very good thing. We could both keep talking and keep telling ourselves that we were merely becoming good friends. Of course, we both knew that deep down, what was happening between us was much, much more than friendship. But it would be a little while longer until either of us was willing to define it.

Time marched on, and we continued talking. Our friendship and connection was blossoming. The first few months or so of our time together was purely over the internet. We talked about everything and talked deeply, yet neither of us seemed ready to make that first move. One night, we were both typing to each other, and Don asked me if I had a strong New York accent. I said, no, not at all. I live in Queens, New York, but I'm not from New York City. I'm from Massachusetts. But since I have lived here since age eighteen to go to college, I don't really have a Boston accent either. He said, "So you have no accent?" "Pretty much," I typed back. I then asked him if he had a southern accent, since he had been living in Florida for so many years, and since he used words like "fixin." He said that although he had picked up southern phrases over the years, that he was born in Whittier, California, and also didn't really have a strong accent of any kind.

So, based on all that curiosity, we made the decision to finally call each other later that same night. We were both very anxious to hear the other speak. Plus, Don had just traded in his sports-car for a "sweet as hell '97 Grand Prix Pontiac, as he called it, and he was really excited to tell me all about it, being a typical guy who was obsessed with everything car-related. I wanted to hear about his car too, but I wanted to hear him speak even more. I still remember how nervous I was when he gave me his number and told me to call him in about an hour. I was home alone that night at the apartment, and I paced back and forth about thirty seven times in the living room area before finally picking up the phone and dialing it, my hands sweating against the receiver.

Him: Hello Camelsocks.

Me: Hi, Don. (pause) This is so weird.

Him: It is weird. But good weird. My fingers were starting to hurt from all the typing.

Me: Yeah. Mine too. So tell me about your car.

Him: Oh my god, it's the best. I'm so excited. My cat Isabelle loves it too. She sits in my lap while I drive. It's the coolest thing. She doesn't even move, just sits there calmly. This car rocks.

Me: I'm so happy for you. I know nothing at all about cars. (pause) Okay. I'm just gonna say it. I'm SO relieved you don't talk like one of "them Duke Boys down in Hazard County." I was really scared you were gonna talk like someone from "Deliverance."

Him: (laughing) Oh, now darlin' - don't you worry yer purdy little head off about things like that...

Me: Stop it. That is frightening.

Him: Okay. I'll admit it too. I was picturing you talking like Fran Drescher/The Nanny, or having some awful Long Island accent. I don't think I could have handled that. (laughing)

Me: Was I right, then? I don't really have an accent.

Him: Yeah, you really don't. You do have a really sexy voice though.

Me: Really?

Him: Hell yeah. I love listening to you talk. I already like this way more than the typing.

That night, we broke our internet chat record of five hours with an epic, championship eight hour long phone call. We spent hours talking about our pasts, families, past relationships. I told him that something had happened to me that was traumatic, but that I wasn't ready to talk about it right now, or maybe ever. He said that when I felt ready, I could trust him. The conversation that night became very flirtatious, and we turned a corner in our friendship, going from just friends, to "friends with possibility."

Kelley Lynn Shepherd

There was an electricity happening. Something new and strange and beautiful. Something not yet defined. When we hung up the phone finally, he ended the call by referring to me as "Bunny-Boo." I had no idea where that came from, so I asked, as I giggled. "I dunno," he said. "It's just what I felt like calling you. My Bunny-Boo. Goodnight Bunny-Boo." "Goodnight Boo-Bear." I don't know where the hell *that* came from either.

"My heart, still beating, whispers, 'where there is shadow, you will find light.'" – Sue Knight Deutsch

Dear Stupid Death Diary,

All the kindness and generosity shown toward me by people over the past month and a half has been astounding and very moving. It's coming from so many different places, it floors me. I've been so scared about how on earth I'm going to survive and keep living ten minutes outside NYC in our apartment, which was my dream and Don's dream for me, to make it as a writer/comedian/actor here one day. We struggled so much financially. Neither of us made great money, and then he died, out of nowhere. The bills keep coming, and I have to pay them alone somehow. We had no life insurance, no savings of any kind, and he was working two jobs just so we could BEGIN to start up a small savings plan to help our future. I lost my health insurance, because I was covered under his. So now I have nothing. And then, all this generosity comes pouring in from friends, FB friends, strangers, friends of Don's that he only knew online. There's this music site called Vanderbilly.com, where guitar lovers hang out and talk on message boards and offer up each other guitar lessons on YouTube for free. Don hung out there a lot, so I logged in and told them he had died, and they were in shock. One of the guys there makes guitars, so he made one to honor Don, then raffled it off on the site. All the money went to me. They are also having t-shirts made up with his screen-name (DShep) on the sleeve, in memory. It fills me with emotion to know they are doing this for me, someone they have never even met.

Meanwhile, my own online friends that I met years ago while planning my wedding at the Message Boards for Brides.com, have begun their own campaign to help me out by making donations into my PayPal account. They have also gotten together and sent me care packages, gift cards, and other really sweet things. Don used to call them "imaginary friends", because I hadn't met them in person. "You talkin' to your imaginary friends again?" he would say jokingly, while walking by me sitting at the computer. We all planned our weddings together on that website, sharing ideas, and talking about our engagements and then weddings. And now, my husband has died. It is just so surreal.

Lots of people also made donations with cards at the funeral, and others have come together in groups to pool a bit of cash together for me. Everyone at Adelphi University, where I teach and graduated in '94 with a BFA in Performing Arts, got together and collected money. Barbara, the Theatre Department Administrator, told me they have something for me when I return to work in a couple of weeks. She and my boss/friend, Nick, the Theatre Chairperson, were so sweet and concerned and caring. Some of the nurses from the ER at the hospital where Don spent lots of his time while on shift also pitched in and collected, and they all signed a huge card to me. Most of these people have never met me, or met me at the funeral. It is just so overwhelming and incredible. I don't even know how to begin to thank people. My mom always raised us on writing thank you notes to people who came to the services, signed the book, gave a card. It is so emotional writing these out, but I really do want to thank people. I have been doing about five of them a day, or as many as I can handle before needing to stop. Thank you, thank you, thank you. This would make Don so happy, to know so many people care.

"Maybe I get to keep that piece that nobody else gets.
Maybe you and I get to share your soul and your heart,
Until the end of time, and then longer.
Much, much longer.
Maybe I need to believe this,
In order to survive." - Me

Dear Stupid Death Diary:

My brother and my dad have been taking Don's car and fixing it up as best as they can, cleaning it inside and out, and getting it ready for someone to possibly, hopefully buy it. My dad doesn't think we will get more than a few hundred bucks for it, since it has so much mileage, is so old, and is in pretty poor condition with lots of issues. He thinks maybe someone will buy it for parts, and I just about lost it crying. For PARTS? No!!! That is Don's baby. He was in love with that car. He would be heartbroken if the person who bought it didn't even LIKE it, and just tore it apart for car parts. I made my brother promise me that they would do whatever they could to sell it to someone who will actually take care of it and drive it. My brother understood. He took me outside to the garage today, and said, "So before I put this on Craigslist and put it up for sale, there's a few things I can switch out of it and give to you, that you can put into the car I'm buying you, so you can feel like you still have a piece of Don or Don's car when you drive it."

He walked over to the floor mats, in the front seat, and told me he would put those into my Bonneville. Then he showed me the

My Husband is Not a Rainbow

Grand Prix logo emblem on the dashboard. "I can take this off and velcro it onto the dash of your car." I followed him over to the steering wheel. "Last thing. The rearview mirror. I can take it off and switch it out, and put the one from Brendan's car in here. I know it's kind of dumb, but this way, when you're adjusting your mirror with your hand, your hand will be in the same place where Don's hand was every time he drove. I know it's stupid, but..."

And with that, I couldn't hold back the crying any longer. "All of that is beyond amazing and not at ALL dumb. Thank you!" I gave him a hug and tried to stop crying. He said something about: "I don't know how to help you, and this is something small I can do, so I'm doing it." Something SMALL??? Buying me a used car is hardly SMALL, and then knowing what it would mean to me to have any tiny piece of Don's car to keep with me. It is just priceless. I have the best brother. Truly.

Dear Stupid Death Diary:

Earlier, my parents were having a conversation about something totally insignificant and small, but it represented the kind of conversations you have after years and years of marriage. It would only come from having decades together, so instantly, my face felt flush as I sat there in the living room, half-listening to them speak. They were talking about what to do with all the many boxes of dishes, kitchen stuff, and other things that came from their home of forty five years and now would be in this condo. Should they put it all downstairs in the basement, or take some out and use it, even though they may have to move again in a year or two? Then they began talking about the dining room set they had since we were kids, and whether or not to sell it, since it didn't fit in the new place.

Kelley Lynn Shepherd

All of a sudden, my stomach was in knots again. Don and I will never have years of furniture to pack, or move, or make decisions about. We will never even have ONE house together, never mind the two places we have lived. All we will ever have is that crappy New Jersey apartment. No kids to think about, or toys to store away for the next one. No future to think of. Just nothing. Nothing ever again. I suddenly bolted up off the couch, because the massive sobbing was about to start, and I ran out of there, yelling out to them, "Gotta go. Sorry." Made it out the door about three feet before I burst into a crying fit. The kind of crying where it's loud and wailing and messy and so hard to breathe or talk. I ran full speed up to the other end of the condo association and found a huge rock by the woods. I sat there and just screamed and cried. Even though I could barely get out words or anything intelligent, I needed badly to talk to someone. I called John and left a babbling voicemail. Called Elayne Boosler and did the same. Called Vanessa. Nobody picked up. So I just cried some more, instead, and kept wishing for a huge boulder to fall on top of me and end this pain.

"When people look at a widow,
They see her smile and her bravery.
When a fellow widow looks at her,
They see the pain in her eyes,
like looking through portholes into an empty room
with debris of her prior life on the floor."
– Janice Martel Hart

Dear Stupid Death Diary:

Everyone knows about Jen and Dave's baby news now, as the word has spread through family to the rest of our relatives. Everyone is talking about new life, new siblings, and new joy.

My Husband is Not a Rainbow

All I can think about is that my life has ended. The life I have always known, and the one we were planning and dreaming about and picturing is just gone. I didn't know it was possible to be so happy for my brother while simultaneously feeling my heart rip outside of itself. I can't say most of this out loud to anyone, because I will sound bitter and jealous and like I'm not happy for my brother. But I am. Truly. It's just that my life has ended, and there will be no new babies or kids or houses or dreams of a family. I'm just barely holding on...

Words About Don

"I did not know Don Shepherd. Not yet anyway. All I really knew of him was that he was coming all the way from Florida to live with my friend, Kelley. I did know how happy he made her, and that was enough for me. When thinking of Don, my mind always goes back to that first day. Don had moved his entire life to New Jersey to be with Kelley, and we were all there to greet him and help with the move. Sounded fairly simple, but bringing his entertainment center up multiple flights of stairs with him and Kevin proved to be more powerful than us. We finally did it, but it wasn't pretty.

That same day, Don had to return his Penske moving truck to 'Who The Hell Knows' New Jersey, and it was decided that I would go with him. Now, with people I don't know, I can get shy and uncomfortable. It's not them, it's me. I feel socially awkward. A tall order for someone like me - Don was tall. Of course, it was more than okay, and I'm glad I got to spend those few hours with him. Yes, HOURS. We got very lost.

As I said, my mind always goes to that first day when he moved in. Strange. We've had lots of great times together after that; road trips, Christmases together, lots of get-togethers with friends over the years, etc. It was sweet and uplifting to see

Kelley Lynn Shepherd

Kelley and Don begin their lives together. I was extremely happy for her, for them. Kelley was, and will always be, one of my best friends. To see her so happy was enough for me."
- John Joseph Cina

Dear Stupid Death Diary:

My dad has been spending so much time on the car that my brother bought me. It is the nicest thing. He has been cleaning it inside and out. He and mom bought me new tires, had fresh oil put in, and had everything in it fixed that needed attention, which I think was a few different things in total. We took all of Don's car tools and safety things and moved them from his car trunk to my new one. His First Aid kit, blanket, and tool box are all back there now. Flashlight, batteries, all that good stuff. It is so funny how, before I met Don, my dad used to do all those things for me that kept me safe and made me feel secure. Then, my husband did all those things for years. Now, my dad is doing them again. It breaks my heart and makes my heart happy all at once. My dad came inside today and told me and my mom, "I know you are both going to think I'm nuts or have lost my mind, but when I was out there just now, washing and vacuuming the car, I stopped for a minute, and I distinctly heard Don's voice say to me, 'Thanks, Pop. Thanks for taking care of my girl. " That's what Don used to call him - Pop. And I don't think my dad is crazy at all. The most important thing to Don was ALWAYS that I was safe, happy, taken care of. I don't "believe" that he said that to my dad today - I *know* he did.

"Life is good, death is not the end, love is all that matters." – Orlagh Green

My Husband is Not a Rainbow

Dear Stupid Death Diary:

The last couple of days, I have spent time with some relatives. Yesterday, my Aunt Ginny (mom's sister) came over and brought me a homemade giant pot of Pasta Boonatha, our Italian family dish that goes back a few generations. It's a huge undertaking to make it, so the fact that she did it for me really means a lot. And it was so yummy.

Then last night, my cousin, (Ginny's' daughter) Laura, picked me up and took me out for dinner down the street at this great little place. We had a really nice time, and we talked a lot about me and Don, and other things too. On the drive home, she wanted to take me to this great local place for ice cream, but they were closed for some reason. So instead, we went to this other place down the street from where my parents live. I told Laura that since she paid for dinner, I would buy dessert. As we started eating our ice-cream, we both paused at the same time. I think she spoke first. "This is gross. Is yours gross?" "Yes," I said, laughing hysterically. "How the hell do you screw up ice-cream? I don't think I've ever had gross chocolate-chip ice cream before, until right now." "I know! It tastes like wood. How is that possible?" We both ate a few more bites, and then threw the rest away, which I don't think I have ever done before in my entire life. As we pulled into my parent's driveway and I started to get out, I said to my cousin: "Thank you so much for dinner!" She yelled back as she pulled away, "Sure. Thanks for the shitty ice cream!"

"Some people say, 'Things happen for a reason.' I say, 'We make reason out of what happens to us.'"
– Nancy Saltzman

Kelley Lynn Shepherd

FB Post: Today is my last day in Massachusetts. Headed back to Jersey and to the kitties tomorrow morning. Not really looking forward to what awaits me and to being in that apartment alone, without Don. It feels so empty and wrong, but I begin teaching in a few days for fall semester, so I need to start attempting this "life" thing once again. My stomach hurts.
LIKES: 55   COMMENTS: 12

Words About Don

"I am one of Donny's nephews. One of his four nephews, to be exact. He also has a niece. I learned to love rock music because of Don. I know his life as one of being a truly genuine man, kindhearted and loving. He looked after everyone with grace and enthusiasm, and always gave the best of himself. He loved his wife deeply, his sisters immensely, and they all loved him the same. He comes from a sassy, outspoken family - but he was my mom's and my aunt's baby brother, and boy do they miss him. He used to come here in the summers with my grandma. She was something else. That is all I will say about that.

But Kelley won his heart, and that is what made us all happy. Don and my mom, Karen, were almost fourteen years apart, a huge age difference, but in personality - no difference at all. My mom used to look after him when he was a baby. When Donny moved to New Jersey, he was in love and glad to leave Florida behind. Kelley is forever our family and forever in our hearts. He told me once that he was proud of the man I had become. Well, I am proud of being the kind of man that he was. You will always be my Uncle Donny, and now, my Auntie Kelley. It is funny because I am only two years younger than Kelley, and ten years younger than Donny, who HATED being called 'Donny,' by the way. But I still get to tease him, no matter what. Forever." - Mark Exlos

"The ebb and flow of acceptance and denial is as certain as the waxing and the waning of the moon."
– Kimberly Conway

Goodbye

Today is the day I say goodbye. No, not to my husband. I don't imagine that I could EVER say goodbye to him. Nor would I want to. He will be with me forever, and saying goodbye to him is simply not in my heart or my vocabulary.

Today I am driving my new, used car over to our old, used car to say goodbye. Today I am driving from my parent's new, rented condo in a new town, to their house on Taylor Road in the town I grew up in, Groton, Massachusetts, to see our house for the very last time. I heard or read somewhere that three of the most stressful things in life are: losing a spouse or child, moving, and losing a job or community of some kind. I can't recall who said this, so it might be total bullshit, but either way, my family has dealt with all three things in the month of July, and let me tell you that I'm pretty stressed out right now.

For the past couple of years, my parents have been dealing with the reality of losing their home. Our home. It is the only home they have ever owned together, the home where my brother and I were raised; the home they have shared for the past forty five years of their lives and marriage. Like many others, they became victims of the housing market and the economy. Because the banks and lawyers are so backed up with thousands of foreclosures across the map, my parents had been living in their home for the past couple years, looking for a new place, and awaiting word on the date of the foreclosure auction. The first auction was held July first. Nobody showed up, so it was rescheduled for a few weeks later. Don died July thirteenth. The funeral was the seventeenth, and by the next week, my parents were back home packing up forty five years of their lives into boxes and moving vans, getting ready for the inevitable. I kept thinking about how Don would have been so helpful with them moving and would have lightened the mood by making all of us laugh while being forced out of the life we all knew. But he is gone, and he won't be making us laugh anymore. At least not in the way I want him to.

A second auction was scheduled for July thirty first. This time, people showed up to possibly buy the home, but when the dumb bank set the foreclosure price astronomically high, the people said, "For a foreclosure home? You've got to be kidding me!" and went on their merry way. (I don't know if they literally said those exact words. I doubt it, since nobody talks like that. But that was the overall tone.) So that leaves the evil bank owning my parents' home and them moving to a few towns over. After staying in the condo with them for a couple weeks now and helping them with all the back and forth trips from the old house and back, today is the day I must go back to MY home in New Jersey, go back to my job after the end of my summer "break," and to try and figure out how the hell to live life without my husband.

But first, I need to take my Pontiac Bonneville that my brother bought me and drive it over to our old Pontiac Grand Prix and say one final goodbye to both the car and the house. It is just something I feel I must do, as I will most likely never see either the car or the house again. Our car, Don's car, will be sold by my brother to, hopefully, some really nice people out there that for whatever reason, desire to have an old beat up car that really loves being in repair shops. The house will still be here, of course, but it won't be ours anymore, so I have no interest in gawking at it or looking at it and knowing that other people now live there, and they aren't us.

My Husband is Not a Rainbow

As I get into my new car for the first time, mom and dad are standing in their new rented driveway of our new life. We say our goodbyes, and my mom and I both cry. My dad pretends to busy himself with dad things, so that he doesn't cry too, probably. The emotions of losing Don, and just having spent the past couple weeks at my parents place that isn't really their place, take over, and I drive off from Lunenburg to Groton, sobbing the whole way there.

When I pull up into our old circular driveway, I look at the stone wall that surrounds it and think about my dad and his late brother, Ray, building that wall together. I'm pretty sure I was too young to actually remember them doing it, but for some reason, I do have a memory of them doing it. Or maybe it's just a picture that I've created inside my head of them building that wall. Sometimes it's hard to tell whether what I'm feeling is a memory or if it's the result of someone telling me the story so vividly, that I can then pull it up inside my own mind. Either way, it's a beautiful stone wall that wraps around the half-moon shaped driveway.

Actually, my dad added on two additional rooms to the house, after he and mom bought it decades ago; creating a dining room and an indoor porch that later became my mom's Mary Kay office, and then finally, an informal living room area that had their gigantic HD flat screen TV that Don loved so much. He would look forward to visiting them just to sit in front of that huge TV, spread out on the comfy couch, and relax with family. He felt so at home and comfortable around my parents, that oftentimes, minutes after us arriving from a trip from NJ, he would fall asleep right on that couch with no problem or effort whatsoever. "I'm just gonna rest my eyes, Boo," he would say with a smile, knowing full well he was going to be asleep within seconds. Rest his eyes, my ass. That was Don-speak for "Wake me up at dinner time!"

Kelley Lynn Shepherd

I get out of the car and walk up the stone walkway to our side door entrance. I look down, and carved into the stone, it says, "Dave, Chris, Kelley, David." Our names are all there; written with chalk or a stick or something; one underneath the other. This makes me cry again, but who cares at this point? Nobody is here but me. All I do lately is cry, it seems, so bring it on. I lift up the outdoor welcome mat to find the key underneath that mom and dad had left for me one last time. My mind flashes back to high school, coming home after being dropped off from my first date with my friend, Scott. I wore a red and black checkered plaid skirt and button down matching top, and my hair was feathered and long, in true 1980s glory. My parents were out that night, so they left the key underneath the mat for me. I recall coming home that night crying, because I wasn't sure of how Scott felt about me. I was once again confused by his inconsistent behavior with me, and my little teen heart couldn't comprehend any of it. I remember how serious I thought everything was back then, how tragic it all seemed when Scott and I filtered out as a couple, time and time again. How I thought my life was over, and that I would never meet anyone else, ever again. I wish that someone had told me, or that I somehow could have known, that none of that would ever matter in just a few short years' time. I wish I hadn't wasted so many tears on what turned out to be a blip, a nano-second, of my life. I wish I was nicer to my parents back then, instead of spending so much time slamming doors or being overly rude or sarcastic; or locking myself in my bedroom all night and ignoring my dad, who desperately wanted to help my constant ridiculous adolescent state. If only I could somehow know that what I would experience and go through as an adult would be so much deeper, so much more painful, and that my parents would be my saving grace. I would have never slammed that door in my mom's face if I had known that. I would have never been such a bitch.

My Husband is Not a Rainbow

When I walk into the house, the first thing I see is the dining room. Then, the kitchen. There is no table. No furniture. No life. All the rooms are bare and empty. The moving vans have come and gone days ago, and now all that is left are blank, ugly walls. I'm crying hard now as I feel my childhood and my innocence and my life being stripped away from me, room by room. I stand on the dirty, brown carpet where the dining room table once was, and I look around at the rooms surrounding me. I picture all of the happy family gatherings that took place there, with everyone sitting around that table, laughing. All the Christmas mornings we would sit, drinking our hot chocolate with marshmallows, eating mom's annual tradition of fried dough with cinnamon and sugar, and doing our scratch off lottery tickets with a penny, anxiously waiting to open our stockings and presents under the Christmas tree. All the meatballs, lasagnas, chicken cutlets, and pasta boonatha's my Nana would make in mom's kitchen; banging pots and pans around at four AM in the morning. All of the Monday night Mary Kay meetings my mom used to hold in her office, where grown women would be singing this ridiculous song in unison, "I've got the Mary Kay enthusiasm all over me today!" My dad, brother, and I, would always find something to do each Monday night, in order to escape these meetings. We would either hang out in the basement and watch TV, or leave the house altogether and go out for ice cream at Johnson's or Kimball's, trying not to return until all the cars were gone from the driveway and the house was once again safe from middle-aged ladies in pink business suits.

I walk down the stairs into the basement, and I remember the slumber party I had down there during junior high school, where we played that game "Stiff As a Board, Light as a Feather," and we were convinced that we had lifted Kari Hawkins into thin air, using nothing more than our mental powers. I look at the pool table in the center of the room and think about how mom would always use the top of it during Christmas season to wrap all the various holiday gifts. She would turn the basement into a mini

Kelley Lynn Shepherd

Santa's workshop each year, wrapping paper and tape and scissors and tags strewn all over the place. On Christmas Eve for the past six years, Don and I would take turns going downstairs late at night to wrap each other's gifts in privacy, so the other person couldn't grab a peek. I would always get so excited just looking at Don's gifts for me, all wrapped up and pretty. I was amazed at what a great present wrapper he was. Don's present-wrapping skills were quite impressive.

I walk into my dad's workshop area and remember all the times we recorded ourselves singing down there, using his music equipment and karaoke tapes to make cassettes of us singing to different artists. Dad's favorite was always Elvis. His singing voice sounds just like Elvis when he sings; it really does. He would spend hours down here, just singing and perfecting himself on those tapes. Even earlier, when I was a kid, me and my dad and my cousin, Tabatha, would spend hours making incredibly silly recordings into the microphone; doing impressions of celebrities, fake interviews, and other things we all found hilarious. Most of the tape would just be us laughing and snorting into the microphone, because we couldn't get a hold of ourselves. My dad would do impressions of people like Richard Nixon, Kermit the Frog, or Jimmy Stewart; and he would interview my cousin and me while we tried to keep a straight face and failed. As I walk back up the stairs, my mind flashes back to our family, huddled in the basement together, awaiting the passing of Hurricane Gloria. It was a big one, and for us, a pretty major deal, since New England hardly ever had storms like that.

Back in the kitchen. I am picturing my mom, my Aunt Ginny, and my Nana; all cooking something together, at one of the numerous family get-togethers with my cousins Tabatha, Laura, and Chad. The incredible smells and the love that came out of that kitchen, and Nana yelling at everyone to get out so she could cook properly. "Get out of the way! Go sit down! Fungu!"

My Husband is Not a Rainbow

There were so many cups of tea made, sounds of laughter, and the warmth of family coming from that kitchen. There were so many parties and just nights where friends would be over playing board games and talking. I remember being a little kid and not wanting to go to bed whenever my parents had company over, because it always seemed like they were having so much fun. "I don't wanna' miss anything!" I would pout. Sometimes they would let me stay up late and watch them play Password or Boggle with our next door neighbors and friends, Chuck and Eve. I always called them Aunty Eve and Uncle Chuck, because they felt like family.

I begin to recall various Easter Sundays as a kid, when mom would hide our candy all over the house for the Easter hunt, and my brother and I would mock how lame the hiding places were. It was all right out in the open. There would be a giant piece of candy on top of the coffee table or on top of the TV. We would walk around with our little baskets, picking up the candy and sarcastically saying, "Yeah. THIS was real hard to find!" When I was three years old, one of my Easter gifts was a stuffed Bunny rabbit that I named "Bunny." How original. It was underneath the sewing machine in the living room hallway. I spotted it right away, and ran over to it and hugged it. I am now almost forty years old, and I still have Bunny. He isn't looking too good. He is pretty roughed up at this point, but I still have him, and he sits on my bed, where I sometimes cuddle him and other times, still sleep with him. My Uncle Frank always hated Bunny, as did most of my childhood and college friends. I would annoy all of them by giving Bunny a voice and making him talk. Then, when they would hurt Bunny's feelings, I would hum the ending music from "The Incredible Hulk," and make Bunny slowly walk away with his head down in shame. Don thought it was the cutest thing in the world. He always felt bad for Bunny whenever I did that. "I'm sorry, Bunny," he would say. "Don't go. Come back. I'm sorry I hurt your feelings. Aww!"

Kelley Lynn Shepherd

Standing in the formal living room, which is also now void of furniture, I picture what it looked like before it was a formal living room. When I was a kid, before my dad had built the extra rooms on the house, this was the only living room, and the furniture was pretty beat up. Dad used to sit in this old-looking, ugly, puke colored recliner chair. There are lots of old pictures of him holding either me or my brother as babies, and napping with us. I remember going to bed on school nights as a kid, then sneaking back out into that living room a couple hours later, where Dad would be watching "The Tonight Show with Johnny Carson." I would convince him to let me watch too, and it always felt like a special thing. I also remember being really little and my brother and I watching TV shows together in that living room. We did this weird thing where we had to become the characters on the show. Whenever we would watch "Laverne and Shirley," we would have to BE them. There was always a big announcement about it, and I would always "call it" first, during the opening theme song. "I get to be Laverne! I called it! You HAVE to be Shirley! Hahaha!!!" My brother would whine, "But I hate Shirley! I don't wanna be Shirley!" "Well, too bad!" I would yell. For some reason, the idea of being Shirley was something truly awful. We also used to get up early on weekends to watch Looney Tunes and Davey and Goliath. And we would get to stay up late on Fridays to see "Different Strokes," "Love Boat," and "Fantasy Island." I still don't understand why the hell two little kids would want to watch those last two shows, but we did. We also loved Sesame Street and The Electric Company. Apparently, I was deathly afraid of the numbers on both shows. Whenever large numbers would flash across the screen, I would run behind the chair and start crying and screaming "The numbers! The numbers!" Obviously, I don't remember this, because I was about three years old, but my entire family enjoys torturing me by telling me and others about it often. To this day, I still hate the number seven. It looks frightening to me, like it's out to get me. I don't trust the seven, especially the kind with the big ole slash down the middle of it.

My Husband is Not a Rainbow

And really, it's no wonder. I'm not the only one. Do you know why six is afraid of seven? Because seven eight nine. (Read that one slowly.)

Looking over at where the TV once was, I laugh at the memory of watching the all-day long broadcast of LIVE AID with my childhood friend, Stephanie, and singing along and strumming on an old guitar using a butter knife. Finally, the last image that flashes through my head about this room is Christmas morning, two years ago. Don and me, mom and dad, and Dave and Jen were all opening our gifts under the tree, and we were almost finished, when I jumped up and told Don, "Wait! I have one more thing for you!" I went into my parents' bedroom closet and came back out with it. It was an electric black guitar. But not just any guitar. It was the guitar that Don had seen at Daddy's Junky Music Store when he took his first guitar lesson with my cousin, Nicky, who teaches there. I had remembered him coming home that day, so happy with the lesson, and he kept talking about this guitar that was on the wall that he just fell in love with. "Oh, man. It' so beautiful. I wish I could have bought it. What a great guitar!" A few days later, I called Nicky and asked him to hold it for me as a Christmas gift. By the time Christmas came around later that year, Don had forgotten all about the guitar.

I walked out into the living room and presented it to him. It was unwrapped with a giant bow around it. He was sitting in one of the living room chairs, and when I gave it to him, his face lit up like a Christmas tree. He was suddenly a little boy. "No way!" he shrieked. "Oh, wow. This is awesome! Wow!" He immediately started fiddling with it and playing it, then stood up and gave me the biggest hug and kiss. "I have the bestest wife ever! My wife RULES!" he said. It made me so happy to see him that happy. You would have thought that I had just given him a million dollars. But to him, that guitar was more special than money, or anything really. After that day, each time he played it, he would say out loud, "Boo bought me this guitar!

Kelley Lynn Shepherd

It's my favorite one ever cuz Boo bought it for me!" I will always remember that look on his face that Christmas morning, in this great little house on Taylor Road.

I leave the living room and walk down the hallway where all of the bedrooms and the bathroom are. I look at the two red sinks in the bathroom that my dad built for the house. He was a plumber for years when my parents first got married, and he had done all kinds of work on this house; both in the beginning, and for years afterward. When my parents bought this home, they paid $11,000. That still makes me laugh out loud. That is what homes cost back then. Can you imagine? Today, it's so common to have two or even three bathrooms in one home. Back then, one was normal. My mom wanted two bright red sinks. She thought it looked classy and liked the idea that her and my dad would each get their own sink. So my dad put in two bright red sinks and did the finish in black and white. It was a very unique looking bathroom.

Oddly enough, I can only recall two specific memories having to do with the bathroom. The first one is the day I got my very first period. (At this point, my male readers are very much allowed to groan or to say out loud to yourself, "OH Christ! I gotta hear about her period??") Just like with grief, this milestone is nothing at all like they show you in books or movies. I remember my Aunt Ginny was over having lunch with my mom, and I had gone into the bathroom and noticed the blood. I was so embarrassed and pissed off that this was happening RIGHT. NOW, with company over, and that I was going to have to yell out for my mom to get me some pads or tampons or something. I don't recall the details, but I think I yelled out for her and then whispered through the doorway, "I just got my period!" "What?" she said, either not hearing me or not believing me, because I was a bit young. "I just got my period, mom!" I said again through clenched teeth. I really wanted to die of humiliation, and then it got worse. There is nothing in the world my mom enjoyed more than embarrassing me and my brother. She did it constantly when we were kids. We would be in the grocery store with her, and she would turn to a total stranger and say very loudly, "Hello, I'm Chris. Have you met my two wonderful children, Kelley and David?" So now, during my moment of greatest adolescent humiliation, my mom yelled out to her sister, in a booming voice, "Our little Kelley is growing up! She just got her period!!!" They both began to mock congratulate each other. "It's a lot of fun, being a woman! You're going to love this, Kelley! Cramps, back aches, mood swings! It's the best!" My Aunt Ginny said sarcastically, as she laughed at my misery.

Mom didn't have any sort of pads in the house, so to further my feeling of total humiliation and "someone please hit me in the head with a two by four," she had to get in the car and drive to the store to get some. I had to wait for her to return, in the bathroom still, as my Aunt continued to share with me the hells of womanhood. When mom got back a few minutes later, she asked me if I needed "help," to which I replied a horrified, "HELL NO!!!" Mom kept asking, because she found it hilarious. "Are you sure? It can be confusing the first time." Finally I yelled out to both of them, "Can you two just please both go away now and stop turning this into an 'Afterschool Special?'" The two of them were both incredibly satisfied with the level at which they had humiliated me, and they walked away from the bathroom door, giggling like school children.

As I look around the bathroom and touch the shiny red sinks, I smile at my second vivid memory there. This one involves that Bunny named Bunny that I just mentioned in one of the above stories. In this memory I have, I was about four years old, so Bunny and I were best friends by then, and I loved him. Well, one day, Bunny looked dirty to me, and I felt like maybe he needed a bath. So I walked into the bathroom with him, and for reasons unknown (or because I was four and not very smart), I dropped Bunny into the toilet. I can actually remember doing this; I just can't recall if I did it because I wasn't tall enough to reach the sinks, or because I really thought that the toilet was like a bathtub and that it would properly clean him. In any case, I reached down with my hands and started to splash toilet water all over Bunny. A few seconds later, my dad walked in. "What are you doing?" he asked, laughing. "I'm giving Bunny a bath," I said, as if that was obvious. My dad smiled and said, "Nooo. That's not how you give him a bath. That's the toilet, honey. Let's get him out of here and dry him off, okay?"

It was a warm, spring day, and my dad took Bunny and laid him outside on the side steps on top of a towel so he could dry out in the sun for a while. A few short hours later, we opened the door to check on the drying status of the stuffed animal that was my best friend, and the biggest tragedy of my four year old life had occurred. Bunny was in pieces; his stuffing all over the grass like a murder victim; his poor lifeless head decapitated and thrown across the lawn without a thought. Turns out that our dog, Tori, had left his doghouse, found Bunny, and decided to viciously tear him apart and eat him. I screamed a blood-curdling scream, ran to my room, and cried hysterically on my bed. My dad tried to comfort and calm me down. "We'll get you another one. It's okay. We're going to get you another Bunny, okay?" "Nooo!!!! " I screamed, getting a head start on my overdramatic personality that Don would always accuse me of having as an adult. "It's not the same!!! I want MY Bunny!! Mine!!!" As I sat there crying like a four year old does, my dad sat there with me. Then, after a while, my mom sat with me, and my dad was gone. "Where did Daddy go?" I asked through my crying fits. "He will be back in a while. He had to go do something."

Turns out, as I would find out years later when my dad retold the story to me, Dad was off doing what really good dads do. He was "fixing" my hurt. Dad had gone out to find another Bunny for his little girl. He was gone for hours. He ended up having to go to five different department stores before he found a stuffed Bunny that looked identical enough to MY Bunny. He wouldn't settle for anything less. When he finally returned and presented me with the new Bunny, I forgot all about my pain and held onto my Bunny for dear life. Everything was great again, and my dad was my hero. For years after that, anytime Bunny would get hurt or his stuffing would start falling out of him again, I would bring him to my dad, and he would perform surgery on Bunny. This happened well after high school, through college, and well into adulthood. Today, Bunny is missing one eye, his stuffing is loose, he is greyish brown instead of the white he used to be, his whiskers are askew and pathetic shadows of their former selves, and his ears are made of bathroom towels that Doctor Dad had sewn on years earlier in one of his surgery sessions. But he is still here. Bunny is still here.

I'm exhausted and feeling the pounding of a grief-migraine as I continue down the narrow hallway to the set of three bedrooms; my parents' room, my brother's room, and my room. I suppose I could just leave and end this house tour right now, but this is the last time I will ever have the honor and opportunity to walk through this house piece by piece, memory by memory - and something inside of me feels like *I must go through this process* of walking through each room ceremoniously, as if I am holding onto each one for just a few minutes longer.

As I walk into my parents' bedroom, I am overcome by the distinct memory of sounds of laughter. It is my laughter and my husband's laughter, and we are lying in my parent's bed, holding hands and cracking ourselves up over something completely silly. This would happen each time we would drive here from Jersey and stay with my parents. They would always give us their bedroom, (after we became engaged) and they would sleep in the basement, or in the smaller bed that was in my old room. For some reason, whenever we got into their bed together, in the silence of the night, we would burst out laughing over something stupid, and then tell each other in whispery voices that we need to not laugh so loud because we will wake them. That would, of course, make us laugh even harder. Also, when you turned off the lights in my parents room, it became frighteningly, unbelievably dark. You could not see a thing in front of you. It was pitch black. Don got up one time in the middle of the night to pee and stubbed his toe on the side of the bed. As he cried out in pain and yelled out, "HOLY SHIT!" I was trying like hell to suppress my laughter. He would make me laugh so hard, making fun of how dark it was, putting out his hands to trying and find me. "Hello??? Am I in the right room? Kelley? Boo? Where the fuck am I???" Often, on the morning after a night we had slept in that room, my parents would ask us very genuinely, "What on earth were you two laughing at in there last night? All we could hear was you two giggling!" I still don't really remember what we were always laughing at, specifically. We just really loved to laugh and be silly.

The emptiness of the room starts to fill up with more memories and visuals inside my head. Like how my parents thought they were so sneaky and slick, hiding all the unwrapped Christmas presents in their bedroom closet, inside lots of large store bags. Or the time that our next door neighbor and friend, Dianne, babysat me and my cousins, Tabatha and Laura, while my parents and my Aunt went out somewhere. At bedtime, she had us sleep in my parent's big bed together. We were pretty young, and we were total smart-asses that enjoyed doing things to torture poor Dianne. So we each grabbed a small handful of hard candy from the kitchen table and hid it underneath the covers when we went to bed. Then we called Dianne into the room by yelling, "Dianne! We don't feel good!" When she opened the bedroom door and turned on the light, the three of us violently chucked pieces of hard candy at her head - assaulting her for no apparent reason, except that we found it hilarious.

My Husband is Not a Rainbow

Making my way over to my brother David's room, I lean myself up against his doorway and recall all the silly sibling fights we had, slamming doors dramatically on each other's faces and calling each other names. For the most part, we got along well though. Something we did quite often as kids, was to sit on my brother's bed and play with his matchbox cars. Now, please understand that there was a very specific way to play "cars," as we called it. First, we would dump out all the many matchbox cars from the giant cubby-like box thing with handles that my brother kept them in. Then, we would each choose a car to drive, and then some of the other cars to symbolize gas stations, houses, stores, etc. Then, one of us would loudly and proudly announce to the other: "I'm coming over!" This meant that we were coming over for a visit to the other person's home. Because that's what you do when you play cars. Then, we would take our hand and move the car across the bed, to signal that it was in motion, and we would make a "brrrmmmm, broommmmmm!!!" sound, which was supposed to be the sound of the car engine. Eventually, the visit would end, and we would say, "I'm going home now," and make the same sounds to drive home. And that was pretty much cars.

The other thing my brother and I also liked to do on his bed was play "Guys." This consisted of our small gang of stuffed animals, including a humpty-dumpty looking thing of my brother's named Big Baby, a spider named Spike, and my Bunny named Bunny. I can't recall if there were others, but there had to have been. Something inside me vaguely recalls a puppy named Dog. Now, for some reason, we called them "Guys," and playing "Guys" was about as exciting as playing matchbox cars was. Each animal had a voice and personality, and we would put our hand on them and move them around and make them talk. I have absolutely no idea what kind of things we made them say, but I will bet it was riveting. My eyes wander down to the floor now, and I recall a particular night when our cousins all slept over, and I was in a sleeping bag on my brother's floor, next to my cousins. The lights were off, it was pitch black, and we were almost asleep, when I suddenly felt something moving inside my sleeping bag and on my leg. I unzipped the bag and squirmed around, screaming in horror as I saw it and yelled, "There's a mouse in my lap!!!" My cousins and brother all laughed so hard at me, but I was truly terrified, and will never forget that feeling of that nasty rodent climbing up my leg inside that trap they call a sleeping bag.

My bedroom. It is time now. This is, of course, the toughest room to stand in and say goodbye to. It represented my childhood, my teenage years, and my adult years too - as I watched all the changes to what the room was used for over the years; including being the place that my Nana slept the last six months of her life when she moved in with my parents so they could help take care of her during her cancer battle. She passed away lying in my bed, peaceful, and surrounded by family. Now the bed is gone, as is everything in the room, except for me, not even caring about the tears that are coming again. My brain jumps back to the 1980s. My childhood. My bedroom walls filled with pin-ups from BOP! Magazine of Duran Duran, Corey Hart, Michael Jackson, Culture Club, Bon Jovi, Van Halen, and Madonna. The memories inside this room are endless, and they slide across my heart as if on roller-skates. I remember how excited I was to get that CASIO synthesizer that Christmas, and how I had a crush on Troy Bayley, and he came over Christmas night and was playing my Casio (that's not a euphemism). The waterbed that I hated, always swishing back and forth each time I moved. Talking on my corded phone from inside my bedroom closet anytime I wanted complete privacy from the parents hearing me.

Writing in my diary about all my heartache and pain. Slamming my door like a champ anytime the parents said anything I didn't care for. Recording Casey Kasem's American Top Forty Countdown, and always somehow getting my mom's voice on there at the end of a song, calling me for dinner. Sneaking my much older, marine boyfriend from Fort Devens into my room and then quickly out my bedroom window when my parents came home much sooner than expected one night. (Sorry mom and dad - you had to find out sometime.) My mom waking up my brother and me for school by standing in our doorways and singing at the top of her lungs the most obnoxious song on earth, "It's time to get up, it's time to get up, it's time to get up in the mor-ning! It's time to get up when the bugle calls! (She would, at this point, pretend to be playing a bugle - loudly.) Get up when the bugle calls!!!" My brother would pull the pillow over his head and yell while laughing, "Ma!!! Stop!!"

Walking out of this room right now means walking out of my childhood. I can never go back. It won't be here, so I can never go into this room again. And with that realization, I lean back against the dirty and empty walls, and just cry. Finally, about twenty minutes later, I collect my emotions and my body, and I continue this exercise in trauma.

With the energy and tone of someone on death row about to walk to the electric chair, I get up and begin the move outside and across the front lawn, out onto the circular driveway, to where Don's car is sitting. I stare it down, my heart beating faster with each second. It is not until this very moment that I finally understand how a CAR can have such an emotional hold over you. My husband loved that car with everything inside him, and now, I have to let this car go. Even though I know it's the right thing, and even though he would want me to do this for safety reasons, I still feel as if I am betraying him or failing him somehow. I feel like I am throwing his precious baby away, and it feels awful.

I walk over to the side of the car. I lean on it. I hug it, like it's a person. The images are like a slideshow in my head. The day he moved in, Super Bowl Sunday, 2005. It was snowing, and he pulled up with a giant Penske moving truck with his car attached, after a twenty four hour drive from Florida. The first two weeks he lived with me, he got three parking tickets, and his car was towed. He had to keep getting up and moving his car to the other side of the street. His tires blew out after a month of horrible Jersey and NYC road conditions. He was cursing out the state, the potholes, and everyone after about month three. "My poor baby," he would say, petting the steering wheel like it was human. "This stupid state is killing my car!"

I open the door and sit down in the driver's seat. Leaning my head on the steering wheel, I rest my hands on each side and keep seeing the images. It is late at night, on our first wedding anniversary, and we had just gotten home from having dinner at our beautiful Long Island wedding venue. After we were parked, he looked over at me and said simply, "I love you, wife." I said, "I love you too, husband." Then he paused and added, "Wanna make out?" and we kissed like teenagers in that car until Don's elbow hit the horn, and we scared the shit out of ourselves, laughed, and went inside.

There were many cat escapades in the car. Isabelle sleeping in Don's lap for the entire twenty four hour drive from Florida to New Jersey. Taking Ginger and Autumn to the vet and hearing them meow in two-part harmony from the backseat cages, with Don orchestrating it with his hands like a maestro. Our ER visit in the middle of the night with Ginger, where we had to return home without her. Trying to shove that giant cat condo in the car from Petsmart. Taking Sammy home from the shelter, just days after Ginger's death. This car meant so much to me too. Don shared it with me, from the minute he arrived with it, into his new life. I would drive it out to Long Island to teach, and he would take it to work his overnight EMS shifts. Sometimes, I would bring him to work and then come get him at six AM in the morning, so that I could have the car.

My Husband is Not a Rainbow

It was time to say goodbye now, and it was so very hard. "I'm sorry, Boo," I found myself saying over and over again as I sat there. I sobbed into the steering wheel and hugged it tightly, and kept holding on for dear life until I knew it was the right moment to get up and walk out of that car and into whatever awaited me. I take one last look at the two cars together, noticing again how much they look alike. I get into my Pontiac Bonneville, wave goodbye to my Pontiac Grand Prix, and bawl my head off all the way to Route 495.

"Goodbyes are only for those who love with their eyes. Because for those who love with heart and soul there is no such thing as separation." – Rumi

FB Post: Just drove five hours back to our NJ apartment, which is now without Don and sad as hell. Got intense migraine from all the crying on the drive. Massive traffic through pounding rain, thunder, lightning, and HAIL!!! Where the hell is MY fucking rainbow??? This sucks.
LIKES: 46   COMMENTS: 12

Dear Stupid Death Diary:

Hurricane Irene is here, and it sucks doing this without Don. I woke up in our bed, and there was water dripping into my eyeball. A huge leak in our ceiling, and water dripping onto Don's pillow, where his head should be. This isn't fair. How am I going to do this - this life thing - without him? Everything in this place is always broken, and he would fix it. That's just what he did. He fixed everything. He made it better. There is no making this better. Him being dead. He made me feel so safe, and now it stings knowing I no longer feel safe, and I'm back to being that scared girl who keeps the TV on all night, because the silence is horrifying. The thought of him never being here again to laugh with about our ridiculous life where everything is broken, to keep each other company in a hurricane, hits me like a ton of bricks. I'm sitting in our bed, underneath the giant leak in the ceiling. I don't move. I just sit there and let the water drip into my eyes.

"Sometimes
I just want to rip apart every synapse in my brain
Because I am so tired
Of the constant knowingness that you are gone."
– Sarah Treanor

Dear Stupid Death Diary:

Today is my first day back teaching Acting and Comedy at Adelphi, and it's been really hard. I'm in the bathroom again, crying, typing this from my phone, hiding in the stall. 'I'm okay until I try to speak, and then I fall apart. Over and over. Everyone is staring at me and whispering. I passed two students in the hallway, and one of them pointed at me and whispered to the other, "That's her. That's the one whose husband collapsed and died." Yup, that's me! Step right up, folks, and look at the Widow Attraction. Next showing is at two PM!! It was scary driving all the way from New Jersey to Long Island this morning, knowing that Don wasn't there anymore if the car decided to go haywire on me or stop running or something. Thankfully, the car David got me is safer than Don's was, but I still feel like something could happen at any time. I hate going through the Lincoln Tunnel and thinking about getting stuck in there. I just feel fear everywhere I go now. Panic and fear. It's like CS Lewis said in his book, "A Grief Observed," that a friend sent me a copy of, and it's the only thing so far that makes any sort of sense. In the book, he talks about how nobody ever told him that grief felt a lot like fear. You got that right, buddy.

It's going to suck going home today and not getting a text or call from Don, asking if I got home safe. I really loved being married. Being alone sucks. Gotta go teach my next class now. Somebody please help me through this.

FB Post: I don't know how to do this grief thing. I thought maybe I could do it, but I suck at it. When I'm home, I want to get the hell out. When I'm out, I feel like I can't breathe and can't wait to get home. I feel like I belong nowhere, and my entire day consists of crying or trying not to cry. I feel sick to my stomach and out of place everywhere. Seeing happy couples together hurts my heart. Will this pain ever go away???
LIKES: 30   COMMENTS: 16

"I walk around with a gaping hole that goes clear through my body where my heart used to be. I wonder why people don't see it and mention it to me, until I realize it is covered by my clothes, the cloak of a widow. People cannot see what I feel everyday."
– Janice Martel Hart

Kelley Lynn Shepherd

FB Post: My incredible friends, mostly Andrew Block, who is producing, have put together this Comedy Benefit show - two nights actually, to help me and to honor Don. There will be two unforgettable nights of laughs, hilarious lineup with headliners Elayne Boosler and Danny Cohen, and my first time getting back onstage since this happened. I'm excited for this. This is for you, Boo!
LIKES: 65   COMMENTS: 46

Dear Dead Husband,

I don't want to be here. I might eat my weight in cupcakes. Someone actually reacted to me saying that my husband had died by joking about their own divorce, and saying that I was "lucky" that I never have to see him again, because she has to see her "ex" all the time. I blurted out, "He's not my EX," and then ran out of the room crying. I feel like my insides are burning. I feel like I'm on fire. Who the hell says that to someone whose world just ended? This isn't anything at all like a divorce. I would do anything in the world to see my husband again. Just one more time. Why do people have to compare pain? I can't even think about it, it just makes me cry. I don't feel like living anymore.

Internal Error

You know how on TV shows, in films, and on really bad, death-related Lifetime Movies or Hallmark Movies starring Meredith Baxter Birney or Tori Spelling, there is always that scene after the loved one tragically dies, where the person left behind has this epic, emotional breakdown? In these films, this usually happens one of a few different ways.

My Husband is Not a Rainbow

A: The grieving person is shown in a montage, with depressing music (R.E.M.'s "Everybody Hurts" is a favorite choice), doing different things like crying while smelling a loved one's shirt, or sobbing while staring longingly out a window.

B: The grieving person is shown crying while simultaneously sliding their body down a wall very slowly, cupping their face in their hands, or...

C: the grieving person, either during the funeral, or hours after, has an angry and irrational moment, where they lose their mind with grief and begin breaking things while yelling at the dead person, shouting things out loud like, "Why did you leave me! How could you die and leave me alone? It's not fair!" This last one is popular on soap operas, where the grieving person takes every item off a table or desk and throws it all onto the floor in a fit of hysterical outburst. Or, they are drinking an alcoholic beverage at the time of their sudden angst, and they throw the glass of vodka across the room, shattering it into a billion pieces.

Well, as a grieving widow, I am here to tell you from personal experience, that those scenes are complete and utter bullshit. Sort of.

In these movies and TV shows, it's all very neat and tidy. There are paths and stages and everything follows some made-up timeline. In real life, none of that exists. Forget paths. Forget stages. I have felt anger, sadness, denial, numbness, and many other emotions all in the same day. Hell, sometimes in the same hour. Grief is not pretty. It is not something you wrap up and tie with a bow and define so easily. It can't be shown with one simple movie scene or with one outburst. It is not black and white. It is foggy and shades of vague. It eats you up whole and throws you into an unfamiliar ocean, where you are screaming and nobody can hear you for miles. The only person you want to talk to is gone, and there's not a damn thing you can do about it.

Kelley Lynn Shepherd

Now, go back to that list above from the movies and TV and their version of what grief is like. Today, I experienced C from that list. Today, I had my first real, screaming, emotional, angry, yelling, irrational, throwing random items, classic meltdown. Only, unlike in the movies, mine didn't happen hours or days after the funeral. Mine happened one month and twenty three days after my husband's death. It happened at one PM this afternoon.

I was online, at the Adelphi website, trying to get some important work done that I needed to do for my semester teaching. I was in the midst of creating a class email list, when suddenly my computer went insane. Popups, virus attack warnings, trojan virus this or that, and something about INTERNAL ERROR!!! It went to my desktop screen, and then this: DANGER! ACTIVATE PROTECTION SCAN NOW!

Fuuuuuccckkkk!!!! This message was familiar to me. I had seen it before. Our computer has suffered viruses four or five times in the past few years. Happens once or twice a year, and there's never any pattern to it. One time, Don was on a guitar site when it happened, another time I was on Facebook. The virus protection is fake, and it masks itself as a program that is trying to remove viruses from your computer, when in fact, activating it will ADD viruses to your computer. It's a phony, malicious asshole. And it was this asshole that began my emotional breakdown. "No! Not now! I have too much to do. DAMMIT!" I screamed to myself and nobody and the air. The crying began, and it was an angry cry this time. It was a month of frustration and disbelief and WHY IS THIS HAPPENING TO ME all balled up into this computer virus. Why isn't Don here? Where the hell did he buy this computer? Where did he used to take it to get it fixed? He used to pick up this computer, heaviest thing on earth, put it in his car, and drive it off to some repair place to get it fixed anytime this happened. "I'll take care of it, Boo," he would say, and all would be well. Now, I'm alone. I don't know where the place is to get it fixed. The thought of lifting this computer and carrying it downstairs, across the street, into the parking garage, and into my car sends me into insane panic mode.

Now I'm losing my mind. I am crying angrily and loudly. People next door can hear me. I don't care. I shake the computer monitor with my hands as I scream at it, then I pound my fists into the desk several times. My crying gets extremely loud. I can't help it. It's been building up. The anger has been building. I miss my husband. "I want you back! Where the hell are you? Why did this happen to you? Why???" I say all this out loud and through massive, impressive tears. I walk into the living room and without thinking, grab my favorite wedding picture of us off the Entertainment Center. I go and sit in his recliner chair, and I hug our picture as tightly as possible. I sob for a solid half hour, not moving from his chair. I try like hell to feel him close to me somehow. I cling on to something, hoping for some shift in the air, anything. I want to hold him so badly, and instead, I'm holding a wooden picture frame against my chest. None of it helps.

I search for signs. There aren't any. "Why won't you talk to me?" I scream at him. "What's wrong with me? Everyone else gets signs. Why not me? Why can't I feel that you are with me?" I stand up and smash the wedding picture into the floor, trying to break both in one shot. I grab some sheet music of his and throw it onto the floor like a child. I am having a tantrum. I want to break everything. I want to hurt myself, but I know I won't. I just want something to hurt as much as I do in that moment. I walk into the bathroom and look at my reddened, old eyes in the mirror. I see the fear of the future looking back at me. I punch the mirror. Hard. Yes. That's it. That feels good. A bunch of q-tips and pills fall out from behind the mirror cabinet and land inside the sink. The mirror is cracked, and I cry through the cracks. I pick up the pills and imagine taking the whole bottle. I

Kelley Lynn Shepherd

know that I won't, but I fantasize about it. I think about not having to feel this pain anymore. How liberating that would be. I feel crazy. I am a lunatic. All those people who keep saying how strong I am - if they could only see me now, alone in my apartment. I have become a cliché. I have become a Hallmark Movie of the Week.

Eventually, I calm down enough to make a phone call, but not enough to stop sobbing. I am crying through words, and I am still so angry. My first call is to mom and dad. No answer. Probably a good thing, since Dad doesn't know the first thing about computers anyway, and I wasn't making much sense at the time to explain the issue to him in a way he could comprehend it. I never know who to call when I am like this, so I usually end up calling nobody. I just simply get through it. This time I called John. This is the second time I have called him in a month while sobbing. He must hate when my number comes up on his phone at this point. I am a mess, and I keep apologizing for it. I am half-yelling at him, "My computer won't work and Don is fucking dead! I hate this! I hate my new life! I don't know where he took it to fix it. Why didn't I pay attention?" I break into sobs again. John calms me down and starts entering different things into Google searches for me to try and figure out if we can get rid of the virus together. He comes across something that tells us to shut down, press F8, then reboot. I do this, and everything disappears from my desktop screen. All the icons are gone, but the desktop looks normal, and I'm able to get back online. John tells me to take advantage of it for now, and get the work done that I need to get done for tonight.

So that is what I do. And right now, it's still working. Functioning. The problem is, the second that I shut down the computer and then reboot it, the pop-ups will probably come right back. On the surface, everything looks normal. Everything looks fine. Just like with me. People assume I am doing okay, that I am "getting better." People are wrong. I am able to make jokes, go to work (barely), continue my sarcastic and now darker than ever humor, write, eat food, sometimes sleep an hour, take care of our kitties (barely), and get through the various days that keep happening and coming up. I am able to function. But underneath all of that, there is a pain that cannot be described, a hurt that can't be fixed. There is a monster and an infant waiting to come out and cry. There is an internal error, and it is just sitting there, ready to pounce. Lurking. Just like with everything else, I will have to deal with it tomorrow. Maybe.

"Should I take a grief day or just slam my dick in a car door?" – Wade Winfrey

FB Post: A letter to me from the Restoration of Sight Bank: "Because of your compassion, a second chance at sight has been given to someone in need of a cornea transplant. This will change a life forever, as Don's precious gifts has done." My selfless, amazing husband continues to change people's lives, even now. I can't stop crying and staring at this letter. He had the most beautiful blue eyes I've ever seen.
LIKES: 77   COMMENTS: 51

FB Post: Weird day. First of all, it's 9/11/11, which is weird. My awesome friend, Jay, who works on Broadway, got me two comp tickets to "Billy Elliott." I took my friend Jessica. I met the director outside the stage door - Jay introduced me. They both warned me that the show would rip my heart out. They were right. Very emotional, but fantastic. Memories of Don and I seeing lots of Broadway shows together. He really loved NYC and Broadway. As I was walking through the city on my way to the busses that go back to Jersey, I ran into a theatre acquaintance on the street. He stopped me and said, "Wow! You look great! Marriage must be agreeing with you!" To which I

said, "Actually, my husband just died two months ago." Which was followed by awkward silence. And then an even more awkward, "Well, nice seein' ya. Goodbye then!" I hate telling people over and over that Don is dead. Each time I say it out loud, it feels like knives are stabbing me.
LIKES: 15   COMMENTS: 6

"My broken heart's still beating. It just makes a different sound now." – Julie Risebrough

Everything Goes In a Basket

I used to nag my husband all the time about his "stuff." All the time. He would come home and throw his stuff all over the place. Keys, chapstick, wallet, random receipts and papers. He would kick off his shoes, and they would end up in a corner of the living room floor. His EMS uniform would come off in pieces, like Charlie Brown pitching on the mound, and then they would land across the room, on the arm of the couch, back of a chair. Minutes later, I would walk around and put all the parts of his uniform in one pile, folded up, throw his shoes in his closet and out of the way, and then take each of the smaller items that he would toss onto the top of the entertainment center, and put them into a small basket that sat atop one of his music speakers.

Later, he would always be so confused. "Where the hell are my keys?"

"They're in the basket."

"What about my Altoids? I know I put them somewhere around here…"

My Husband is Not a Rainbow

"In the basket. It's all in the basket."

Then he would shake his head at me and laugh. "Basket. Everything's a basket with you. Why does everything have to go in a basket?"

"Because it's organized, and you always know where it is. It's ALWAYS in the basket."

"But I know where I put my stuff. I don't lose it until YOU move it. Just leave it where I put it, Boo."

"But it doesn't go there."

"Says who? You? Who cares where it goes, as long as I can find it."

"I care. The top of the Entertainment Center isn't for a pile of random items. Just toss everything in the basket."

He always made fun of me and my baskets. He would walk around, kind of mumbling to himself and nobody in particular, "Basket … Jeesh… freakin baskets… you'd put ME in a basket if you could!"

"I heard that!" I'd yell back. "And yes, I would. But you wouldn't fit."

Right now, I would give just about anything to have Don walk through that door and start carelessly throwing his stuff everywhere. If I could have him back again, he could leave his things scattered all over the floor everyday, forever. Well, okay. Maybe not. That seems unsanitary. But I would love nothing more than to hear him making fun of my baskets again. Today I walked down the block to the little bodega store that Victor runs. I had to get some cat food and boring things, and I hadn't been in there much since a couple weeks after Don died, when I walked in there with my mom by my side and said to Victor, "I have to tell you something. My husband, Don, who came in here all the time to get us the newspaper and snacks, he talked to you all the time - he died." Victor was shocked. "Don? Oh no!" he said, and tears came to his eyes. Since then, his store has been one of those painful places for me to go back to. Like the mechanics shop down the block, or the Chinese place we always ordered from. All these places were places we frequented, and places where Don took the time to get to know the store owners and workers. And now they all missed him, and when I go in these places, they look at me with sad eyes. But I went in because I wanted to give Victor one of the prayer cards from the funeral. When I give these to people, it seems to help somehow, or makes them feel like they are a part of remembering him. It gives them something physical to take away from this horrible reality.

So I walked in there, and Victor was there with the other Middle Eastern man who runs the store with him. At least, I think they are Middle Eastern. To be honest, I only know that Victor's name is Victor because Don told me, matter of factly. I have no idea what the other dude's name is, but he looks like a younger Victor, so I'm assuming they are brothers. Or cousins. Maybe Don mentioned his name to me one time, I don't know. I am suddenly wishing I paid attention to these people like Don had; that I had the patience and the common courtesy to make friendly conversation with them; learn their names; and actually give a shit about people, like Don did. I feel like such an undeserving jackass as I hand Victor and the nameless one their prayer cards and say, "Here. I wanted you to have these, just because."

The store is empty, and the two sweet men look at the prayer cards with intense eyes, reading the nice poem we chose on the back and memorizing Don's face on the front with their minds.

My Husband is Not a Rainbow

The three of us stand there in silence for what seems like a long time. It should be awkward, but it isn't. They are both thinking about Don. Finally, Victor looks up and says to me, "Your husband. I still miss him. I miss seeing him." Then he shakes his head in that disbelief sort of way that I have become used to seeing from people. The nameless one says: "He was so nice. So, so nice. Such a nice man." Part of me wants to scream out loudly, WHAT THE HELL IS YOUR NAME??? But I feel that this would be an inappropriate time to ask. I can never ask. It's too late. I wish I could ask Don, because I know he would know the guy's name. But I can't ever ask Don anything again, at least not in the way that I want to.

After a few moments, Victor takes the prayer card and hangs it up on the wall behind him. The nameless guy takes his prayer card and carefully places it into a small basket by the cash register. *He put Don in a basket.* I pay for my items and walk out. As soon as I hit the street corner, I begin to laugh and cry at the same exact time.

FB Post: What an absolutely beautiful evening of love, hope, and laughter. I'm so moved by the amount of support you have all given me and my wonderful husband. There are simply too many people to thank, you are all amazing. Special mention to comedian Jim Gaffigan, for his total surprise cameo performance. Wow! I'm still speechless. I love you all very much.
LIKES: 204   COMMENTS: 71

Dear Stupid Death Diary:

Tonight I went back onstage and did stand-up for the first time since Don died. I think I did about fifteen minutes or so, but it was all such a blur, that I'm not even sure. I told the story about

Mary calling Don a rainbow, which was a huge hit. She even came to the show, and she was laughing a lot at that story. I talked about my phone call with AT&T, and how they kept asking to speak with my dead husband on the phone. I talked about stupid and hurtful comments that people make to widowed people, and I talked about many other things. It felt so good to laugh and to hear others laugh with me and because of words I was saying that came from pain. It was validating to see all the love coming from that room. My friend, Andrew Block, worked so hard to put this together, and I'm forever thankful. Lori Sommer hosted the show beautifully, and she was the perfect choice to do it. There were raffles and prizes. Debra Carozza donated lots of great items, and she and Rodney Ladino ran the raffle onstage. The most unexpected part of the night was when Jim Gaffigan showed up and did about twenty minutes onstage. Our headliner, my friend Danny Cohen, knows him and asked him if he would come by and be in the show. I got to sit and talk with him afterwards. He's a super nice guy. I'm still very stunned right now with all that happened tonight. So many comedians performed, and I sat there nervously watching them. My eyelids were sweating. My friend, John, filmed my set and will make a video later from it after we do the second show in October. I was so floored by all of it. I just wish Don was here, which makes no sense, cuz if he was here, there would be no show. So, I wish there was no show. But since there was, it was amazing.

"When your life suddenly changes forever, your only option is to live in the moment, and value each step."
– Judy Taylor

My Husband is Not a Rainbow

I Turned 40 and Who Cares Cuz You're Dead

When your husband dies unexpectedly, old plans change into new ones. Everything just becomes about me "getting through it." The old "my husband is alive plan" was for us to go to mom and dad's together for the weekend. They were going to throw me a huge fortieth birthday party with loads of family and friends. Then Sunday, we were going to the party of a very good family friend named Thelma, who shares the same birthday date as me, September twenty sixth. Today, when I turn forty, she will turn one hundred. So, we were all invited to her one hundredth birthday party. Well, turns out the one hundred year old made it for her one hundredth birthday, but the forty six year old man didn't live to see forty seven, or to see his wife turn forty. People die. Plans change. The revised "my husband is dead plan" still had me going to mom and dad's, but I was driving the five hours there alone, in the car that my amazing brother bought for me so I'd be safe. Instead of that big party, I asked for them to make it small and mellow. (I would have preferred non-existent, but nobody was on board with that) So, just me, my parents, Jen and Dave and Brian, and my Aunt Ginny and my little cousin, Faith, who Ginny was babysitting for the weekend. We did lobsters and steaks on the grill, and mom made her famous red velvet cake, the same one she makes every year on my birthday, my brothers, Jen's, and Don's.

At first, I was okay. I wouldn't call it a happy day, since right now, there is little to no joy inside me. If I laugh for few seconds, it's a different, dark laugh that is filtered in pain and sadness. Mostly, I'm just walking around in a fog, with a constant headache from the endless crying and grief stress. So we ate delicious lobster with drawn butter, and my dad grilled the steaks to perfection out on the deck. I was even able to bribe a hug, kiss, and an "I love you, Auntie Kelley" from Brian. His price? One black olive. This kid lives for black olives. He will eat the whole can if you let him. Everyone gave me cute little cards with gift cards to Target and Trader Joe's inside, which was really nice. Then, it was time for cake and the traditional "forty" gifts. Years ago, my mom came up with this crazy thing where she would wrap up the number of gifts corresponding with the person's age on big milestone birthdays. She and Aunt Ginny did it for Nana, their mom, on her eightieth birthday, because Nana used to love opening gifts. When Don turned forty, mom wrapped forty gifts for him too. Now it was my turn.

Mom brought out a big laundry basket filled with tons of wrapped gifts and placed it in front of me. Then she cut the cake that was being eaten to celebrate my life. Suddenly, I felt like I couldn't breathe, and like I was inside myself looking out, and like everything was in slow motion, and I slowly got up and left the room. I don't even remember the act of doing it, but I know it happened. I ended up in the bathroom, trying to catch my breath, crying, and missing him so badly, it was hard to focus. It felt so wrong and so sad and so awful to be celebrating life when Don doesn't get to live it anymore. How can I feel happy and eat cake when his time was cut short for no reason? Out of nowhere, I started picturing him lying on that cold, hard floor inside the Petsmart. Dying. Collapsing. Alone. While I was asleep. I started to hyperventilate and go into another panic attack.

From inside the bathroom, I can hear the laughter and chatter of my family. I hear someone say, "Just give her a few minutes alone." They are mourning too, but it's different. They get to have moments, like now, when they aren't thinking about Don; when every single part of their heart isn't being ripped out and consumed by thoughts of him. They lost their son-in-law, their brother-in-law, and it's so awful, and the pain is so real, but they get to walk away from it and turn to their own spouses to talk about it and have support, and be grateful that it wasn't them that was widowed. For me, there is nowhere left to run. I'm trapped inside of this hell, and the one person I want to talk to, who would comfort me better than anyone else, is dead.

My Husband is Not a Rainbow

Once the flashes of my beautiful husband lying on the floor start to fade out a bit, I train myself to breathe again, and I come out of the bathroom and sit back down. Mom asks if I'm okay and says we don't have to do this now if I don't want to. My eyes are teary, and I can't really say words, because I'll break down again. Little Brian appears out of nowhere and looks inside of the laundry basket. A basket filled with presents; pure heaven for a little boy. He picks one up and starts unwrapping it. "I open because Auntie is sad," he says, and he unwraps each and every gift, one by one, and then hands them to me. It is the most perfect and beautiful thing anyone has ever done, and he doesn't even know he is doing it. He is just being a kid. At that moment, I didn't want to celebrate anything. I didn't want to open presents when my husband is dead. I didn't want any focus on me when I feel like I've been under a microscope since he died. So the plan changed. This plan had my not yet three year old nephew opening up pairs of socks, stationary, lip gloss, and more things he couldn't comprehend, and handing them to me with a confused look. He didn't care that the gifts were not for him, he just liked the act of opening them. And opening them was the absolute last thing I felt like doing. It was beautiful.

The next day, we celebrated Thelma's one hundredth birthday with a catered party at a nice venue. I was back in the fog again. I couldn't stop picturing Don in my head. I do that all the time. I see him in my mind, or try to feel him touching me, try to hear his laugh somehow, feel a memory. I mingled and talked to people, but I don't remember much of it. I just kept thinking about how he should be here with me; how he was looking forward to the party; how much he liked Thelma. "I hope I'm that cool when I'm a hundred!" he would say about her. He would talk and joke all the time about what he would be like as an old man. It was a running theme with us. He relished in it. He would tell me, "I can't wait to be a grumpy old man! I can say and do whatever the hell I want, yell at kids for no reason to get off my lawn, act insane - it's gonna rule!" He always imitated himself talking to me when we are both old; using this really spot on cranky old guy voice for himself. He would say, "Come on now Kelley, we gotta get to the Golden Corral, the Early Bird special ends at four!" He would pretend to be bent over and holding a cane. He cracked himself up at the thought of the two of us being old together. I would say, "Please stop. You're scaring me!" and that would make him do it even more. These are the things I was thinking about as Thelma gave me a hug. I pictured Don bending down to hug her, because he was so tall and would have to bend way down to hug a lot of people. I ate the piece of one hundredth birthday cake in silence as I thought about my husband being dead. The sugar both numbed and comforted me all at once. Happy Fortieth Birthday, me. I am the loneliest person in the world.

"Widowhood means you have felt the physical weight of his old shirt at night as you sleep in it, and you still keep right on breathing." – Michelle Miller

FB Post: Just returned from a weekend trip to Woodstock that my friends took me on for my fortieth birthday. We rented a house and spent time together. Thank you so much to John, Jessica, Andrew, and Rodney for the cake, the food, the games, the comfort, the friendship, and most of all; for making me laugh so hard last night that my stomach hurt from something other than crying. I wasn't sure if I'd ever laugh like that again. An unforgettable weekend. I love you all.
LIKES: 56   COMMENTS: 34

Words About Don

"Don Shepherd! Wow! What a great guy! When I heard that my daughter, Kelley, was communicating with a guy online, and from Florida, I wasn't sure if it was a good idea. Me being from the old school way of thinking, it gave me concerns. Who is this guy? Well, at the time, I had a source that enabled me to have a full background check done on Don, and he came out as clean as can be. In this day and age, I was doing this for Kelley - you just never know. I have always trusted Kelley's instincts and decisions, but as her father, her safety is high on my list.

Kelley and Don spent a long relationship online and over the phone. It was becoming clear that it was or could be special, and so it was. The first time I met Don, I just knew he was a good-hearted and genuine guy. I could just feel it. We met at their apartment while he was visiting her, and he and I went right to work on taking care of a mouse issue she was having in her kitchen. He dove right in with me, got behind the fridge, and we started working together as a team to cover up the spaces in Kelley's walls. I remember thinking right then that it was like we had already known each other for years. He was just so easygoing and easy to be around.

As time went on, they got engaged, and then married, living right on the NYC/NJ border. I always felt that she was safe being with Don. He was so caring and really the kindest person you could ever know. It didn't take long for me feeling he was my other son.

Don was fun to be around. He laughed a lot. I never saw him in a bad mood or mad about something. If he was ever bothered about something, you would never know it. He was a rare find, and I knew he would take care of Kelley, which he did always. It was comforting for me knowing that they got along so well, that he treated her so well, and that Don supported her with her career goals in the jungle of NYC. He was always there for her.

Was Don my son? Well, not by blood. But he was a part of our family, and I did look upon him as my other son. What a great guy! I think about him often, and miss him - I always will. "
- Kelley's dad, and Don's "Pop," as he used to call me

Mirrors

A couple times per year, I get my hair straightened by this really sweet hairdresser who runs and operates a salon from inside an apartment building. She rents a very small studio apartment and uses it as a hair salon. She is young and from Japan. She has no help at all. It's just her in there. The place is super tiny and feels claustrophobic. She plays the weirdest, creepiest music you have ever heard in your life as "background" noise. For real. I have no idea what this music is, but there are often sounds of animal noises, clanking and banging, and people screaming as if they are being viciously murdered. Oh, and her salon is completely out of the way. It's way downtown near Avenue A, which is about nineteen subways and forty seven hours from New Jersey on a good day.

But here's the thing; the place is always packed with customers, friends deciding to get their hair cut on a whim, and an energy that comes from Izumi herself. It's always a challenge to get an appointment. She is very busy. Before making my appointment, I had emailed her to let her know about what happened, because I can't stand walking into places or situations with people that then proceed to attack me with a million questions about his death. I am so tired of telling the story of how it happened to different random people over and over again. I hate reliving that awful morning, and I hate having to answer questions that I cannot answer, because I still don't know the answers, and I might not ever know the answers. *Did he have heart problems in his family? Was there a history of heart attacks? Did he have any symptoms? He was in EMS, right? But this happened at his other job, right? Wow, that's so ironic, isn't it, that this didn't happen in the ambulance? Were you alone when you found out? Did he ever go to the doctor? Did you have life insurance? Where will you live now? Was there an autopsy done? What were the results?* On and on and on…

After getting buzzed into the building, Izumi gives me a look that says that she read my email about Don, and I sit my fat self down on the chair that is made for normal-sized people. I absolutely hate going to the hair salon. I hate it because you are seated in a cramped, tight seat that your ass sticks out of on both sides because you are so damn fat; and you are placed in that seat with a gigantic full-length mirror directly in front of you, taunting you with how disgusting and huge you have become and how much more weight you will continue to gain, because you suck at coping with your new life.

On an average, ordinary day, I hate this hair-straightening procedure, because you have to sit in this chair for four hours. There is absolutely nothing to do but read yet another magazine. I reach into my shoulder bag of magazines that I brought with me in preparation and begin reading an article in Redbook about a 9/11 widow with two daughters. Her husband worked in the World Trade Center and never came home that day. For some reason, the magazine opens to this article, and I just start reading it. Even though Don and I never got to do more than talk about having kids or adopting together one day in the near future, and even though the way Don died is completely different than the way this woman's husband died, for some reason, her words resonate with me, and I completely relate.

In one part of the article, she talks about mourning all the things her husband would be missing; important days in their children's lives, milestones, her getting a job as a Science Professor, something she had always wanted to do. I can't stop thinking about how she woke up that morning, and her husband went to work and then never came home. Just like mine. All of a sudden, the tears are coming down my face, and I excuse myself to go into the creepy, tiny bathroom. This bathroom is the size of an airplane restroom, and as I pee and then try to navigate standing up again by grabbing onto a small rack for towels nearby, I realize I'm so damn large, that it's hard to get UP from being seated in this small space. I start crying harder and stay in there for a few minutes, hating my new life and how I am coping with it. I think again about all the people who have told me how "strong" I am, and I think about what a lie that is. It's a fucking lie. What does it even mean, really? Why am I strong? Because I'm not dead yet too? I am not sure what it means, and I don't feel strong. I can't even stand up after peeing in a creepy salon bathroom.

I start thinking about how so many other people deal with loss and death, how they drink or do drugs to dull their pain, or take so many meds they become numb, or fall into a depression that maybe they never come out of. I think about the bag of Cape Cod chips I ate in one sitting the week after he died and the box of Wheat Thins with Alouette garlic and herb spread I devoured a few days ago. The tater tots sitting in my freezer that I can't wait to heat up and bake and get them to the perfect state of crunchiness that makes my pain disappear. The chocolate chip ice cream that is even crunchier with sugar cone goodness. I wipe my tears and look at my fat chins in the bathroom mirror, as some woman screams bloody murder to a synthesizer beat in the speaker behind me.

The next four hours in that chair feel like a decade. I feel like an alien or a monster sitting there. I'm a blob with mirrors everywhere. Suddenly, I hear Izumi talking to me. She is telling me about her father, who died suddenly last May after he fell off of a roof. I am half listening to her gentle soothing voice, and half not. I feel as if I have been drugged. That feeling like when you are on cold meds and have had no sleep. That is how I feel every day since July thirteenth. Drugged.

Finally it is over. I get into a cab back to 42nd street, and the ride seems to take forever. It is now almost eleven thirty PM and we are sitting in bad traffic in Times Square. The cab is stopped right in front of BB King's, and I start to remember all the times Don and I went there to have a drink or dinner and listen to a great Jazz or blues band. I remember how much he loved the Sunday Beatles Brunch we went to that one time, how he talked about the guitar player for days afterwards. There are hundreds of people on the streets of New York City, loud and happy and filled with life and hope. There is a young looking couple that is smiling at each other and hugging tightly.

The cab doesn't move. Their hugs and their love are taunting me as I think about the many, many times Don and I hung out in NYC and how much he loved it there. I think about how he will never see it ever again and how I will never go for a night out with him ever again. I think about how young we were when we first started talking and falling in love and how we had that same goofy smile for each other. They are a new couple. You can tell by the gleam in their eye and by the feeling of hope as they practically skip down the street together. I instantly hate them because they get to exist together. I hate their laughter and their joy. The tears are coming hard now, and as I pay the fare and run out of the cab, I realize that I haven't eaten anything all day. There are many days since his death where I simply don't care enough to eat, or where I eat nothing until five PM, and then I eat about eighteen terrible things all in a row. Right this minute, my comfort comes in the form of a Burger King chicken sandwich and fries, and I stuff it into my bag as I get on the bus to go home to New Jersey. Please just get me the fuck home.

By the time I finally get home and eat my sad dinner at my computer alone, it is after midnight. My time clock, emotions, and my life are all so fucked up right now, and I don't much care. I am just glad to be home, where I don't have to sit in a hard chair and stare at my own failed self in the giant mirror. There are no mirrors in my apartment. There is nobody here to tell me that my hair looks really pretty or that they are happy I arrived home safely. There is none of that. There is only french fries.

"Loneliness is my companion. Emptiness overwhelms me. I wonder just how long I can be strong."
– Margaret Mccoy

Dear Death Diary:

Just returned from my first attempt at a Widowed Support Group. It was an epic fail. I found it on Facebook, and it was run by this older woman who holds support group dinner gatherings for widowed people at a diner out on Long Island. From New Jersey to Long Island is pretty damn far, but I really am desperate for someone to talk to. So I got in the car and drove in the dark out there, sat in horrid traffic, and got there almost two and a half hours later. Took me twenty minutes to talk myself into going inside. Once I did, I immediately regretted it. They asked my name and gave me a name tag sticker to put on. I was told to go inside to the private back room of the diner. There were about forty people there, all very much older than me. I looked ridiculous. Everyone stared as I aimlessly wandered around looking for a place to sit like it was the high school cafeteria.

My Husband is Not a Rainbow

I sat next to a woman who had to be eighty five. She looked at me and said in a loud voice with a horrible Long Island accent, "How long has it been for you, dear?" I told her three months. She replied, "Well I hate to burst your bubble, but it's going to get so much worse!!!" My bubble? What bubble? And WORSE? How much worse??? After that, it DID get worse, inside that diner. It became a contest on who had worse grief and pain. They all went around in a circle and complained and almost bragged about their pain. "My Richard had the cancer so bad, he suffered for seventeen years!" "Well that's nothing. My Joseph had the Alzheimer's, and he didn't remember our grandkids." When it was my turn to share my story, they all looked at me like I was an alien. Then one of them said, "It's okay. You're so young. You'll find another man, dear." It was so condescending. I'll find another man? Like he was a library book, and I can just get another one. He was my husband, you jerks! Just because we didn't get the chance to have grandkids or kids or a house or retirement, does NOT make my love any less valid. I excused myself to use the restroom, and then I fled the hell out of there. I sat in my car and just cried in the parking lot before driving home. How was any of this helpful or healing? There had to be a better way. Better support. I sat in the car repeating out loud "I will NOT be like them. I will NOT be like them. I will NEVER be like them." Is that what awaits me as a widowed person? Sitting around some crappy diner once a week and comparing our misery? Telling newcomers that it won't ever get better? Or implying that their love isn't as real because they only had four years of marriage together before death? This cannot be what is out there for me in this life. It can't be. I won't let it be.

Kelley Lynn Shepherd

The Courtship

In the late 1990s, this wonderfully strange man named Don Shepherd and I were quickly, yet very slowly, becoming very close. Each and every conversation that we had together was filled with the hope and joy of a young and new relationship. We were blooming, and the words that we typed and spoke on the phone to one another practically skipped themselves out of our mouths or onto the computer screen. We were getting to know each other, we were happy, and we were falling into love.

Somewhere about a year or so into our friendship, I started to ask Don, in a very casual way, what this was that we were doing. Was it a relationship? Was it friends? What is this? He would usually reply by gently asking me if we could meet in person soon. He knew that something awful had happened to me, but he didn't know what it was. He only knew and sensed that it made me extremely cautious about men in general. Even though that was true, what he didn't know was that my greater fear in meeting him was that he would reject me. That he wouldn't be physically attracted to me because I'm fat. And I was fat because this traumatic thing happened to me. As much as I wanted to meet him, I just wasn't ready. He never once pushed me. He was very laid back about all of it, saying over and over again, "We will meet when you are ready to meet. I've got all the time in the world, and you need to know that you're safe with me."

Eventually, Don moved out of the house he was sharing and got his own apartment in Largo, Florida. He was working part-time at Cadillac as a car mechanic while working with Sunstar Ambulance in EMS and taking night classes to get more certifications to work nationally, I believe. Meanwhile, over time, the lease that Sarah and I had in Forest Hills would end, and we would be forced to move out. I found a place with my college friend, Jay, in West New York, New Jersey. It was literally eight minutes outside NYC, and my view from the street was the NYC skyline. Amazing.

After lots of different temp jobs and weird jobs and all over the place type jobs, I started as an Adjunct Professor in September of 2000, teaching theatre. This would be the second time that Jay and I would be roommates, as we had our very first New York apartment together in Prospect Park, Brooklyn, back in 1994, for about three years. As time went on, Don and I continued to get close and talk almost every day. Sometimes we would call, sometimes we would type. We also exchanged mailing addresses and started to send each other things through the mail regularly; cards, letters, care packages, movies, and even mix tapes on cassette. I got him really into movies, and would send him my old VHS tapes and make him watch them and then report back to me what he thought. I had never met someone who had so little movie watching experience as him before. It was so weird. He had never seen "The Godfather." How is that even possible?

We had cute, nauseating little pet names for each other, and we were both pretty flirtatious with one another. We would talk late into the night, only hanging up when we were seconds away from falling asleep. I got him into films and Yankees baseball, he got me into tennis and guitars. We took on each other's interests, shared a lot of the same interests (like music), and we loved talking to each other. To help you better understand our relationship during that time, and to help create a timeline of events for our long-distance portion of the relationship, I have typed out word for word just some small snippets of a few of the letters and cards that were exchanged over the period of time that we grew our relationship, up until finally meeting in person in 2002. Here is just a tiny sample of how our love grew, through the mail:

Kelley Lynn Shepherd

No Valentine could ever express the way I feel about you. However, I did use a lot of tongue licking the envelope. Happy Valentine's Day Kelley. Love, Don

Hi Bunny. Just a little card because I miss you and am thinking about you. I also made this for you. It's a mix tape of rock songs and love songs. Rockin love songs. Hope you like it. Love, Don

Happy Birthday, you lowly Human. With Disinterest and Boredom, my cat Isabelle

Happy Birthday, BunnyBoo. Presents will be a little late this year. Sorry. Isabelle wouldn't get in the box. Love, Don

Hi Angel. Just wanted to send you a little bit of money, because I know how hard it is to get by for you out there in NY area paying rent by yourself. Use this to help pay bills or for whatever else. Also sending you this baseball card, since I know you love Derek Jeter. I miss your voice. Love, Don.

Merry Christmas Kelley. I hope it's your best one ever. The Christmas Bear inside this box is so cuddly and big, and I know you'll be hugging him at night when you sleep. Love, Don.

Hi Birthday Angel. I couldn't smoosh any cake into this box for you, but I hope you love all your other gifts I sent. You're the bestest ever. Love, Don.

Dear Don, Here are some more Peanuts comic strips, cuz we both love those. I'm sorry I can't be there, but I know that we will figure out together a way to finally see each other, and I look forward to seeing what we have together. I miss you. Love, Kelley

Hi Sweetheart, I hope you like my little box of fun. I just felt like sending you some silly things and gifts for your new adventure at

EMS school and studying. I hope it takes your mind off of chemistry for at least a while. Sent you more of this month's picks from Kelley's movie shack. I had two copies of "Return to Me," so I'm giving one to you. I'm also sending you "American Beauty." It's like a beautiful piece of music. I hope you love it as much as I do. Enjoy your school supplies and don't trade your apple with some bully for Twinkies. I miss you so much, even though we haven't met yet. Minor details. Your Angel, Kelley

Hi Boo. I hope you love your gifts. I wanted to get you the new George Harrison CD, but everyone was sold out of it. I'm really excited to see you finally, and I know it will happen. Merry Christmas, BooBear. Love, Kelley

Hi Cuddlebear, I really want you to know that I love talking to you, and I'm so anxious to see you in person. I'm just really scared. You're an amazing person, and I really appreciate all the late nights you have sat on the phone with me and comforted me when I am upset. You are strong and smart and sexy, and you just mean the world to me. You are extremely important to me, and you always will be. Love, Kelley

Cuddlebunny, just a short card to remind you that you are "bootiful" in every way, and that I can't wait to meet you and be able to reassure you in person that I think you are gorgeous and you have nothing to worry about. I love everything about you. Love, Don

"When I look back, I will always remember how our love is like an endless summer…blissful, glowing with a warm heat, sun-kissed and everlasting."
-Sarah Treanor

Kelley Lynn Shepherd

FB Post: We are going to make you proud tonight, honey. Mom is driving up, and so many friends are here for our second comedy benefit show. We even have Elayne Boosler on the lineup as our headliner! You never got to meet her, so I guess this is the next best thing, her doing this show. So many people love you and will be there tonight to show you that. I hate that we have to do this at all, but I'm so touched that it is happening. Until Forever. Xoxo…
LIKES: 98   COMMENTS: 105

FB Post: I honestly don't think I would get through this awful, sad time in my life without the friends I've been honored to know. That's the truth. Elayne Boosler, you are a true comedy hero of mine and a true friend. Andrew Block put together two special evenings I will never forget. Lori Sommer hosted them both beautifully. So many people to thank, so much love. Don and I both say thank you. I am floored and overwhelmed.
LIKES: 109   COMMENTS: 56

Dear Dead Husband:

I am too emotional to write anything that makes any sort of sense publicly, so I need to talk to you. Do you realize what happened here? During this comedy show in your honor? Here is what happened: Elayne Boosler, legendary comedian, whom you loved and wanted so badly to meet, got up onstage in NYC and not only headlined the show, but she ROASTED YOU, Boo! You were roasted in classic Dean Martin Roast style by Elayne Boosler. I am not sure if she even realizes how much that means to me and to YOU, to be roasted by one of the greatest in comedy. Maybe she was listening when I mentioned that you loved the Dean Martin Roasts and that I bought you the whole set for Christmas. Maybe she just knew, because she is an amazing friend. After the show, she was so, so sweet. She came up to me, and she was truly concerned. She said in a slight whisper, "Was that too much, hon? Are you okay with what I did up there? I hope I didn't go over the line." Over the line? What line? HELL NO! What she did is exactly what you would have wanted, Boo. And I hope like hell you could somehow hear it and be aware of it and laugh your head off.

 One of her best moments came when my friend, Lori, who was hosting, started to hold up the "light" on Elayne, which meant her time was up. She couldn't believe it. She went on a hilarious tirade. "Really? You're giving me the light? You want me to get off the stage? My time is up? Really? (pointing at me) Where's she going after this? She doesn't wanna leave, trust me. It's not like there's anyone waiting for her back at home tonight. I can stay up here another hour. She isn't going anywhere." Another joke I laughed so hard at was when she was describing you, Boo. "Kelley's husband, Don, sounded like the sweetest man. He loved cats. They had two of them, and he cared for cats on his days off. He also loved going to see Broadway shows with Kelley, and … (looking at me) are you SURE this guy wasn't gay?" I still can't believe I am friends with Elayne, but I am, and she is really good people. I so wish you could have known her. I wish even more that she could have known you. Everyone should have the honor of knowing you. I love you, Boo.

"We still have good to do.
We still have love to share.
We still have life. Let's make it count."
– Annie Nebergall

Kelley Lynn Shepherd

Flying While Fat

One thing that has become evident throughout this whole horrific ordeal of losing Don is that I have some pretty amazing friends. Two of those great friends are Dave and Marina. They are married, with two great boys, and they met one another over two decades ago in our college days at Adelphi together.

One night, a few weeks ago, I got a text from Marina saying, "Dave and I are going to New Orleans for his fortieth birthday, and we are taking you with us. We want to pay for your hotel and your flight and everything. We just want you to come and see a new city and hear the great music. No pressure, but don't say no. Please come!" I was so touched. And floored. And overwhelmed by the idea of hanging out in a strange city with a bunch of married couples and me, the widow. The very thought of that made me sick and sad inside, and the last thing I wanted to do was ruin everyone's trip with my sadness and misery and grief triggers. So I told Marina I would think about it, and then I thought about it.

Turns out that while I was thinking about it, my other awesome friends Andrew and Rodney were also planning a separate trip to New Orleans for that same weekend. This changed everything for me. Two friends that wouldn't be coupled up? Yes, please! And there it was. A trip to New Orleans.

Thursday, October twentieth. We are going. I get into a cab and head to Newark airport. It's a super early flight, and I hate flying. Let me be more specific. I hate crashing. And when I fly, all I think about is crashing. If there is a noise of any kind, I am one hundred percent sure that something must be wrong with the plane. When there is turbulence, I am convinced that death is soon to follow. The last time I flew, I was with Don, and we were taking a vacation to Florida together to visit where he used to live. I remember him gently laughing at me and shaking his head like he always did at my crazy antics. He always accused me of being "overdramatic," when in reality, I was simply stating how I felt. I was never trying to be dramatic. If we were on a plane, and the plane was shaking back and forth nonstop in a frightening manner, I might say to him, "Boo, are we gonna die? Why is the plane shaking like that? Why isn't the pilot saying anything? We are going to die, aren't we?" And he would respond calmly, "No, Boo. We aren't going to die. We are fine. It's just some turbulence. You're so overdramatic." Then he would see that I was white as a ghost, laugh at me some more, and then take my hand in his. "Here. Use my arm to pinch and squeeze if you need to. It's okay if you ruin it. I have two of them."

Then, as I would sit there squeezing his arm, he would patiently and quietly explain to me how a plane works, why there is turbulence, and why it is normal. "It's just the plane going through some wind. Think of it as a tiny bump in the road when you're driving. That's all it is, Boo. We are perfectly safe. Keep grabbing my arm." He would always explain everything to me in a logical way, so that it made sense, and so that I didn't feel as scared. And he was never condescending about it either. He never made you feel like you were stupid for not knowing something, yet he usually knew more about most topics than I did. By the time we landed, his arm would be all red and scratched up to bits with my fingernail marks. He never complained. He would smile and say, "See Boo? We are here, and we didn't die."

This time, there is no Don here to make me feel safe. It is just me. When it's time to board, my heart starts pounding as I walk down and finally find my way onto the plane. B-34... B-34... Where the hell is it? I walk for what seems like days, until I finally reach the aisle I will be panicking in for the next few hours. B-34 is all the way in the back, across from the bathrooms. Great. So not only do I get to have anxiety for three hours straight, I also get to smell the poop of various strangers. Awesome. A... B... C... here's even more great news! I have the B seat, which means I'm in the middle. So now I get to feel extremely claustrophobic, stuck in between two people I've never met and don't care to ever meet. I can feel the panic in my throat.

I toss my bag up above and then slide my fat body into the middle seat. My huge thighs fit into the seat, but there is a tiny bit of "spillage" hanging out the side. I feel like a sausage link. There is nobody in the window seat, and an older business looking guy with a laptop is in the aisle seat to the left of me. He seems unfazed by me and my fatness. As I sit down and try to locate the seatbelt, I start to realize very quickly that I am too fat to buckle it. Is that possible? Last time I flew was about a year and a half ago, and I buckled it okay then. There is no way in hell I've gained that much weight since then. How is it that I can't get this belt on? Okay, hold your breath, I tell myself. Try again. Again. Again. One more time. Do not make a scene. Do not make it obvious that this won't buckle. Am I going to have to ask for that seat belt extender thing? Am I THAT person? Please don't let me be that person.

And then, it happens. Just as I am feeling like I couldn't possibly ever feel worse or more embarrassed with myself for simply existing, it happens. Minutes before takeoff, a woman boards the plane. A last minute passenger. She makes her way down the aisle until she gets to 34-C. She is the missing person who has the window seat. Our eyes lock for a second. She gives me a look that expresses disgust. Then she says in a really, over the top, Long Island accent, "I'm over there." "Okay," I say as I pretend to remove my seatbelt that wouldn't close from underneath the magazine that's on my lap to hide the fact that my seatbelt isn't closed. I really deserve an Oscar for this performance. I get up and stand in the aisle so that she can get in. She isn't even halfway in, and she is already looking annoyed

My Husband is Not a Rainbow

that I walk the earth. I sit back down and again, pretend to re-buckle my seatbelt, putting the magazine back in my lap again. She sits down, buckles her belt, then lets out a huge sigh. Then another one. She undoes her belt, stands up quickly, and proceeds to step over my entire body to get to the aisle of the plane. (The business dude was in the bathroom.)

I would have moved so that she could get out, but at that point, she was pretty much finished with even acknowledging me as a person. She stomps up the aisle to the front of the plane, and seconds later, she has a whole circle of crew surrounding her as she tells them of the horrible monster that is seated beside her. I can't hear what is being said, but I can see it, and it's very obvious. Every few seconds, one of them looks over at me. They keep talking. We are supposed to be taking off now, and we aren't taking off, because a gaggle of strangers are discussing what to do about my state of fatness. I start sweating, feeling anxiety building, and I am seconds away from crying. Why is this happening? Why now? Am I really going to have a Kevin Smith incident and get thrown off this plane for being too fat? I suddenly start picturing myself, an hour in the future, calling Marina or Andrew, and making up some story about why I'm not going to be able to go to New Orleans. There is no way in hell I am telling them that I was too fat to fly on a plane! Is this actually happening? I can't stop sweating. I feel like I've just committed a crime. I feel so guilty and awful and angry. I want to run away.

34-C lady stays up at the front of the plane, and this very security-official-looking Staff Member guy starts walking down the aisle toward me. He looks very serious, as if he is about to confront a possible terrorist. I am Osama Bin Laden now, and I have eaten one too many cheeseburgers. Bin-Lard-en. I can't breathe. He leans into me, and he says in a whispery voice: "Ma'am, we have encountered a problem. The passenger in the seat next to you is feeling a bit crowded and uncomfortable. She says you are spilling over into her seat." He looks at me, as if I'm supposed to come up with some magic solution to my being fat. What the fuck does he want me to do? Should I instantly lose thirty pounds so she can be more "comfortable?" Should I just spontaneously disappear into a cloud of nothing, so that I don't inconvenience this poor, victimized woman? What the hell do they expect me to do about this? I say nothing, and the tears start coming. They are the silent ones that just trickle down the face slowly with no control.

People on the plane start looking at their watches, getting impatient, wondering why the hell we haven't taken off yet. If these people want me to volunteer to get off this plane, that ain't happening! First of all, this Long Island chick is TINY! She is about five foot three and weighs about two vanilla wafers. She is skinny minny, and even though my thigh fat stuck out of my seat a tad, it wasn't even close to touching her perfect, little body. She had plenty of space in her little bubble of a life. Second of all, I just had my husband cremated. I just made the decision to donate his organs. I just lost everything I thought I had. I DESERVE to go to New Orleans, and I am NOT getting off this plane! I want to scream at all of them that my husband is dead. I want to cry my head off until I get my way. But I can't. I am paralyzed. I can't move or speak. I'm frozen.

A few seconds later, 34-C lady comes back to the aisle. Her arms are folded, and she is just standing there. Suddenly, out of nowhere, a steward appears. He looks at my face and seems to recognize that I'm in some kind of pain. He gently says, "How about if the two of you switch seats? You could sit Window, and you can sit middle. You might not feel so crushed if you're not pinned into the window." I say, "Okay, I'll sit in the window seat," and 34-C says, "I don't think that will work." We say it at the exact same time, like some sort of terrible airplane choir. I ignore her, move over to the window seat, sit down, and make the motions with my hands to pretend to put the belt on again.

My Husband is Not a Rainbow

And then a small miracle happens. I hear the clicking sound of the belt. It closes! I don't know why the hell the middle seat belt wouldn't even reach my damn waist, but this one not only closes, I have extra room. Whatever the reason, for a second, I feel victorious. I feel justified in my ability to sit on a plane and not harm others.

Then I wait. This is ridiculous. I know I am overweight, but this is insane to me. I am not crushing this woman. I am not even touching her. I am pretty sure she has come into contact with other fat people in her lifetime. I bet she has a husband at home who is alive and well, and who she probably doesn't appreciate at all. She gets back into her seat, hesitantly, and puts her belt back on. Without ever looking at me, she says to the steward, "Okay. I guess this is a bit better."

And suddenly, it is over. I am allowed to stay on the plane. A few minutes after we take off, she says to me in a faint and unconvincing voice, "No offense or anything. I just need my space." I want to scream at her that my husband had a heart attack and died, and really make her feel like shit. I really want to. But I don't. It will accomplish nothing, and I'm much too exhausted. Besides, she would never understand or care what I'm going through. To her, I'm just some lazy, gross, fat woman. It's that simple to her. For the entire three hour flight, I stare out the window and do the silent crying. There is a lot of turbulence, and I grab the tiny ledge and pretend it's Don's arm. I clamp my eyes closed and chant inside my head, "It's just wind. It's just wind. It's air pockets. Pockets of air. It's okay, Boo. We're okay. We didn't die, Boo." I say this to myself over and over, like a prayer. I just keep repeating and repeating Don's words until we are safely landed on the ground. As we are de-boarding the plane and walking through into the airport, 34-C is about three people in front of me. She gets on her cell phone and says dramatically, "Oh my GAWD! You would not BELIEVE what I just went through on this plane! You'd better not be late picking me up, because I need a drink NOW!" I run into the nearest bathroom stall and cry loudly and fiercely, the way I have wanted to for the past three hours.

"Anxiety. Panic. P.T.S.D.
They are real. So very real.
Once you are inside that tunnel,
It feels impossible
To locate any doors." – Me

FB Post: I'm in looooove with "Naaawlins!" It's like stepping back in time. A whole other world. Of all the places I've seen in life, I think Don would have loved it here the most. Truly bittersweet. I wish I could show you, Boo!
LIKES: 38   COMMENTS: 10

Dear Dead Husband:

I'm inside my hotel room in New Orleans. Dave and Marina got me my very own room. Being here with them and the two other couples that came - it's reminding me of how much everything has changed since you died. Our core group of friends, we don't really fit anymore. I don't even know why really. It's just all different and lonely. Everyone went their separate ways. Or maybe it just feels that way for me. I don't know. I'm too tired to do anything about it. Being here is like a weird dream. Foggy, but different foggy than things have been since July thirteenth, when my world died. You should be here. This place is filled with music. It is literally everywhere. In the streets and in the pubs and just in the air. The food is incredible too. The spirit of the city is vibrant and alive, and nothing matches the way I feel. I love it here, but I feel like I don't belong. I really love my

My Husband is Not a Rainbow

friends for bringing me here. I start crying when I think about how supportive everyone has been the past couple months. My mind is all over the place. Usually I get homesick when I'm on vacation. Right now, I don't want to go home, ever again. I hate home. It is not home anymore. You are my home, and my home is dead.

FB Post: Back home. The jig is up. Back to reality and ugly Newark airport. Funny thing though. After 4 days of incredible food and massive overeating, that seat belt still fit fine, and there was no woman next to me complaining about my too-large existence. Had a great time. Parts of it were hard. Very hard. Looking over and seeing all the couples holding hands or the couples I was with kissing or just having fun together. It felt lonely to know that I am no longer a part of that life. That my partner would no longer be holding my hand or laughing with me or hearing a new band in New Orleans. BUT - I went to New Orleans. And I'm so happy I had that experience. Thank you Marina, Dave, Rodney, Andrew. Love you all. We will always be friends, for life.

Next Page Rainbow Illustration: Kristen Reeves enjoyed Don's company in Country Clare, Ireland. Man, this dead guy gets around...

Kelley Lynn Shepherd

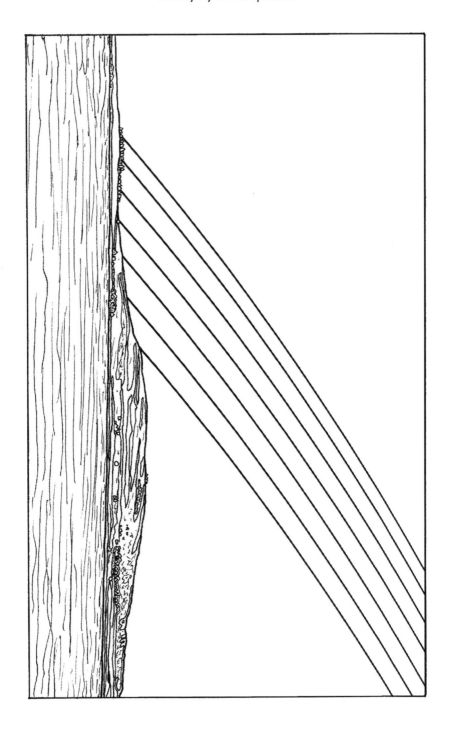

My Husband is Not a Rainbow

Dear Stupid Death Diary:

It's late October, and my wedding anniversary is tomorrow. I was supposed to pick up Don's ashes today. I haven't felt strong enough to go get them or keep them at my apartment yet, so his EMS supervisors said they would hold onto him in the offices there, until I was ready to come and get them. My friend, Herbert, is going with me in case I break down or something, then he can take over and drive us home if that should happen. I didn't go today because something much more fun came up instead. Today, I am filming another comedy video with my friend Opie for his YouTube channel. We are going down to Occupy Wall Street so I can pretend to be one of the protestors, make a fool of myself, and have fun. Oh, how I love doing stuff like this. The ashes will have to wait.

"Once you touch the face of truth, it forever changes who you are." – Christine Schnider

FB Post: Here is a sentence I never thought I would write: Just finished shooting an interview for GBTV (Glenn Beck TV); a conservative online satellite TV network. I was interviewed about the Occupy Wall Street video. It will air on their network after editing. I can just hear Don laughing his ass off at me right now. "Glenn Beck gets you exposure? Priceless!" The video came out great, and it was such a blast to film. I NEED to do more creative and fun things like this much more often. It is pretty much the only time I feel happy and not consumed by grief.
LIKES: 78   COMMENTS: 23

Kelley Lynn Shepherd

"The change that occurs in widowhood is what I refer to, and with a great deal of sarcasm, as 'involuntary evolution.'" – *Hope Robbins*

Dear Stupid Death Diary:

Went to pick up Don's ashes today with my friend, Herb, an actor friend of mine that I got to know while doing extra work on a couple of films. I felt so nervous getting the ashes. I suck at this widow thing. Took me almost four months to be able to even consider picking up the ashes. It's like I'm terrified of having them near me or something. When we walked into the EMS offices, there was a banner honoring Don, a plaque in his memory, and then a memorial picture on the counter. I didn't expect that. It's weird seeing a picture of your own husband with words that say "In Memory of." It makes my heart hurt. Joe, his manager, said, "Wait here. I'll go get Don. I have to warn you, he is very heavy. He was so tall. There is a lot of him." The guys here are hilarious and joke around constantly. They start telling me how they took Don on one last ambulance ride - a full day of 911 calls. They buckled him into the passenger's seat in his cardboard box, and then put the country station on that he hated and sang along, since he couldn't argue or turn it to classic rock. I started laughing and wishing like hell I had met these people when Don was alive and not like this. Why do I have to meet people because he died?

Joe came out with a large cardboard box. It was tall, like Don. Not what I was expecting to see. He said, "You ready?" He was right. The box was heavy, and my husband was inside. He made a few more jokes about his tallness, then told me to stop by anytime, to keep in touch. Herb and I walked to the car, and Herb held Don in his lap while I drove. Talk about weird. I took Herb out for lunch. PF Changs again. I still can't go anywhere that Don and I used to go to. During lunch, all I could think about was that my six foot three husband was sitting in a box, and I wanted to be in a place alone so I could really let that sink in. And then cry.

(hours later) I am home alone with the box. I open it, and I half expect a Jack in the Box type thing to pop up and scare me. Instead, there is a large canister inside the box. I take the canister out and open that. Inside that, there is a large plastic bag that holds the remains of my husband. I feel like I'm looking at cocaine or doing something wrong as I cut the top of the plastic with scissors to make an opening. I need to get some of the ashes out and into something smaller, so that my friends and I can toss some of him into the bay tomorrow. I suddenly become very overwhelmed and feel sick to my stomach and run to the bathroom and throw up. Again with the throwing up. Then I cry a lot. My fingers and hands smell like death and bones and weird, awful things. This is horrible. Beyond horrible. Why didn't anyone tell me how fucking horrible this would be? I take a small plastic cup and put it inside the ashes bag, like a scoop. I put a spoon in there too. I cannot deal with this right now. I put Don on top of the Entertainment Center, and I try to pretend he isn't there each and every time I walk by him. I put my head down when I walk through the living room and avoid all eye contact. Nothing about this is comforting to me in any way, shape, or form. The whole thing is totally freaking me out.

"Where once you stood, majestic and tall…
You now reside in this box.
All your parts,
Collapsed into broken dust,
And I,
have never been more alone."
- Me

Kelley Lynn Shepherd

Don In a Box

So there we were, my friends and I, standing at the edge of the sea earlier today. We were in Sea Cliff, Long Island, across the street from where Don and I got married. There is a beautiful bay there, and we took pictures there on that day, in 2006, not even five years ago. It felt to me like somewhere I needed to scatter some of his ashes. Today is my wedding anniversary - my first one without him.

So we stood there. We were, if nothing else, a bunch of confused morons, trying to figure out the logistics of throwing our loved one into the bay. He was inside that box, and in that box was that canister, and in that canister, was that plastic bag. Inside that bag was the saddest and most ridiculous thing I had ever sat my eyes on. My husband. This big, strong, tall, amazing man who made me feel safe and loved and who made me laugh - was reduced to ashes. Dust. Particles. Sand. If I'm being one hundred percent honest, he looked like Duncan Hines brownie mix. He loved brownies, but he preferred Ghirardelli, so let's go with that.

It was the most heartbreaking, hilarious thing in the world. Devastating beyond all reason. It was so damn sad, what we were doing, and so foreign and strange to all of us, that it then became funny. That is what happens when something is so awful and so traumatic, that you cannot even really process it. It becomes funny. At least, in my world it does. So we made it funny. We started to call it "Don-tossing," like an Olympic sport. "Okay, who wants to toss Don first?" We made a small semi-circle by the edge of the water. It was me, Jessica, John, and Sarah. We stared at one another awkwardly and tried to figure out what the hell came next. John mocked my green plastic cup and spoon. "Classy," he said. "I'm sure this is exactly how Don would want to be remembered." I was laughing hard. Too hard. It was that nervous laugh that comes with tragedy. I was laugh-crying.

My Husband is Not a Rainbow

There was so much Don in that canister, that we began scooping him out little by little and putting some of him into the plastic cup, which became our tossing weapon. We all laughed at our extreme awkwardness and tried to imagine what Don would have said if he was orchestrating this somehow. "Will you idiots just toss me already? Jesus Christ. It's not rocket science. Do it!" Finally, we uncomfortably took turns tossing my husband into the water, each person with about half a cup of Don. There was a lot of Don, so we kept tossing. It seemed like he was multiplying in that canister. Sarah tossed. I tossed. John. Jessica and Sarah. John and me. No matter how many times we tossed, he just wouldn't go away. He wouldn't leave. When we finally made the decision to end the tossing event for the day, there was still more than half a huge bag left of Don in that canister. It was unreal. It was nothing at all like in the movies.

There was a lot of crying, a lot of laughing, and a lot of love. We ended the day with a beautiful gourmet dinner at Sarah's husband Julio's restaurant "Sage Bistro." My friends held me up today, and that is the only reason I didn't collapse into a pile of nothing. A pile of dirt, flailing around in the wind.

Dear Stupid Death Diary:

Having a bit of anxiety right now. About my future. About Christmas. How I'll get through it without him. I want to run away. I'm not sleeping well. I have so much guilt and panic and fear. How could I have been asleep while my husband was collapsing and dying? Why wasn't I there? I keep picturing him alone, struggling, calling my name, wondering where I am. What if he was in pain? I have nightmares about it. Or, I sleep a couple hours and then wake up and remember all over again, that he is still really dead. He dies in pieces everyday. I have nobody to talk to who really understands. All the widowed people I have found are eighty years old. I don't relate. They are talking about

Kelley Lynn Shepherd

retirement and great grandchildren - we never even made five years. I don't remember ever being this sad. My wedding anniversary. It used to be my favorite day. I'm so empty, and I already feel like people are tired of hearing about how much I miss him and miss my life. I saw, by accident, a post on a friend's Facebook about a dinner party that was two married couples they invited over, and I realized I wasn't invited. This was a party I would have been invited to if I was still married. But my husband died, and this was a couple's thing, so I was ignored. It hurt seeing their pictures all smiling and laughing and knowing that I'm not part of that anymore, even though I did nothing to deserve not being part of that. I'm not a part of anything anymore. Another "friend" private messaged me with all kinds of judgments and saying how my posts are depressing, and I shouldn't share so much, because I'm depressing people. Well guess what? The widowed people I've met online keep asking me, begging me, pleading with me to keep on posting things about what this is like and how brutally hard it is - because nobody else is saying it. So I will. I told my "friend" to stop following my page if it depresses her so much. Then I told her that it must be nice to be able to give advice to a widowed person and then to go climb into bed with her husband, who is very much alive. Get back to me when you have a clue about what this might be like.

I hate being in this apartment alone. I take a shower, and I'm terrified I will fall and die and be found four days later, eaten by cats. What if I have a heart attack like he did, and I'm here alone? What if I choke on food? I'm not eating anything really hard or crunchy in case I choke and I'm all alone here. I don't want to be one of those ladies who has "fallen and can't get up," and all the EMT's laugh at me while I lie there dead on the kitchen floor. I miss him calming down my panic and laughing at me. He would be laughing at me right now, and then he would comfort me. I miss his comforting presence. I don't know how people live in this kind of pain and fear. The only thing worse than trying to get through the day and work and life, is trying to get through the night. It hurts to be awake, and it hurts to be asleep. Everything in between is a fog. I feel like I am just stuck in mid-air and uncomfortable in my own skin always. Will there ever be any peace?

Words About Don

"I met Don in EMS school, then eventually became his EMT partner on the ambulance at Sunstar in Florida. He was so easygoing and used to laugh at many of the things I did. One thing that sticks out, is how he would always anticipate my next move or thought when it came to treating a patient. I never had to ask for much, because he always had it waiting for me. Blood sugar? Check. He was already doing it. IV 20 gauge? Check. It was already on the bench seat, along with the 1000 bag of saline and other accoutrements.

I have worked with many partners, but none compared to Don. He was one in a million; the one everybody wanted to work with. Whenever we walked into a hospital, people greeted him warmly and lovingly. Everyone liked him. I remember one call we ran. I had been threatened, for what seemed like months, by every intoxicated patient/person we encountered. One day we had this little old man, who, when we were strapping him onto the backboard, started threatening he was going to kill me. Don looked down at him and said: "You'd better take a number, buddy. She's got almost the whole county ahead of you." He could diffuse any situation.

Don came up with a great line to describe the mindset of some of our more, non-emergency patients. "Panic now - Think Later." Among my favorite memories is anytime my husband would call, and Don would ask to speak with him. They both played 'Advanced Squad Leader.' I would hand him the phone and say

Kelley Lynn Shepherd

'You know, I can just give you his number so you can call him yourself.' He would reply: 'You could, but it's free to talk to him when he's already calling you.'" - Maria Mantek

FB Post: This weekend, I will be honoring my husband with his best friend, Rob, and lots of other friends in Largo, Florida, where Don lived for most of his adult life before moving with me. We will sprinkle ashes at Clearwater Beach, say some words, and then watch Don's favorite football team (Tampa Bay Bucs) together at a pub. If anyone would like to attend from that area, please message me. Going to be another emotional weekend. I love you Boo.
LIKES: 78   COMMENTS: 11

Dear Stupid Death Diary:

Been a beautiful but rough few days. Staying with Rob and Mindy at their house while we honor Don this weekend, on his birthday (November six). He would have been forty seven, but instead, he will be forever forty six. Had pina coladas and coconut shrimp outside at a restaurant on the beach. All the times I was here with Don, and he told me how amazing the beaches were here, the white sand and the water so clear. All the times I was down here visiting him while we dated each other. Now I'm just sad, missing him. Florida makes me sad.

Watching "Ghost" on the TV at Rob and Mindy's in the bedroom I'm staying in here. When I saw this in the movie theatre ages ago, I thought it was stupid and dopey. I remember laughing out loud at the end when she finally "feels" Swayze, because I thought he looked like Lester the Lightbulb. I still think the movie is dopey, but this time, I'm crying my head off. Stupid "Ghost."

My Husband is Not a Rainbow

We did the ashes today at the beach. It was really beautiful. Made a circle with Rob and Mindy's family and few other local friends, told stories and memories of Don, and then tossed a bit into the water down by the Pier. Don would absolutely LOVE that I flew down here to do this for him, that we made a whole separate memorial day for him down here, in addition to everything we did in Jersey. I'm so happy I did this and so sad that I had to. It feels so weird hanging out with Rob without Don here. One of my favorite parts of the past few days was when Rob and I were driving somewhere, and "Living On a Prayer" came on. We both knew how much Don hated that song, and hated Bon Jovi's voice, and pretty much hated anything "Jersey." Don used to imitate Bon Jovi singing, "Tommy used to work on the docks..." in this exaggerated, whiny voice. Well, when it came on the radio in Rob's car, I did an imitation of Don imitating Bon Jovi. Rob just about fell over laughing - his laugh was loud like Don's, and his whole body shook like Don's, and he said happily, "Oh my god! That imitation was PERFECT! You sound just like him! It was like he was back for a second! That was great!" Yes. That was pretty great. Missing him with other people is a hell of a lot better than missing him all by myself.

You Could Be A Foot

Social Media is pretty fantastic. I really can't knock it, because I have received a lot of comedy work, connections, and career forwards from being on social media. I met Elayne Boosler through Facebook. I met Opie and started doing YouTube videos on his @OpieRadio channel by talking to him on Twitter. And now, when my husband is no longer here on earth and I'm lonely as hell each night and up with trauma-induced insomnia, I turn to Facebook to find other people who are lonely and need someone to talk to. However, sometimes people act like idiots when using social media, which can create a lot of problems.

Kelley Lynn Shepherd

Since Don died, there have been a number of tiny incidents involving postings on Social Media. I say tiny, because in the grand scheme of things, they don't REALLY matter. But I say incident, because they do affect me and make me upset, so they must be valid. There are too many to count, but a few of them stick in my mind. Some jerk on Twitter wrote and rudely asked if every tweet from now until death would be about my husband's passing. It annoyed me. Every tweet is NOT about that, first of all. I actually post about lots of other things too. But guess what? My fucking husband just died. Not even five months ago. So yes, I am going to talk about that.

Second, I hate the term "passing" when talking about death. I just loathe it. It's one of those words people always whisper when they say, "Oh yes, her husband...he passed. So tragic." He passed. Passed what? A kidney stone? The Bar Exam? He DIED. My husband died. That is what happened, and it's okay to say the word. And stop with the whispering. I am aware that he died. There's really no need to whisper. Lastly, this Twitter douche doesn't know me or know anything at all about my husband or our relationship. So for him to judge me and what I choose to put on my Twitter page, is silly.

Months ago, I posted on Facebook this: "Need to attempt this life thing again without Don. Not looking forward to it. Wish me luck!" A lot of people did wish me luck, told me to hang in there, and a bunch of other really nice things. And then there was this comment:

"Be glad you have your health, Kelley. Remember that some are living with diseases which make it difficult to just get out of bed. I've got rheumatoid arthritis, but some have it worse." Well, alrighty then. What the hell is THAT supposed to mean? What does your rheumatoid arthritis got to do with my husband's death or ANYTHING for that matter? Nothing. I don't see the connection. Because there isn't one. They are two completely

My Husband is Not a Rainbow

different issues. It makes zero sense to bring up one when talking about the other. I suppose the purpose of saying something like that is to make me feel "grateful" for all the things I could be dealing with that I'm not dealing with. But honestly, I never saw the point to that argument. It's like when you were a kid, and you didn't want to eat your vegetables, and your mom would say, "Eat everything on your plate! There are starving children in Africa!" Okay. Whether or not I eat my green beans, they will still be starving. Me eating or not eating my food has nothing to do with them being starving. Starvation will always be an epidemic, and the only way to combat it is to help them! Send donations. Put programs together to help solve the ongoing issues. And guess what? These beans are still disgusting, and I'm still not eatin' em.

So If I tell you my husband just died and you say, "Well, at least you don't have rheumatoid arthritis!" I'm going to look at you like you're fucking nuts. Unless you leave it as a comment on Facebook. In that case, I will just THINK you are fucking nuts and say nothing and then write about it in my book later on. No, I don't have arthritis. I also don't have lupus, lyme disease, or a weak bladder. And hey, at least I'm not headless! You know, some people are walking around earth without a HEAD! So be grateful you have a head! And legs. There are some people who have no legs. And if they grieved the loss of their legs, would you say to them, "Well, be grateful you've got a torso! You know, some people don't have a torso! Or eyes. At least you have eyes! I know a guy with no eyes, no torso, no legs, no arms, and no face. He's just a foot. So be grateful. You could be a foot."

I mean, where does it end? Your problems are your problems, and my problems are my problems. The death of my husband is what I happen to be dealing with. He is gone forever, and my life is forever different, and every day, I'm trying to get up and figure out another reason why I should stick around. I'm sorry if, at the moment, I'm not feeling very grateful for my lack of rheumatoid arthritis.

"I don't understand the need that some people have to compare pain. If I tell you that my wife died just 4 weeks after her diagnosis, and you come back at me with some story about someone you know who suffered longer with the same illness before dying – what am I supposed to say? 'Okay – you win! That pain is worse than my pain.' There are no prizes when everyone is dead." – Joe Harris

The Thing That Happened

It was the year 2000, and I had recently moved out of the apartment I shared with my best friend, Sarah, in Forest Hills, to a shared apartment with my friend, Jay, and his boyfriend at the time. Sarah and I loved Forest Hills, but they doubled our rent when the lease was up, so we could no longer afford to stay. So I moved in with my good friend from college, Jay, to an apartment in West New York, New Jersey, which was literally about eight minutes outside of New York City. It was the gorgeous city skyline view from the street that sold me on the place. Plus, it was a basement apartment, so it was a bit more affordable. I had my own room. I was working a bunch of horrible part-time jobs to try and survive, and I was not doing well in the love department. Yes, I had been talking to Don this whole time, but we still hadn't met, and despite all the flirtations and gifts and mix tapes by mail, I still wasn't sure if he would bail on me once he saw me in person.

My Husband is Not a Rainbow

I was fat. Very fat. Extremely fat. I had let this traumatic event that had happened to me almost four years before ruin my life. Food became my depression, my friend, and my shield of armor. Not only did I not trust or believe that Don would not run away screaming once he saw me in person finally, but I also had a hard time understanding why he would even like me to begin with. In our many conversations, both by phone and instant messenger over that year and a half or so, he knew that something was deeply wrong inside me. He asked me a few times if I would tell him about it, and each time, I would just shut down. I would only say that, yes, something awful had happened, but if I talked about it, I might never stop crying. He didn't push me. He didn't ever push me.

And then one night, I was walking home from the bus after a late night shift at my job doing merchandise for Broadway shows, when I felt someone following me. There was a creepy presence behind me in the form of a young man, and I just got a very bad feeling. I took my building key and got it ready, resting it between my thumb and finger, so I could poke his eye out with it, if need be. I started walking faster. So did he. Faster. Faster. I felt him within reach, so I walked inside the Chinese food place on the corner. It was still open, and I figured if I went somewhere public, he won't know where I live and maybe he would stop following me. I was trembling. He looked me straight in the eyes through the window of the restaurant, he mumbled the word "bitch," and then he took off down the street. I waited until he was blocks away before entering my building. Don and I were scheduled to chat that night when I got home from work, so I logged onto the Instant Messenger, once in my room and safe, and started typing back and forth. Right away, he knew something was wrong, so I told him what had happened. He comforted me and talked about it with me for a while, and then we switched topics. He had to work early the next morning EMS shift, so he was starting to sign off. He kept asking if I was okay and if he could call me. I played it off like I was fine, but he knew better. He typed "I feel like there's something else going on here tonight. I feel like this is more than just this creepy guy that scared you. Like it maybe took you back to that traumatic thing that happened to you. Do you want to talk to me about it? I think it would be good for you to talk about it with someone."

I was starting to cry and have flashbacks about that night, so I told him I was okay and to go to bed because he had work tomorrow. We hung up. Five minutes later, my phone rang, and it was him. The following dialogue exchange is our conversation, from my memory, all these years later. Due to the extremely personal and traumatic nature of this conversation and event, some names have been taken out entirely, changed, or not mentioned. Some specifics have been left out or slightly altered in order to protect myself, but this was the conversation that made me certain I could trust Don Shepherd with my life and that he would one day be my husband. You should also know that a big part of me did not want to include this story in the book at all, because this is not what the book is about. But in the end, I felt it was absolutely necessary to include this, in order for you to fully understand why Don Shepherd was so special and how he brought me out of despair and showed me love. How he saved me. How I fell in love with him on this night, during this call, when I knew with everything inside me, that he would always keep me safe. And why losing him made me terrified and hopeless and standing on shaky ground all over again. From my memory:

Don: Hi Boo. I know you said not to call you, but I can tell something is really wrong. Will you please talk to me about it? You know you can trust me, right?

Me: I know. (sobbing) I'm just scared. I've never told anyone before. Well, that's not true. I called up one of those anonymous hotlines a bit after it happened, and the woman on the phone made me feel like such an asshole. She made me feel like I was stupid and like it was my fault what happened. She made it worse. So then I told nobody. I just kept eating and being depressed, because I didn't know how to tell someone. And then I dated people that were bad for me, and I kept gaining more weight, and I'm so afraid you're going to run away like everyone else when you see me.

Don: Oh, sweetie. That isn't going to happen. I know what you look like. You've sent me pictures in the mail. You are beautiful, and I'm not going anywhere. I don't care about your weight. I care about you and this hell you are going through. Why don't I ask you some basic questions, and if anything gets uncomfortable, you tell me, and we will stop. Okay?

Me: Okay.

Don: Okay, good. So this thing that happened to you, it was about four years ago you said, right? While you were living in your first New York apartment after college?

Me: Yeah. We were close to our lease being up after being there a couple years, and my roommate had gone home to visit his parents for a few days, I think, so I was by myself in the apartment.

Don: Okay. And you had been dating someone for a little while?

Me: Uh huh. I had met this guy at one of the theatre shows I was doing. He came to the show as a fan. He told me I had gorgeous eyes and that my eyes were going to get him into serious trouble. He gave me his business card, and we started dating. It was only for a few months, but I was so stupid. I had never really been in a real relationship before, just dating guys here and there in high school and college and after. But nothing was ever someone who seemed to love me. This guy was always complimenting me, and so it felt like something more than it was. I didn't notice the red flags. Like, we had nothing in common. He was kind of possessive of my time. Things were moving kind of fast sometimes. He asked if he could stay over for the weekend while my roommate was away. He lived about an hour away, and he made the whole thing sound so innocent, like it was just for convenience, and we could rent movies and cuddle. We hadn't slept together yet, so he assured me that wasn't what he was after. He had this way of saying things and making it sound like it was no big deal.

Don: Okay. Like what kind of things?

Me: Like, a couple weeks before my roommate went out of town, he came up with the suggestion that maybe I should just give him my spare key to my apartment, so that way he could get there before I got home from work one night, and he could surprise me with dinner . I was such an idiot. I didn't know any better. Nobody had ever called me beautiful so much, or looked into my eyes the way he did, so I gave him my key and said okay. I thought it was innocent.

Don: You can't blame yourself for that, Boo. You were under the impression that this guy was in love with you, that he cared about you, and that he wanted to set up a romantic date. So what happened next?

Me: So about a week goes by, and he is headed upstate for the weekend to visit his parents. While he is away, I get a weird phone call from someone claiming they are a friend of his, and that they want to warn me about him. They start telling me that it turns out his parents had died in a car crash over a decade ago, and that I can look it up if I want to. This person tells me that my boyfriend had actually gone upstate to see another girl - apparently he was dating both of us at the same time for months. I asked this person why they would call and warn me about all this, and they said because X is not mentally stable. He is not right in the head. That he has been in and out of mental hospitals for some time now. That he can be violent and mess with my head. She said that if he calls me again, I shouldn't pick up the phone. Just let him fade out of my life.

Don: Holy shit. So now this bastard is walking around with your apartment key, and there's nothing you can do about it?

Me: Yes, except that I somehow completely forgot I had given him that key. That is how much of a fog I was in with this relationship. After her phone call, I followed the instructions, and I just tried putting him out of my head for good. I considered myself lucky to have gotten a warning, and I tried to move on. And it was easy, because I didn't hear from him for about a week. Then my roommate went away, and he called that day. I didn't pick up. He called again a few hours later. I didn't pick up. He kept calling and leaving these desperate messages about how he was sorry for whatever he did to hurt me, but please call him back because he couldn't live without me. Finally, I picked up the phone and told him to stop calling me and that we were finished. He seemed to be aware that his friend had ratted him out, because he kept apologizing. I hung up the phone. He left voicemails begging me to take him back. I ignored him, and I STILL never remembered that this guy had my key the whole time. It just never entered into my mind. It's like I gave it to him in a trance, and then instantly forgot about it.

Don: Okay. That's understandable. You thought you might be in love with this guy, or that he was in love with you. My stomach is in knots right now, because I have a very sick feeling that I know exactly what is coming, and I have to interject right here and just let you know that it really sucks to be on the phone with you having this conversation, because I really want to hold you and tell you it will be okay. I want you to feel safe.

Kelley Lynn Shepherd

Me: I do feel safe with you. I have never told this story with this much detail before. A couple close friends know what happened to me, but hardly anyone, and literally nobody knows the whole thing. I just never felt comfortable enough to say it out loud

Don: I want you to feel that you can tell me anything, because you can. And I won't ever judge you. I will always comfort you and support you and try my best to help you get through it. Remember to let me know if you want to stop talking about it, and we will stop. But I'm not hanging up this phone tonight until I can feel a hundred percent that you feel safe. I don't care if I have to stay on the phone with you all night long, like Lionel Richie. I'll take a nap at work in the morning. Tell me what happened after he left the voicemails. You're okay.

Me: So the next day, I didn't hear any more from him, and so I started to think that maybe he got the hint and would be out of my life for good. I went to sleep that night, and everything was normal. The next day, I didn't hear from him either. That night, I was lying down, watching TV, and I guess I fell asleep at some point, because I don't recall the act of actually going to bed. And then...

Don: Okay, Boo. Listen to my voice, okay? You can do this. You can tell me. I think it's important that you say it out loud as much as you can handle, because you have held this in for years, and it's hurting you so much. You can trust me. Is that when he used the key to break into your apartment?

Me: Uh huh. One second, I was asleep, and then the next second, I felt someone's hand cupping my mouth and my eyes opened, and there he was, on top of me. He kept talking. He wouldn't shut up. I think he might have been on something, because he was acting crazed and manic and really, really scary, and I had NEVER seen him that way before. Never. I had on a long shirt and underwear, and he yanked my shirt up and started getting really rough with me.

Don: You're doing great, Boo. Keep talking if you can. If not, just sit on the phone with me. It's okay. You're safe now (His voice was starting to break, because at this point, he was crying too.).

Me: I was half asleep, and it was dark, and I was trying like hell to yell or scream, but he kept covering my mouth each time. And then the room got fuzzy, and I started feeling weak, like I was fighting and fighting him, but it didn't matter. I felt like I was underwater and trying to lift bricks off me, and he is a very small and skinny guy. It made no sense. I think he had put something on his hands to drug me or make me sleepy. I really don't know. It had a weird smell where his hand was, sort of like alcohol but not. Like chloroform. I think there was a rag or sponge or something in his hand. It felt wet, and I kept going in and out of full consciousness. My body wasn't moving right. It felt like I was made of Jell-O. He told me to shut up. He kept saying shut the hell up. Then he started looking me right in the eyes and saying all this fucked up stuff with my arms pinned above my head.

Don: You're safe, baby. You're safe... I won't let anything happen to you...

Me: He said that I was a fuckin' tease, and that his other girlfriend upstate lets him fuck her in the ass all the time, and they don't use protection. He started mumbling all this stuff about how she is HIV positive and has all these STDS or something, and then said, "And now, you will have them too..." I screamed no over and over again, and I remember trying to bite his fingers. But I was sooo weak. My legs and arms felt like they were made of rubber. I was screaming, "Get the fuck off me!" and I was crying hysterically.

Kelley Lynn Shepherd

Don: You're doing amazing, Boo. Do you remember what happened next?

Me: Yes. I thrashed all over the place, trying to break free. I got my hands near the floor lamp that was next to me. I grabbed at it by the bottom where I could reach it, and I was about to try and tilt it over and smash it on him so I could get away, but he caught the lamp before it hit him. He sort of half-laughed at me, and then told me how what he was about to do was all my fault. And then, just like that, he was pushing my underwear down and then pushing himself into me.

Don: Oh, honey…

Me: He was screaming at me and insulting me as he was raping me. He said if I told anyone, they would never believe me, because I was dumb enough to give him my key. He called me a dumb stupid bitch and a whore and a prude in the same breath, and just had such rage in his face, like he wanted me dead or something. This person that kept saying how gorgeous I was and who looked like he couldn't hurt a flea, wanted me dead. I tried pretending it wasn't happening. I felt weaker, and my legs were so tired from thrashing around. He called me worthless and a disgusting fat pig. He kept talking, telling me how he had lied to me for months and was sleeping with his ex-girlfriend the whole time. Living with her off and on. And how dare I not return his calls or try to break things off with him, when I should be grateful that someone like him would even look at someone like me. That I should be dead. That he would leave me for dead in my apartment, but I wasn't even worth killing. That if I told the police or anyone at all, he would find my family and harm them too. He started saying these things as he was choking me. He began choking me. And then stopping. And then doing it again. I don't know how long it went on, because it just kept happening. I felt like I passed out a few times, and maybe I did. I can't be sure. But I remember waking up or coming to one of the times, and I was being choked.

He kept pushing into me violently, and it hurt. I was screaming and crying, but the noise didn't come out the same as before. I don't know why nobody heard me. I felt like my sounds were muffled. Nobody came or called or knocked on the door. I couldn't understand why nobody was calling the police. This is what was going through my head while he did this to me. I also thought that I might die. I thought that he might end this by killing me, and that would be it. That he would choke me unconscious, and I'd just be gone. I would be just some dead girl that somebody finds and then forgets about on the news.

Don: Kelley, you're the most courageous person that I've never met. I mean it. You have so much courage. I wish I could hold your hand right now, dammit. I hate that I can't be there for you right now. Do you want to stop? Or do you want to tell me the rest, Boo? It's up to you.

Me: If I stop, I don't think I'll ever be able to start again. And I don't really want to tell this horrible story more than once. So let's keep going...

Don: Like I said, you're the bravest person I know. Deep breaths...

Me: Deep breaths. So then... he stopped thrashing into me, and he sat on top of me and looked me right in the eyes. Then he took out the key to my apartment and held it up over me. He started laughing, and then he said, "I hate you." (crying)

Don: Jesus, this guy is beyond sick.

Me: I know. And I can't believe I didn't know. He said it totally matter of fact. Just, I hate you. He took the key, and he shoved it up inside me, tearing me and making me bleed. He did that maybe ten times, I don't know. I felt so dizzy again, like I was going to pass out again. Nothing was coming out of my voice. No sound, even though I kept screaming or felt like I was screaming. I started to accept the fact that I was going to be killed. I didn't want to be killed, but I didn't know what to do about it. I felt like my sounds and this whole thing was happening in a vacuum. He really must have drugged me with something, because I feel like if my screams were as loud as I remember them being, then someone would have called the police or come knocking, but nobody did. So maybe my screams were faint. I just don't know.

And then it got worse. He threw the key across the room, and he spit on me. He spit into my face, and it went in my right eye. Like I wasn't even human. I was this thing that he could dump his sickness into and then leave broken and damaged forever. He kept raping me and had this look of rage that was frightening. And then he had this lighter... I don't know where he got it... but I saw him flicking it at me, and I smelled the smell. He kept holding it onto different parts of me for a few seconds at a time, he made scars and skin irritations and fears that are still there today. I don't know why he was burning me in slow motion, but he got off on it. He would place it above my nipples or under my breasts, then move it around to my labia area. I felt like I kept falling asleep, so I kept waking up to this horror, over and over again. I don't know how to even describe what that feeling is like. To keep waking up and being in the middle of this nightmare. To this day, it is terrifying to fall asleep and terrifying to wake up.

Don: (who was trying not to let me know he was crying pretty hard) Yeah... I'm in such awe of you... that you have carried this around all this time... this is huge trauma. You're doing amazing, Boo. Tell me the rest...

My Husband is Not a Rainbow

Me: It was so sick. He kept doing things with the lighter, and then that, combined with raping me and choking me, made him "finish." I couldn't move. I felt frozen and stuck in place. And so dizzy. The room smelled like burning death and rubbing alcohol. At some point, he mumbled something as he stood up. Something about, "You're such a fucking cunt." I don't really fully remember him leaving. Or what I did next. I think I just lied there for a long time and cried.

At this point during our phone call, Don and I sat in complete silence together, exhausted from the re-living and telling of this awful event. We were both crying, and I was sobbing hard. The way that he was talking to me that night on the phone - it was like the most comfortable blanket. It was the sound of trust and safety and total security and love. Every time he repeated, "listen to my voice" or "you're doing great," I believed him, and for the first time ever, I felt one hundred percent safe in sharing this hell with another human. He let me cry for a while, and at this point, it was maybe three AM. And then he did and said the thing that made me know he would one day be my husband and that I could trust him with my very life.

He said, "I want to stay on the line with you for a while. All night and into the morning, if necessary. I will call in sick to work. I do not want you to be alone right now. Not after telling me what you just told me. You're safe now, Kelley. I won't let anything happen to you, I promise. And I want to say thank you for trusting me with everything you just shared. I know that was really hard. We are going to sit on the phone together until the sun comes up, okay? And then we'll make some breakfast, and then we'll talk some more. You did it, sweetheart. And now, next time it's the middle of the night, and you get scared or triggered, I want you to call me, and I'm going to get you through it. Now you can finally start to heal."

Kelley Lynn Shepherd

We talked into the morning and right through our breakfast and lunch. I told him about the aftermath of the rape - how I would go to work, come home, and sit in the fetal position against the wall in the corner of the living room, shaking and terrified. How my roommate had no idea what happened, and how oddly ashamed I felt, so I kept silent. How I was afraid to sleep or take a shower, because what if he came back somehow. How I took my first shower at the gym instead of at home, and how I silently sobbed as I scrubbed the dirty filth of him off me. How I could feel his spit in my eye and taste it in my mouth, even after brushing my teeth six times in a row. How everything smelled like it was burning flesh. How I stayed up night after night, eyes wide open, listening for the sound of a key opening a door, grabbing my stuffed animals like a scared child. How I ate mindlessly day after day, and packed on weight, convincing myself that my shield of fat would protect me from hurt forever. How I called a rape hotline number in the middle of the night one evening, and began to tell my story. And how the woman on the phone reacted when I told her that I had given him the key that he used to break into my apartment with while I slept. "That's not a break-in," she said unsympathetically. "You gave him consent to enter the apartment. That wouldn't hold up in court." Court? Who the hell was thinking about court? I just needed someone to tell me I'm not an idiot. I asked her why she was being so harsh with me, and she said, "These are the kinds of things you will be asked if you press charges. They're going to grill you like you did something wrong. And you giving him a key doesn't look good." I told him how those types of comments are the exact reason why women don't speak up when this happens to them, and how when someone who choked you and burned you while raping you says they will harm your family if you tell anyone, you sort of believe them.

I kept talking. I told Don everything. How I stayed silent year after year, because how do you tell someone something like that? The words just wouldn't form. And with my parents, I was convinced that if I told them what happened, they would force me to come back to small town Groton and never return to my beloved New York City ever again. I was also a bit afraid of what my dad or brother might do to my rapist. Honestly. I thought they might find him and kill him, and then my dad would be in jail, because I made a stupid decision and gave a lunatic person my apartment key. It just felt a hell of a lot easier to keep this to myself and never talk about it again. Pretend it never happened. The problem with that, of course, is that it doesn't work.

About a month after the rape, our lease was up, and we moved out of the apartment. I made the decision to leave New York for a few months, and go stay with my parents in Massachusetts, so I could find a job there and save up some money for my next New York apartment move. The lease ending came at the right time, because every second spent in that apartment after the rape was traumatic and horrific. Going home to mom and dad's was just the thing I needed. I would be out of the place where it happened, and I would feel safe again. But that wasn't so simple. Being home was good, but it didn't stop the trauma. I had nightmares and flashbacks, often. My sleep was non-existent. There were many times when I came close to telling my parents, because I was in such pain and was having trouble hiding it, but then I would always chicken out. Or I would fear that telling them meant I would have to stay in Massachusetts forever. So instead, I held it all inside, and slowly became someone who was more than one hundred pounds heavier than before. I was a shell of my former self. I was walking around afraid of every little noise, scared of men in general, and terrified that I would never feel safe again.

After working a couple of full time jobs at mom and dad's for about seven months or so, I was able to save up a few thousand dollars, which would be enough to start looking for an apartment with my best friend, Sarah. That is when we moved to Forest

Hills, and soon after, when I began talking with Don in that AOL Music Chat Room. He would become the thing that brought me back to myself again. He would also be the one who would teach me about the meaning of real and beautiful love.

"Be afraid. But do it anyway." – Hyla Molander

FB Post: There are a lot of Don's things that I am keeping, because I feel they should stay with me, or they make me feel close to him. There are other things I am not holding onto, and it's been very important to me to do something meaningful with each item, and not simply sell it off or donate to something with no personal meaning. One thing he loved was his Playstation 2, and the many games he had. It made him so happy to play those games, he looked like a little boy playing them, all serious and focused while playing Call of Duty or whatever else. I was going to just sell the games, but that didn't feel right. Then it came to me. I'm going to donate the Playstation and all the games to his two Air Force/military buddies, Jake and Carol. Jake used to play video games with Don while serving together back in the day, so it's only fitting that he have them now. The Playstation and the games will go to all the other men and women who are deployed out there, so they'll have some games to play. I'll be sending them out tomorrow to the base Jake is at now in New Mexico, and I can't think of a better thing to do with these games, than share them with soldiers and active duty Air Force. Thanks to Carol and Jay for helping me put this together. I know this is exactly what Don would want for his precious video games that I always used to make fun of.
LIKES: 98 COMMENTS: 65

My Husband is Not a Rainbow

FB Post: Had a dream last night that my husband never died. That he was alive, and we were at the Yankees game together at Yankee Stadium, with incredible box seats right behind third base. I would give anything for that dream to be true. Do you know how HARD it is to get seats like that for a YANKEES game? (Come on, that was funny.)
LIKES: 44   COMMENTS: 21

FB Post: Music was Don, and Don was music. He owned lots of guitars, and he strummed and played them as if it freed his soul. They were his most prized possession. He currently has seven. Two of them, I am holding onto - the black electric guitar that I bought him for Christmas a couple years ago, and his acoustic. Since Don and I are both lefties, my hope is one day learn to play guitar, on Don's guitar. Four of his guitars are sitting at my parent's place right now, waiting to be picked up by my cousin Nicky. Nicky runs an incredible music program in Massachusetts called BAND GIG. People of all ages, kids to adults, get together and learn rock songs and form bands. Then they play all over the local towns, in organized events. It's sort of like "School of Rock, except that my cousin Nicky is way cooler than Jack Black." Nicky is going to put the guitars in the rehearsal studio where the kids come to play music. This way, they are being used by people who will love them, and also staying in the family. If any of Nicky's students are interested in buying one of the guitars, he will sell it to them. Don loved Nicky, and loved his music program, and it makes me happy knowing that his guitars will be taken care of by people who love music as much as he did. So that leaves one more guitar. It's going to David, over at Vanderbilly.com, the incredible guitar site where some of the guys got together and raffled off a guitar in Don's honor when he died, and gave the money to me. David lost his home and lots of his music instruments in the horrible wildfires that happened recently in Texas. He deserves to have this last guitar. With the help of another member there,

Chris, we are going to ship it to him as an early Christmas gift. Don would be SO happy with these decisions, I just know it. His music and his kindness will live on forever. Merry Christmas, David and Don.
LIKES: 167   COMMENTS: 56

FB Post: Tonight was already so hard, and then it got harder. My first Adelphi Stand-up Show at Gotham Comedy Club without my husband there to support and cheer us on. Then it went from hard to impossible. Just as I was leaving the apartment to go into the city for the show, I checked my mailbox. The detailed autopsy report on Don's death was in there. Five months we have been waiting for this thing, and it comes as I'm walking out the door for this very important evening that my students have been working so hard on all semester long. "Cardiovascular Disease," along with a lot of other medical jargon, listed as cause of death. I already knew this. The widowmaker heart attack. Silent and deadly. But somehow, seeing it in print absolutely shook me up and floored me. All these graphic descriptions of body parts and harsh language. I cried for over an hour. On my way into the city, on the bus, and at the pub I met John and Jessica at before the show. This hit me like a boulder. I know I shouldn't blame myself, but I can't stop. What if this could have been rectified with a simple doctors visit or heart tests? I shouldn't have let him keep that second job. It was too much. We should have eaten better food. I should have been better. I feel like this is my fault, and I just want him back so badly. I'm so sorry honey. You moved your entire life for me, and I failed you big time. How can I ever be okay with that? I feel like I let you down.
LIKES: 4   COMMENTS: 32

FB Post: Wow. This Christmas thing is hitting me hard. There's no escaping it. The lights, trees, presents, happy families, love…

it's everywhere. I don't think I've ever been this sad. How do I get through the next couple days? It's not even Christmas Eve yet, and I'm already overwhelmed, suffocated, exhausted, invisible, and missing my husband so deeply. This is awful.
LIKES: 9   COMMENTS: 44

"Grief is an elevator with no floors. An escalator that won't stop. A merry go-round forever. Grief is that friend that won't take a hint. It sleeps on your couch and doesn't pay rent. It's a scream and a whisper. A push and a pull. A stab and a dull." – Me

Dear Stupid Death Diary:

I'm crumbling fast. Seeing that autopsy report has got me in a downward spiral. And now Christmas. So glad the fall semester of teaching is over. I feel like I will never be normal again. It's so hard to do things like work a job or talk to humans. I just want to cry all the time, or I feel panicked or intensely sad. Thanksgiving was so hard. I really don't even remember most of the day, but we were at my cousin's house. Some of the people there hadn't seen me since he died, so there was lots of awkward "sorry for your loss" or worse, zero acknowledgement of anything. Almost nobody talked of him or spoke of him. Nobody said his name at all. Why do people try to pretend that he never existed? I don't get it. Some family members mentioned our Nana in conversation - missing her, stories, etc. But no mention of Don. Then I got lectured about religion from a family friend that I barely ever see, and I ran out crying and couldn't breathe right. She said something about his death being God's will, and I said very nicely that if that comforts her, that's great, but I don't really believe in that. She practically yelled at me, "Well you'd better start believing it, or you'll never see your husband ever again. You'd better start reading your Bible." I didn't really plan on coming to Thanksgiving dinner to be threatened about the Bible today. I said nothing. But it hurt. I don't understand why people have to be so hurtful and insensitive. I just don't understand it. I would never in a million years dream of saying something so mean to someone whose husband just died. It really baffles me.

"There is just one thing that the grieving crave, more than any other thing - and it's usually the one thing that is very much lacking by other humans; compassion." - Me

Dear Stupid Death Diary,

It's Christmas Day, and I'm trying to pretend it isn't. I don't even feel like writing about it, but I guess if I'm going to document this loss on a regular basis through writings, blogs, and more and turn it into a book - I should probably mention my first Christmas without Don. It's heartbreaking. It sucks. I told my parents that I can't do it this year. Like, I really, actually cannot do Christmas. So they got the three of us a hotel room overnight at Foxwoods Casino, and we are here gambling and ignoring Christmas. Nothing says Christmas like slot machines! We are trying to not think about the holiday. It's not working. It's pretty much ALL I can think about. My heart hurts.

"The hole I am in is so deep, that I don't recall anything ever existing around it. Life has ended, and I don't much care."
- Bryan Ascavol

My Husband is Not a Rainbow

Dear Stupid Death Diary:

It's New Year's Day, and I think I'm falling into a deep depression. I have a few online folks I can talk to who are widowed, but it doesn't feel like enough, and they are so far away. I feel so alone. I feel like my friends are sick of me. I'm at my parents place because of the holiday break, and last night, we went to a New Year's Eve dinner party at our friend's house. Everything seemed okay at first. Then it wasn't. A few minutes before the Dick Clark countdown to midnight, I felt sick to my stomach. I had to get out. Panic attack. I leaned over to my mom and said, "We have to go." I ran into the car and sat in the backseat waiting for them. I couldn't say goodbye or anything. I was shaking and filled with anxiety. My dad got in and put the radio on. I snapped at him. "Turn that off, please. I can't hear the countdown. I can't hear that right now." When we got home, I ran into the bedroom and cried myself to sleep, refusing to acknowledge any counting of days or weeks or months where my husband doesn't get to live.

That's where the panic came from. During the countdown, I suddenly thought about how my husband would never know another year. 2011 would be the last year he would ever know. He would not see another President get elected or another sunset over New York City. He would never meet our niece that is due to arrive in March. He won't be a dad, or play another guitar chord, or hear another song. No more great movies or Yankees games. No more tomorrows. Just gone. I absolutely refused to take part in any countdown that magnifies all of that.

Dear Death Diary:

It's a new calendar year, and Don is still dead. I moved my wedding ring from my left hand to my right. Not for any real reason, other than I got tired of random men commenting on it, and saying, "So you're married?" and then I'd have to explain, "Well, he died." "Oh, so you're single?" Yeah jerk, I'm not interested. And saying out loud that he died or that I'm not married anymore makes me so damn sad. So I moved it so that strangers stop assuming I'm married. I feel married. So what if my husband happens to be dead? I still feel married, and I will call myself married and feel married for as long as I want to. I don't really care what anyone thinks about it.

The other thing that happened is that next week, I have my first appointment with a grief counselor named Caitlin. How I got to Caitlin is a long story, but I'll try to keep it short. My friend, Frank, who is one of my comedian friends and has been through a huge amount of trauma and death himself, has been pretty much begging me for the past month or so to call his grief counselor, whom he loves. "Please just try," he kept saying to me. So I finally call her, and her schedule is booked solid, and she can't take me on as a client. So she gives me the name of a colleague of hers, and I go see her in Manhattan. She was very nice. I pour my heart out to her for over an hour, telling her my tragic tale of woe, and she listens. Then, after I'm done, she says casually, "I'm not sure I can help you, because I'm not a grief counselor. That's not my specialty." Perhaps you could have told me this BEFORE I launched into my death novel??? Just sayin'.

So then SHE refers me to one of her colleagues, and I call this woman, make another appointment, and meet her in the city at her offices. She is also quite nice and lovely, but her fees are way above what I can afford. Actually, what I can afford is zero, and she is way above zero. She looks at me and says, "I know someone who can help you. Let me give her a call and tell her about you, and I'll email you in a few days with her contact info. I really think you'll be a good fit." So a few days later, I get the email, and it has Caitlin's number. And even though at this point, I felt like giving up after three failed attempts at finding a human who will help me, I called her. She had a soothing voice on the phone. She sounded like a real person who wasn't putting on some crazy "doctor" aura. We made an appointment, and I start seeing her next week. I feel bad for her, having to deal with my crazy, fucked-up, widow ass. I hope she is up for the challenge.

"Grief isn't a race, and there are no rules on how to do it. Take it day by day, hour by hour, minute by minute if you have to. You may not feel better tomorrow, but down the road, you'll look back and see the progress you've made." – Stephen Glasgow

FB Post: It is with great excitement and nervousness that I announce my very first (and probably only) solo play: "My Husband is Not a Rainbow," has been accepted into the Networks One Act Festival, and will be performed by me at The Barrows Theatre, NYC, in March. Details to follow shortly, but the festival is a competition, so I will need your support. Please come and vote for me to continue through to the semi-finals, and then into the finals! Performance dates coming soon! Thanks.
LIKES: 76   COMMENTS: 43

"It is not in the stars to hold our destiny, but in ourselves." – William Shakespeare

Kelley Lynn Shepherd

Dear Stupid Death Diary:

I was uninvited to yet another gathering this week. This time, it was a bridal shower. I guess I understand, because who wants the sad widow at their bridal shower? But still, it hurts to be ignored, and I hate it so much. I heard second hand from someone else that was invited that I had been "uninvited," because "the bride just thought it might be too depressing having me there." Nice. Have any of these people ever considered how depressing it is FOR ME to be stuck in this reality, with myself, twenty four fucking seven, forever??? I'm so sorry that my life makes you uncomfortable for an hour out of your day, but please try being me. I came home and ordered Chinese food, and I'm planning on drowning my depressed self in some sour cream and onion chips. At least my kitties still love me. For now.

FB Post: For all of you who helped me to see a private grief counselor, thank you. It took me a while, and I went through three before finding the one, but I absolutely love her, and I'm sort of convinced she is a gift direct from Don. She gives me a hug before I leave to make sure I'm okay, she makes me tea, and she reads my blog! She said she wants to come to the One Act Festival to see my show too. She really genuinely cares about me. When I was worried because I feel like I'm not progressing enough, and I'm still in so much pain, she said, "Are you always this hard on yourself? You have been through a traumatic, sudden, life changing loss. The fact that you are going to work, coming here, writing, creating, and generally reaching out to people is amazing. You are doing very good things, and even if the only reason you can find to get out of bed in the morning is so you can tell your husband's story - well, then, make that your reason, because it will keep you getting up each day. And then one day, maybe a couple years from now, tomorrow will get a tiny bit easier. Until then, keep sharing Don with the world. It is SO healthy, and you're helping people." That made me feel so

much better than I've felt in months. For once, I feel like I can talk about Don and be sad and share stories, and have someone, a professional, tell me that it's *healthy*. What a relief, in this world where everyone makes me feel like I have lost my mind, for simply loving and missing my husband. She is awesome. I think I have a girl-crush on her.
LIKES: 76   COMMENTS: 17

The 9/11 Shift

It was a perfectly gorgeous day in NYC that day. I got onto the bus that went from New Jersey into Manhattan, to then take the train from Penn Station out to Long Island and out to Adelphi, where I was working for my second year as an Adjunct Professor. We were on the bus, when suddenly we heard a weird noise that sounded like a crash and felt like an earthquake. We looked over to our left, at the NYC skyline on the Hudson River, and saw what looked like smoke and flames coming out of one of the Towers. None of us knew what was happening, and as we got dropped off in the Times Square area of the city, there was mass chaos and general confusion. It was as if everyone on the streets was trying to figure out a mystery or puzzle. "I think there was a plane crash." "Someone just said the World Trade Center is on fire!"

Eventually, cops pushed us onto the trains at Penn Station and out of the city. On the ride over to Long Island, I was with my friend Marina, who also taught there. People were on their phones, and someone yelled out, "Another plane just hit the other tower!" We reached our stop in Garden City, and we went to campus, figuring classes would be cancelled. We walked into the library, where hundreds of students were gathered watching live news coverage of the towers. We walked in just as the first tower started crumbling. And then the second. It was mass hysteria. People's phones stopped working, and I remember there was only one landline working in some random faculty members office. There was a huge line of people waiting to use this one phone to let family members know they were alive. I reached my own family around noon that day, I think. I was able to tell them quickly that none of the phones were working, and that I'd be staying with Marina on Long Island for a couple days until we figured out how to get home, but I was alive.

At this time, Don and I were still talking daily, and still had not met each other. He also had never been to NYC in his life, so he didn't know the layout. So here he was in Florida, hearing the news about the attack in NYC, and he knew I went through the city to get to work, and he couldn't reach me. I think it was a couple days before I was able to reach him or to hear my own voicemail and see that he had called several times and left multiple messages with a shaky voice. When we finally talked on the phone, he was so relieved. And determined. He said to me with a very serious tone, "I was very worried, Boo. It is just such a helpless feeling being all the way down here. Knowing I can't DO anything, and I didn't know if you were okay. We need to meet soon. I can't do that again. I don't want to be away from you like this anymore. We need to meet soon so that we can confirm what we know is real, and then take steps for us to be together in the same state and zip code. I want to keep you safe. I promised you that. You must have been terrified. I know I was. Thank god you're okay. I thought you might have been dead, Boo."

It was the events of 9/11 and the horror of what could have happened to me, to any of us, that pushed our relationship forward and made us both want to take a risk on each other, finally. That day, we started making concrete plans for Don to fly to New Jersey and spend a few days with me. I was beyond terrified about this, but it was time. He had been so patient with me, and although it would actually be 2002 before he would fly to NYC to meet me, it was finally going to be time.

My Husband is Not a Rainbow

"I knew when I decided to love you fully, with all of my cells, that I was risking everything."
- Sarah Treanor

FB Post: Today was Valentine's Day. Perhaps the saddest thing about this day, as a widow, is the feeling of being forgotten about. My husband is not here with me, and it sucks something awful, but my friends made sure I wasn't forgotten. Thank you Sarah, my oldest childhood friend, for spending the day with me, eating pizza takeout, making fun of the world, and sending me back home with lots of homemade food in little containers I can freeze. Thanks to Jessica, who sent me a sweet email, even though today is HER birthday. Thank you to one of my male students, who came up to me right before the start of Acting class, handed me a yellow rose, and said, "I know Valentine's Day is stupid, but I'm sure the first one without your husband is really hard. I hope this helps." I wanted to hug him inappropriately, but I felt that might not be the best idea. Finally, thank you to my friend Ginger, who had a dozen roses shipped to me today, so that I would get flowers on Valentine's Day. I really don't know what I would do without my incredible friends. Today sucks, but because of you all, I don't feel invisible.

LIKES: 105   COMMENTS: 56

FB Post: My brother and Jen just had a baby girl! She is a little bit over 7 pounds, and I wish I could go and meet her, but since I'm 5 hours away and working, it will have to wait a few weeks. I wish Don could meet his new niece. Makes me very sad, because I know he would have been amazing with her. He was so good with our nephew, Brian. He loved that kid so much. Welcome to the world, little Jillian!
LIKES: 79   COMMENTS: 84

Ghost Sex

I have a rather disturbing story to share. At least in my mind, it is disturbing. The other day, I made my second attempt in this post-Don life at finding a satisfactory and helpful in-person support group for widowed people. So far, this has been a close to impossible task. The first group I went to, which was more than a two hour drive to get there, ended up being an epic fail where lots of really old people sat in a circle comparing their misery. I felt completely out of place, because they were talking about retirement and great-grandchildren, and social security benefits. Instead of feeling better, I left there in tears, determined to find something with a bit more hope.

A couple of days ago, I found a group of "forty five and under" widows that meets up two times per month at a local community center for talking, support, coffee, and refreshments. I decided to take a chance and go, with the hopes that it would prove better than my previous experience with the cast of *Cocoon*. This group was certainly a very different experience than the first group, but I won't be going back again.

It started out pretty normal. I was welcomed into the group as a new member, and everyone seemed very cordial and lovely. We sat in folding chairs in a large circle and began the meeting with a reading about loss and grief. They asked me if I wanted to share my story, and I did. It felt weird saying that my husband was dead out loud, because it always feels weird every time I say it. The people in this group were around my age, and some were even younger than me. I started to relax and feel as if maybe I had finally found a group where I fit in.

Then the tide turned. The conversation turned spiritual. Then it just turned *weird*. A young woman, who looked to be in her thirties, began talking about her most recent interaction with her dead husband. She said she was lying in bed, when she suddenly felt him near. Then, out of nowhere, she began describing in graphic detail how her dead husband "came to her" again, wanting to have sex with her. My reaction to these words, which was a lot like a character from a *Loony Tunes* cartoon, seemed to be in the minority. Everyone else in the group was listening intently and nodding their heads, as if this was information they had heard before. The woman continued her story, and then went on to "instruct" the rest of us on how we could also have sex with our own ghost husbands and partners. Since nobody except me seemed put off by this topic, I didn't move or breathe. I sat there, paralyzed and probably in shock. As she began to use hand movements as part of her description, circling the outside of her lady-parts with her bony fingertips and over her mom-jeans, I felt the insides of my stomach churning. I cringed in my folding chair and pretended I was somewhere less awful, like a "Drop a Refrigerator on my Face" Convention. I began singing nursery rhyme songs in my head, as a feeble attempt to drown out the horrific images she was forcing onto me. The other widows in the group began mirroring her movements, so now there were fifteen-plus women in folding chairs, tracing circles around their hoo-has, in rapid succession. The lead cult-woman began telling the others to "feel the essence of your partner inside you," and "let go of society norms, and let your lover invade your special place." She stood up and made her way around the circle like a yoga-instructor, giving tips to each individual on their ghost-sex efforts. At this point, one or two of the ladies started lightly moaning. Another one said in a whisper, while touching herself through her long floral skirt, "Oh, John!" The leader praised her, clapping while further encouraging her, "Good! Good, Becky! Tell John you want him to enter you now, and then make it so!" I half-expected a film crew to appear out of nowhere and for someone to do the big reveal of the hilarious practical joke that was clearly being played on me. Except that didn't happen. These women were very serious and very into the moment. As for me, I needed to get the hell out of there and make my grand exit before any of these women were able to, god forbid, "finish."

Most of them had their eyes closed while performing this "sex with a ghost" ritual, so they couldn't see me trying to suppress laughter. They also didn't really notice much when I got up and pretended to get myself some coffee and continued walking all the way out the door and down the hallway and out of the building and back to my car. When I reached the inside of my car, I laughed loudly and fiercely and said out loud to the cold, night air, "Wow!!! What the hell was *THAT???*" After collecting myself for a few minutes, I thought a little bit about what I had witnessed. In general, I think I am a pretty open-minded person. However, I did discover, in my thought-process, that ghost-sex is where I draw the line. Maybe if you're going to have a group where you all sit around and touch yourselves through your clothing while pretending you are having sex with your partners who are dead, you might want to put that somewhere on the flyer. Calling that a "support group for widows" is tad bit misleading. Also, I share a lot about my dead husband with others, but our love life and sex life - that belongs to us. Why on earth would I want to get into our sex life in a room filled with people I just met? To me, that is sacred, especially now that he is dead. The times we had together, intimately, will remain with me forever. Plus, I could literally hear Don's voice cackling with laughter at me while I was sitting in that circle, *"Run, Boo!!! Get the hell outta there!!! These people are NUTS, and this is super creepy!!!"* Hey, to each their own, right? I'm not judging, but if I were, that shit was *weird*. So, just in case anyone is keeping track - that is *two* widow support groups so far. The first one I left crying. This one I left laughing. I guess we'll call that a victory.

"Everyone has a grief all their own.
Some drink or eat too much. Some don't eat at all.
Some work or feel too much. Some don't feel at all.
Some sleep around too much. Some don't sleep (or screw) at all.
Eventually, you figure out what helps get you through
And what pours salt into the forever open wound."
– Carrie Johnson

FB Post: Well, after two emotional, back to back night's performances, my one-woman show, "My Husband is Not a Rainbow," made it into the semi-finals at the Network One-act Festival! I'm so excited, and thank you so much to everyone who has come out so far to support it! This kind of material is so raw and personal and really exhausting. But in some ways, it feels like exactly what I should be doing right now. Telling the truth about grief and life after the death of my beautiful husband. Next stop: The Finals!
COMMENTS: 23   LIKES: 97

"We all need a refuge from our grief, but we need the battlefield to win the clash." – Rachel Kodanaz

Kelley Lynn Shepherd

FB Post: My one-act did not make the Finals. I'm very sad, disappointed, and somewhat surprised. My goal was to use this play to get exposure for my story/blog/book and for industry people to see it and see ME. Making the finals was important, because the finals audience is filled with industry agents and casting people. I feel defeated. I really wanted this to get seen. I put everything I have into this piece, but I guess it wasn't enough. Going to go drown my sorrows in some Girl Scout cookies. Thin Mints and Tagalongs, to be exact. Thanks to everyone who came out and voted.
COMMENTS: 67   LIKES: 32

Dear Dead Husband,

I'm so sorry, Boo. I feel like I failed you. I just want to tell your story to everyone on earth, and I'm not able to do that in the way that I want to. I wish more people would listen. I'll have to find another way. Doing this festival gave me a reason to get up in the morning - something to look forward to. Something to get me out of this hell-hole apartment so I can stop thinking about you being dead all the time. So I did a play about you being dead all the time, which makes no sense, but somehow, it was better than sitting here at home, knowing you're still dead all the time, forever. Mostly, it was another way to honor you. I'm sorry I didn't do better. I love you.

Session Snippet

Caitlin: It's good to see you. Your one-act was very powerful. It was such a revealing mix of raw stand-up comedy and vulnerable, real life in the face of death. It was really very brave stuff.

My Husband is Not a Rainbow

Me: Thank you so much for coming to see it. That really meant a lot to me that you were there. I've been in such a funk since not making the Final round of plays. It makes me want to cry every time I think about it.

Caitlin: I know, honey. I didn't see all of the plays, but from the bunch I saw along with yours, they were very good - but none were quite as raw and brutally real as yours was. I think that some people just aren't capable of sitting through something that real. Or maybe they aren't sure if it's real or not; how much of it is fiction.

Me: Yeah, some audience members came up to me after my first two performances and asked me if it was real, if my husband really died. That confused the hell out of me. Why on earth would I make this shit up? And HOW? I could never write anything like this if I wasn't living it. And why the hell would I want to? I just feel defeated.

Caitlin: Do you feel like you accomplished what you set out to do?

Me: Not really. Sort of. I mean, it moved people. But I wanted it to be seen on a bigger level and for people to really comprehend how awful this is and how it's a struggle every single day. And I feel like I just miss him even more now, somehow. I don't know why. I hate this.

Caitlin: Here are my thoughts. I'm wondering if, by writing an entire play about what it's like to grieve your husband and what you're going through these past nine months, then having to rehearse that, go through the process of performing it multiple times, and then having it stripped from you suddenly, like Don was stripped from you - if, in a sense, you maybe felt like you were re-living the whole thing all over again.

Kelley Lynn Shepherd

Me: Yes. Maybe. I think so. (crying hard) I wrote it that way on purpose, you know, as a theatre device to show the harsh contrast of my life. Having the play begin with footage of our wedding and the vows - and ending with me standing there with his ashes. Because that's what it is. I got married, I was supposed to build a life with him - and now I have ashes in a can.

Caitlin: Yes, and for the audience, that was a very powerful theatre device, and that message got across. But for you, that's your reality. You're literally standing there with his ashes on that stage as the lights go down - and then you're going home to sit there with his ashes. So, it didn't end for you when those lights went out, and maybe putting a spotlight on that, literally and figuratively, was just a lot for your heart to take.

Me: Yeah, the worst was after the play was over, and getting all my stuff together backstage, and I just had the biggest meltdown. It was like I realized, in that moment, that I have to go home to this now. Maybe I was expecting some sense of relief from putting this onstage, and the relief never came. Instead, I was kind of terrified at the idea that I don't get to walk away from it like the audience does. This is forever (more crying).

Caitlin: Yes. I think you created something up there that was way more powerful than maybe you even imagined or could predict. It's pushed you right into the nucleus of this grief hole. I think this play has opened up some things for you that maybe we need to work through, some of those deep emotions about loving and losing Don.

Me: I feel like I failed him. (sobbing hard) I keep apologizing to him at night. I keep saying I'm so sorry. I'm sorry...

My Husband is Not a Rainbow

Caitlin: That makes a lot of sense. You didn't fail him, Kelley. But I know why you feel like you did. I think you poured your heart out to these people, these audiences - and by them not voting you into the Finals, to you, it was as if they were rejecting *him*. They were saying no to Don. You were screaming out to them to please hear your beautiful story, to please hear your love for this wonderful man, and they basically said, "Yeah, that's nice. NEXT!"

Me: Yes! I just wanted everyone to know how great he was, and how fucking hard this is. And how empty it feels to go from promises of a lifetime together, to going home with a can of dirt on your Entertainment Center. I still can't believe this happened sometimes. I just can't believe it. It took me so many years to find him. Why was he taken away?

Caitlin: I don't think there is an answer to that question that will ever make sense for you. But I do know that doing this play was courageous, and writing it and performing it was brave, and it has led you to this extremely vulnerable place, where maybe we can start to really dig deep into these grief thoughts and help you to process and move through them.

Me: I don't feel courageous. I feel like I failed, and I'm just so tired. I feel like I don't want to do anything anymore. What's the point?

Caitlin: I know. Grief is hard, hard work. It's exhausting. On top of working your actual job, trying to stay afloat, and dealing with your new reality. I think you've been so focused on ways to honor him since he died - writing, performing, the blog - that maybe it's just recently that you've really started to focus on *you,* and on the deep, hard work of feeling the grief and feeling the hole of his absence in your life.

Me: I feel his absence every single second. There's literally no time when I don't feel it.

Caitlin: Yes, and so accepting every offer from friends to take you for dinner or lunch, doing plays, working two jobs (I know you have to financially), driving to Massachusetts to visit your parents on weekends, creating art, these are all keeping you out of the apartment for as long as possible, so that you show up late at night and go right to your room and log onto Facebook until you're tired enough to maybe sleep. And then the sleep doesn't happen most times anyway. Get up and do it all over again. Anything to stay out of those suffocating walls, right?

Me: Do you have cameras in my apartment? How do you know this?

Caitlin: Because I know all about finding ways to not sit inside the awful silence of losing someone to death. The problem is, eventually, you have to sit in it.

Me: I don't want to…

Caitlin: I know. It's going to suck. Hard. But I will be here with you, sitting with you, and helping you process through everything. Try and get some rest the next few weeks. Maybe only leave the apartment four nights a week instead of five or seven. See how long you can take being there with your thoughts, and let me know what happens when you don't run from them. You're going to be okay.

Me: Okay. I don't believe you, but okay.

I'm In Love With a Dead Guy

Today is March thirteen, 2012, and it has been exactly nine months since my husband died. It's been nine months since I have felt him hold me or touch me, or take his index finger, put it on the tip of my nose, and go "BEEP!" He really loved doing that, and it was so incredibly silly. We would pass each other on the way to the kitchen, and he would stop and go "Beep!" on my nose. It's been nine long months since I've heard my husband speak words to me, or laugh with me, or start his sentences with, "You know…" while folding his arms across his chest. Nine months since he sat in his favorite chair while I would present him with various fun "prizes," like candy bars and toys. Nine months since he tapped his fingers on my arm or leg to the beat of the music while trying to learn a new guitar chord. Nine months since he put his key in the door while coming home from an overnight shift, snuck in slowly, so as not to fully wake me, and say out loud while pointing at each of us, "One kitty, two kitty, and a Boo. Everyone is safe."

For the past nine months, I have eaten meals alone. I've watched movies without pausing them every ten minutes so we can give each other mini-reviews throughout, "You like it so far? Cuz I love it!" "Yeah! This is awesome!" For the past nine months, I have been to the grocery store and only bought foods that I like, avoiding the aisles that contained all of his favorites; telling myself not to look too long at the Special Dark Bars or the Barq's Root Beer, or you might cry. For nine months now, I haven't been able to ask him his opinion, or get his advice, or his take on something I've been writing or performing or doing. For nine months, I've shut off the bedroom light with no fanfare, instead of racing my husband to be the first one into bed. He would usually beat me and yell victoriously, "HA HA! I'm in bed first! I win! You have to shut the light! Ha Ha!" For nine months, I've been throwing my hair up in a wet ponytail after my shower, instead of Don gently towel-drying it for me while standing in front of me, humming some made-up song.

It's hard to comprehend that it's been nine months in this life. It feels like an eternity without him. Each day that goes by feels longer; like just another twenty four hours that I don't get to spend with him. It also strikes me that nine months is the length of a typical pregnancy, and that in the time since my husband has died, another family member has been born. Our brand new niece, Jillian, came into the world on March seventh. After my mom called to tell me she had been born, I hung up the phone and started crying. I felt so alone and so sad for Don, who would never get to meet this beautiful little girl. He will never get to meet anyone ever again. Jillian's birth is one of the first, significant things that have taken place, completely in the span of time that Don hasn't been here to know about it. Nine months is a long time. He doesn't know a lot of things. He doesn't know that our dear friend, Rodney, got married, and he didn't get to see the unique and beautiful ceremony where Andrew married them. He missed Sarah's fortieth birthday party, and he doesn't know that John is in college now, taking film courses; or that his best friend, Rob, got yet another promotion. He doesn't know that a Comedy Benefit was put together in his honor, or that I went to New Orleans, or that Posada retired this year from baseball. My husband has no idea that I'm driving an entirely different car, or that my parents are living in a different town. Enough time has passed since his death for me to write a play about my experience with grief; and to be performing it in the Network's One-Act Play Festival. Don will never get to read my blog, or my book about him, or know all the things I am trying to do just to honor him and my love for him. He has missed so, so many things.

Nine months is a long, long time. And then, when you think about it in terms of life, it's not a long time at all. Nine months behind me, still a lifetime to go. When you marry someone, you just assume and hope and *think* that you'll be together forever. You don't think one of you will lose their life this way, this soon. And so when that happens, and you are left here on earth without that person that you vowed to be with for life, it is an extremely confusing time. Most people become widowed when they are old, and while it is still very sad to lose your spouse at any age, they don't have to face *decades* of a future without their love. Everything you do and everything you are is intertwined with that person. To lose them suddenly, is to throw you into mass chaos. Who am I now? What am I doing? Where do I fit? What does it all mean without someone to share it with? *What is the point without love?* I vowed to love this man until forever; until "death do us part." But what if only one of you dies, and they die at age forty six? Where does that leave the other? Just because he is dead, does not mean I love him any less. In fact, my love for him has never felt stronger and more alive than right now. My husband is gone, and I love him. I do not know how to stop loving him, and I don't know that I would ever want to. But how do you continue life when you are in love with someone you can no longer be with? I wish I knew. My heart is stuck on forever, and I don't know how to *not* love my husband. I am in love with a dead guy. Tell me – what am I supposed to do with that?

Dear Dead Husband,

I've been casually looking for apartments, Boo. My horribly paying teaching job just isn't cutting it alone, and I can't afford the lavish lifestyle of this luxury New Jersey apartment anymore (I know you would laugh at that, since our apartment is crap). I need a roommate. I don't want to get a roommate, but I need to in order to survive. I need to move out of New Jersey and maybe back to Queens or somewhere much closer to where I teach on Long Island. Doing this commute makes no sense. Nothing makes any sense. I hate looking for places to live without you. I never know what questions to ask or if I'm being taken advantage of. We were supposed to be getting a nicer place to live together, and now I'm doing so many things I don't want to do, because you are not here. This sucks, and I miss you.

I Have Lost my Mind - and my Pants

When you wake up one morning, and your husband is randomly dead, there is a long period of time where you feel as if you may have lost your mind. There is a "fog" that covers you and protects you from the unbelievable reality that is your life now. This fog keeps you in a constant state of "Huh?" and you forget things over and over, repeat yourself, and just generally behave much like someone with memory loss or no brain cells. This must be how it feels for Kim Kardashian every single day. Empty.

In the first few months, when the fog was still very heavy, I was scatterbrained beyond belief. I would leave the house for work five times, forgetting something new each time. I would get out to the parking garage and realize I didn't have my phone. Then I would realize I didn't have the remote for the garage. The third time, I made my way across the street seconds later, it was because I had forgotten my phone AGAIN!!! I would walk inside, grab my phone, and walk back outside. Realizing I didn't have the remote, I would go back inside the apartment to get it. When I picked up the remote off our entertainment center, I put down my phone and walked out of the apartment without it.

On a completely different day, my toothbrush somehow ended up in the freezer for an entire afternoon. There was another day where I thought I lost one of the cats, and was looking everywhere for him and sobbing, only to realize he was sitting on my bed, in plain sight, looking at me like I had finally lost my mind. He was wrong. Yesterday – I finally lost my mind.

My Husband is Not a Rainbow

It was sixty forty five AM, and I was just about ready to leave for work. The first class I teach is Stand-Up Comedy at nine AM, and the morning commute traffic can be insane, so I leave myself at least two hours to drive out to Long Island. Before I left the apartment, I double-checked my hands and my shoulder bags to make sure I had everything. Purse, teacher bag filled with paperwork and worksheets, garage remote, cell phone, keys, water bottle, cats are fed, lights are off, TV/computer off… okay. I think this time I've got everything. Time to go.

Please keep in mind while reading the rest of this story that I am someone who has just been through a sudden and traumatic loss, and I don't sleep much anymore. I probably get an average of two to four hours of sleep per night, and most nights it's closer to the two. So, perhaps my brain is not functioning properly most of the time. This is important to remember as I continue…

I walk into the elevator, go down to the lobby, and walk outside. It is a really nice day. A bit cooler than usual, somewhat brisk. There is an older man who walks by me with his dog. He looks at me, then he stares at me strangely. I wait to cross the busy street. He looks back at me again as he walks away. I think nothing of it and mutter to myself and also out loud, "Asshole."

When I cross the street to where the parking garage is, there are about eight or nine people standing and waiting at the bus stop there. Most are busy on their phones or not paying attention, but a couple of them start laughing. One woman points at me. I click the remote, walk into the garage, open my car door, and sit down in my car. I start the engine, and when I do, my elbow sort of slightly makes contact with my leg and knee area, brushing against it softly. It is at this point, and only at this point, that I finally realize why people are looking at me.

I'm not wearing any pants.

Kelley Lynn Shepherd

Let me repeat that, just in case you thought it was a misprint or some bizarre error. *I'm not wearing any pants. No pants.* Somehow, impossibly, I had left my apartment, went outside, crossed the damn street, and gotten into my car WITH NO PANTS ON! I had on a bra, a brown shirt, and some lovely cotton underwear. And shoes. Somehow, I managed to bend down, inside my apartment, and put on a whole pair of shoes without realizing I did not have on pants. And they weren't just flat loafers or something. Oh no. They were sneakers. That were tied. I sat down and tied my sneakers, with bare legs, apparently, and didn't notice the no pants.

How exactly does one leave their place of residence without realizing they are not fully dressed, you ask? How does one not FEEL that their legs are, in fact, naked, and that they are, indeed, sans pants? THAT, my friends, is the grief fog. Here I was, under the impression that I was improving. I thought the fog was starting to lift. And then I looked down and saw no pants.

The worst part of this story (or the best part, depending on how sick your sense of humor is), is that I now had to take the same exact journey across that same street, back up that elevator, and into my apartment so that I could GET said pants and then put them on. I had to embarrass myself a second time, this time with full knowledge of what was about to take place before this nightmare would be over. And so I pressed that remote, lifted that garage door, and up came the view of the crazy widow with no pants on. All those people at the bus stop waiting for the bus? Still there. Still staring at me. The man walking his dog? He walked by yet again, and I muttered: "Sorry I called you an asshole." I sprinted across that street faster than any fat girl has ever sprinted before, and into the building and back up the elevator, and then put on the pants.

Then, I had to come outside, into the world of humans once again, and cross that same street again now, for a THIRD time, this time with pants on. There I was, my purse over my shoulder, acting all professional, waltzing across the busy street, as if I'm NOT the same lunatic woman who JUST crossed the street a few seconds ago, twice, with no pants on. "Widow crossing! Widow crossing! Go back to your homes, folks. Nothing to see here. Nothing to see..."

I don't think I have ever been so humiliated in my entire life. Actually, I know I haven't. But, at least I now have THE greatest, most humiliating, real-life example of that thing we call *widow brain*. And now I'm wishing I could go back to the days where I was putting my toothbrush in the freezer. Those days seem a lot more sane than leaving my apartment and getting into my car with no pants. Widow of the Year.

"Widow Brain is a real thing.
All cognitive thought goes right out the window.
Unless you thought you threw it out the window,
but really, it is somehow inside the washing machine instead.
Good luck getting your brain back. It left on a train called death."
- Me

FB Post: Watching Yankees Red Sox on 100th Bday of Fenway. First full game without you. Kenny Singleton is commentating, so I know this is the perfect game to watch, since he was your favorite. Swisher just hit a homer, and so did Chavez. Wish you were here to banter with me and call our brother and dad and just laugh into the phone like you used to do everytime Yanks slammed a homer or Boston did something dumb - I miss that stuff so much. Yanks are doin' great Boo! Love you xoxo.
COMMENTS: 23   LIKES: 14

Kelley Lynn Shepherd

FB Post: Today I want to say thank you to all of the new "brothers and sisters" I've met here on Facebook. Also, to the first widow support group I have been to that doesn't suck. Thank you to Kathryn Douglas, for providing a weekly place to go and meet other people my age who have lost their spouses. The first widow group I went to back in month 3, was so horrible, I didn't think I would ever try again. Then I did try again, and it was a comedy of errors. Then I found your Long Island groups on Facebook, and you are a gem. So thank you, Kathryn and all my new in-person friends in the widowed community. I find myself looking forward to Wednesday nights now, because I have this amazing group of friends who understand me when I say words. That feels nice.

Also, my widowed friends on FB, there are too many of you to tag, and that fact alone makes me sad. In society and out there in the world, the young widowed are a minority; a blip on the radar. It's tough to find ANYONE who is going through what you are going through at this age. While all your friends' lives are beginning with marriages, kids, and futures - the lives we knew are over. So thank you - for being the only people who understand what this really is, for never judging, for staying up typing and talking at ALL hours of the night when I feel the most alone, for always confirming that I'm NOT crazy - I'm just in pain, for being a friend. Much love to all of you today, tomorrow, and everyday. In the loss of our loves, we gained a family. Grief creates the strongest bonds, and even though we all wish we never had to cross paths, we did; and I love you guys.
COMMENTS: 40   LIKES: 110

FB Post: Our kitty cats constantly look at me like, "Where's the other guy? What'd you do with him? We've discussed it, and we liked him way more than we like you. We don't care for you. You suck."
COMMENTS: 14   LIKES: 23

FB Post: Dear General Public: Please don't call me "single." It is sort of insulting, and it implies that I had a choice in the matter. My husband didn't leave me, I didn't leave him, our love is still love, and this new reality was forced upon me. I am not single. I was widowed at 39 years old. There is a ginormous difference. Thank you.
COMMENTS: 21   LIKES: 87

FB Post: The hardest and saddest part of performing in a comedy show, is coming home to my empty apartment, with nobody to share the "high" with. The best part is doing comedy with people I admire and hearing those loud laughs that just come from the gut. So many people came up to me after the show and either just hugged me, shared their stories of loss with me, or said something that made me want to keep going and keep doing this. Thank you Michael Karen for putting me on this gig and trusting I would do well, and thank you Jessica Kirson for saying what you said to me tonight. I can never hear my husband tell me he is proud of me ever again, but it's sure nice to hear it from someone whom I consider an amazing friend and an INCREDIBLE comedian. It was an honor to open for you tonight, and I love you.
COMMENTS: 34   LIKES: 102

My Husband Finally Spoke to Me. He Said: "Leave Bon Jovi."

My husband and I were very similar. He believed in things that were logical. If it was reasonable, made sense, or could be proven, then it was true. He loved science, and he made me love it too, whenever he would teach me something new. He was always teaching me something, because he loved to soak up information in books, by watching endless documentaries, or just by paying attention to people when they talked. We had many discussions about religion, faith, God. Fascinating topics, really. Don and I loved to talk about stuff like that while lying in bed together. We would ponder life, death, and everything in between. Neither of us really believed in the concept of Heaven or Hell, and we didn't see The Bible as anything more than a collection of interesting and far-fetched fables written by man many, many years ago. But we both believed in the idea of "something more," and we believed that God was a force of Love and all good things. I remember during one of our bedtime talks, Don told me, "You know, if there is a God, I think our pets have the closest access. I think they have a completely different awareness than we do. I would bet anything that Autumn is talking to Isabelle and Ginger when she meows nonstop at the ceiling. Either that, or she's clinically insane."

Isabelle was Don's cat, his baby, that he had for years in Florida and then brought up here to live with us when he moved in. She died at fifteen years old, weak and sick. Weeks later, we adopted Autumn and Ginger, two kitten sisters. We lost Ginger to an enlarged heart at only age three. Ever since then, Autumn stares at the ceiling in our hallway for HOURS sometimes, meowing loudly like she is talking to someone. After Don died, her meowing intensified, and her ceiling chats have gotten more and more frequent. Now this is one of those things, where, if I were to tell someone about my cat who sees dead people, they might want to have me institutionalized. But all I can tell you is that it's real, and she really does this, and it's freaky as hell. I don't know what I believe about some things, but I know that there are often things that just can't be explained. And after today, I'm thinking maybe Don was right. Maybe our pets do have better access to the other side. Or maybe I need to be institutionalized. It's still up in the air.

Going back to science, there is this: Energy. Energy does not die. This is a fact. Energy lives forever, cannot be destroyed, and we are all made up of energy. So if energy never dies but stays alive forever, what happens to us when WE die? Where does that energy go? What form does it take? Are we all just pieces of the universe floating around out there? Do we become stars? Chickens? Salt shakers? Coconut-cream pies? The ocean? (Whoever became a salt-shaker in their second life must have been a real douchebag.) I don't know. None of us know, except for the dead people, and maybe the animals. I'm not big on religion or following a bunch of rules or going to church or using "God" to tell people how to live their lives or judge others or ANY of that. To me, God is Love. And in truth, the origin of the word "God" was that it is a verb; meaning *to love*. I believe in Energy. I believe in a higher power of some kind. What you call that is up to you. Some people call it God. Mother Nature. Spirits. Afterlife. Angels. The Universe. It doesn't really matter. People should believe whatever it is that helps them get through the day.

What gets me through the day right now is a hell of a lot different than it was ten months ago, when my husband was still alive and here on Earth. Ten months ago, If someone had said to me that they were going to see a Medium, I probably would have said, "Oh. That's nice." Then I would go home and think to myself how that person must have lost their mind or question how the hell anyone can fall for that kind of garbage. Actually, I probably wouldn't have given it a second thought. Just like I never gave a second thought to the fact that I could hold or hug my husband anytime I wanted to. I could eat dinner with him, see a movie with him, be intimate with him, feel loved by him. The instant all of that was stripped from me, everything changed. Forever. I changed. First, his love changed me, and then his death changed me again. Ten months ago, I never would have considered a session with a Medium. I would have laughed at it, mocked it, and put my cynical spin on it. But it's amazing what you will do when you are faced with the harsh reality that your husband is *never again coming home*. One thing I will say about religious people and those who believe in God, is that they seem to have an easier time accepting death. Think about it. If you really believed that your loved ones go to "a better place" or that it was part of some Divine Plan, (neither of which I believe to be true at all), that's a lot more comforting of a thought than what someone like me believes; which is that nothing at all happens after we die, and that there is no reason for anything except for the reasons WE make of things, what WE do with our lives here on Earth. To me, this is it. I am open to the idea that maybe there is some sort of "life" in another form after we die, but I don't know exactly what that is or what it means. If we all become rocks or blades of grass, what the hell kind of future is that to look forward to? Am I supposed to be excited about that? If I see Don again one day, will we both be blades of grass? Will some drunk father kill us with his lawnmower wheel? What will become of us? Nobody knows.

After months of talking to other young widowed friends on Facebook, most of whom had "felt" their late spouse's presence in many ways since their death, I started to feel really sad, because I haven't had any experiences at all where I felt like Don is "with me" still. A good friend of mine had gone to see this Medium / Psychic / Healer several times, and she swore by the woman's accuracy and realness. So, after over-analyzing it to death and panicking, because that's what I do best, I finally made an appointment, or a "session" with this woman. I was told by people to talk to my husband out loud before the session, to let him know that I need for him to come through for me. I have never felt like such a jackass in my entire life, but I took out our wedding picture, put on his wedding ring over mine, and started talking to him as if he were right here. I asked him to please help me believe that he is somehow still here with me. No, that doesn't make any of the pain go away or make me miss him any less intensely, but at least I would have some confirmation that maybe I can still have some sort of different type of connection with my husband forever. That at the very least, I would always have *that*.

My Husband is Not a Rainbow

When I picked up the phone to call her, I couldn't stop shaking. I had a similar feeling the very first time I met Don in person, after we had been talking online for over a year. I thought my heart would literally fall out, and then the instant I saw him, it was as if I had known him my whole life. Something similar happened on this call. I was so nervous, and the feeling of not having a clue how this works or what to expect started to overwhelm me. Then she introduced herself, explained a bit about what she does and how she "reaches" over to the other side and talks to spirits, then asked me a few mundane questions about the weather and things, just to start picking up on the energy through my voice. What happened next I will type below, pretty much word for word, or as much as I can remember. It is a dialogue like nothing I have ever experienced before, and I was a bit in shock for a whole day afterward, and it took me a while to process it all. I will type out the actual dialogue that occurred, and then underneath certain exchanges, I will put my inner-monologue *reaction* to what she was saying to me **in bold.** Let me also just make clear that this woman knew absolutely nothing about me when this phone call began. The only thing she knew was my first name to make the appointment. She didn't know that my husband died, how old I was, how old he was, none of it. Here we go…

Her: Okay, Kelley. Several people are starting to come through that all want to talk to you or are here for a reason. I'm getting a father or a fatherly figure. But your dad – he is still alive, correct?

Me: Yes, he is alive.

Her: Is it your father-in-law? He is an older man, like 70s or 80s, and he is standing on a golf-course or near a golf-course.

HOLY FUCKING SHIT! This was Moment One where chills went up my spine. Don's father lived on a golf-course, and had

a heart-attack and died on a golf-course. How could she possibly know that?

Me: *That must be my father-in-law then, but I never met him, and my husband and him were not close.*

Her: *That doesn't matter, that you've never met him. He is here to bring me to someone else who wants to talk to you. Sometimes when the loss is recent, the spirit doesn't know how to move in this world yet, so someone else "goes to get them," so they can speak with you and be reached.*

Goes to GET THEM? How does that work exactly? "Don!!! Your wife's on the phone from Earth! She wants to talk to you!" This is WILD!!!

Her: *You lost someone recently, correct? Within the past year?*

Me: *Correct. Almost ten months ago.*

Her: *It was sudden. It was traumatic. They died all of a sudden, very quickly. They weren't sick or anything. Was it your husband?*

Me: *Yes.*

Her: *Okay. I have him here. His father is standing next to him. There is also a small woman, very fragile and frail looking, very tiny. She is also old and standing with him.*

Me: *That is his mother. She died a couple years ago.*

Her: *She is here with him. They are together.*

My Husband is Not a Rainbow

Oh, he must LOOOVE that! She was a total pain in the ass his whole life, and he ran away from her – now he is stuck with her for eternity!

Her: Okay there is someone else. It's someone's grandmother ..yours, correct? On your mom's side of the family. Did she pass away?

Me: Yes. (I start crying. This is just so weird.)

Her: It's okay. She wants to tell you that she knows how hard this has been on you, losing him, and that she is sending you a big hug and food. She also says that she thought your husband was an amazing person, and she really loved him for all the times he helped her with her medication questions and health things. He was very kind to her.

Her: Okay, there are some things your husband wants you to know. He says the reason you haven't felt close to him is because he had a lot of trouble "crossing over" to the other side. His crossing over was peaceful, and it was quick, and there was no pain, but when he got here, he was confused, and he was just as shocked as you were that his life had ended. He felt lost on the other side. There were three angels that helped him, and one was his dad, and mom. I'm also getting a strong male figure, someone young, either a brother or a best friend maybe?

Me: He had a half-brother that died young. He didn't know him though.

Her: He knows him now. They were all Angels for him and helped him cross over. The sibling, the brother, also had a peaceful crossing. Your husband also wants you to know that he is so sorry there was no chance for you to say last words to each other, and he wants you to know how much he loved you and will always love you, and appreciated you, and was so grateful *for you in his life. He is also saying that every single thing you did since his death, he approves of and he is happy with. He said he could not have ever done a better job himself. The way you have conducted yourself has been amazing. He is proud of you.*

He is proud of me. He always used to tell me that. ALWAYS. To hear it again, even if it's coming from a third party, is just so beyond meaningful to me. Now I really cannot stop crying.

Her: You didn't have children together, but he says the reason for his death was heart related, and it came from his dad's side of the family, not his mom's, and that his father's father had it too, and if you had a son together, he would have also probably had it. He says it was just one of those things, and that you couldn't have done anything to save him. He wants you to stop blaming yourself. He said, "Cut it out. You gave me everything, and I was happy. I'm sorry if I didn't tell you that enough." He really wants you to know how much he loved you. (pause) Now I'm picking up on some pets around him too. Getting a very strong large cat vibe or small dog. Did you have pets together?

Me: Yes. A few. Two that died and two are here now with me.

Her: The one's there with you are sort of tiger-or-multi-colored right? A boy and a girl? And there are two girls here with him...

Isabelle and Ginger. Sure, this woman could have googled me and then read my blog, which pretty much tells the entire story in detail of Don and me and our life. Don't think I haven't thought of that. I AM the greatest cynic alive. But the way she was saying all of this stuff, it really FELT like it was coming from a genuine place, and also felt like it was coming to her AS she was saying it. Plus, there were SO many tiny details that there is just no way she could have known. At this point in the conversation, I'm a sobbing mess and just listening with wonder and in awe of this whole thing, quite frankly. It is a lot

to process and take in. Some stranger is on the phone, whom I have NEVER met, and she is talking to my dead husband!!! WHAT???

Her: *The female cat that is with you, she likes to sit in high places or meow or talk in high places? When she does that, he is near you. He hasn't been here long enough yet to know how to reach you, and that's why you haven't felt his presence a lot, but you will soon. But pay attention to your pets, because they have access we don't to the spirit world.*

(This is getting out of this world weird now. That is the EXACT same thing that Don said to me while lying in bed that night, about our pets having access to God and life beyond. AAAHHHH!!!!!!)

Your other cat, the male one, he scratches some sort of case that belonged to your husband. An instrument or something.

(WTF? How could anyone know this? This is SO random of a thing to know. Okay. This woman is clearly on a different plane, and it's scaring me. Everything that I thought I believed or didn't believe is now being questioned with this one statement about a guitar case. And then my logical side kicks in, my inner-cynic, and I think, "Nah. There MUST be some explanation.")

Me: *Yes. He played guitar, and you're talking about Sammy. I have one of Don's guitars that I kept, and it's in the case against the wall in our bedroom. Sammy always goes up to it and tries to use it as a scratching post.*

Her: *He is doing that because he feels him nearby that case, cats are better at dogs at picking up energy forces. But your husband says to please make him stop doing that, because he's ruining the case.*

Kelley Lynn Shepherd

(Now I'm laughing, because that is exactly something Don would say. He took SUCH good care of his things and was very particular about them being touched, moved, or fooled around with. This is INSANITY!)

Her: He is telling me that he feels badly that he couldn't leave you with anything when he died. He says that you two didn't have much financially. He had no idea that his heart was sick, or he would have prepared better so that you wouldn't have to struggle so much now. He feels terrible about this, because he wants for you to be safe and always taken care of. He hates that he, as your husband, wasn't able to provide you with that. He keeps apologizing for that, and says that he will try and do whatever he can from the other side to help you - putting good people in your path, making sure the right people see your talents. The spirits can sense and see things that we can't, and he is telling me that you will not struggle forever, and you will be very successful. Are you a writer? Have you written plays?

Me: I wrote a short play after he died and performed it, and yes, I'm a writer.

Her: He said that something you wrote or are writing will become a book, and that the book will be very successful for you. He also is saying something about you facilitating large groups of people. Something in your future that will be part of your success, it has to do with you either talking or lecturing or something in larger arenas, venues. I'm seeing humor.

Me: I'm a stand-up comedian, is that what you're seeing?

Her: It could be that, yes, but it's going to be more than that. He is telling you to keep going, keep doing what you love, it is going to become something bigger. He sees lots of traveling and speaking or comedy engagements, but with a bigger message.

My Husband is Not a Rainbow

He says you are just beginning to get recognized, and that you will be known by many soon, and that these speaking engagements will be inspirational. Something inspirational and humorous. He is saying that he believes in you, and he thinks you have amazing talent. He says you have the talent of a Gilda Radner or a Tina Fey. He said you are going to live to be an old lady and be known like Betty White. He said Betty White.

Trippy. Don loved Betty White like crazy, and I love Tina Fey like crazy, and he always compared me to Gilda or said I reminded him of her and her "unique" presence and talent that is like nobody else. It is so strange that she would choose those three people as examples, when she really could have said just about anyone.

Her: Have you gained weight or had weight issues? He is coming through saying to "please stop" with the hating yourself over your weight. He says you need to understand that you are so so beautiful inside and out, and stop beating yourself up. He says he knows you are so sad and you are grieving, and will be for a long time, and he understands. He misses you too. But he wants you to keep doing what you love. He says he will do as much as he can to protect you and keep you safe. He is asking about the female in your life that has helped you. Is there a female recently that came to you or you came to her, who has helped you emotionally?

Me: I think you mean my grief counselor.

Her: She is either a friend or yes, a counselor or teacher. He brought you together. He wants you to know that he is taking care of you and still learning how to communicate with you, but he will always find ways to take care of you. He says this is why you trust her so much, because he brought her to you.

Kelley Lynn Shepherd

OH. MY. GOD. *So it's not my imagination that she seemed really "special" or like a gift in some way. That is also why I feel closer to him when I see her, because he chose her for me.*

Her: Okay he is saying something about baseball, and that he wants to watch the games. Put the games on, he says. He says for you to wear his shirt and go back to Yankee Stadium. He says for you to know that he is at peace, and he is okay, and that you will be okay one day too. He says that you were the love of his life, and that he will never stop loving you or taking care of you. He also says he is glad you are leaving... Bon Jovi? Something about the band Bon Jovi, and you finally leaving... does that mean anything to you?

Me: (laughing) Yes. He hated Bon Jovi, and he hated New Jersey, and hated everything New Jersey, which is where we lived and I live now. Bon Jovi is a private joke between us, because I would always call him and blast "Livin On a Prayer" whenever it came on, and he would say, "Are you done now? Great, now that's in my head all day," and then hang up. I think he is saying he is happy I'm finally leaving New Jersey and moving back to New York.

So that was my very first Medium experience. You might think I'm a lunatic or that I need to be put away for believing some of this stuff, but let me tell you, I didn't believe ANY of it before that phone call, or before my husband died. So please don't judge me too harshly, for when you never get to see or talk to your husband ever again, you will do just about anything to be able to feel his presence, even for a half hour. I don't know how to explain what happened during that phone call. The things she said... the details... knowing nothing at all about my life and then being so accurate in that way. There was more to it, but I left some of it private, because a few things she said are too personal to share with the world. But after years of being so sure of myself in thinking that nothing at all happens after we die, I can tell you one thing I do know for sure, and that is this: I don't know shit.

"There is this place we can't see with our eyes...
It is made of energy.
All the people we lose from here, go there.
They can see us, but we can't see them.
Some call it heaven, others call it universe.
I call it home." – Christina Rasmussen

FB Post: Watching the Yankees game. Because my dead husband told me to.
LIKES: 76   COMMENTS: 11

Dear Stupid Death Diary:

I took a cab ride the other day, because I had to, because I was coming home super late in the city, and because my husband is dead and can no longer meet me somewhere and escort me home when it's super late at night and creepy on the subways. I don't feel comfortable on the subways alone after about midnight or one AM, and Don would either have been with me on the subway in my old life, or I just wouldn't return home that late if I was alone. He would almost always meet me places, even if it was totally out of his way, because he wanted me to be safe, and he didn't like me walking through subways and city streets alone with creepy dudes out there that are up to no good. So I took a cab to be safe, and the cab driver was hitting on me all the way home to New Jersey. It made me so uncomfortable, and then while he was talking and kept staring at me through the rearview mirror and giving me this look like he wanted to do creepy things to me - I decided in my head - that I would have him drop me off a few blocks from my apartment, because there was no way in hell I wanted this fuckface knowing what building I lived in. He was asking me, "Are you married? Are you single? Did you go out tonight? 'Pretty lady like you out so late alone.'" That is creepy. Yeah, I'm alone because my husband is dead, and I still have a life and go out sometimes with friends, or I have to be out late for a work gig or whatever, and then I have to come home alone. Anyway, I tried writing down his info and name somewhere, but I had no pen, and my phone was on like three percent, so I couldn't get it to function without shutting itself off. So I had him drop me off at the Chinese place around the corner, then got out and picked up takeout, because that's how I cope with stress and pain and feeling unsafe. Then I went home and literally cried while I ate my chicken lo-mein. Sometimes I hate being female, especially without my husband here. He was such an advocate for women and such a feminist in a lot of ways. He knew people, other than me, in his life, that had lived through tremendously horrifying rapes or sex assaults or attacks at the hands of truly awful men, and he was the kind of guy who never let that be okay and who stood up for women like me and believed us when we would tell our stories of being victimized or treated like sex objects - and he called men out on this behavior, often. He did not put up with mistreatment of women, children, or animals. I miss him standing up for me, and the world feels so much more terrifying without him here.

He's Dead. I'm Pissed.

This morning, I woke up with a brand new emotion: Anger. Yes, I have been angry since my husband's death. I have been *pissed*. But this was different. I literally woke up, sat up, and felt an instant wave of violent anger. And the same way that an infant cries on instinct after waking up wanting their bottle, I broke down sobbing and wanting my husband. The sobbing became louder, and then weirder, and then it turned into cries and half-screams. It just wouldn't stop. I wanted to punch somebody, everybody. I wanted to take away someone else's world so that they finally *get* what this feels like. I wanted to burn our bed down and write all over the walls and take a knife to my wedding dress that's been hanging in his closet – taunting me. I wanted to senselessly shatter and murder and hurt things, because my life has been shattered and hurt and murdered. "It's not FAIR!" I screamed like a child, and then fell forward in our bed, stomping at the mattress with my fists.

It is now almost two PM, and in just a couple hours, I have to put on the "professional" face, and go out there, be funny onstage, and then be a motivational leader for my twenty two Adelphi students, who will be nervous as hell tonight and looking for my support. But where's my support? Who do I get to lean on for strength? Tonight is my stand-up comedy students' big Comedy Show at Gotham Comedy Club in NYC. We work on their sets all semester long, tirelessly, and it all leads up to this. Their first big professional show.

I am so fucking angry. I'm pissed that I pulled back the shower curtain this morning, and lying in the tub was a ginormous dead cockroach that the cats must have killed. I can't bring myself to pick it up with a napkin and throw it away. I am so goddamn terrified of bugs and rodents and things. There are three light bulbs out in my apartment. Two in the kitchen, and one in the hallway. The ceilings are so high, that I can't even reach them standing on a stepstool, and I'm so annoyed that my husband's more than six foot three frame isn't here to just *do this shit for me.* I'm sick of all the creditors calling, the lawyers, the hospital bills that are ENDLESS and don't stop; and how the hell can it be over $23,000 for an ambulance ride, and less than a freakin' hour in the ER that ended in him never waking up??? I'm sick of dealing with paperwork and red tape and after-effects of death. I'm so tired of facing the daily piles of *stuff* inside our apartment

Kelley Lynn Shepherd

and not knowing what to do with it and not caring and feeling sad and feeling beaten down by *things*. I am so mad that I have to avoid my living room, and that nobody comes over here anymore. Nothing happy has happened in this apartment since he died, so I immediately picture the day of his death, sitting here with my mom and about eight friends, letting the reality of our new hell marinate. My living room is now just a death room. It's the place we all gathered when he died. I can't even go in there without shivering. I'm tired of staring at his Ashes in a fucking Christmas tin on top of the Entertainment Center. I'm sick of thinking about what to do with the remaining ashes, I'm so over trying to be meaningful and inspirational and motivational, when I just want to die. I'm sick of my bathroom being a pharmacy, filled with pills to help me sleep, stop me from thinking, stop my headaches, get rid of the intense physical aches that are everywhere, and make me feel human again. Waking up groggy or driving to work on two hours of sleep for an entire ten months is really getting on my nerves.

I'm really angry that something as huge as having a life-altering experience with a Medium that makes me feel a bit of hope that maybe there *is* more after life than just death – does absolutely nothing to help my day-to-day existence here on Earth. I'm still just as alone and just as lonely as ever. I still have to live out the rest of my days without my husband. I am so annoyed that I have nowhere to put my love for him. I am so over looking at pictures and watching video clips and recalling memories, all in an effort to *feel* his presence again, to feel his love. None of it works. It is all a lie. He might be with me in spirit, but what the fuck does that do for me right now, when I want his opinion on this show tonight? Or when I want to lay in bed with him on a Sunday afternoon and watch a baseball game. Or feel him kissing me again. Tomorrow will be ten months since I have felt him do anything, say anything, be anything. I am so angry that I have to write this, that my life is now *about* this, and that nobody will ever really understand. I want to hurt something, but I know it won't help to stop me from hurting. I want to look into my husband's eyes again. I want to know what it's like to be together forever. I want to have a fifth and a tenth and a fortieth and a fiftieth anniversary. I want to grow old and cranky together. *Why the fuck did this happen???*

"When angry, count four. When very angry, swear."
– Mark Twain

Session Snippet

Caitlin: So, have you been spending any more time at home, inside the apartment?

Me: Yeah.

Caitlin: And what happened as a result of being forced to sit with your emotions?

Me: I started getting really fucking pissed off.

Caitlin: At Don?

Me: No. I'm rarely mad at Don. He doesn't want to be dead. I'm pissed off that I'm a widow. I'm sick of this being my thing. I'm tired of going into widow groups and hearing other horrible heart-wrenching stories about more depressing shit like my depressing shit. I'm sick of my regular, normal, non-widowed friends not understanding, and I'm sick of somehow expecting them to understand, when I know they can't, and I know they are trying as best as they can, and I love them, but everything is just different now, and I don't fit in with anyone. I'm tired of missing him. I'm tired of not caring about anything anymore. Of gaining weight and not caring. Of eating meals that consist of microwave popcorn at one PM for breakfast, or Wendy's drive-thru on my way home from work, or gorging on chips and coke and candy at insanely late hours of the night while watching mind-numbing TV to stop thinking about my crappy life. I'm just sick of all this shit. I want to punch something.

Caitlin: So punch something.

Me: Huh?

Caitlin: Punch something. Safely. Go buy a punching bag and put it in your living room and punch it. Punch your pillow. Drive to work and park your car far away and scream and punch your steering wheel. Just don't be driving while punching. The anger is there, because the anger needs to be released. It won't go away until it's released. So let it out. Release it. In a healthy way that's not harming you or someone else. Did anything specific happen to make the anger come out stronger?

Me: Just everything. Bills. Bugs. Life. Our crappy apartment. Driving two hours each way, each week for the only support group I can find for younger widowed people. Anxiety about my car breaking down. About having no money ever. About my future, what the hell I'm gonna do. All the stressful stuff was funny when Don was here. He made everything funny and easy, and we would just make fun of everything together and laugh. Now it just sucks, and there's nothing funny about being this broke and this hopeless feeling. I think I got angry because I was just so damn tired of being sad.

Caitlin: Do you feel overwhelmed by all the grief emotions? Is it hard to make it through a work day, through the day at all?

Me: I guess so. I'm just used to it. I just feel like I don't want to be home, or at work, or out with friends, or anything. I don't want to be anywhere. Except for wherever Don is. That's where I want to be. Why is this pain so awful? Is it ever going to stop?

Caitlin: No. I don't think it will ever stop entirely.

Me: Well that's fuckin' uplifting.

Caitlin: That's what I'm here for, kiddo. Uplifting. Grief is an expression and a direct result of love. As cliché' as it sounds, it's the cost we pay for loving someone, loving anyone. So, I don't think that you ever really stop grieving someone that you love. You and Don had an extremely special and beautiful love, and it was much too short, and so your level of grief is equal to your level of love. Your love was huge. Your grief is huge. But Kelley, it will get easier. It will shift into something different than what you feel right now. You're going to have a life that has more joys in it. But it's going to take a long time to get there, because your love and your grief are immense. It's important that you let yourself sit with these feelings right now. Write about them. Keep coming here. Talk them out. And you know that if you are ever feeling overwhelmed, or you need to talk, you can email me, and I'll call you back as soon as I can.

Me: I feel weird bothering you when I don't have an appointment.

Caitlin: Please. You're not bothering me. This is what I do. You are under my care, and I care about you. I'm also going to ask around and see what I can do about finding a widow support group for you that's closer than a two hour drive each way. (looks at her watch) Shit!

Me: (laughing) What's wrong?

Caitlin: We just went over by an hour. I don't care normally, but I have to be at a work function, and I'm late.

Me: But I thought you cared about me...

Caitlin: Yeah, yeah, yeah. I care about you, but I need to care about you from afar right now. I'm late. Come on. (pushing me out the door) Get the fuck out!

(We both laugh hysterically.)

Caitlin: You okay? I need to make sure you're okay before I send you out into the streets of Manhattan. Always make sure you're aware and alert when you leave here. Grieving people can be in a fog and are very vulnerable to being robbed, attacked, things like that, when they are zoned out in their heads and not paying attention to their surroundings. I need you to be okay and alert before you leave here.

Me: Can I hug you?

Caitlin: Of course. You need hugs right now. You need to feel safe. Now go home and punch something. Keep punching it until the anger alleviates. Then let yourself rest, because living and grieving at the same exact time is exhausting. Get rest. And go beat the hell out of something.

"Car therapy has worked for me. I've beaten my steering wheel so hard that I bruised the palm of my hand. I've cursed at my dead spouse for dying, shouted along with angry punk rock music, and let out primal screams through tears while driving. And I haven't been arrested. Yet." – Tim O'Brien

It's Great to Finally Meet You. I Love You.

So it was August of 2002, and the events of 9/11, along with over three years of having an undefined relationship through phone calls, care-packages, and AOL instant messages, finally led Don Shepherd and me to the day we would finally meet. After much preparation and planning, we set up a week-long visit in late August, so that I could take Don to see the famous U.S. Open tennis tournament, one of this favorite things on earth.

I was living in New Jersey at the time, and had moved out of the roommate situation and into my own place, up on the third floor. It was decided that I would take the bus from West New York into the city, take the subway to Queens, meet him at the airport, and then we would take the bus and subway back to my apartment. Because Don was such a gentleman, he insisted on booking a hotel room in nearby Edgewater, but I told him he would most likely be cancelling that room and staying at my place. I wanted to grab and cling onto every second I had with him in person before he had to get back on a plane again and go back to sunny Florida.

My self-esteem was low. I was panicky. This was the first guy, since the rape, that I not only trusted and liked so much, but I felt like I might be in love with him. He had also spoken of similar feelings, so we figured that we should probably meet each other if we were going to be in love and all. I jumped on the bus to meet him, nerves and all. My hands were sweaty, and my heart was fragile. I was terrified. What if he rejected me? What if he thought I was too fat, or wasn't attracted to me at all? All of this went through my head on a loop, as I arrived at the airport.

I walked in and waited over by baggage claim. Before 9/11, you used to be able to go all the way up to the Gate to meet your party and wait just outside the doors there. After 9/11, however, they changed all the airport security in NY and NJ, and you could no longer do that. You now had to wait in Baggage Claim. Don wasn't familiar with this rule, I didn't think to tell him, and he had never been to NYC before. So that day, when he flew out to me, I was waiting in Baggage Claim, and he was waiting just outside his Gate. Both of our cell phones were ancient, and I think we had spoken earlier in the day just very quickly to say that we would meet up when he got off the plane. From what I remember in my mind, we didn't do texting or anything like that back then. Maybe others did, but I don't think Don and I did. Or if we did, both our phones were flip-phones and not the kind you could easily text from. Basically, our mode of communication with one another at the time was less than stellar.

So when he arrived and stayed on the other side of the gate, we couldn't reach each other, because our cell phones had no reception. We were both panicked, thinking that the other one had blown them off or not shown up. I remember going into the public restroom and crying my eyes out, convinced that I had been stood up, all the way from Florida. I couldn't get any reception on my phone, and it was also about to die, so I was having trouble checking it. Finally – I stopped a passenger that was going into the gate for a flight, and I begged him to please pass on the message to a very tall man about six foot three or more, they might see there, that he needed to come down to Baggage Claim, because they wouldn't let me up and through the gate. A short while later, I saw my future husband walking toward me through the double doors and onto the other side. Into my arms. We both cried from the sheer relief of finally meeting one another and out of sheer frustration in thinking we had just been stood up. Don was wearing a dark blue t-shirt, and he was so tall and so huggable. I wanted to hug him forever. "Hi Sweetie," he said. "It's great to finally meet you." I kept hugging him for what seemed like a lot of time. He took my hand in his as we walked through the airport, chatting and laughing as if we had known each other our whole lives.

On the bus ride back to my apartment, my hands were so sweaty still. I was shaking. Don put his hand out toward mine and said, "Take my hand. Everything's okay. We're okay. You're so beautiful. I knew you were beautiful, way before I ever saw you, but you are really very beautiful, Kelley. We are going to have a great week together."

Immediately, somehow, I went from panicked to completely relaxed. Then Don started making me laugh by mocking the bus we were on, and New Jersey, specifically Newark. "It's not breaking my heart to be leaving this dumpster-smelling city," he said as we passed through the strong-smelling part of town. When we arrived in West New York, just minutes outside of NYC, Don's face lit up as he saw for the very first time, the gorgeous NYC skyline view from my street. "Now this is more like it!" he said. "I don't think I could ever get tired of looking at that city skyline." We went inside, and I had prepared for him a great lunch feast; my Nana Mary's famous bow-tie lasagna with meatballs and ribs on the side, garlic bread, and chocolate cake. Everything was homemade, and I had worked on it all the entire day before. We sat at my kitchen table and ate like an old married couple. He moaned with exaggerated pleasure as he tasted the sauce and meatballs, and blurted out, "Holy shit! Will you marry me?"

The week went by too fast, as we tried to get in as much of the NYC experience as possible in a few days. On night one, we went to the Pier in Manhattan and took a sunset cruise that had a live jazz band on board. It was so beautiful, and as we sat there gazing at The Statue of Liberty and the orange sun slowly leaving the night sky, we shared our very first kiss. This man that I had been talking to nightly, for over three years, was finally here, and he was kissing me. We fell into each other's arms and sighed with happiness. Later that night, when we came back to my place, we sat on the couch and listened to music. Don could talk forever about music, and I felt like I could listen forever. We played CD after CD, and talked through the music as Don used my legs, knees, and arms as pretend guitars for him to strum chords on. Everything felt so natural, and everything led right into the next thing, without any thought or worry. When we went to sleep that night, things became intimate, and we made love with each other for the first time. This man who had sat on the phone for hours and talked through my rape with me, was looking into my eyes and asking me gently, "Are you okay?" before moving to the next physical thing. He knew what a big deal this was for me. He knew I needed gentle arms and trust. It was beautiful. It was loving. For the first time in a very long time, I felt respected, cared for, and loved.

The rest of our week together flew by in an instant. We spent two days in a row at the U.S. Open, and Don showed me the art of running from tennis match to tennis match, based on who was playing who, and how competitive of a match it would be. He knew how to find the best matches for us to see live. "Oh, this one will be a good one! These two have the same style of play, this has a great chance of going five sets!" he would say as he took my hand and ran us through the large crowds of people to find a seat amongst the general admission bleachers.

We walked up and down Fifth Avenue, went to a couple great local restaurants, went to the Bronx Zoo, and rowed boats in Central Park. Before we knew it, it was time for him to go back to Florida. We talked about how we would keep flying out to visit one another, and he offered to pay for my first trip and all remaining ones down south. We made plans for me to go down there that next February or March, for spring training baseball. And when it was time to leave him to go up to his Gate area at the airport, I couldn't help but start to cry.

My Husband is Not a Rainbow

"Aww, Bunny-Boo, don't cry," he said to me softly. "We're gonna see each other very soon."

I hugged him tightly as he started picking up his bags to leave. "I gotta go, Boo. Thank you for the best week of my life. NYC is awesome, and this trip just sealed the deal for me on what I pretty much already knew."

"Oh yeah?" I asked. "What's that?"

"That I love you. It's really great to finally meet you, and I love you."

"I love you too, Boo Bear." Everything inside me melted.

He started to disappear from my view slowly, and he yelled out one more time, much louder than the first time, "I love you, Boo!!!"

And as I watched his tall, strong, handsome body walking away from me and getting smaller and more invisible in the crowd, I already missed him. I never wanted to have to say goodbye to him, ever again.

Words About Don

"I think that what I would like to say about my brother is this: with all the adversity he faced during his youth, my brother innately had a gift that could not be bought or bartered, could not be removed or dissolved. He was TRUSTWORTHY to all of his family and those he considered his friends. A rare personality trait that not all can lay claim to." - Karen Exlos, Don's sister

Kelley Lynn Shepherd

I Need To Be Touched. But Please Don't Touch Me.

Can we talk about a very sensitive subject? Would that be okay with you? Because quite frankly; this topic makes me incredibly uncomfortable, and with all the many things I have shared with the world lately, I still find myself stalling and putting off discussing this. But it's time. So here we go.

Human touch. Sex. Intimacy. Hugs. The holding of hands. Making out. Placing one's head in the center of someone else's chest and lightly humming almost subconsciously, because you are so happy lying there. Back rubs. Neck rubs. Hugs. Did I mention hugs?

A husband who looks directly into your eyes and says, "You look beautiful." The stroking of one's long hair. The washing of hair in the shower. Wrapping a towel or his jacket around me. Affection. Massages from someone who wants you to feel good. Feeling the love in the tips of his fingers, in his arms grabbing me gently from behind as I cook dinner, in his hand resting on my knee as he figures out a guitar chord. Hugs. Amazing, safe, wonderful hugs.

When you lose the love of your life in an instant, you find yourself doing a lot of crazy things in a desperate attempt to try and connect to them again, to feel their presence. Everybody will keep telling you the person is "always with you," and maybe he is – but here's the thing: *he isn't HERE with me. It isn't enough. I want more.* Lately, the type of sadness and grief I've been feeling is different than before. Along with the intense crying, has come a physical "reaching" for him. Sometimes I stand in our kitchen, say his name, and put my arms out as if I'm hugging him. Or I will hold our cat, Sammy, a tad too close, just to feel *something* against me. Or I will grab the tin that his leftover Ashes are in, sit in his favorite old chair, and just rock in the chair while trying to pull the ashes as close to my chest as possible, and pull me as close to his chair as possible. It sounds sick, I know. But all I can tell you is that it's an urge, a *need,* and when it happens, I don't fight it.

I got in my car one night and drove out to a large park nearby that has a baseball field in the middle. I don't know why I went to that specific place. My heart just brought me there, and suddenly, I was driving there. When I got there, I sat in the grass on my knees and just sobbed. I called out his name. I screamed. I wailed. And I was silent. It helped, and it didn't. None of these things ever help me to feel him again, to physically feel him. They don't work. But they get me through a moment, and sometimes, that is my only goal. And sometimes, a weird force is driving me to do these things, and it definitely isn't me.

To have the knowledge that you won't ever physically touch or be touched by your husband again, is a sad thing to be aware of. It's heartbreaking, and after almost eleven months of nobody touching me or being affectionate with me, *empty* doesn't even begin to describe the feeling inside me. Other people have tried to be affectionate with me. It affects me in strange ways. For some reason, whenever my parents hug me, I feel like I want to cry. I get extremely sad. Maybe because I know they are missing him too, they are in pain too, and that everything will be different forever. Friends and relatives try to hug me. Some people hug me like it's their mission to make me better. They grab me and hold me for much too long, and they rub my back or say something like, "Awww it's okay. Let it out." They act like they are the Grief Whisperer, and their magic hugs will send me reeling into a mountain of tears and set me free.

Here is where it gets complicated. I hate being touched by people. I mean – *I hate being touched by people.* I'm not talking about friends or close family members hugging or kissing me, that's fine. I am talking about everybody else on earth. Massages, manicures, pedicures, spa days… all of these things make me shiver with an awkward, creepy feeling. Most people find a nice pedicure or massage relaxing. Almost every female I've ever spoken to enjoys this sort of thing. These things were offered to me by many as a stress-reduction after Don's death. I can't think of anything more awful or uncomfortable than some random stranger touching my feet while I have to sit perfectly still in a tiny cramped room, surrounded by other people's nasty feet sitting in bowls filled with murky, gray water.

Manicures? Yuck. Sitting there, being forced into conversation with an old Russian lady who has a moustache and is painting my nails while telling me about her grandson's chess match, is not my idea of a good time. The two times I was forced into getting a manicure, my instinct was to reach up with my freshly-painted hand and punch the manicurist in the face. Someone rubbing a green sandpaper-like mask on my face, or wrapping me up in some weird-ass seaweed thing, and making me sit there to clear out toxins and shit – no. That is not ever happening. Not in my world. Take your spa gift certificate, and give it to someone who enjoys hanging out with fifty strangers in germ-infested rooms that smell like warm ass-crack. Give it to someone who doesn't mind that nine hundred other people's ballsacks and clammy vaginas have sat on that very same bed of arugula treatment, or whatever the hell it is. Just get the hell away from me with your touching.

I am not a touchy-feely person. I have to know you really well to feel comfortable with you showing me affection. I have never been into casual sex, one-night stands, or anything like that. I can't *be* with someone unless I know that they care about me deeply. So I don't want a hug from just anybody. I want a hug from Don. I cannot have that ever again, and I'm not quite sure how to be okay with that.

Eventually – in time – I will grow and heal and really start living again, one day. I will rebuild my dreams. I will figure out how to be happy, or a new version of happy. I will adjust to this new, bizarre life that was handed off to me. But human beings need affection. We need to be held. We need that physical connection to someone. How will I ever get past the concept that my husband will never hold me? What do I *do* with this insane paradox of strong feelings; where I *need* to be touched, but by the one person who cannot do it? It is perhaps the biggest oxymoron of all-time:

I really need to be touched. But for the Love of God, please don't touch me.

Seven Years Long (Distance)

So, the man first known as Wayabovepar and the woman first known as Camelsocks would talk to one another for over three years before finally meeting in person. After the initial meet-up in New Jersey, it would be another four years before Don Shepherd would pack up his belongings, his cat, and his life into a Penske moving truck and make the drive from Florida to our new life. Seven years total, from the day we began typing back and forth, to when we would officially begin our lives together in the same zip code.

The months and years after Don flew to meet me in Jersey passed along quite slowly, and we got closer emotionally. There were several trips back and forth, me going out to stay with him in his tiny apartment in Largo, and him coming to stay with me in my slightly less tiny apartment in West New York, New Jersey. There were tennis matches, Yankee games, dinners, NYC touristy stuff, NYC non-touristy stuff (spending hours in small guitar shops in the village, or talking with a musician/guitarist after a blues show downtown), Broadway shows, off-Broadway shows, off-off-off Broadway shows, Central Park trips, and walks, and rowing of boats in the Great

Lake, and much more. In Florida, we drove to Orlando, attended a mystery dinner theatre night, went to comedy clubs, walked Clearwater Beach at night, picked out seashells, and ate at places like The Waffle House and Golden Corral, just to make fun of them. Most of all, we laughed. We made each other laugh so often, it just became expected. We really enjoyed each other's company, and our time together felt precious. That being said, Don was a very logical and smart type of person. He was a planner. And so after that first time we met in person, Don started silently planning so that we could have a life together. He picked up extra shifts on the EMS crew. He saved money and put money away each paycheck. He started asking me what bills I needed help with, because he knew my cost of living was extremely high, and I didn't make much money. He began sending me romantic or silly cards with checks inside, regularly, for a couple hundred or more dollars. He was already thinking forward, and he thought of us as a team, a partnership. He did everything he could to ensure that eventually, we would be together.

One day while he was visiting me in Jersey, he started pulling up a website that had info on getting his EMS license in the state of New Jersey. I asked him what he was looking at, and he said matter of factly, as if it was obvious, "Well, if I'm going to move to New Jersey, I might want to have a job here working EMS. And so I need to get my license and figure out the process for that." I responded, stunned, "You're moving to New Jersey?" "Ummm … yeah. This is where you need to be for your career and life, Boo. There's nothing for you in Florida. Besides, you'll melt like Frosty the Snowman in that heat down there. You won't last ten days. This is where you live, so it's where I need to be." He kissed me on the forehead, whistled some tune out loud, and walked in the other room. After that, it was just always known that he would be the one to move, and that we were working toward that happening. It would take four more years, after the time of our initial meet up in person. Three years of talking, then four years of flying back and forth. Seven years total. Don moved slow when it came to life planning, but he moved with purpose. By the time moving day arrived, he had saved up close to $10,000 for our new life together. He knew it might take him a few months to find work in New Jersey or New York. He knew he had to pay for classes and testing for EMS licensing. He knew that life in this area was way more expensive than what he was used to, and he knew that his hard-earned money would be gone within months, inside the vulture that is New York living. He knew, and he planned. And even though I was the one who lived there already and knew my way around, he always found ways to make me feel safe and taken care of. He always made me feel as if everything would be okay.

Somewhere during those last four years of flying back and forth to see each other, Don flew up from Florida, my parents drove from Massachusetts, and they met one another. I had a massive mouse issue in my apartment, and I was terrified. Within minutes of meeting one another, my dad and Don took over my apartment and started closing up all the holes in the walls and taking care of the issue. Don jumped right in to help, and he and my dad worked together as if they had been partnered up for years. About an hour after meeting him, my dad said to me about Don, "That is a very good man. You did great with that one. I can see him being a part of our family, and I would love to have him as a son-in-law." My mom was beaming from ear to ear also. They both loved him and began to think of him like family. And soon, we would become family for real, through marriage. But before any of that, he had to move in with me first, and turn my apartment into a home. It would take time, but we were on our way.

"Everyone can master a grief, but he that has it."
- William Shakespeare

Kelley Lynn Shepherd

FB Post: Today feels endless. Life feels endless. Today I miss him and ache for him so much, I can hardly move. Most of my time is spent finding ways to distract myself from the pain. And then sometimes, I can't. Sometimes there is nothing I can do but feel the intense pain, and there is literally nothing worse. Some nights - the pain and the love is so strong, I can barely get a breath out. My God, how I miss my love.
LIKES: 12   COMMENTS: 7

FB Post: I don't know how to do this anymore. How to make it on my own. I really don't think I can do this. My car went in for oil change today, turns out I have transmission leak, gasket issues, fluid leaks, and front axle is broken. Going to cost me almost $500. I can't do this anymore. I can't live on the money I make. I can't find more work than the job and a half I already have. I'm a ball of stress and grief every day, walking around with a migraine and no sleep. My husband is dead, and I look like death. I feel like death. I want to be death. Please don't call social services on me. I'm not going to do anything to harm myself. I just don't want to be here. It's too hard. Life is too hard without Don in it. He made my life so easy and so beautiful. He put me at ease daily. He made sure all the pain in the ass things were taken care of. I'm never going to be able to move out of this shit apartment, the bills keep piling up, his hospital bill is coming at an alarming rate, so many bills and paperwork crap that I haven't dealt with yet. I'm over this. No health insurance, no life insurance, no backup of any kind. I'm trying like hell to do this, but I'm failing. My husband is dead, and I'm failing at life.
LIKES: 20   COMMENTS: 26

FB Post: Everywhere I go, I see ambulances. 5 or 10 times per day. Ambulances. I live 5 minutes from the hospital where he was lying there, dead forever, and the ambulances drive by my street constantly. People are sick or dying in an ambulance all the time, and they are just everywhere, always. I can't escape them. And every single time I see or hear those lights and sirens, or pull over for one in traffic, I picture my handsome and kind husband, all dressed up for work in his blue EMS uniform. I picture him kissing me goodbye for the day, or coming home to me at the end of the day. And then I picture him going off to work in one of those ambulances. And then I picture how he went off to his other job at a Petsmart that day, and how he collapsed, and there was no ambulance in sight. And then I picture that store manager telling me how he was maybe on the floor there in that aisle for a few minutes, and then I picture him being alone and cold and frightened, and then I picture him riding in the back of an ambulance, when it finally arrived, and being the one on the stretcher this time. And I picture him coding, and I picture what that ride might have been like, and I picture him hurting and in pain, and I picture a bunch of strangers, calling time of death on my husband. When I see ambulances, I get this nausea feeling in the pit of my stomach, like I'm being punched. Sometimes, when I'm driving by the hospital, I pull over to the side of the road soon after passing it, so that I can cry or try to get myself breathing normal again. I feel panic at the site of ambulances, and I feel a billion little deaths, churning inside me, like a storm.

Why did he have to be in EMS? Why couldn't I have married a Glass Sculptor? Or a Jelly-Donut Filler? Or an Auctioneer? Or anything else that's completely random and that I wouldn't have to be faced with a billion times per day, every second, forever??? This shit sucks.
LIKES: 69   COMMENTS: 55

Kelley Lynn Shepherd

Schadenfreude - A Husband's Revenge

Don loved to laugh at me. He really enjoyed chuckling and pointing out to me that I tend to exaggerate everything, that I'm a "drama queen" (one of his favorite things to say to me was, "Stop being so overdramatic, Boo."), or his favorite thing; that I had gotten myself into a situation that would eventually turn into a trainwreck of epic proportions. If there was ever anyone that loved watching a good dose of *schadenfreude* (the term for laughing and delighting in others small misfortunes), it was my husband. He was one of those "I told you so!" douchebags, but he always said it as he was laughing, good-naturedly in my face. I participated in The NJ Sharing Networks 5K Walk/Run for Families and Friends of Organ Donors and Receivers. It was something I wanted to do to honor Don and in memory of him. And what did I get for my troubles? The entire day, I could literally hear my husband laughing gently... no, cackling... at me and at the situation I had once again gotten myself into and, in his eyes, deserved. My husband came to me in the form of his laughter, and he was there to get Sweet Revenge. I'm sure of it.

Somewhere around September or October of 2010, a friend of a friend was trying to put a team together of people who wanted to participate in a 5K "Walk for Hearing," a charity that benefited The Clarke School, a school for deaf children. This friend of a friend worked with these kids at this school and was recruiting as many people as possible to join her team. Apparently, she did an amazing job in convincing a whole bunch of us to do this walk, because for some reason, our whole group of friends agreed to do it. I vaguely recall filling out some sort of application form online, registering for it, and saying, "Okay. That sounds fun." I also sort of remember getting our friends, John and Jessica, involved in this event as well. Looking back now, I'm pretty sure I was drugged at the time. Whatever the case, one thing that I neglected to do was to inform my husband that we were doing this walk, until this conversation that happened maybe two days before said event: (dialogue is from memory, but I pretty much remember this like it was yesterday, so it's extremely close to the actual conversation that occurred.)

Him: Boo, I think I'm gonna play some tennis on my day off, Sunday, and then I was thinking of maybe heading down to the music store to check out some of the new lefty guitars that just came in. Then maybe we can get dinner or something.

Me: You can't on Sunday. We have plans. I thought I told you, sorry. We are doing the Walk for Hearing for Missy's school in the city.

Him: (with most perplexed expression of all time on face) We are doing the *what* for *WHAT?* And for *who???*

Me: Walk for Hearing. For Missy.

Him: Who the hell is Missy?

Me: Missy. Kevin and Michelle's friend. You've met her before. You know who she is.

Him: No. If I knew who she was, I wouldn't have just asked you who the hell she was. (still confused) When did I agree to do this thing? Was I on crack at the time, because this is not something I would agree to do – ever.

Me: No. (laughing) You didn't agree to it. I signed us up for it. John and Jessica are doing it. Kevin and Michelle. All their friends. It'll be fun.

Him: I don't think you know what the word *fun* means. Getting up at six AM on a Sunday to go on the bus and then onto the subway to go into the city and WALK for no reason on my only day off, in no way, sounds *fun* to me.

Kelley Lynn Shepherd

Me: It's not for no reason, Boo. It's for kids who can't hear.

Him: Uh-huh. Please explain how me walking in the cold and rain at an ungodly early hour against my will is going to magically make them hear again. Can't I just write them a check and stay home and sleep?

Me: No, cuz I already committed both of us to doing it. (laughing at him) It's really not that big of a deal, hon. Let's just go and have a good time.

Him: Why do you hate me?

Me: (laughing) I don't hate you, Boo. This is just one of those things that married people do. It's part of marriage.

Him: Oh really? Married people forcibly sign their spouses up for 5k Walks? Funny. I don't recall that being in our vows.

Me: It was in the fine print, Boo. You'll be fine.

Him: Did you read the fine print, where it also said that if a mean spouse enters you into a 5K Race against your will, that is acceptable grounds for divorce? Cuz I think that's in there too.

The day of the Walk for Hearing was really raw, cold, and rainy. We had to get up super early to get into NYC for the early start time. Don was grumpy and exhausted and sort of pouting and whining the entire time into the city. My husband was not a whiner. He normally just went with the flow and would have a good time wherever we would go together. On this day, however, he was clearly annoyed, in a playful way, and wanted me to know it. When we got into the city, we started walking the wrong way for about four avenues and then had to turn around and go back. I remember Don walking with me on our way there and saying, "Jesus, Boo. We just did a freakin' 5K on the way to the 5k. This sucks. I'm cold. I'm tired. Can we go home yet?" He was purposely trying to irritate me in order to give me payback for roping him into this. It didn't work. I just kept laughing at him and his silly whining. When we finally got there, Jessica was also extremely unhappy to be anywhere except in bed, sleeping on a Sunday.

During the walk, Don kept complaining about his sneakers. The trails and paths were very rocky and hilly in some spots, and he never got used to that up here. He always missed the flat roads and paths in Florida for walking, biking, everything. "Ah, my feet are killing me. I'm getting blisters. Can we leave yet? How about now? Now? Or now?" I remember making fun of him for being such a baby. I believe I said, "Aren't you an EMT? Weren't you in the Air Force? You can't handle a little walking in a light sprinkle? Come on Boo, suck it up!" He looked at me with daggers in his eyes, and we kept moving. When it was finally time to go, hours later, we had to walk more blocks and avenues back to the bus to take us to New Jersey. The second we walked in the door, Don kicked off his sneakers harshly, fell into our bed face-down, and mumbled something under his breath. "What did you say?" I asked him. "Oh nothing, Boo. I just said that I'll get you back for this misery you've caused me today. I will get my revenge when you've forgotten all about this. I will never forget, Boo. Goodnight. Wake me up when my feet stop throbbing or when you've completed making the delicious homemade meal you surely owe me for making me take part in this travesty you call *fun*." Jesus. And he calls *me* overdramatic?

And that's just how it happened. I never even saw it coming. When the Sharing Network called and asked me if I'd like to participate in this year's walk for families of donors, I figured it would be a really nice way to honor him and pay forward his kindness to others. So I said yes. And about two months before, I started to let everybody know that I wanted to start a team, and that I wanted everybody to walk on my team. It would be great.

Kelley Lynn Shepherd

We would be Team Shepherd. We would get t-shirts made up. We would cheer each other on during the walk. We would hold up signs and yell Don's name and say things like, "GO TEAM SHEP!!" People from all over the land would come out to join my team for Don. And at first, that is exactly what it seemed like would happen. Family, friends, and even some acquaintances and connections seemed genuinely excited to be part of the Walk. "I'm so there!" they chimed in on my Facebook posts. "I would love to walk on your team! Count me in!" they bellowed. Before I knew it, I had a minimum of fifteen to twenty people that really seemed as though they were going to do this with me. It was exciting.

And then, about a week before the walk, it suddenly became clear that out of all the people who said they would like to walk with us, only two would actually be doing it; my friend, Sheila, and my mom. Turns out, my dad's knees and legs had started to give him problems in the last few months before that, and he couldn't walk long-distances, so he was out. The walk turned out to be on the same date that John and Jessica were on vacation in California. Lots of other friends had family obligations, weddings, graduations, you name it. Andrew and Rodney and Sheri wanted to come, but didn't realize how far into New Jersey it was, and had no real way to get out there. Very quickly, our enthusiastic group of supporters started to dwindle into nothing. "Team Shepherd" was now three people and a homemade sign that I made that listed everyone's name that made a donation. And because we raised so much money and so many friends and family donated in Don's memory ($1460 and counting), I now felt obligated to do the Walk, even though at this point, it seemed a bit.. well... pointless. Three of us? Really? That's kind of lame. But all these people gave money, and they are going to want to see some pictures and know that we were there and we did this thing. The night before, I heard it was going to be ungodly hot and humid for the Sunday Walk, and I honestly just wanted to cancel and not even do it. But then I remembered all the people who supported me, and realized I was stuck doing it, whether I wanted to or not. I didn't really have a choice in the matter. And that was the first time I heard Don laughing at me.

It started out as a light chuckle that evening, and then it began to progress the next morning and throughout the entire day of The Walk as a loud, bellowing, "HA HA HA HA HA!!!! Have *fun,* honey!" in your face kind of thing. I tried to ignore it at first, but then I just couldn't. There were too many elements that pointed in the direction of this working out exactly the way that Don had planned it to. The weather was hot as hell. The high was 87 that day, and very humid. Every surrounding day before and after was in the low 70s. And just as my husband and I had to walk a 5k before walking the 5k, my mom and I did too. The parking situation was atrocious, and we were led to a giant lot that was at least a mile… or four… from the Event itself. When we finally found the starting location, they made me stand in a "pre-registration" line to get a number, even though I had already registered online in order to avoid standing in huge lines at the event.

The sun was blazing as I stood in this line for minimum of thirty minutes to receive my number. Before we even began walking, I started to notice that my sneakers felt really tight. I don't recall them being too small for me in the past, but my toes felt like they were being squished into my shoe. As I stood there with my tight shoes in the hot sun with my TWO teammates, I heard him laughing again. "Ha ha ha! You thought this would be FUN! You thought you'd get fifteen people to do it with you! But they didn't show up. They were SMART and did what I suggested in the first place. They stayed home and wrote a damn check! Ha ha ha!!! Oh, this is awesome! Go ahead and walk, Boo! Go on… it's FUN!" I could literally hear him inside my head or my heart, or wherever evil, late husband spirits with a twisted sense of humor speak to you.

Kelley Lynn Shepherd

And as me, mom, and Sheila walked along, the heat became unbearable, and my toes felt like they were on fire. The water we were drinking to stay hydrated went from semi-cold to lukewarm to sweaty hot. I felt sticky and nasty and gross. When we crossed the finish line, after what seemed like decades, the only emotion I was feeling was the intense pain coming from inside my shoes, where I knew I had developed blisters on my toes, just like Don. The walk was over, and then we had the second walk to our car. I was convinced that my feet would just burn right off of my body. I kept hearing Don and his sarcasm, "How exactly is you walking in the nasty heat going to get some poor soul a kidney any faster?" And he was right.

Was the event more than that? Yes. It was. There were close to six thousand people walking and running. Families. Kids. Dogs. Strollers with babies in them. Teams of people all wearing homemade t-shirts to show their love for the person they were there representing. Lots and lots of stories. So many stories. One woman I met was part of a very large team of people, probably at least thirty people, all there in memory of their friend who was struck by a car and died. There was a man there whose brother had lost his life in a freak work accident, and his lungs ended up going to one of the man's best friends at their job. I met a father who just lost his twenty one year old daughter to a violent crime committed by a college guy who was apparently obsessed with her. There were people there that had received organs and were walking with the families of those that gave them life. Perhaps the most surreal moment for me was having people ask me why I was walking, who I was walking for, and then hearing myself say out loud that my husband was dead. I never quite get used to hearing my own voice say those words. It seems like someone else talking and not me.

So, in the end, just like everything else surrounding my husband's death, nothing is the way that I pictured it would be. In my mind, I pictured this walk being life-changing and motivating and inspiring and beautiful and so many other things like that. In some ways, it was those things. But it was subtle. I do think things like this are much more powerful when you can rope a whole bunch of your friends to experience it with you, like Missy did on that day that will always make me laugh. Maybe next year, more people will be able to take part with me, and we can start to make it a yearly tradition. Or maybe I will take my husband's advice of staying home and writing a check. Who knows. The only thing I do know is that I need to stop expecting that things will turn out a certain way. Things never turn out in the way you thought they would. Not even close. This is not a good or a bad thing – it's just true.

But when I got home later that night and harshly kicked off my sneakers, I saw two big blisters, one on each pinky toe. I limped into the bedroom, and I fell into our bed face-down as I felt my husband's laughter all around me. He was laughing at me, and he was enjoying himself.

It was schadenfreude. It was marriage. It was the sweet revenge of a husband who never forgot that day. Whatever it was, it was there, and it was real. It made me feel close to him the entire day as he found joy in my misery; and to me, that was all the reason I needed to do a 5K in his honor.
But maybe next time, I'll just send a goddamn check.

Dear Dead Husband:

Yankees have won eight in a row, and are in first place. Met my new possible roommate yesterday and will go see his apartment tomorrow. Hoping this is the right move for me, but nothing feels right without you. Sat in again with the guys at "The Some Guy Show" podcast and my friend Jay Such. Everytime I spoke during the podcast, they played sad widow music. It was hilarious, and being a guest on podcasts and doing other comedy stuff is such a great thing for me right now. Did my third comedy video yesterday with Opie on his YouTube channel. You would love this. Wish you were here to combat all of the jerks making hateful comments online and social media. You would set them straight. I just get upset and cry. I feel like a broken record, always trying to express how much I miss you. But I miss you. SO. DAMN. MUCH. I love you. I love you. I love you. It will never ever be enough times for me to say it or type it or know it. I love you. Xoxo

Session Snippet

Caitlin: You seemed really upset in your email before coming here. What happened?

Me: I just can't believe it's been almost a year of this crap. This pain. And I'm trying to cope the ways I know how. Doing silly comedy videos, trying to take my mind off things for five seconds, and lots of writing in my blog about how this feels. But I keep getting assholes who make nasty comments on my videos or in my blog. It bothers me.

Caitlin: What kind of things are they saying?

Me: One person wrote me a nasty private message about the comedy show material I did months ago, in the show we did honoring Don. She said that it must be nice to use my husband's death for "entertainment," and that she thinks it's tacky of me to write a book about him, and that I should stop trying to get attention.

Caitlin: Why does this bother you so much?

Me: Because anyone questioning my love for my husband, or my intentions, or my grief feels so violating and awful. To say

My Husband is Not a Rainbow

I'm "using " his death - when writing is one of the only things that makes me feel a little bit whole again - it just hurts. Do these people think I wanted this life? That I want fame out of this? Jesus. I just want my husband back, and that's never going to happen, so I'm trying to use words to help people and help me. When I do a video or a blog piece, and I get fifty positive comments, and then two or three that are negative, why do I always focus so hard on the negative ones? Why can't I let them go? They bother me so damn much. They sit in my head, and my stomach hurts, and I feel nauseous.

Caitlin: Because that's just human nature. Two people don't like me? Well, why the hell don't they like me? We all want everyone to like us, but not everyone ever will. Plus, when you have lost your person, the person who was a witness to your talents and who uplifted you and made you feel good about yourself all the time, sometimes it's hard to remember or to see all the good things that HE saw in you. So your self-esteem is lowered, it's taken a big hit, and that's when predators attack best.

Me: But why are people so mean? What the hell did I ever do to them?

Caitlin: You showed them a mirror into who they truly are, and they don't like it.

Me: I don't understand.

Caitlin: You are a truth-teller. In your writing, in your comedy, in your life. You always speak and write and live the truth, even when it's brutally honest and raw and real. There are a lot of people out there who cannot handle that kind of truth, or who are too weak themselves to live in that kind of truth, who don't have the kind of courage that someone like you has to live in that truth, so they attack the truth-messenger. I know it's hard to see it this way, but when those people attack you, it actually has nothing at all to do with you, and everything to do with them and their character.

Me: But I'm not brave at all. I'm just hurting and trying to find ways to help myself. The person I used to talk to every single day and night about my day, is gone. I have nobody at the end of the day, so that's why I reach out so much. I can feel my own desperation. It's like I'm trying to feel that feeling of my person validating and supporting me by getting it from others online, and it's just not working. It feels so personal when they are mean.

Caitlin: Next time it happens, I want you to try and see it differently. Look at it in a new way. Next time you read an attack or anger at your words, I want you to think about it like this: you pissed them off. How incredible is it that something you wrote could evoke that kind of powerful response or emotion in someone? You enraged them, which means that you made them feel. Who cares if they didn't *like* it. You're pushing buttons. You're hitting a nerve. And when you anger or upset people or make them look inside themselves and their ugliness, you are touching them, and they don't forget. Let them hate it! In order for them to hate it, they have to read it, and in order to read it, they have to have made the choice to do that. Because you touched a nerve. You're on the verge of something big here with your words. Believe that.

My Husband is Not a Rainbow

"That unemployed, failed loser probably typed that garbage about you after watching the video from his mom's basement, with one hand on his dick and the other inside a bucket of KFC. He only wishes he could be as hilarious or as talented as you. But he never will be, so he attacks. When's the last time HE was featured in a comedy video for a huge radio personality? Oh, that's right. NEVER!" – Don Shepherd, in 2010, reacting to the rude comments on my first ever YouTube comedy video on the @OpieRadio channel

Dear Dead Husband:

You are love, and love is everything. One year ago today, you died, and I still don't know how to live without you. I do know that when you are good to people, they remember. And holy shit, were you ever good. They remember how you treated them, and then they pay it forward. If only you could see the avalanche of love and kindness that you have inspired. I started a thing, a new tradition, to help me get through this day. "Pay it Forward for Don Shepherd Day" will now be how I refer to July thirteenth. I have asked people all over to do something kind in your name and to post their stories on my Facebook page. I'll be writing a huge blog about all the stories, every year, from this day forward, forever. There are over one hundred stories so far. I'm so touched, but not surprised, that your life has caused people to be kind. My love, my heart. My beautiful, dead husband. I love you, Until Forever…

Kelley Lynn Shepherd

Amnesia

If there is one thing I have learned as a student in this new life that was handed to me by force, it is this: I don't know a damn thing. The Grief Monster is in charge here, and much like *Charles In Charge,* grief wants to rule "my days and my nights, my wrongs and my rights." Except this isn't a really bad TV sitcom starring Scott Baio and an awful laugh track – it is my very real life. Eventually, *Charles In Charge* was cancelled, because it sucked. This new life I have will never be cancelled, no matter how much it sucks. And it's also the only show on television. It is on every single channel. I have a broken television that I can never ever turn off, and I simply have to learn to deal with it.

July thirteenth was the one-year Anniversary of Don's death. Have I mentioned how much I loathe the phrase "anniversary" when talking about my husband's death? It makes it sound as if it's a great big party, or something to celebrate with balloons and cake and ice-cream, instead of the worst day of my entire life. (I'm guessing it wasn't the best day for my husband either.) I chose to face that day by creating a holiday out of it and calling it "Pay it Forward for Don Shepherd Day." I asked friends and family and total strangers, pretty much everyone on earth, to do something kind that day for someone else in honor of my husband's generous nature and who he was as a person everyday. I also asked them to tell me the stories of what they did, so I could read them, and make "Pay it Forward for Don Day" an entire chapter in my book. My hope was that in creating this type of day, it would not only help others, but also remove the horror of having to sit with and deal with re-living the worst day of my life, one year later, and that I would instead have something hopeful to focus on. Did it work? Yes. And not at all. I still felt shaky and panicky all day on July thirteenth, and I woke up at six forty three AM, the exact time that my phone kept ringing and ringing and eventually waking me up just one year before, informing me of my new, terrible life.

As we gathered later that night with my mom, my dad, my Aunt Debbie and Uncle Richard, and our friends Cheryl, Thelma and Nancy and Ron; celebrating Don's life by eating his favorite homemade chicken parmesan, garlic bread, salad, brownie sundaes, and root beer; I was able to somehow get through the evening. The constant barrage of emails, private messages, texts, and a few phone calls saying, "Thinking of you today," or telling me an incredible Pay it Forward story, kept my emotional breakdown at bay. But it was still there, just waiting to pounce. The Grief Monster never goes away – he just waits until that one second where you finally start to think, "Maybe I'm going to be okay today," and then he attacks violently and with no warning. He makes your stomach churn and gives you intense headaches that start at the center of your eyeball and pound against your temple nonstop. He gives you the shakes and that feeling like there's a brick in your chest, and everything you do is so heavy. Every breath is so thick. You want to explain to people and to earth and to your job that, yes, you are aware it's been an entire year since your husband died, and yes, you are still grieving. You want to scream to the world that "NO!!! I'M NOT OKAY YET!" or order them politely to please stop rushing you into the next phase of your feelings. "I'm not ready!" you want to tell them. But they aren't listening. They are eating brownie sundaes and laughing in the next room as you anticipate The Grief Monster's next unpredictable move.

On Tuesday, July seventeenth, I woke up feeling physically ill, and that damn headache was back again. I woke up crying. I didn't want to or mean to. It was involuntary. Stretched, yawned, and cried. Why was I feeling so lost that morning? I put on the news. Ninety six degrees today, with heat index of one hundred and ten. Why did that sound like an echo to me? There was a certain smell in the air. It was the smell of humidity. It was the smell of something familiar and awful. It was the same smell that was in the air just one year ago today, the day of my husband's funeral.

Grief is a fucked-up thing. Everytime you think you are moving forward, it stops you cold. In the days and weeks leading up to the one-year mark of his death, my mind went reeling back to last year at this time. Not only did I relive the actual day that he died and the horrors I went through on that day, but I also relived and questioned all the surrounding days and weeks around that day. When you lose your spouse in a sudden and tragic way, and it happens in a flash, you want to give significance to things that had no significance at the time. You didn't know he was going to die, so how were you to know that every single thing you did would be the last time you would be doing it? Over the past few weeks then, my heart and brain had been on overload, trying to figure out the pieces of the puzzle that made up his last few weeks and days on earth. When was our last kiss? When was the last meal we ate together? The last time we were intimate? The last time we hung out with friends? When did we laugh together? When was the last time he strummed his guitar for me? What was our last conversation about? What was the last thing I said to my husband? I honestly had no idea. The night before he died is like a vague cloud of nothingness. It was a typical evening in an ordinary married day. We were both exhausted. He was sitting at the very desk where I typed, and he was online and texting to a friend. I was talking to him. Smalltalk. I was watching something on TV. I don't recall what. We talked some more. Or didn't. I don't remember. And then, just like that, it was over. The memory fades. Either I fell asleep or he did or we both did. There was no goodnight kiss that night. There was no goodnight anything. The night just sort of came to an end, and he had to be up at four thirty AM the next morning for work. He knew how much trouble I had sleeping, so when he left that early, he would never wake me. And so he left. And he went to work. And while I lay there asleep, he lay collapsed on a

My Husband is Not a Rainbow

Petsmart floor. And then when I finally woke up, his life had already ended.

People ask me all the time how I got through the funeral, or how I wrote and delivered a Eulogy for my husband. Easy answer. I got through it, because I wasn't really ever there. Physically, I was there. But I was in deep, deep shock at that point, just four days after he died. I stood in that room, with my husband in a casket behind me, and I pretended that none of it was happening. I was not able to comprehend the sheer horror of what had transpired or what was to come. There was a cloud over my head during that funeral and in the weeks and months afterward. Now – one year later – the cloud has lifted, and I am left with a very frightening reality. It hurts like hell now, and knowing that there is nothing I can do but just "walk through the fire," as my grief counselor so perfectly put it, makes that pain even more unbearable. There is no running away. No escaping it. The only way out is through. *The only way out is through.*

So in my state of panic and terror and sadness, I made an emergency call to my grief counselor. And we talked. And, like she always has a way of doing for me, she gave me a bit of hope. She doesn't say anything magical or even "fix" things for me. Because there is no such thing as fixing this. It cannot be fixed. But she tells me the truth, and she does it in a really smart and compassionate way, and that is so much more than a lot of other people do. I told her how for months, I couldn't remember anything at all about the funeral. It was like a big blank space in my memory. It was the same for my first birthday without him, his birthday, Christmas, Thanksgiving, all of it. A big, gigantic mass of vague. That is how I got through all of those days – I was protected by the cloud. I told her that grieving feels a lot like being a patient who is recovering from amnesia, and all of the painful details of important days and events in our life, like his services, are coming back to me now, in flashes. It doesn't even feel like I am re-living the funeral. It feels as if I am there for the first time. If you asked me six months ago to tell you the details of Don's services, I would have stared at you with fog in my eyes. Now? There are so many things that I clearly remember about the funeral. Things that I wish would go away, things I will never forget, things that a thirty nine year old woman at the beginning of her wonderful marriage should not have to think about. But here they are, stuck inside of me forever...

I remember being in the backseat of my parents' car while they drove us from Massachusetts to New Jersey, and texting back and forth with Opie. He sent me a private message that said, "You're strong, and you'll get through today. Lean on your family and friends." I remember him sending out a tweet to all the fans of their radio show on Twitter that simply said, "Our friend Kelley Lynn is attending her husband's funeral today. Please reach out to her if you can. She will need it."

I remember shopping with my mom for an outfit to wear to my husband's funeral and how strange and terrible and weird that sounded to say out loud. The sales woman asked me, "Anything I can help you with todayyyy?" in a way too bubbly voice, and I remember wanting to answer, in that same phony way, "Why YES! What goes better with my husband's casket – red or blue?" I will never forget trying on that cranberry sleeveless blouse, liking it, and immediately thinking, "Don would love this on me." Then realizing, of course, that Don would never love anything on me again.

I remember how disgustingly hot it was that day. High 90s. It was sticky and humid and disastrous. I remember getting there early and the funeral director asking me if I wanted Don's wedding ring. He informed me that when my husband is cremated, "That ring isn't going with him. It belongs with you." He handed it to me, and I kept touching it all day long, rolling it back and forth in the palm of my hand, as if doing so would

My Husband is Not a Rainbow

make all of this go away. I remember the smell of death flowers and awkwardness and pain as I walked into the big main room where he lay there in his casket. The American Flag was draped over half of it, and my husband didn't look like my husband. His face was puffy. His eyes looked weird. They were not his eyes. They looked swollen shut. His arms were thicker than normal. His hands were placed in an unnatural position that he would have never put them in. He seemed uncomfortable. He had this creepy look on his face. It was a combination of stillness and fear.

I remember talking with friends in front of, to the side of, and all around that casket, never once acknowledging it. If I ignored it, then it wasn't really happening. If I kept telling myself, *"That is not my husband,"* then maybe it really wouldn't be. I remember bits and pieces of conversations with people as songs from Aerosmith's *Toys in the Attic* and the Beatles *Abbey Road* and The Who's *Quadrophenia* played in the background. They told me that during the "viewing" portion of the afternoon, I could have whatever music I wanted playing. And that is what Don wanted. Aerosmith.

I remember talking with one of Don's EMS brothers, Matt, and how shaken up he was and crying. I kept thinking, *"Why am I comforting HIM? I'm the wife, and I'm not even crying. What the hell is wrong with me?"* I recall that when I mentioned how Don looked nothing at all like himself because the Organ Donation people "took so much – he isn't even recognizable," he corrected me by saying, "Don't word it that way. They didn't *take* anything. Don *gave.*" Right. He gave. I gave. I gave away my husband, and now he looked like Frankenstein instead of my Sweet Boo-Bear.

I remember everyone sweating and constantly wiping their foreheads and fanning themselves with anything they could find. My dad asking the funeral director to please turn up the air-conditioning and them telling us over and over, "It IS up!" I remember being in the bathroom with Don's good friend, Meg, before the service and telling her that I just got my "friend" (my period), and how Don would be laughing at me, because he always said that it showed up on the most important days for me and ruined everything. And there it was. Right on time.

I remember so clearly, such small and unimportant details. My dad asking the pastor for directions to the nearest Dunkin Donuts so he could go and get his morning coffee, and how he tried to make me eat a muffin, and I just couldn't. The funeral director asking me which pictures I would like placed on the back of my husband's casket. The guest book and fancy pen by the door that reminded me of weddings; people signing their names as if this was some happy occasion to remember down the road.

People. There were endless amounts of people. The heartbreak in my friend John's eyes, the crack in Kevin's voice, the knowing look from my boss and friend, Laura; who had lost her own brother and father only four months apart, just five years ago. The comedian friends that showed up and made dark jokes and made me laugh inappropriately. Standing in the hallway with Jessica Kirson, Danny Cohen, and Jonathan Fursh, saying that one of us should get up there and "do a comedy set." The woman who walked up to me and said, "You don't know me, but I know you from the comedy circuit and Facebook. I just had to come here today and honor the love that you and Don had and the life you had together." She was, at the time, a complete stranger to me. We hugged and have been friends ever since. Thank you Mindi.

Watching Don's sister, Karen, and her husband, George, walk into the room after their long drive from Ohio and thinking to myself, *"Don, your sister is here! Come on out here and talk to your sister!"* The faraway look in her eyes as she tried to convince me, and herself, that his death was quick and therefore, more peaceful. Feeling the urge to hug her over and over again, to somehow fix this hurt for both of us, and feel a piece of Don through each other. Seeing Don's best friend in the world, Rob, and his wife, Mindy, after driving from Florida to attend the service. Watching as Rob came out in his EMS uniform to honor Don. Watching as all of his EMS brothers and sisters slowly filled up the room, all in uniform. In the back, a whole bunch of doctors and nurses, all coming directly from their shifts and in their scrubs. An entire group of employees and friends from his part-time job at Petsmart, where he collapsed just four days earlier. Watching as EMS and Air Force lined the walls and held flags up throughout the service. Feeling my face turn hot as the soldiers and Air Force members kept saluting me, acknowledging me, looking me directly in the eyes as they performed their procedural ceremonies.

I will always remember the beautiful and heartfelt words that were spoken about Don by so many people. His boss Joe, who offered Don a management position multiple times, only for Don to shrug his shoulders and say, "No thanks." He didn't want the stress. He wanted to come home to his wife each night and not think about work anymore. He wanted to leave work at work when he punched out for the day and not be the guy who had to deal with all of his workmates' personal dramas while he was just trying to enjoy his time with me. Our friend Kevin, whose words were touching and funny and spoke of the true love Don had for me and my family and his friends. Mary, who runs the adoption for kitties center at the Petsmart where Don volunteered his time, telling endless stories of Don's love for animals. Meg and Don became close friends when they were EMS partners on the ambulance, and her speech spoke of how amazing Don was as an EMT, and how he made everyone else feel safer. Rob told some great stories about his days on the ambulance with Don, and how they would banter and purposely try to annoy the other. So many words of love spoken. Mine was last, of course, and I barely recall delivering it. The highlight was when one of the Air Force members took a spill and passed out right in the middle of my speech. *Does anyone know if there's an EMT in the house?* After the chuckles from the guests in the crowd, about twenty five EMS people all gathered around the Air Force member, got him water, and quickly took care of the situation to mild and scattered applause. Turns out he was having a bit of heat stroke.

I will never forget sitting in that front row and feeling outside of myself as the Air Force members folded up the American flag, played TAPS, and delivered their touching speech that before then, I had only seen in the movies. A young African-American pretty lady handed me the folded up flag, and she said, "On behalf of the President of the United States of America, we thank you for your service." I remember my brother sitting next to me, and when I cried, he started rubbing my back gently. And then there was a line. A long, endless line of loved ones, friends, family, colleagues... all there to say we love you, and his life mattered. The line seemed to never end, and the people kept coming and coming. "We're sorry for your loss," as they bent down to my chair and hugged me, then Don's sister and George, then my brother and Jen, my mom, and my dad. The words continued from many. "So sorry for your loss." My cousins and their families; my Aunt Ginny; Nicky and his wife Julie; all coming from far away to support me. My dear friend, Vanessa, who had changed her flight for an important business trip to make sure she could be at the funeral for me. The faces I went to college with at Adelphi over twenty years ago, all back together in one, horrific place. Holly, Meghan, Kim, Debra, Matt, Vinnie, Rodney, Jay, Andrew... it was so surreal. I remember each time I turned around, there was a new person to hug, another face to look at, a different soul to hear.

Once everyone had cleared out, they left us alone with Don. I will never forget my mom saying to him, "Thank you for being such a wonderful husband to our daughter. We love you always." My dad, standing by his casket, his body shaking, and his words not being fully formed or able to come out. I remember what my mom said, what my dad tried or wanted to say, and I have no idea what I said. What do you say to someone that you know you will never see again who doesn't even look like themselves and is lying there not breathing and looking a little bit like Frankenstein? There's not much to say. As I walked out though, my only thought was, *"How can we just leave him here all alone?"* That simple thought crushed my insides. It was the same feeling I had when I left him in that tiny room at the hospital. It just seemed like the cruelest, most unimaginable thing to do. When we left the funeral home, I was escorted out and led through men and women in uniform forming a canopy above me with their swords. A long line of Hackensack Medical Center ambulances led the way and formed the most beautiful processional I have ever seen. They drove lights and sirens, down New Jersey streets, which were closed off for Don, and we were brought to the nearby Vanguard Healthcare, where Don worked and where we all gathered for after-death refreshments.

At the food gathering, I recall talking to people and mingling as if it were a normal event. As if my husband would join us any minute at his place of work and make some comment about idiot New Jersey drivers making him late. As Sarah and Julio served up gourmet food from his Long Island restaurant that they lovingly prepared, and people talked and laughed and drank coffee and soda and ate cookies around me, I really wasn't getting this. It wasn't sinking in. Not yet. And not for a while. Today – I attended my husband's funeral for the first time, and finally *looked* at what was inside that casket. Today, I didn't turn away. In some ways, today was the worst day of my life, because even though it happened a year ago, this time, I was there. This time, I remembered.

Kelley Lynn Shepherd

Dear Stupid Death Diary:

I am so tired of this. I don't fit in anywhere. I'm single. But I hate being single, because I'm widowed, and it's so very different. No, I don't want to go out to the clubs and flirt with men. No, I don't want to just sleep with someone because I can. Actually, the idea of another man touching me makes me want to shove pencils in my eyeballs. No, I don't feel a sense of "freedom" and like I can now do whatever I want because my husband isn't here to "tie me down." How insulting. I was more free with my husband than I've ever been in my life. He encouraged and supported my every aspiration. I can't breathe without him. I'm not free. Nothing about this is freeing. I'm suffocating, and nobody notices ever. No, I don't see how your divorce is the same, because you also didn't have a choice in the matter. That's valid. That's fine, but it's still nowhere near the same. The end of a marriage does NOT equal the end of a human being's LIFE. I'm so tired of the comparisons. Stop trying to make it a contest.

The other day, I attended a mini-reunion of sorts with some old work friends from way, way back. All females. We hadn't seen each other in many years. Most of them knew about what happened with Don - that he died. There were about eight of us, and we met up at a local restaurant. I didn't want to go, but sitting in my apartment alone is worse, so I went, because I thought maybe it MIGHT be okay to catch up with people who didn't even know Don, so maybe it might be less painful, or I could forget I'm widowed for five minutes or something. It was awful. I felt like I was from another planet. NOTHING they were talking about was anything I could relate to or anything that I was going through. It started when they all began talking about their husbands and how long each had been married. Some of them made light-hearted jokes about their marriages or how long they had been married. Jokes about how it had been "seven years but feels like twenty!" or "Some days I just want to kill

My Husband is Not a Rainbow

him, I swear!" Part of me wanted to shout out, "Hello??? Widowed person here! I JUST lost my husband to death! Maybe jokes about killing your husband might not be the best way to go at this time. Know your audience! Have some compassion!" They were so unaware, and it was like they were talking around me. I felt dizzy and sick and tortured, like I was sitting in chains. Nobody said Don's name. Nobody mentioned that my entire life had been altered and changed forever. They said nothing and made a toast with their bloody marys and wine to how great everyone was doing in their perfect married universes. One woman practically climbed over my limp body so she could get her wine glass arm into that all-important toast.

Two of the women had since been divorced, and they both seemed very angry about it. One of them made a casual comment to me about how her divorce was harder than MY HUSBAND LOSING HIS LIFE, because "at least you get closure with death. I don't have any closure. So, I do know how you feel." I sat there in silence, picking at my roasted potatoes with my fork. There were so many things horribly inaccurate about her statement, I didn't even know where to begin. And since I didn't have the energy to make waves or have a confrontation, because I felt my face turning bright red hot and felt the tears welling up, I said nothing. I ordered chocolate chip pie to help swallow my pain.

So the married ones all spoke of how long they had been married. When it came to me, I said flatly, "Four years and nine months. And then he died." Nobody offered up apologies. Nobody said, "I'm so sorry that happened." Nobody said a damn thing. One woman cleared her throat awkwardly, another one took a sip of her champagne, and then a third brought up the topic of children. Fantastic. They all started pulling out pictures of their kids and sharing them with one another. Talking about milestones and graduations and colleges and such. One woman was buying a new home to have more space for the newest kid.

Kelley Lynn Shepherd

Another was having issues with her two kids fighting a lot. A third complained about her husband working two extra hours last week and not being home to help with dinner. I gritted my teeth as I thought about my widowed parent friends who would never have any *help* with dinner or anything else from their husband or wife, ever again. It was beyond awful. And then, it got worse. One of the ladies asked me cheerily, "How about you, Kelley? How many children did you and your husband have?" I sat there for a beat, not knowing how to respond without fire shooting from my insides. Why would she assume that we had kids at all? And also, you don't say a word to me the whole lunch, but now, because I might have children, I'm suddenly of interest to you? I took a deep breath to stop myself from murdering her, and then said plainly and matter of fact, "I don't have any kids. We wanted them, and we were talking about starting a family soon, but he died before it could happen." Again, there was no acknowledgement of my pain or what I just said. Her immediate reply to my words was a way too happy, "Ohhhhh!!! Well that's good that you didn't have children! It would be so much harder for you if you did!" She turned her face away and began talking with the other ladies, because they were fellow mom's and wives, and therefore, more significant than me and my silly childlessness. I hid my tears by viciously buttering a dinner roll while my head was down and then announcing to nobody in particular when my eyes were leaking, "It's my allergies." After that, the conversation turned toward family vacations, adventures, and other things that were no longer a thing in my life.

In that crowd of friends who used to be friends, I have never felt more alone or unwanted. Nobody did anything wrong. They are not bad people. Extremely insensitive people? Yes. But not bad people. It's just that the lives they are living are no longer the life I have. The things they are experiencing are not things I will ever experience. I have nothing to add to this conversation, and my husband's forever absence never felt more under the spotlight. I tried to go back in time to a place of nostalgia, early work days, hanging out with old friends I knew in younger years. But going backwards isn't possible. Going to a place that feels like home, or feels familiar, no longer exists when the life you knew is over before it began. I had nothing to say to these people, they had nothing to say to me, and the realization of that is just one more thing on the long list of things I now have to grieve. Who says you can't go home? I do, Bon Jovi. I say it. And this delicious bite of sugar says it too, as I plant my face in the chocolate-chip pie with whipped cream. It's the only place that still feels familiar.

"When the dream that was, no longer can be,
You have to dream a different dream."
– Christina Rasmussen

Quarters, Dreams, and Chapstick

Here's a Riddle: What are you left with when your husband drops dead, and there is no warning, no will, no money, nothing you owned, no children, no "estate," and nothing of monetary value in the crappy little New Jersey apartment you rented together for seven years?

Answer: A bottle of guitar polish, some old chapstick, and a book of dumb State Quarters.

I said it was a riddle. I never said it was *funny*.

Exactly one month from today, I am moving. Leaving New Jersey and going back to New York. Forest Hills, Queens, to be exact. For weeks now, I have been putting the life that Don and I shared, into boxes. Bags. Suitcases. Piles. This box goes to mom and dad's place for storage. That one goes with me to my new apartment. This bag gets thrown away. That one gets donated to The Salvation Army. This one, I might sell. On and on and on, making emotional decisions at lightning speed as the days count down to when I must be gone from this room, this neighborhood, these walls. Time will not wait for my grief. Life will not be patient while I consider, yet again, whether or not to keep his favorite chair. (I'm keeping it, dammit!)

When you're grieving and dealing with your spouse's "stuff," everyone is an expert. People attack you with their opinions. Everyone knows what you should do. "Only keep ten items," they say. "Anything you haven't used in the last six months gets thrown away!" they bellow. "Be brutal! Get rid of everything!" they order, before returning home to their husbands and wives who are still alive and well. People love to tell you how you need to do things, what is best for you. Do this. Do that. Keep this. Throw that out. Move on. Cleanse your soul. Get over this. Make space for new things in your life. You can't grow with all this junk surrounding you.

And that is where it gets messy. When your spouse is alive and breathing, his dental floss or his nail file or his ratty old t-shirt might very well be *junk*. But when he is dead? It is everything. It is the only thing I have. There is nothing else. Just stuff. Each item becomes a tiny piece of him, something that is still somehow alive. Something I can keep. I study the dental floss like a CSI-investigator, pulling at the long string and trying to place my fingertips in the same place where he placed his the last time he used it. I unzip the old duffle bag that is sitting in the corner, wipe off the dust, and unveil the old ratty t-shirt that is inside. He played tennis wearing that ugly thing. Two days before his heart stopped, he was running around a tennis court in ninety two degree heat. I sniff the shirt like it's a fine wine, searching for his scent somewhere. Could it still be there after one year? Am I imagining that I smell him faintly? The plastic water bottle he drank from rolls out of the bag and onto the hardwood floor, taunting me. I pick it up. I fill it up with fresh water. I do not wash it first. I want to put my lips where he put his. I want to feel him through my thirst. I feel crazy as I take the first sip. It doesn't make me feel close to him. I feel so far away.

How can I simply discard his things? It was *his*. It feels like I am throwing him away. It *feels* like he is dying again. How the fuck do people *do this???* I have to stop now. It's too much. Tomorrow. I will do this then. Separating our life into boxes and bags is too exhausting for words. I need to quit my job so I can stare at this Swiss army knife, or that silly uniform pin that says 'EMS," and decide what to do with it. These are awful choices, and I have to make them. I want to just leave everything here and run away forever. I also want to take everything with me and hold onto it for dear life. But I can't. There are deadlines. There is rent to pay. There is reality.

The Entertainment Center in our living room. There is a little box sitting on top of it, which has a bunch of random items inside. I open it, with trash bag at the ready, feeling simultaneously victorious and like a murderer each time I throw another item away. Old pens. A piece of paper with a couple of music notes written on it. The startings of a song he was writing? Something he was learning? Seeing his handwriting gives me the chills. For a second, he is here, and I am home again. There is a tiny bottle of guitar polish. He was always cleaning and taking care of his many guitars. I mocked him incessantly for treating his instruments as if they were people. The polish is old and probably expired. But he took such good care of his things. How can I just carelessly toss it away like he was never here? Like he never even existed. I will come back to it. I can't decide now.

The Book of Quarters. It has been sitting here, messing with me for weeks. Don collected State Quarters. He put them in this official looking book called, "State Series Quarters: Complete

100 Coin Set." It took him years to build up the collection. He was almost finished with it. He still needed six states. I remember him taking me into two or three different places in the town of Falmouth, Massachusetts while we were on our Cape Cod honeymoon. He was anxious to see if they had the missing states. He desired to complete his book. I laughed at him and his silly hobby. I found it lame. We had a conversation during our honeymoon that went like this:

Me: I don't understand why you collect quarters.

Him: (mock-pouts at me while folding his arms and pouting his bottom lip) Boo doesn't like my hobby. It's fun. It's just something I do.

Me: But what's the point? They just sit inside this book that you never even look at or acknowledge. It just sits on a shelf and serves no purpose.

Him: The purpose it serves is that I enjoy collecting the coins.

Me: But why? They aren't even worth anything. I don't understand how that is fun.

Him: Well, Boo, you don't have to understand everything I do. It's really not all that deep. I just like it, that's all. It's really no big mystery.

Me: Oh. Well that's dumb.

Him: Yes, Boo. (laughing at me) I'm sorry my hobby is dumb to you and that it annoys you so much. Actually, I'm not sorry. Annoying you is fun. Let's go into this store. I still need the Montana Quarter. Come on Boo… (grabs my hand and walks me into store enthusiastically) You know you want to look at coins with me. Isn't this fun?

My Husband is Not a Rainbow

Me: No. It's dumb. (mock-pouting back at him)

Now, sitting here with this stupid book of coins, I feel guilt and sadness and pain. The logical part of my brain wants to take all the quarters out of the book and put them into my giant change jar, the one Don and I always threw change into over time, and then used it for laundry or tolls or saved it up and changed it in for actual dollars when we needed to. What the hell am I going to do with this Quarter Collection? I don't collect coins. I will never collect coins. I have zero desire to collect fucking coins. But for some damn reason, I can't seem to make myself toss these dumb quarters into the jar and be done with it. For some reason, it feels like stealing. Like I'm stealing his hobby. Like I'm mocking him while he's dead. It seems really unfair. Then again, they are just coins. Why is this so hard? Why am I making it so hard?

I wrestle with it for hours. I still can't decide. I need to do laundry, and I have no change. The guilt creeps back as I steal from my dead husband and his harmless little hobby. I post my dilemma on Facebook, knowing how humorous it is, and knowing I will get many responses. Immediately, people start in with their opinions. People are getting emotional. Other widowed people who have their own individual issues with their loved one's items are becoming affected by what I decide to do with these quarters. Now it weighs on my mind and the minds of people in cyberspace. The world is on the edge of its seat. Never was a book of quarters so damn entertaining. What will happen??? Will the widow make the right choice? Will she do right by her husband? There were too many people screaming and typing in my ear. I couldn't think straight, and I just wanted to be done with feeling. I took the few quarters I needed to do my laundry out of the book, did it, and decided to deal with the rest in the morning. I felt unsure about what to do, and honestly, only one person could tell me the right thing, and that was Don.

Kelley Lynn Shepherd

Last night, I went to bed. Last night, I had a dream. It was the first time that my husband "came to me" in a dream, since months and months ago. There were two dreams where I "felt" his presence there, where it felt like more than just a dream. Both of them happened two or three months after he died. Last night it happened again. In the dream, I was lying in bed on my side like I always do. I felt his arms around me. He was spooning me, and my hand grabbed his as it reached around my waist. He was here.

"Your hands are dry, Boo. You should use some of my Chapstick on them. I still have some left. It's in that little box on the entertainment center. Just rub it on your palms. It will help. You never used to have dry skin. I had dry skin." His voice was calm and reassuring. I was safe again. All was well.

"Why are you wasting time talking about dry skin and chapstick? There are so many other things to talk about. I can't believe you're here." My voice is shaky and scared. I'm crying.

"I'm always here for you, Boo. We don't have to talk at all. I just want to lie here with you. I think that's what you need right now." He sighs into the back of my neck. I never see his face in this dream. He is behind me, and I feel him. His hands. His touch. His warmth. I feel him.

"I don't want to move, Boo. I don't wanna move from this bed. This apartment. This room. If I leave here, and I go somewhere new, it will be somewhere that you never were. I don't want to be anywhere that you never were. We were supposed to leave here together. I'm scared." Now I'm sobbing loudly, and his hand wipes away my tears. He rubs my back.

"I know you're scared. I'm not going anywhere, Boo. And neither are you. You aren't leaving me. You're leaving this shitty, stupid, messed up state and going back to New York, where you belong. Just remember – wherever you are, that is where I'll be too. I know it's not the same as what we planned, but I'm here. You need to know that." He sounds like an Angel.

"I wish I could believe that. I wish these dreams would happen everyday. I wish I would stay with you forever and never, ever wake up." My voice sounds like an alien.

We lay there in silence for a while, until I stop crying. The whole time, I feel his arms around me. He doesn't let go. Finally, I ask. "Are you mad at me?"

There is no hesitation in his response. "Of course not. Why would I be mad at you?" He seems hurt that I would even think such a thing.

"Because I threw away your stuff. And because of the quarters. You loved those stupid quarters." I'm sobbing again. Ridiculously hard. These fucking quarters have made me lose my goddamn mind.

"Remember what you said on our honeymoon? They are dumb. They are just dumb quarters. What are you supposed to do with a book of quarters, Boo? They were *my* hobby. Not yours. Use them for laundry. Throw them in the jar. Like I told you years ago, it's just a hobby. It's not that deep. You do what you need to do honey. With everything. What's mine is ours. It's yours now. I'm dead. I don't need a book of quarters. And you're alive. And laundry needs quarters. Use them. They aren't important. You're important. I love you." He starts to disappear now. His fingers unlock from mine.

"I hate when you leave. I hate waking up. Please, please don't go. I love you so much." My pillow is drenched with my reality. My pain. My life. There is no response. He is gone. I'm awake.

Kelley Lynn Shepherd

Just like that. I lay there for minutes and try like hell to get it back. But it's gone.

After a while, I walk into the living room, feeling as if a train just ran me over. I pick up the small box I had looked at yesterday, the one with all the random items inside it. I look at it and shake it, and it appears to be emptied. Everything was removed by me before. I sit in his favorite chair, exhausted and spent. Some time passes. Then, out of nowhere, Sammy meows. He meows again. He looks at me and keeps making noise. He is like Lassie with an important message. Something tells me to get up. Look again. I pick up the box, just for kicks. This time, the bottom of the box is not the bottom of the box. There is more. Another layer; like one of those boxes of chocolates with the paper in between. The corner is sticking up, so I pull it. Underneath lies some junk, or the greatest thing on earth, depending on who you are.

Chapstick. His chapstick that he used every single day for his really dry skin and lips that never quite got used to the air up here. I take off the cap, and twist the gooey, waxy substance into a ball, so it's floating just above the top. Putting out the palm of my hand, I gently rub the chapstick back and forth across it, in a calming and slow rhythm, erasing my dry skin and my fears and my guilt with each stroke. Finally, I put it to my lips and feel the texture go over my mouth, knowing that once, long ago, it was on his mouth. Knowing that I felt him in that dream and that it wasn't just a dream. Knowing that I can be at peace with my choices about his stuff, that isn't just junk. Knowing that with every State Quarter I put into that washing machine, I have his permission, and that wherever I chose to go in my life, from now on, he would follow me. He will follow me. This I know, and this I choose to believe.

Session Snippet

Caitlin: How are you doing with preparing for your move?

Me: I hate it. It feels like I'm putting him away in boxes and discarding him forever. I hate being in that apartment, but I hate the idea of going somewhere else too. Yesterday, one of my co-workers at the college said that it's good that I'm moving, because now I can "put all this behind me," like Don was some wife-beater or serial cheater that I should be ashamed of or something. I don't want to put him behind me. I refuse.

Caitlin: Good. Don't listen to that woman or to anyone that tells you those things. That is the archaic way of thinking. That is really old-fashioned grief-thinking. Listen to me. You do not ever have to let go of your husband. Not ever. That is not the goal here. It never has been.

Me: (burst out crying)

Caitlin: What's wrong?

Me: Nothing. You're just the first person who has said those words to me. Everyone keeps telling me I have to move on, I have to let him go, I have to get past this. You're the only person who has said that I don't have to do that. I don't think I could live in a world where I had to do that, honestly. It's just too damn sad for me not to have him in my life, in some form.

Caitlin: Of course it is. You do not need to let go of your husband, and you do not need to stop loving him. That is not the goal. The goal here is for you to process through your emotions and then eventually be able to live a life again. A life that you create and build. And in that life, Don will be there. He is a part of it. He is a part of you now, so it would be impossible to let him go.

Kelley Lynn Shepherd

Me: This is literally the greatest thing you have ever said to me.

Caitlin: Part of what we are doing here, our work here together, is to help you create that life for yourself, and then to help you to shift the relationship that you have with Don, because you will always have a relationship and a connection to him. We just need to figure out, in time, what that new relationship looks like and where he now fits in your heart and in this next part of your life.

Me: But I'm not ready to shift him anywhere. I don't want him to go anywhere. I still feel married. I'm still in love with him. The idea of ever being with anyone other than him makes me sick to my stomach. I want to throw up thinking about it.

Caitlin: I know, honey. I'm not asking you to do anything at all right now, except what you are already doing. The shifting will happen naturally, and we will both know when it is time to start figuring out that change in the relationship. You will feel married as long as you feel married. You will date - IF you date - when you feel like it, and no sooner. Don't let anyone rush you through any of that. You are always exactly where you need to be in your healing.

Me: But I'm scared to not feel close to him anymore. I'm scared of him disappearing from my life. I don't want to shift him. I want him back.

Caitlin: I know. You're not there yet. And that's okay. We will keep coming back to it. All you need to know right now is this; the connection between you and Don will never go away. You get to keep him in your life, and you get to keep him in a very profound way. It's called "continuing bonds."

Me: What does that mean?

Caitlin: It basically challenges the old way of thinking about grief, which was that the bereaved had to "let go of" the person who has died. Continuing bonds means that death ends a life and not a relationship or a connection, and so your connection remains and shifts into something that makes more sense, now that the person is no longer physically here. You do not need to let go of Don. Ever.

Me: ...and this is why I love you. Thank you.

FB Post: My husband just got a letter in the mail. Jury Duty. He has Jury Duty. I'm going to send a letter back, along with a copy of the Death Certificate, saying, "Dear Jury Duty Morons, my husband Don will not be able to make Jury Duty, because he is dead. Thank you for your consideration in this matter." I can just see Don shaking his head right now at the stupidity of New Jersey.
LIKES: 89   COMMENTS: 65

I Don't Need Anything ... Except This Chair

One of my very favorite comedy films of all-time has always been *The Jerk*. As I continue to pack, lift, go through piles, clean, organize, fill boxes and bags, and generally prepare to move out of the apartment my husband and I shared our life in for seven years, I feel a little bit like Steve Martin's character, Navin, as he left his mansion and his lovely wife Marie (Bernadette Peters). My dad and I used to quote this scene constantly when I was a kid, and I can still watch it a hundred times, and it always makes me laugh. Basically, Navin is grabbing lots of different items in desperation as he leaves his house, while simultaneously announcing how he does not need each of the items he is grabbing. An ashtray. A lamp. His dog. The chair...

Kelley Lynn Shepherd

The comedy comes from the fact that by the time he walks out of his mansion, he is juggling about eight different items in his hands as he continues to claim that each item is for sure, the very last thing that he needs.

Don has been dead for a year now, and I'm saying goodbye to the only home we have ever known as a couple. We never lived anywhere else together. We never got to own a home or have kids or reach our goals. We weren't there yet. It was only the beginning – until it was the end. Our life was here, in this crappy, dusty, tiny apartment. We had dreams. We had a future planned. We also had no money, no savings, and no idea when we would be able to get out of New Jersey like Don wanted to so badly. And in just a few days, I will be leaving, alone. And let me tell you – it hurts like hell to go.

Moving is a goddamn nightmare. Moving while grieving is a hellish nightmare. Moving out of New Jersey is an impossible, hellish, awful, terrible, evil nightmare. After all this time, I am finally starting to see why my husband hated this state so much. *"It's a pain in the ass to do the simplest thing here,"* he used to say. *"They are ass-backwards, and things that should be easy, you gotta break your damn back to accomplish. Why is EVERYTHING so difficult here?"* He never understood why you couldn't miss your exit and just turn around. Or why you had to *pay money* to simply park your car in a space. Or why they never fixed the potholes that would ruin his car. He could never grasp the concept of the jughandle, the mafia-mentality, or the "Jersey Shore" obsession. *"The beaches here suck,"* he would say. The bike and golf clubs that he used all year long in Florida – stayed in our storage closet here, barely used. The lifestyle was different. He didn't like how everybody was on top of each other here. It's always crowded. Filthy. Old. Moving from Florida to here, his car insurance doubled. His rent doubled. There were so many more expenses here than what he was used to. It was stressful just to live. He was always working his ass off, yet we never got ahead. He loved NYC, and he loved me. He knew I needed to be here, so this is where we were. But he really hated New Jersey. I used to take that personally. Now, after jumping through hoops trying to move the hell out of here, I truly understand.

The place I am moving into in Forest Hills comes complete with a roommate. It also comes with a beautiful king-sized bed, dressers, nightstands, couches, desk, and everything else you can think of. It is furnished, and so I cannot take much with me. Because of this, for the past month, I've been trying to figure out ways to get rid of my bed, two sofas, Entertainment Center, kitchen table, coffee table, and annoyingly large dresser. I put them on Craigslist. Freecycle. I even made posters and put them up in our building, and then walked them into the mom and pop stores all over our neighborhood. The items were all listed as being FREE, provided you come get them and carry them out of here yourself. Good luck finding a parking spot. It'll never happen. And if by some miracle it does occur, and you park within a mile of the place without issue, have fun trying to fit the ginormous items through the small doorways, and down the three flights of stairs. Nobody showed up. Nobody wanted my things. For FREE!

Okay. Fine. I will donate them. Surely a woman's shelter or The Salvation Army would be *honored* to have these items, right? Wrong. Turns out the Salvation Army only has one guy available to pick up donated items, and he isn't free until mid-September. The shelter doesn't take any items from families who have cats, due to possible allergies. (*Seriously?*) Well, Kelley, you may say- why not just leave the furniture on your curb? Surely, someone will come and pick it up! Not in good 'ole New Jersey! In my neighborhood, you are not allowed to leave any large items or furniture in the basement or on the street. If you do, you will be fined. And then killed. The town will come and pick up your items for you, but only on Tuesdays between the hours of twelve forty five PM and one seventeen PM, and only on partly cloudy days, and only if it's not raining. Or sunny. Or hot. Or cold. And they won't come up the steps to your apartment to get the items. They will only pick them up on the curb. Oh, and they will only pick up three items at a time. Are you fucking kidding me? What kind of dumb-ass racket are you people running anyway? How is this convenient or logical in any way whatsoever? And *what the hell am I going to do with all my crap???* Eventually, I had to let my friends know that I needed help. And when I did that, they came running, and the process of getting rid of my things began. So did my extreme emotions.

First up, our good friend and Don's long-time EMS partner on the ambulance, Meg, showed up and tore apart the two sofas. She literally took box-cutters and a mallet and destroyed the damn things. Don would have really appreciated that and found it awesome. Me? It was really weird watching the couches that we bought right after our wedding, the couches he always sat on when he strummed his guitars, being turned into sawdust. *"They are just things,"* Meg reminded me. And she was right. I just had to constantly remind myself of that. Meanwhile, I took the mallet to the dresser and showed it who was boss. Two seven-hour days later, and our lungs filled with dust, we had accomplished something. We had bonded in our violent destruction of innocent objects. We were one. (Okay, that last part is ridiculous. It's late, and I'm just tired. We weren't *one*.)

Next, my friend John came over and helped me go through Don's hallway closet, a project that, if I had done by myself, would have left me frozen by intense emotion at the discovery of each new item found. With him there, I was able to control that, continue, and talk about it with him instead of crying in a corner alone.

My Husband is Not a Rainbow

Today was the biggest project of all. Two gay men, a married guy driving a church-owned box-truck, and a widow – all working together as the weirdest moving company ever to get all the pieces of junk that was once my furniture out of the apartment and into some dumpster somewhere. In preparation for all of my friends' arrival, I woke up this morning and moved what I could into the living room so they would have easy access to it all. Then, I stopped. Looked around. Another empty room. Just like last year, standing in my parent's house, empty, just days before it would no longer be their house anymore. Once again, it all hit me. The flood gates opened up, and I broke down. An hour later, I cried again, this time while talking to Rebecca on the phone about the details of today. That time, I was overcome with gratefulness. Thankful for the many ways friends like her who have helped me. So I cried.

Just hours later, my crew arrived, and we were eating the pizza I ordered and drinking the soda and bottled water I provided them – a tiny thank you for all they were doing for me. And then we got to work. Bobby, Jay, Ben, and me. Slowly removing the pieces of my life into a truck donated by Ben and the church his wife, Rebecca, goes to. It was messy. It was funny. It was strange.

When we found an empty trash bin outside, and Jay came up with the idea to "borrow" it for a few minutes so that we could use it to put all the many loose pieces of wood from our couches and Entertainment Center and dresser that had been hacked to pieces the days before, I suggested that may be considered stealing by our neighbors. Then Bobby came up with an ad slogan for our new fake Moving Company, "Need movers? Have no values? Call us! We are 'QuestionableMorals.com!' We have no conscience – Right or wrong, we get the job done!"

Later, when we removed our mattress and bed frame, we discovered Don's gun in a case underneath the bed. This wasn't a surprise to me, as I recall him telling me he had brought it up here from Florida. It sat under our bed for seven years, never coming out of its case. Don was in the Air Force, and he enjoyed skeet shooting – even won some trophies for it in competitions. So, it was some sort of skeet-shooting rifle. When I told the men that I wanted to open the case and look and see the gun inside, again we started creating fake future newspaper headlines:

"Widow Accidentally Shoots Herself with Dead Husband's Gun. Gay Friends Watch in Horror."

Or my favorite:

"Young Widow Found Dead After Gay Friend Accidentally Mistakes Gun for Microphone. Local Church Held Liable."

(Not to worry. Later in the day, I phoned the local police station and informed them of the situation and that I found my deceased husband's gun while packing. An officer came over and made the gun go bye-bye.)

Today I cried. Today I laughed. Today my friends were amazing, as they have been throughout this never-ending nightmare of losing my wonderful husband. Today I stood in our living room and saw my never-reached future and my bittersweet past. I saw the things that we bought together and used together and lived in together – carted away.

You would think that the emptiness of the rooms would make the place seem more impersonal. It didn't. It just made me sad. Made me think about five days from now, when I close that door forever, when I walk out of here for the last time, and how I won't be with my husband when I do that. None of our things made it out alive. Our couches. Dresser. Tables. All the small

My Husband is Not a Rainbow

and big things we owned together – gone. Cut up and thrown into a truck.

The only thing that made it – the only thing that is coming with me – is his chair. His silly, stupid, dumb, horrible, wonderful chair. I made fun of it all the time. He loved his chair. He brought it with him from Florida. His La-Z-boy chair. The chair he napped with the cats in. The chair he took care of me in for a week when I threw out my back. The chair I sat in the first time I flew out to Florida to visit him, when we were dating long-distance. I sat in his chair, and his cat Isabelle jumped right into my lap. Don smiled and said, "She loves you. She doesn't usually do that. She loves you, Boo." It's the chair that I called ugly on more than one occasion. We dubbed it his "Archie Bunker chair." And now, as if I'm being punished for mocking it so openly, I am left with it.

As I leave this apartment and move into this new one, I am forty years old, and I am starting my life all over again. I am left with no husband. No money. No health insurance. No security. No safety net. No plan. What if my new roommate hates me? What if he regrets letting me live there? What if he dies like Don did? Then where will I live? What if my cats freak out and hate it there, and he kicks us out? What if I get sick and can't pay my bills? What if I lose my job? What if I can't think of any more panicky questions? What if...

And so, as I attempt to fall asleep tonight in my husband's favorite, lame chair that is now my lame chair, I am reminded again of that classic scene in *The Jerk*. And when I leave here in a week, I will need to remind myself that, like Navin, I don't need the Entertainment Center. Or the dresser. I don't need our couches. I don't need anything.

Except this chair. This chair... and my kitties. And I don't need anything else. Not one other thing. But as I close the doors on

New Jersey and open them to New York and to this new part of my life, I'll tell you a secret. And the secret is this: I'm terrified.

FB Post: Tonight is my last overnight at the apartment. My parents are here to help me clean before the movers come, and they are staying in a hotel down the street. I was going to go with them, but I'm feeling compelled to spend my last night here, where I shared a life with my husband. Already walked into most of the local stores and said goodbye to the store owners, and later tonight, when it's dark and NYC is shining in lights, I'll take that last walk along the Hudson River and sit at the bench Don and I used to always sit at and talk, hold hands, kiss. Bringing some of his ashes with me, and I will sprinkle some by the bench and the river path. Can't possibly litter New Jersey any more than it already is, right? Man, this is goddamn heartbreaking.
LIKES: 102   COMMENTS: 51

Following Page Rainbow Illustration: Okay, this is weird. Somehow, Don ended up hanging out on this dude's ass. Not that there's anything wrong with that...

My Husband is Not a Rainbow

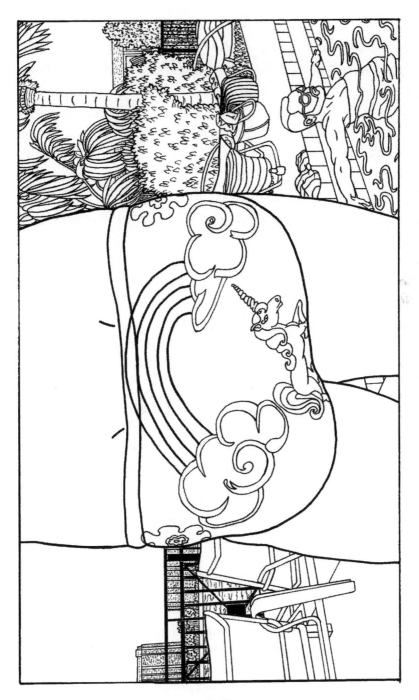

"Losing your partner or spouse is never just losing your partner or spouse. The secondary losses that come with it are endless and heart-wrenching. Having to move out of your home, or having to stay in it without them. Being forced to let go of so many things you don't want to lose…Finances, jobs, security, friendships, family who no longer wants to hear it – the list goes on and on, and it's incredibly stressful and exhausting. Most days you just feel like giving up. But you can't. Because you're alone now, and nobody's going to take care of this shit for you. And just at that moment when you want to lie down and die, is when some asshole who knows nothing at all about your reality, tells you, in that casual and thoughtless way, to 'Get over it.'" – Widower Who Chose to Remain Anonymous

A Super Bowl to Remember

It was Super Bowl Sunday, 2005. After a few years of dating long-distance, and lots of planning and saving money, it was finally happening. Don Shepherd was finally on his way to me, to live with me, and to begin our forever time together. He had packed up his entire life into a Penske yellow moving truck, attached that to his precious Grand Prix Pontiac, and taken off, his cat Isabelle sitting in his lap for most of the twenty four hour drive.

It was February, and there were several snowstorms along his route, but he kept on going - only stopping for food and gas breaks. He chose not to do a hotel stay, but to drive it straight through. I thought he was nuts. He said, "The sooner I get there, the sooner we can start our lives together, Boo." I was nervous, excited, and anxious, hoping everything would go just right. This would be the first time I had ever "lived with" a guy, and so we had discussed our mutual desire to marry each other, and that this would eventually lead to a proposal. So, I knew that was coming, I just didn't know when or where or how. Even though I was anxious, it was more about being anxious that he would find a job he liked, that he wouldn't hate it here, those types of things. I was never once anxious or terrified about our future together. Loving Don, or his love for me, never scared me. It was comforting, beautiful, and everything that made me so very happy.

My friends Kevin, Michelle, John, and Jessica all met me at my apartment, and we all awaited Don's arrival. I had made homemade lasagna, sauce, meatballs. I tried to clear out as much space as possible in the tiny closets and in my room (our room), and everywhere else for him to enter into my life. And we waited…

When that Penske truck pulled up, I was standing outside by the street, because he had called to inform me he was close to arriving. We had parked John's car in front of my building, ensuring us at least one space for the moving truck to go. Once he was finally safely into the space, he got out of the truck and stretched his long arms and legs. We fell into a hug and lots of short kisses. "You're here!" I kept squealing. "I can't believe you're really here!" He responded with equal enthusiasm through his exhaustion, "I'm here, Boo! And I don't have to leave this time! No more goodbyes!"

Everyone unloaded the truck. John, Kevin, and Don made multiple references and jokes about Don's ungodly heavy Entertainment Center that had to get up three flights of stairs, and would end up in our living room. I mocked Don's old-looking, Archie Bunker recliner chair as we placed it in the corner of the living room. Stacks of boxes got taller and taller. Wider and wider. We could barely see each other across all of the boxes. Isabelle hid under the bed and remained there until later that evening, when she finally felt comfortable enough to make her appearance. John and Don drove to the Penske place to return the moving truck. It was fifteen minutes away, but somehow, they got lost for almost three hours. When they finally returned, Don officially began his hatred of all things New Jersey. "You can't make a wrong turn in this stupid state! Good luck to anyone who is lost around here! You do one little thing wrong, you end up in a vortex, never to return again!" he sighed heavily as he finally ate my homemade lasagna.

Hours later, when our friends had left, and the two of us sat there surrounded by boxes, there was a calmness that came over the atmosphere. A knowing that life would now be happy and safe, and that my days of having to fall asleep in the bed alone were over. There would be someone there now to hold me when I had a nightmare, to support me when I needed them to, and to share all of life's adventures. The idea that I would get to do all of these things for someone, for him, too, was thrilling. It made my heart happy. We sat there, tired, holding hands, and with boxes so high around us, we could barely walk. But I didn't feel suffocated. There was chaos all around us, but I didn't feel scared. My apartment was in shambles and turned upside down, but I didn't feel anxious. No. As I looked at the man who would eventually become my husband and saw him next to me in our living room, smiling at me with content and peace in his blue eyes, I felt like I had finally come home.

"I draw great comfort in honoring my wife's memory that when we married, we promised to spend the rest of our lives together. My wife did spend the rest of her life with me, and for that I am eternally grateful."
– Greg Roman

Words About Don

"Don and I worked on an ambulance in Florida for a couple of years. Don was a great partner to work with on an ambulance. When we got on a call, he handled the patient care and movement until he found something that I needed to do as a paramedic. I would get information and start on the report while he did his thing. We worked a high performance unit where we either worked a 10 hour shift, or if we did 10 calls, then we were done with our shift, and we would go home for 10 hours of pay, as if we had worked 10 hours. Don would drag me through the hallways at hospitals and nursing homes. If I was in the front of the stretcher, he would run me over with it (Don was 6 inches taller than I am). We both loved 80s music and would be blasting the songs when we did not have a patient on board. We would change the words to songs to make them fit what we did or plan to do in the future. We talked about retiring together and going to a nursing home so we could harass the nurses. Our plan was to be the grumpy old men.

Don then decided to leave me to move to NYC to be with a woman he met online. I told him it would never work, and he should just stay and work with me. He did not listen (normal for him), and he left me for her. As much as I did not want to forgive him for it, he asked me to be his best man at the wedding, and I could not say no and stay mad at him. So I got to go to NYC to meet his bride and help him get hitched to the partner thief (Kelley). She was really sweet, and I could not be happier for him. Her family was one that I knew Don would love forever. The worst day of knowing Don was the day he passed away. I still remember the call from Kelley; I was heartbroken that my best friend had left us that day, way too soon. To a great friend and EMT, thanks for the memories old man (AKA Putz)." - Rob Smith, Don's best friend

Widow: Party of Four

I'm supposed to be happier. I'm supposed to be getting "better." I should be "grateful" for having such a great love in my life in the first place. Some people never experience such a love, you know. I was very lucky to end up in such a nice, new living situation – with a wonderful, genuine, new roommate. I need to be thankful.

At least, this is what everybody keeps telling me. Or implying to me. Or saying to me with their judgmental, no clue what they're talking about because they haven't ever lost a spouse eyes.

My Husband is Not a Rainbow

So why the hell do I feel so sad? Ever since moving to my lovely, amazing apartment in the sky in Forest Hills, I feel this wave of nausea over me, like something desperately needs to get out. It feels like I will burst into tears at any second. But I never do. Don't get me wrong. I was sad as hell in my old apartment in New Jersey. I was surrounded by our past, by "stuff," and I felt like I was suffocating. Choking. I was miserable. But there was a certain, sick comfort in that horrible misery, because I was living in the place where my husband and I shared our life together. We ate there. Slept. Kissed. Napped. Laughed. Cooked. Had Christmas parties and get-togethers. Brought adopted, rescued kitties home. Cried and grieved over those kitties when they died. Tried again. Brought more pets home. Loved them deeply. Had talks about having children. Had minor arguments and discussions about what our future would hold, where we would live, would we ever have a family? We were a team in that apartment. We lived a life in that apartment. We had dreams in that apartment. We wanted *out* of that apartment. We breathed air in that apartment. It was dusty, unclean air, and it was an overcrowded, cramped, ancient, pain-in-the-ass place to live. But it was our pain-in-the-ass place, and it meant something to us. Sometimes, it meant everything.

Living in that apartment for the past fourteen months since Don's death, I have been overwhelmed and consumed by piles. Piles of our past. Piles of migraine-inducing emotions that left me heavy at night and unable to sleep. Piles of unpaid bills, unplayed guitars, unrealized dreams. Part of me didn't want to ever leave. But I had to. If I didn't, that apartment would have killed me. My spirit and my will to keep going would be gone. Too many ghosts in the corners. Too much dust had piled up. There were so many piles of our "stuff," that there wasn't any room in there to grow. If I had remained there any longer, I would have emotionally exploded from too much pain.

Kelley Lynn Shepherd

This new apartment brings with it a *new* kind of pain. It is different than what I felt before, but it is just as harsh and just as stabbing. Sometimes it feels worse, because I feel guilty for feeling it at all. This is the neighborhood I wanted to live in. There is a beautiful sunset and a crazy-good view of NYC shining in lights at night from my bedroom window. The people here are friendly and say hello. My commute to work has been cut in half, and my stress levels are down some. My roommate is a guy I found on Craigslist, who took me and my kitties in, and is a really nice person. Life feels lighter, and I can feel the breeze now. I am no longer suffocating in piles.

And yet…I just want to cry. I want to cry because my husband cannot see the glorious sunset. He cannot eat cupcakes with me at Martha's Bakery on Austin Street. He can't have a great burger at Bareburger or get a beer and watch the Yankees game with me and Vanessa. My husband cannot see how happy our kitties are here or how *hard* I'm trying to love them in the same, incredible, selfless way that he did. Can he see me brushing them? Can he hear me talking to them and telling them how much we miss him? Does he laugh when I sing our silly songs to them and annoy them? I don't know.

People say that he can feel these kinds of things, and maybe he can. But I don't know. And even if he can feel them and see them and hear them, it's not enough. It's just not fucking fair, and it's not enough for me. I want to touch him. I want to hold his hand and look at that sunset together. I want to take long walks in my new neighborhood with him and talk about how we *finally* made it out of that crappy Jersey place. I want to make dinners in this awesome kitchen and sit at the dining room table with our friends and play board games and mock life. I want to make him all his favorites, like chicken parmesan and Swedish meatballs and Shepherd's Pie. I want him to be here, dammit! And it *sucks* that he isn't. I don't want to be alone. I was alone for decades before I met him. I struggled and paid bills alone and carried my own damn groceries and luggage and *everything* – alone, before I met him. I got married so I wouldn't have to be alone ever again. So I could be part of a team. The best team in the world. Marriage. It's not fair that he only got to be around for the struggling parts of our life. And it's not fair that my teammate is just gone. He is gone, and this place is beautiful, and I just want to cry.

In our old Jersey neighborhood, there was nowhere to really walk to, no real life in the streets, aside from a random little pharmacy or store here and there, so for the past year or so, I sat home a lot at night. Inside. Alone. In my new home, however, life is all around me. People are everywhere. They walk their dogs, and they buy fresh fruit at the Farmer's Market, and they laugh as they stroll along the crowded streets that are filled with stores and cafes and bars. When I am busy with friends and I have plans, things are much more tolerable. The grief gets pushed down, or at least distracted enough by good conversation, jokes, banter, fun. It is all that time in between working and having plans that makes me sit in a fog and think about what it might be like to let myself slowly freefall from my twenty one story window, high in the sky.

Weekends. One of the many examples of "things I used to love that I now dread." Friday nights are all about couples. Dating. Love. Saturdays and Sundays are made for families. Kids. Relaxation. Movies. Beaches. Malls. Time spent with those you share a home with, a life with. This weekend, my roommate went away with some friends, and I was here alone for the first time. I had asked a bunch of people if anyone had plans, but it seemed as if everyone was busy. On Friday night, I was sitting here at the computer, looking at Facebook to kill some time. My screen was filled with people talking about their wedding anniversaries, summer vacations, kids' birthday parties, marriage issues, and general family life things. I couldn't look at it for one more second. The words, "Happy Anniversary!" sting in my chest, even in type. Sometimes it's simply too much to cope with, and I have to just get away from everyone's happiness and joy for a while.

The Yankees game was on, and I started to watch it here in my room, when suddenly it felt extremely depressing to be watching a Yankee game alone in my room. So I went out. Walked around the neighborhood. Figured, maybe sitting in a Sports Pub, watching a Yankees game with other humans, was a bit less pathetic than being alone.

I was so very wrong. From the second I left the safe, cozy, bubble of my apartment and entered into the world of humans outside – love attacked me and snuck up on me along every corner. Life was everywhere. Relationships. New ones. Old ones. Good ones and bad ones. Couples on first or second dates having awkward conversations. Having *no* conversations. Making out and making plans and making *"I want you now"* eyes at one another. As I turned onto 72nd Avenue, a young gay couple was lost in each other's pupils. A block away, an obvious husband and wife well into their 80s walked side by side, extremely slowly, in their matching walkers. Seconds later, I was struck by the force and energy of a couple with their four children. They were standing outside of a frozen yogurt place, giving their complicated order to the woman standing in the walk-up window. The man was rubbing the woman's back as she placed the order. He grabbed all the cones and handed them to each child, then instructed them in his heavy accent to sit on a nearby bench. They seemed overwhelmed but happy. He was very loving and patient with his little kids, the way that Don would have been if we had a family.

My heart skipped a beat or seven as I turned the next corner and noticed a woman, desperately trying to get the attention of her man as she followed him, cursing loudly. He was ignoring her as he chatted away on his cell phone. She looked exhausted by life.

He looked clueless and like he didn't give a shit. Why the fuck do *they* get to be together when they clearly don't even appreciate each other? Why do they get to have more time to continue to fuck up that relationship, when my husband and I had a perfectly awesome one and it was TAKEN away for no reason? It doesn't make any sense.

Sitting there inside The Irish Tavern with my Diet Coke and my Yankees game – it hit me how alone I truly am. One couple in their thirties or so was talking up another young couple. The husbands were laughing and joking around about their wives. The one guy was a Salsa-dance instructor for a local studio. "I can't even get my wife to go dancing," he said to the other, as he gave his wife a knowing and teasing glare. "She just wants to come here, have a drink, and watch the game." "Well yeah," she shot back. "Screw the dancing. I'm tired after a long day. I want margaritas." They all smiled and talked about mutual restaurants and dance clubs they had all been to in the area, and then the one woman who didn't like dancing said, "I can hardly see the game from here. What's the score?"

The way that the tables were placed in the pub, it was apparently awkward for them to be able to see the Yankees game from where they were sitting. I could see it fine from the four-person booth the hostess had seated me in earlier. There was some chatter between them, and then one of the women came over and very nicely asked me if they could switch tables with me so they could watch the game. I don't know why they assumed that I *wasn't* watching the game also, but they did. Maybe it was because I was alone, by myself, and maybe people would never think that someone would have a reason to go to a sports bar alone on a Friday night to watch a Yankees game. But you *do* have a reason when the person you watched every single game with is dead, and when you can't look at sunsets or foliage, or eat delicious food, or experience new and amazing things without feeling a pain and a stab inside you each and every time.

Kelley Lynn Shepherd

There is nothing at all wrong with watching a baseball game alone. But when you *have* to watch a baseball game alone, because the other half of your team no longer breathes air, *that* is devastating.

Before I could even respond to her request, I quickly got up and walked out of the pub. I may have mumbled "sure" or something of that nature. I honestly can't recall. I just know that I felt so lonely at that very moment, and I felt so lonely on the long walk back home. When I got into my bedroom, I sat in my husband's recliner chair, pulled the quilt with the pictures of us and our life all over it into my body, and cried.

When I was living in our old place alone after his death, I felt suffocated inside the apartment. Now – I feel suffocated outside. A loner in a world filled with love. A single soul – trying to fill the space and time with cups of coffee and walks and drives around town. A widow, sitting in a booth for four.

Technically, it is "better" to be in this gorgeous environment than in the stifling one I was in before. Making this move was something I had to do, and it was the right thing to do. But is it worse to be alone surrounded by the past you shared together – or alone surrounded by the future you will never share together?

Like I said before – it's a different kind of pain. In this new world of "better things" for me, I feel so hollow, and I miss him more than ever.

*"Less time ahead than I clocked behind.
Caught in a minefield and crossing blind."*
– Alex Rivera

Dear Dead Husband:

Things have been so damn hard lately. I feel super depressed. I just want to lie down all the time or do nothing. I do a lot of staring into space. I go to work, I do the things I need to do, but I feel like I am nowhere, really. I just don't see a time when this will ever get any better, and it seems like nobody can really tell me otherwise. Even Caitlin seems baffled by me lately, by my intense sadness. I don't remember ever being this sad before. On a good note though, - I'm going back to our favorite place in NYC today - Central Park - on this first day of Fall, our favorite time of year together. Like Billy Idol once said, "It's a nice day to start again. It's a nice day for a Gay Wedding ..." Oh, that's NOT what he said? Well, screw him then. He's lame anyway. Your nephew, Mark, is getting married today, Boo! I know you will be there with us, somehow. I love you.

Here Comes the Rain Again

It all started with Facebook. I'm going to blame Facebook, because my husband hated Facebook, so he would have been the first one to blame the site for causing this rollercoaster ride of emotions that has been jumbled inside my screwed-up head for the past three days. A few years ago, at my continued request, and because he wanted to reconnect with an old high-school buddy from California, Don joined Facebook. He hated it. He rarely posted anything, and whenever he did, it was something sarcastic like, "Well here is my once a month status update. Can I go now?" He never did find his friend from high-school, but he did reconnect with his nephew, Mark, who he had lost touch with over the years that they both became adults. Mark was now in his thirties and living in Ohio. Connecting with Mark was sort of a big deal, because Don's family was and *is* very strange. It's a weird dynamic. They aren't particularly close, hardly anyone keeps in touch or communicates, and there is a lifetime of severe dysfunction that nobody seems to want to cut through or acknowledge ever. Don was really happy to find Mark on Facebook. I remember him telling me, "He's just a great guy. Always liked him so much. You would love him, Boo. You two should meet, you would love each other." The three of us stayed connected via Facebook, talking and laughing and sharing pictures and comments and exchanges.

And then, one day, out of nowhere, my husband was gone. Dead. Just like that. When I posted the news on Facebook shortly after I found out myself, Mark was the first person from Don's family to contact me. I don't recall what he said on the phone that day, because it's all a blur and always will be, but I do remember that I was instantly comforted by his voice, his presence, his being. The same way I always felt with Don. Safe. Loved.

Over the next few months and as time passed, Mark continued to reach out to me. Beyond the funeral and the first week or so, nobody else in Don's family kept in touch with me or stayed in contact. But Mark did, and it meant everything. I desperately needed something to hold onto, a branch to grab. Something or someone that was somehow connected to Don by blood, because we never got to have kids together, so I didn't have that person to look to and say, "He is sooo much like my husband," or "He really has his eyes." And when you lose your spouse in a split second, *you need to have that connection.* An extension of the one you love – breathing and alive. And there it was, in this incredibly sweet man named Mark. Don's nephew. My nephew. As time went on, I started to feel strongly that Don really wanted me and Mark to connect, and that we were forming a bond by phone and emails, having never met in person, because he planned it somehow, and he wished it. He told me so that day he signed onto Facebook. He told me that I would love his nephew. He was right.

But what my husband couldn't have known is how much knowing Mark would help me. How much Mark would not only be a link to Don for me, but also someone who could *truly understand* what I'm going through. Ironically enough, Mark himself, years earlier, had also lost his love. The same way. He had a sudden heart-attack while they were pumping gas at a gas station. So when we would talk on the phone and he would tell me, "Sweetie, I know that right now it feels like you will never be able to breathe again… I know…" He really *did* know. And he was one of the very lucky ones, because he found love again with another amazing man, and on Valentine's Day 2012, he became engaged to his new fiancé, Russ.

One night a couple months ago, Mark and I were talking on the phone, and he said that "We are family, and Russ and I would love it if you would come to our wedding. I would love to meet you finally." Wedding? But wouldn't that be in Ohio, where you live, I asked? "No honey. Gay marriage isn't legal there. We are coming to New York City. Central Park."

My heart skipped. Or stopped. Or something. Of all the places where they could be getting married, it would be in NYC. Where I am. And of all the places in NYC they could have chosen, they chose Central Park, which was my husband's absolute *favorite* place in all of New York. As a couple, we absolutely loved going there together. We would hang out at the tennis courts and watch people play. We would sit in the bleachers and watch random softball or baseball games. We went to Strawberry Fields. Sat on The Great Lawn and watched a free summer Jazz concert. Ate ice-cream and drank lemonade from the vendors.

Kelley Lynn Shepherd

But our very favorite thing to do in the park was to rent out one of the rowboats on the Great Lake and paddle all around for an hour or two. Don would row me around, and I would sit. It was romantic and sweet and offered the most gorgeous view of the city high-rises from the center of the water. One of my plans, inside my head, has been to row a boat out there soon and scatter some of his ashes in the lake. Except I haven't been able to make myself go back to Central Park at all since he died last year. Until this past weekend. There was a very important wedding I needed to be at, and nothing was going to stop me from meeting this sweet, wonderful man. "Yes!" I told him. "I would love to come to your wedding. There is nowhere I would rather be."

So this weekend, I went to my very first ever gay wedding. I also met my nephew for the first time. And as it turned out, there were many more unexpected "firsts," parallels, memories, flashbacks, and signs along the way. Mark and Russ flew into JFK airport, which is in Queens, New York. Two weeks ago, I lived in New Jersey. Now, I live in Queens, a mere ten minute drive from the airport, meaning I could pick them up. The airport happens to be the exact same airport where I met my husband for the first time ever – back in 2002. Don was wearing a dark blue t-shirt, and he was so tall and huggable. I wanted to hug him forever. "Hi Sweetie," he said. "It's so great to finally meet you."

I stood there at JFK, Friday morning, waiting for my nephew to come through those exact same doors that Don came through all those years ago. And again, there was a long delay. I felt the same kind of nervousness that I had felt meeting Don that day. I waited. I paced. And then suddenly walking toward me, was a very tall, huggable, sweet man. A man in a blue t-shirt. A man that resembled Don. As he got closer, my heart flashed back to hugging Don and never wanting to let go. As Mark gave me a huge, never-ending hug, he said, "Hi Sweetie. It's so great to finally meet you." But this time, I was the only one crying. I couldn't stop. There I was. Hugging Mark. Hugging Don.

Saturday. Wedding Day. The air felt different. Lighter. From the second I woke up, I felt like something was on my side that day. People were being extra nice to me. Saying hello. Holding doors. Going the extra mile. It was as if my husband *knew* how hard and emotional this wedding was going to be for me, and he was doing everything in his power to show me he is here and he is making things a tiny bit easier. I got dressed up and got on the subway to go into the city. About four stops in, a tall man in a blue EMT uniform gets on. He is with a woman who is also an EMT. They work for a New York City hospital, and their uniforms are strikingly similar to the one my husband wore. They sit down across from me. The woman puts on her iPod and listens to music, ignoring the man. The man looks at me gently, as if he somehow understands. I try to look away, but I cannot. I keep running my fingers over the green heart necklace my husband bought me. I feel safe. A few stops later, they get up to exit the subway. As he is leaving, he looks into my face and nobody else's and says simply, "It will be a good day." He winks at me and at nobody else, smiles, and leaves the subway car.

I meet Mark, Russ, Mark's very sweet sister Cathy, and about seven other incredibly warm and friendly friends and family members of the groom and groom at their hotel, and we all walk over to the park to catch up with the officiant who will perform the wedding ceremony. It is gorgeous outside. A bit warm. Near 80 degrees, which is warm for the first day of fall. There were warnings on the news of afternoon showers, but the skies were sunny and nice. As the officiant walks us all over to the area outside where the ceremony will be, I notice we are getting closer and closer to the Great Lake. I start to see all the happy couples in love, rowing their boats in the lake where Don and I rowed every single fall for years. We literally stop at the exact spot where we used to rent out the boats, and there is a pavilion there, where the intimate and beautiful ceremony is being held. Of all the many, many places inside of this ginormous park, the ceremony will be held right at this lake. Our spot. Our favorite spot. Don is here.

My heart is beating outside my chest. As the officiant begins speaking his words to start the ceremony, I listen intently. Then I don't. It's too much. At one point, he says something about how life's moments are so much more meaningful when you can share them with the one you love. I feel myself shaking. It takes everything inside me not to cry right there. I try to breathe through it, and I hear Don's voice in my head. He says, "Look at the lake, Boo. Think about us rowing around in the lake and laughing. I love you." I watch Mark's face, and the smile in his eyes is the same as Don's was on our wedding day. The love in the air and inside everyone witnessing this union is so big. It is so big, I feel as if my heart will explode. I focus on Don's voice. "I'm right here," he says. "Look at our lake. You can do this."

After the ceremony and pictures and things, I am very close to breaking down. The emotions are just too much, but I'm trying to hold it together. Mark notices this and comes up to me, asking if I'm okay. I say yes, but I mean no. He gives me a long hug and says in the most calming voice as I cry into his shoulder, "He is with us. He is here right now, and he is with you always. Always. Don't you ever forget that." So many people have said things like that to me that were very similar, but in that moment, from *that* person, on that day – it was comforting, and I needed to hear it.

The rest of the day was spent walking up Fifth Avenue and seeing the popular sites of the city – Tiffanys, St. Patrick's Cathedral, Radio City. Since I live here, it just sort of naturally happened that I was kind of "leading" everyone around as we walked. They followed me, so I led. And as I walked up Fifth

My Husband is Not a Rainbow

Avenue, pointing out all the different stores and places of interest, I suddenly recalled holding hands with Don and walking up Fifth Avenue that first day that we met and I picked him up at the airport. After making him lunch at my apartment, we went into the city all day long and did the same touristy walk I was now doing with his family. There is no weirder feeling in the world than being with your husband's family members in the absence of your dead husband. It is bizarre and heartbreaking on so many levels, and sometimes, while being with them this weekend, it would hit me over the head without warning. The unfairness of it all. Why couldn't we make time to get to know these people when he was still alive? Why does he have to be dead in order for this to occur?

Later that evening, we had dinner at The Russian Tea Room. It was there that Don decided to say hello again and sort of remind me that he is still "around." As we walked into the restaurant and were being seated, one of the servers recognized me and called out my name. Her name was Janine, and we were both Theatre Majors together in college, but she left after the first year. We got to talking, and she asked me, out of nowhere, if I am a paramedic. "No, but my husband was." "Oh, well I saw you and your husband a couple years ago walking in West New York. He was in his uniform and you were holding hands." Turns out, she lives in West New York, the very small town in New Jersey that I *just* left two weeks ago, after living there for seven years with Don, and twelve years total. The fact that I ran into this girl in the first place, that she lives where we lived for years, and that she SAW us two years ago walking together was all a bit too much for coincidence. I thought about the EMT on the subway, and how he winked at me and smiled and said what he said. I don't know what was going on here, but it felt like one overlapping hug from the universe.

The gang from Ohio wanted to see Times Square all lit up at night. So we walked towards it and then through it. It was a beautiful day that had turned into a beautiful night. Slight breeze. Clear sky. As I walked along with Mark, he said suddenly, "Oh, I just felt a raindrop." I replied that I had been getting signs from Don all day, but if it started pouring on us right now in the middle of Times Square, that would be a downright guarantee that he is *right here with us*. Why? Because on October 27, 2006, our wedding day, the weather was beautiful and clear. No rain. Gorgeous. Our reception ended around eleven PM at night. I will never forget leaving The San Souci in Sea Cliff and walking to our own car to drive ourselves to the hotel. We thought a limousine was a dumb thing to waste money on, so we drove our own damn selves to our hotel, him still in his tux and me in my wedding gown. As we were walking out to the car, suddenly there was a roar of thunder. Loud. Seconds later, lightning. And then, the sky opened up in a fierce way, and the biggest torrential downpour you could imagine came out of nowhere. Fast. Don and I laughed hard as we got completely soaked, and it continued raining and storming like that overnight and into the next morning. Our wedding day was beautiful. Our wedding *night* was a monsoon.

Walking through Times Square, Mark and I looked at each other knowingly as a loud rumble of thunder came from the sky's voice. Then, the most amazing and wonderful pouring, driving rain fell from above. We all huddled and stood underneath one of the many marquees in the city. "I can't believe this," I said to Mark, laughing. "It's JUST like our wedding night. And now he's sending you one on your wedding night too. We are all together. This is amazing. He sent us a monster rainstorm." "He sure did," said Mark as we both looked up into the night sky.

As I said my goodbyes to everyone, I felt the rush of tears coming. I wouldn't be able to hold back much longer. Yes, I had cried and broken down a couple times during the day of emotional events for me, but I was always keeping it at bay. Crying was one thing, but the last thing I wanted to do was ruin

My Husband is Not a Rainbow

Mark's wedding day by turning it into a sob-fest funeral. So I tried like hell to control myself, keep it together. But now was my time. I saved my last big hug for Mark, because I knew it would start the emotional wave for me. And as I walked away from the group, letting the rain fall onto my clothes and skin and face and not caring one single bit, I heard Mark call out from a block or two away, really loudly and sweetly, "I love you!"

I love you. He said "I love you." I stopped in my tracks in the middle of Times Square. In the middle of New York City. In the middle of the pouring down rain. My heart was instantly transported back to the end of that first week I had finally met Don in person. We were back at the airport, and it was time for him to go back to Florida. At that point in our relationship, our long-distance "something" was strong enough for me, but Don had not yet quite figured out his feelings for me, because we hadn't met yet. I knew I was in love with him before meeting him, but it was never said out loud. Not yet. But on that day, at the end of our amazing week together in New York City, we held each other and cried. I will never forget letting him go and letting him get on that plane, and how I wanted to stay like that, holding him, forever. And as he started to walk away from me, and I was just out of reach, he said those three powerful, incredible words. For the first time. "I love you."

And for the first time all weekend, I walked in that pouring rain, and I let each drop of water mix in with my tears. The rain and I cried together. We laughed and we cried. We cried hard, and we didn't stop. Walking and crying. It just kept coming. Endless buckets. From the sky, from my eyes, from the deepest part of inside my heart.

Cried my soul out in the middle of Times Square. It was New York City. Nobody cared. But Don knew. He knew it all. He was there. It was a good day.

Kelley Lynn Shepherd

*"It's not one huge step that promotes healing.
It's many intentional single small steps."
– Susan Hannifin-MacNab*

Session Snippet

Me: I'm not ready for Christmas again this year. I'm still not ready. I thought I might be, but I'm not. I don't think I can go home to my family and do it. It's too hard.

Caitlin: Honey, why are you even thinking about this right now? It's barely October.

Me: I don't know. I just feel like I'm failing at everything. Like I should be over this by now.

Caitlin: Over what? There is no "over this." You know that. You've said that to me. We will walk through your grief together, but there is no "over" anything. You're progressing just fine.

Me: I love Christmas too much to hate it for the rest of my life because my husband died. So I need to run away from it, so that when I go back to it, I don't resent it and hate it and feel angry about it.

Caitlin: Then that is what you will do. Maybe stay in New York City this year, do something with friends that's non-Christmasy. We'll figure it out. How is your new place? Do you feel different since being back in Forest Hills?

Me: Yeah. No. I guess. Everything still sucks. I thought maybe I would miss him less or something, but I don't. I almost miss him more now, because I'm not being suffocated by "things." His stuff. So now I guess it's less panic attacks and traumatizing stuff, like I don't have to drive by that damn hospital anymore. But I just miss him, and I want him to be my roommate instead of my roommate being my roommate.

Caitlin: That makes complete sense. Do you feel resentment toward your roommate?

Me: Sometimes. But it's not really about him. It's more about having resentment that I have to have a roommate in the first place. Like, here's this guy that took me and my two kitties into his apartment, and it feels like I'm some charity case, like I can't do anything on my own anymore, after my whole life of doing everything on my own.

Caitlin: That must be very difficult. Do you find that people treat you like a child in a way? Like you can't make decisions?

Me: Yes. Like, because my husband died, I'm suddenly some idiot who isn't capable of knowing basic things about life. It's like everyone forgets that I've been on my own since I was eighteen years old, and I've been a career person and a wife, and generally, just a very well-rounded, self-sufficient, independent person.

Caitlin: And now?

Me: Now, I feel like I'm a burden.

Caitlin: I can see how you could feel that.

Me: People invite me over out of pity. People want to include me in things because I'm alone. My roommate took me in because I'm in a bad way. I just feel like such a burden, and I'm not anyone's priority anymore. That is the saddest fucking thing. (crying) I just feel like I should feel better after moving, and I'm just so damn sad, and I miss him so much, and I miss being someone's priority, instead of a burden and an afterthought. When is this pain ever going to go away? When?

Caitlin: I don't have an answer for that. I'm sorry. I wish I did.

(Long, uncomfortable silence.)

Caitlin: Are you going to be okay to go back home? I don't want you leaving here until you feel okay enough to go.

Me: I'll be okay. Thanks.

Caitlin: Keep going, Kelley. The pain will get less harsh. I just can't tell you when. But it will, because you're doing the hard work to make sure of it. I promise.

Until Forever

I question everything. I'm suspicious by nature, and even after feeling my husband come to me several times in the fifteen months since his death, both while awake and while asleep, I *still* try and justify it or try to reason with it and make logical sense of it. I still feel like someone is pulling the wool over my eyes each and every time it happens. But my husband, in his typical way, refuses to give up on me. He keeps coming back, and there is nothing more powerful or emotional than receiving just a few moments in time with the one that you lost. To feel them, to hear them, to touch them again – it is like nothing else in the world. It is magic.

Last night was magic. It started as a laugh. I heard him laugh, just as if he were sitting here beside me. Then he said words to me, and suddenly I was typing to my friend, John, what *my husband* wanted me to say. I was like his secretary. It was bizarre. They were his words, and I was typing them. And I saw and felt him standing behind me, looking over my shoulder as I typed and laughing his big laugh, just like he always used to do in real life.

I was on Facebook late at night, bored and goofing around. A funny status update I had posted about people who always threaten to leave the country if so-and-so becomes President had somehow turned into a free-for-all random discussion between a few of us that were up late and dazed. John and I were talking about the playoffs, and he typed something about how the Orioles would win against the Yankees and then win the World Series. Just then, in that instant, I heard Don's laugh. It was more of a cackle really. It was him laughing at his friend, John, for saying such a thing, and just like that, his energy was in the room with me. It was strong. He wanted to be there to bust on John, our Mets fan friend who hates the Yankees, just like old times.

After he laughed, I heard him say to me, "The Orioles? Oh please! Make him feel bad, Boo. Ask him how he can root against his dead friend's favorite team and still sleep at night." I laughed out loud as I typed my husband's sick and twisted humor into the Facebook thread. He was here, stronger than ever now, and he kept laughing and cheering me on during this entire exchange:

John: O's will win the World Series.
Kelley Lynn: You know, Johnycakes, the least you could do is root for your dead friend's favorite team. Yup. I went there.
John: That's cold blooded.
Kelley Lynn: No, what's cold-blooded is you rooting for the Orioles over the Yankees – your friend's beloved team. Your friend who is dead. lol.
John: Hard to turn off 35 years of Yankee dislike.

Kelley Lynn Shepherd

Kelley Lynn: I heard Don laughing in my head, telling me to make you feel guilty and mess with you lol.
Kelley Lynn: Is it hard to turn off Yankee dislike? It's hard when your husband randomly dies too. (Sniff sniff...)
Kelley Lynn: You have no soul, Cina.
John: I'm all soul, baby.
John: He's still laughing at me. And it still hurts.

I went to bed last night with a pounding headache. And, like often happens, I had trouble falling asleep. Thinking about Don. Missing him deeply. Questioning the validity of just feeling his presence earlier in the evening. Filling my head up with endless thoughts about life and death and love. At some point, I did fall asleep, and Don came back to me again in my sleep. Some would call it a dream. Some would say it's more than that. I will never know for sure how to define these things, I can only tell you what I felt and what happened. This is the dream that transpired:

I'm feeling lonely and alone, which are two separate things, so I decide to go see a movie and get out of the apartment for a while. I walk down the streets of my new neighborhood in Forest Hills to the theatre. It is fall. It is crisp. The air and the avenues are filled with life and energy and couples walking hand in hand. They are happy and laughing and oblivious that it could all be taken away for no reason. I want to murder each and every one of them. There are people everywhere. All around me.

I walk up to the ticket booth and say, "One ticket, please, for a movie." I actually say that in the dream. *One ticket, please, for a movie.* No idea what movie I'm about to see in my land of slumber. I guess it's not important. Suddenly, to the right of me, there is a voice. It is my husband. He pulls out his wallet and says to the ticket guy, "Make that two tickets for a movie. Can I sit with you, Boo?"

My Husband is Not a Rainbow

I don't answer. I just stare at his face. I look into his deep blue eyes that I fell in love with all those years ago, and I swim in them. I marinate in them, trying to memorize their shape and their beauty. I'm aware that I'm dreaming, and that it won't last forever, so I try to slow it down. I want to stop time and just stand there with him in that cold, crisp autumn air that we both loved so much. Finally, after five minutes or an hour, I speak. "Is it really you?" My eyes are already tearing up, and he just got here. "It's really me, Boo. It's been a while since we've had a date night. Just you and me. Come on. Let's go inside and watch the movie."

He takes my hand, and I sigh as his familiar, strong finger tips interlock with mine. We float hand in hand into the theatre. All of the people, the crowds, the couples that were there when I arrived – are gone. Nobody is inside this movie. It is just us, and it is mesmerizing. It's a miracle. We sit down toward the back of the theatre, and he hands me some popcorn that appears out of thin air. A large beverage sits in the cup holder, waiting. Neither of us looks at the movie screen. We are fixated on each other and on this time we have together.

I start spilling out anything and everything to him. I feel like he has been gone for nine hundred years, and there are so many things to say. I can't choose, so I say it all, "I moved out of our apartment, Boo. I left New Jersey, and I'm in New York, and it's so nice, and I should be happy, but I don't know how to be without you. Everything I do now is without you here on earth, and I don't know how to give any of it meaning anymore. I feel like I'm pretending when I'm with people and lonely as hell when I'm not with people. Everything in between feels like a migraine. I'm so tired."

"I know, Boo. You're doing so well. I'm so proud of you. It kills me to see you in this kind of pain, but it also means you are processing things. You're not running away from any of it. You are getting through this. One awful second at a time." His eyes are tearing up. Mine are crying buckets.

"Why are we at a movie theatre?" I ask him. "And where did all the people go that were outside?"

"Because you came to this theatre the other night by yourself, and it made you sad, so I wanted to replace that memory with this one. So now, when you come back to the movies alone, you can think about this night instead of that night, okay?" He puts his arm around me and scratches my back like he used to do. "Scratch, scratch, scratch," he says in his silly voice as his hand moves up and down my back. I can't stop staring at him.

"But this isn't a memory. It's just a dream. None of it is real, right?"

"Does it feel like it's real?"

"Yes. You feel real right now, and my heart is pounding, and I love you."

"Then it's real. Popcorn?" He pops giant handfuls of popcorn into his mouth and eats them way too fast, just like he used to do at home.

"Slow down, Boo. You'll choke, and I won't know how to save you." I used to always say this to him, but it made much more sense when he was alive.

"I'm dead, Boo." He gives me his best deadpan, smart-ass reply. "Choking is no longer an issue." He hands me the drink, and I sip it. Root beer. His favorite.

"So can I ask you stuff? What's it like where you are now? Are you energy? Are you an Angel? What happens to us? Do you

My Husband is Not a Rainbow

miss me?" I start crying again. I don't ever want to let go or leave this movie theatre with the non-movie or leave this dream or this vision or this *thing* that is happening.

He holds me tight. "If I told you any of that stuff, I'd have to kill you." He cackles at his own joke.

I'm still crying. I pick up the popcorn tub and throw it on the floor like a child. "It's not funny!" I yell at him for the first time ever, and my tears won't stop now. "None of this is funny to me. You don't have to be down here and suffer this pain and this agony and this fear. You don't have to walk around with a huge chunk of your soul missing. You don't have to face the rest of your life and sickness and old age and other people you love dying – without the person you were supposed to be with forever! You get to be a spirit and dance on clouds and make cameo appearances and fly around the atmosphere like fuckin' Tinkerbell, while I have to sit here and be madly in love with a dead guy who I can only feel for a few seconds in my dreams. It's not fucking funny, and I wish you *would* kill me, because that would mean this pain would finally end, and I could just be with you all the time forever. I hate you."

I am sobbing into his Yankees t-shirt now. Hyperventilating. He holds onto me tight until I can breathe again. He looks into my eyes. He says these next words with extreme importance. He isn't laughing anymore. "This is why we are in the theatre alone, Boo. So you can breakdown in private. It's just you and me. Outside these doors, the people and the happy couples and holidays and love and life are all there. They are all there waiting. Someday, Boo, you will want to be there too. Right now, you are living, but someday, you will *want* to live again. I promise. I would never lie to you. I love you. Go at your own pace. Take all the time you need. I will be here for as long as you need. I am dead, but I am not gone. Our love is never gone. You need to carry me with you everywhere you go. Trust that it's real. Believe it, and I will be there with you. I know it's not the same, and I know it sucks, but it *is* real. Don't ever let go, Boo. Remember what we wrote in our vows?"

"Until forever."

"That's right. Not *'til death do us part.* Until forever. And that is how long I'll be with you. When my heart stopped, it traveled into yours, Boo. My heart is your heart. Your heart is mine. Until forever."

There is a pause. "How come you were never this romantic when you were alive? Suddenly you're Robert Frost now. Holy Shit!" I'm laughing again, and so is he. "Not romantic? What are you talkin' about? I uprooted my entire life to that goddamn shit-hole New Jersey so I could be with you. That's romantic." He shakes his head and smiles.

"Movie's over, Boo." He starts to get up and takes my hand to help me up too. "What movie?" I say sarcastically. "We didn't see anything!"

"Sure we did. We saw a lot. It just wasn't on the movie screen. It was real."

We walk hand in hand outside of the movie theatre and into the large hallway. We stand underneath a sign that reads, in big red letters, EXIT. This is the end of our date. Our time. Our dream. Our whatever. It's time to go now, or time to wake up, and as usual, I am dreading that moment when I am forced to return to the harsh reality of him being gone.

He reads my heart and he says, "Stop thinking about it, Boo. You're going to wake up and start questioning and doubting everything all over again. Just stop. Believe. Trust me. Our time on earth together is done, but our *relationship* is never over. Not ever. It's just different. You always used to say that marriage is like a secret. The greatest secret between two people that nobody else will ever truly know about. Well, now we have a new secret. You and me. Now we have this. I'm not going to say goodbye, because it's not goodbye. It's until next time. Until forever."

He gives me a kiss that I feel in my toes. I would give up everything to feel it again. He starts to slowly walk away. Once he is a good distance from me, he turns around and yells out, "By the way, tell Johnycakes that if I ever catch him at Camden Yards waving around one of those stupid orange rags and rootin' for the damn Orioles, there's gonna be some serious Hell to pay. Ass-hat." I laugh out loud hearing him use one of his favorite insult terms again. Asshat.

I don't remember this dream ending. I don't know how it ended, and maybe that's how it was designed. No ending. No end. Just me standing underneath that EXIT sign. Not yet ready to *want* to live life again.

Not ready to face the people. Not wanting to go outside. Just staying right there. In that place. In that hallway. In that dream that wasn't a dream. Just taking in the profound words that my beautiful, dead husband said to me and letting them sink in. Letting the magic seep into my bones. Like when you see a really good movie with someone. One of those films that make you think and feel. Make you wonder. So you just stay there and watch the credits roll – and you revel in the tiny miracle that just occurred on that big screen in front of you. Was it art? A dream? An escape? Or was it real?

Who cares? Let's just stay here and be perfectly still, so we can remain inside of our secret for just a little bit longer.

Kelley Lynn Shepherd

"I will not let your death steal our forever love." – Jason Miran

Words About Don

"I met Don when I got hired at Hackensack Medical Center as a critical care transport nurse. Don was assigned to the unit. For two years, I spent a good chunk of my waking hours with him. To me, the highest opinion we can hold of each other, as providers, is when we look at someone we work with and think 'I would let them take care of my family.' Don lived up to that standard everyday.

As a person, Don loved to laugh. He had a great laugh. He loved 'South Park' and Mel Brooks. He found the humor in the job. He laughed at me. A lot. Oh god, did he laugh at me. He laughed at himself the most though. I feel like everyone who never got a chance to meet and know Don has been cheated. And my heart breaks for Kelley and for his family. I can never thank them enough for sharing Don with all of us. " - Meg Chandler

Please Don't Choke on That Popcorn
(at the movies together, sometime in 2005)

Me: Thanks for coming to the movies with me, Boo. I know you hate going.

Don: I don't hate it, Boo. There's just other things I like better. But I love you bestest.

Me: Aww. That's why you live in New Jersey now!

My Husband is Not a Rainbow

Don: Yeah. For eight months and seventeen days now. Not that I'm counting or anything.

Me: Very funny. Hey, the good news is that it's only about twenty five more years until we can retire and move to Florida, like you want!

Don: Yes!!! I can't wait! (starts coughing while eating popcorn)

Me: Boo, please don't choke on that popcorn. I wouldn't know what to do or how to save you. And then you would die, and I would be sad.

Don: I'm fine, Boo. Nobody's going to die.

Me: Yes they are. Everyone is going to die. All of us.

Don: Well, nobody's going to die right now, here, in this movie theater

Me: What if I died, Boo? What would you do?

Don: (laughing) I don't know. What the hell kind of question is that?

Me: What if I didn't die, but what if I choked on these Corn Nuts right now that I'm eating? And I lost my vocal chords, and I had one of those creepy voice-box things for the rest of my life. Would you leave me?

Don: No, Boo. I wouldn't leave you. But it's irrelevant anyway, because it would never happen. If you started choking, I'd be here, and I'd stop you from choking and save your life, like that time I almost had to at your parents' house with the potato salad. I'm trained in all that, Boo. You'd be safe with me. That being said, how the hell do you eat those Corn Nuts anyway? They're like little rocks covered in BBQ flavoring. Your teeth will fall out eating those things.

Me: What if all my teeth fell out, and I had no teeth. Would you still stay with me?

Don: Yes, Boo. But hopefully you'd get some dentures or something, right? You wouldn't just be a toothless thirty four year old woman. That would be weird. Where do you come up with these questions?

Me: But you'd stay with me, right? Even if I was toothless…

Don: Yes, dear. Are these previews ever gonna start, so this insane conversation I'm stuck in can be over?

Me: We still have about ten minutes before the movie starts, Boo. We're early.

Don: Fantastic. Is it too late for me to change my mind about this whole 'sharing a life together' thing? Where's that Penske truck? I need a ride back to Florida (shaking his head at me).

Me: See? You *would* leave me! I knew it!

Don: I won't ever leave you, Boo. Not ever. You really think I'd move my entire life up here to freakin' Jersey, if I wasn't a hundred percent sure about us and about you? Please stop worrying about me leaving you. It won't happen. I know other guys have done that to you in the past - but I'm not them. I would never do that to you. I love you. Now the previews are starting. Finally!!! Can we table this riveting discussion of possible ridiculous scenarios for me leaving you for another inconvenient time?

Me: Of course! Thanks for putting up with my crazy.

Don: (shakes head and laughs at me, kisses me on forehead)

"Out of 7 billion people on this planet,
The one single person I need,
Left." – Nanette Bergerac Koomen

Dear Dead Husband:

Today would have been our sixth year wedding anniversary. Instead, it is my second one without you. There are no words to describe the hollowness I feel without you here. This was our day, and I never know what to do with it, because it all feels just so sad to me. We celebrated you the best we could today. We have amazing friends, Boo - but you already knew that. I love you so much. Forever your wife, me xoxoxo

FB Post: Holy Shit I miss my husband. Sometimes I feel like I'm going crazy. Why is it that every single time it feels like it MIGHT be getting a tiny bit easier for 15 seconds - it immediately gets way harder again? The past few days have been soooo freakin' tough, with Hurricane Sandy, and just feeling so alone. Just want to scream, but I'm too tired. I want my best friend back. He would hold me and laugh with me and stay up late and let me annoy him and make everything okay again. I feel like nothing will ever be okay again. Fuck you, Death.
LIKES: 5   COMMENTS: 11

Kelley Lynn Shepherd

Dust In the Wind

The past few days have been an emotional, upside-down, tipsy-turvy rollercoaster of events, all with the strange and unexpected theme of sand. Dirt. Earth. Dust.

It all began with my Wedding Anniversary. Six years. Well ... *would have been* six years. According to the official Widow Book of Etiquette and Proper Behavior, I'm supposed to talk in past-tense now because my husband is dead, right? Well, excuse me if I forgot. Of course, I didn't forget that he's dead. I *never* forget that, not even for one second. What I do forget though, is that I am no longer married. That I'm no longer his wife. That hurts to say. Hurts to type. Breaks me in half sometimes. *I'm not married.* I certainly feel married. Maybe I always will. Nobody left anybody else. No divorce. No break-up. None of that. Just lots and lots of love. And then, of course, sudden death.

Strange thing about getting married, when you are making wedding plans and you choose your venue, you never really think that only five years later, you'll be standing across the street from that venue by the water, holding pieces of your husband's remains in a green tupperware cup. You never think you'll be making plans to take turns tossing him into the sea with your friends. You never ask yourself, "Hey! I wonder if this would be a good place to scatter his ashes sometime soon!" None of those things ever really cross your mind while in the ecstatic whirlwind chaos that is blissful engagement and wedding planning.

As it turns out, Sea Cliff, New York is the perfect place to scatter your husband's ashes. It is beautiful, charming, subtle, and peaceful. It's a quiet little town on Long Island that somehow doesn't feel like Long Island. It has character. It has love. And now, it has Don.

My Husband is Not a Rainbow

Last October, on my first Wedding Anniversary since his death, on October twenty seventh, we came to Sea Cliff together, and tossed some of Don into the sea. Me, John, Jessica, and Sarah. Good friends. The best. We were all scared. Nervous. Unsure. Rookies. It was only three months after his death, and none of us had any sort of experience with scattering ashes. The only time I had ever even seen the topic of ashes or remains depicted, was on TV shows or in movies. Well, let me tell you something: *It is NOTHING AT ALL like in the movies.*

This weekend, we went back. Saturday, October twenty seventh. Back to the water. Back with more ashes. Back to the sandy beach to put some dirt inside the sand. A slightly revised crew this time. John, Andrew, Vanessa, and me. Good friends. The best. This time, it was less about the scattering of ashes, and more about returning to the place where Don and I spent the happiest day of our lives. Across the street from our wedding venue, in the sand, on the day we married just six years before, we stood. We laughed. We talked. Remembered. This time, there was no tupperware cup or spoon or group-tossing Olympic event. This time, I brought a little bit of Don with me, inside my purse, in a tiny sandwich Ziploc bag. Only the best for my husband.

For some reason, I began to feel weird about emptying the ashes I brought into the sea. I don't know why. It just felt so blah. Or maybe we were all having a nice time, and I knew if I went *there* to that place in my heart, that I couldn't recover, and I might be sobbing the rest of the afternoon. "I don't want to," I hesitated. Andrew gently insisted, "You brought the ashes for a reason. You should do it. Go do it. We will wait up here for you. If you don't do it, you'll wish you did." He had a point. So with that, I walked down to edge, where the sand meets the water. I opened up the baggie and slowly let the ashes touch the sand and blow into the sea. The dust started dancing in the wind. The water from my tears merged with the sea water, the ashes from Don merged with the beach sand. It was poetic. It was lovely. It was terrible.

The tide turned, as I knew it would. My heart shifted, and suddenly I was sadder than I remember being in a while. I walked back up to my friends. "Are you okay?" John asked. No. He continued, "This was nice though. He would approve of this. He would like this." I started to question everything while crying. "I don't know *what* he would have liked! I woke up, and he was dead. We never talked about burials or cremation or *anything* like that." I started to feel dizzy. "But he chose *you*, and he trusted you, so whatever you decided to do was the right decision, and he would love it," Vanessa offered. We began walking back up to my car to drive over and meet the others at the restaurant for lunch. Everyone was hungry, but my mood had altered, as it often does with grief. I felt lost. Hopeless. Defeated. I wanted to go home and sleep forever.

And that is when we saw it. The sign. The evidence that he was with us, that he was trying to say, "Lighten up guys!" He was trying to make me laugh at the exact moment that I *absolutely had to laugh*. It was big as day. There were lots of other cars in the parking lot, but this was directly behind my car and nobody else's. "You gotta be kidding me!" said Andrew as he cracked up laughing. "Was that there when we got here?" we all questioned. I don't think it was. Either way, it was there now, and it was large and pointless and dumb. And it made us laugh like hell. Don was sending us a very important message through graffiti, and the message was simply this: BALLZ.

Ballz. Spelled with a "z" for extra comedy purposes. After that, the rest of the day was light and fun and wonderful. We met up with Rodney and Sheri and Sarah at the same restaurant as the year before, we ate delicious food, and we shared stories and memories about the guy we all loved. Our friend. We talked about signs and death and life, and it was just like old times. Together with my friends, keeping my husband alive.

Sunday, October twenty eighth. I drove to the funeral services of Eva Kotovnikov, the beautiful mother of my dear friend, Marina. She had suffered from the horrible disease ALS, and departed this earth much too young. The funeral was in Hartford, Connecticut, a two hour drive from where I live in New York. It was the very first funeral I attended since my own husband's. My incredible friends, Marina, and Dave, her husband, had been there for me since the first hour that I lost Don. It was time to put my own pain aside and be there for them. It was not something I even decided to do. I just sort of got in my car and started driving.

Since Marina's family is both Jewish and Russian, the services were too. When I arrived for the memorial service, the main room was already full, as if I were attending a service for Whitney Houston or some other big-time celebrity. There was a second room with a large TV-screen, where I was seated with at least a hundred others. We all looked up at the big screen. Many people were crying. The Rabbi was saying words in Hebrew. Sometimes in Russian. I had no idea what was going on, what was being said, but I felt love. I felt that the Rabbi perhaps knew Eva personally and was genuine in his speech and his emotion for her. He introduced Marina by saying, "And now, I'd like to introduce Eva's daughter, Marina, who would like to say a few words." There was a pause. Marina slowly made her way up front, took out a piece of paper, and said, "Good Morning. I would like to say a few words." It struck me as funny, the way she echoed what he just said seconds before. Her comic timing, even at her own mother's funeral, was perfect. In reality, it probably wasn't all that funny. But when something is so awful and so traumatic that you can't process it happening, it then becomes funny. So I suppressed my laughter and listened and watched my friend as she honored her mother. I thought about how many people would come up to her afterwards and tell her how brave she was for speaking at the service. That is what they all said to me after I wrote and delivered the Eulogy for my husband. And maybe she would tell them what I told them then – that it wasn't a choice. It wasn't a decision I made. I did it because I had to. I had to honor my husband. He deserved that, and everyone needed to know how amazing he was. Marina had to honor her mother, and she did it beautifully. And as I left there and got in my car to follow the processional to the cemetery, I began to flashback to my husband's funeral. I told myself to breathe. It will be okay. This isn't about you. Stop thinking about Don. Focus. Just breathe.

The burial ceremony was like nothing I had ever witnessed before in my life. Family and friends gathered around the plot where Eva would be buried. In the center, the Rabbi was there, and again he read words and verses in Hebrew and Russian, and he performed chant-like phrases in a sing-song manner, and again I didn't understand any of it, but I felt love.

Then, the cemetery workers, right there in front of everyone, went to task lowering the casket into the ground. I stood next to my friend, trying to comfort her, feeling helpless, trying to breathe. Dave came over and put his arm around me, and we stood together. As Eva started to disappear from view, I whispered to him, "How are your kids doing?" "Much better than me," he said with tears in his eyes. Me too, I thought to myself.

Once the casket was lowered, the Rabbi asked anyone who wanted to participate to form a line. And with that, everyone around me started to move toward the giant pile of dirt next to the hole in the ground. A huge pile of dirt was there, and shovels stuck out of it on all sides. Together, like a community, one by one, the people picked up a shovel, scooped up some dirt, and tossed it into the grave. I was mesmerized. I was terrified. I was shaking. It was beautiful. It was insane. It was horrifying. It was love. And for the third time that day, I had no idea what was going on, but I suddenly understood.

I have no idea why, but it reminded me of that last scene in *How The Grinch Stole Christmas,* where all the "Whos down in Who-Ville" hold hands and begin to sing. Amidst the horror and sadness of their holiday being taken away from them, their response is to sing these ridiculous, beautiful words that make absolutely no sense. And that is what these people did. They took their shovels and their love and their respect and their tears and their grief – and they tossed it into the ground. So many people participated in this bizarre ritual. Almost everyone. Toward the end, when the casket was almost all the way covered, a few good men were left shoveling furiously, until the loving act of kindness was finished. Until the body met with the dust.

Body. Dirt. Dust. Soul.

I couldn't hold back anymore. I finally lost it. I started to cry, and I couldn't stop. I was crying for Marina losing her mother. For her kids losing their grandmother. For Dave losing his mother-in-law and having to see his own wife go through this kind of pain. I cried for the little kiss that Dave gave his wife on her forehead to comfort her. Cried for Marina's dad, Felix, who just lost his wife, his soul mate, his best friend. Cried because someone as young as me shouldn't have to know what it's like to lose a spouse and be having the urge to comfort someone who is older than me, but still too young to lose a spouse. Cried for myself, because one day, I will lose my mom, and nobody will be there to kiss my forehead and help me through it. Cried for the life inside that casket. For the image that sits in my heart of my own husband lying in a similar casket. Cried for the hours and days and weeks and months of grief that my dear friend is about to endure. Cried because death is so final, and life so fragile. I left that cemetery, and I cried almost half the way home.

Monday, October twenty ninth. Hurricane Sandy. The worst weather-related thing to happen to New York and New Jersey ever. The storm that brought frightening, hissing winds. Pounding rain. Flooding waters. Horrific surges. Land met water. Waves invaded land. Water took people, and homes, and lives. Sandy blew sand through my window sideways. Chairs flew across the street. A stop sign smashed through a car roof. Beaches disappeared. The Jersey Shore half gone. The Rockaways, Howard Beach, and Long Branch – decimated. Five million people left without power. Or heat. In the cold. Darkness. Afraid. Clinging to rafts. Rescued by boats. Grabbing their pets and pictures. Leaving their dreams and their shops and their homes behind. Earth met water. Water destroyed. Buildings turned to dust. Sand. Dirt. Wind. Like John Travolta once said: Oh Sandy…

And somehow, in all that madness and flying debris, my little corner of the neighborhood stayed perfectly safe. My roommate, my kitties, and me – we were okay. The wind was louder than hell and made my heart skip. The crackling sounds and the popping noises of transformers blowing up in the Manhattan sky gave me panic. Being twenty one floors up and watching sand and dirt fly across my window brought me anxiety. But in the end, I was spared. I was okay. I got lucky. After speaking with some people on the other side of the Hudson River, I learned that my old neighborhood in New Jersey was flooded. Roads were down. The basement of my old building filled with water when a pipe burst inside. I could have been there. Scared and alone in that dusty old apartment. But I wasn't. I moved out two months ago, because my dead husband kept insisting that I leave New Jersey and move back to New York.

My Husband is Not a Rainbow

It might sound silly, but I feel like he protected me from harm. I don't pretend to know how these things work, and I certainly don't think I'm somehow special. I don't have a clue. I just know what I feel. I just know that while everything around me was falling apart and coming undone – I felt calm. I was safe. I felt like my husband's arms were wrapped around me tightly, and he was saying, "Shhh! It's okay. Don't worry, Boo. I got your back." I know that while towns and neighborhoods just two or five miles away from us are completely underwater, we didn't even lose our power. I know that I got out of New Jersey just in time. And I know that last year, just a month after he died, I went through Hurricane Irene all alone. Frightened. Hopeless. That night, I sat in our awful, uncomfortable, old bed and sobbed loudly as a giant leak dripped into a large bucket. I heard the endless ambulance sirens going by into the night, and I was terrified. Tortured by the sounds of the trucks he worked on everyday as an EMT – the trucks that couldn't save him. That sound gave me stomach pains and made me want to die. I thought, "How am I ever going to get out of here? I can't live like this. Please help me, Boo."

Monday night, when Hurricane Sandy gave us her most ferocious, there were several devastating house fires just miles away from our apartment in the sky. There were many hospital evacuations nearby, due to massive amounts of flooding. I cuddled with our kitties and told them not to be scared – that poppa is looking out for us. I heard the endless ambulances that were circling the area, nonstop, for hours. The sirens got louder and louder as they continued to go to their destinations and save people. And for the first time in fifteen months, the sirens didn't make me feel awful. They didn't make me nauseous. For the first time in a very long time, the ambulances didn't sound like torture or death or massive anxiety. They sounded like a lullaby.

FB Post: Day 9 after Storm. First day back teaching. Long Island is a mess. Still NO gas stations. Passed 6 of them, all closed except one on Grand Central, line was 3 miles down highway. Most of my fellow co-workers/professors still don't have power or heat. Lots of students not coming to class. No car/gas. One student texted me that his house is gone. It's crazy out there.
LIKES: 78   COMMENTS: 34

FB Posts: Obama wins. I should be happy. But what is happiness when you have nobody to share it with? My husband is not here to hug or to celebrate, nor was he here to vote with, as we did in the last election, and so, I'm going to bed. I guess I'll attempt this life thing again tomorrow. Tonight, I'm done.
LIKES: 51   COMMENTS: 28

"Helping others who are grieving is a profound experience that opens you to a larger realm. You begin to see what a universal experience grief is and the personal growth that grief offers us. That is the silver lining of grief."
- Abigail Carter

You Might Be Them. Lessons from Don, Election Day, and Sandy

Yesterday, on Veteran's Day, my husband Don; an EMT, an animal activist, and a United States Air Force Vet who was born on Election Day; went to The Rockaways, in Queens, New York, to help take part in Hurricane Sandy Relief efforts.

Except that he didn't. He couldn't. Because he's dead.

My Husband is Not a Rainbow

But in the sixteen months since his death, I have felt his presence in my life and in my heart countless times. Just like in his life, he shows up whenever I need him. He shows up to comfort me, to help me, to make sure I am safe. So yesterday, when I volunteered to serve food, drinks, and generally help out in Far Rockaway with the good people of *The Gibbons House* in Maspeth, New York, it was really my late husband doing the work. It was that part of him – that kind, selfless, generous soul – that lives on in me now. He is a part of me now, forever, and he is what led me there yesterday. He also led me to learning some really life-changing lessons over this past week. Lessons that connected Veterans' Day, Election Day, Hurricane Sandy, and our values as people in an unexpected way. Lessons that I did not necessarily see in the horizon. Lessons of surprise and purpose.

November sixth. Election Day. There are certain, very specific times when I can literally *feel* and almost clearly see his presence and his being with me. His birthday – election day – was one of those times. As I walked the two blocks to my voting site, my mind and heart recalled doing a similar walk, hand in hand, with my husband, four years ago in New Jersey, as we made our way to the local high school poll site to vote together for Barack Obama. There was such excitement in the air that night, such a feeling of wonder and hope. This time, my vote was the same, but I did it alone and with an empty feeling in my chest. The feelings of hope had been replaced by intense sadness and reality. How could my husband, someone who loved history and politics so much, be missing all of this? The realization that he would never live to know who our next President is, or ANY President ever again, hit me like a chainsaw as I exited the building. And that is when I saw him…

A voice from around the corner, at the top of the stairs that led to the street and sidewalk entrance of the school. He was yelling to nobody and everybody. Screaming at the top of his old, tired lungs. From his wheelchair. "Goddamn liberals!" he judged. "Lazy, no good unemployed trash, lookin' for a hand-out. Get this socialist negro Muslim out of the White House! Put him back to Kenya or wherever the hell he's from! Jesus Christ!" He was ranting endlessly, and people began walking *around* him and sprinting down the stairs to get out of his way. He looked into all of our eyes, accusing us of destroying his world, his vision of what America should be. He threw his cigarette down by his feet, on the cement, as he stammered in one last cry for attention, "Goddamn country has gone to Hell." Well, alrighty then. This guy was like Archie Bunker, minus the charm, likeability, and TV show. Total silence.

As I stood next to him at the top of the cement stairs, only a short distance separating us, I wanted to punch him in his eyeball. I wanted to duct tape his mouth shut and make him shut up for five seconds so I could tell him how incredibly wrong he was. How judgmental and rude. I wanted to tell him that my husband was a Vet who served in Desert Storm. That he was an EMT who saved people's lives everyday. That he held down not one, but two jobs just to support us, and that he collapsed and died while helping innocent animals, volunteering on his one day off. I wanted him to know that today would have been his birthday, if he was alive and here to see it, and that I'm a teacher and a struggling artist who works my ass off and still has no health insurance because my husband is gone. I wanted to find out why the hell a cranky, bitter douchebag like him gets to live a long and miserable life, while someone as wonderful as my husband gets screwed over by death.

And then, out of nowhere, I remembered Don's favorite t-shirt. It was one he had made up for himself by my friend, Dave, who creates logos, t-shirts, and signs in a sign shop business. On the front of the shirt was the symbol for EMS. On the back, it said, "I'm not here to save your life. I'm here to prolong your miserable existence." My husband used to think that was the funniest t-shirt on earth, and he loved that message. Me? I never really got it, because I wasn't an EMT, so how could I? But standing there with that miserable prick of a man in the wheelchair who was judging my life based on absolutely nothing but his own ignorance, I suddenly understood exactly what that t-shirt meant, and why Don found it so hysterically funny.

I started to recall all the many times he would come home from work, telling me about the patients he had to deal with that day. The drug-addict who spit in his face and tried to punch him because he was so jacked-up on cocaine. The teenage girl who was so drunk when EMS arrived on the scene, she threw up all over Don three times as he gave her much needed care. The old, angry, half-senile woman, who simultaneously peed down his leg and cursed him out violently, because she had no interest in being taken away by ambulance. There were hundreds more. People who were not pleasant to deal with, but who needed help nonetheless. It was the exact reason my husband loved animals so much. Animals never judged or criticized or insulted. They just wanted to love and be loved. That's it. That's all. Simple. Don used to always tell me, "Boo, if my patient is an asshole, I still have to help him. I can come home to you later on and bitch and complain about what a fucktard he was, but when I'm on the scene, there's a job to do, and everybody gets the same treatment. That's why I can't get emotionally involved. If I did, I wouldn't be able to properly do my job. And if you think about it, who cares if the guy's an asshole? He still needs help."

Yes, I suppose he does. So with my husband's heart and words on my mind, I walked over to the ginormous prick in the wheelchair, and I asked him matter-of-factly, "Do you need help getting down these stairs?" Suddenly, two young-ish looking men appeared out of nowhere, teaming up with me to get this old fuck down the stairs to continue his mission of misery on earth. "We can do this. You want us to lift you down, sir?" they said, unaware of the sharp tongue they were about to receive.

Kelley Lynn Shepherd

"What is this, some kind of do-gooder's convention? Now that you voted for Obama, you gotta help the old cripple? Forget it! I'm fine."

The two men looked at me and I looked back. We all somehow silently agreed what would happen next. This asshole was going down these stairs, like it or not. As we started to slowly roll and lift him down, one step at a time, two other strangers joined in to assist. It was an all-out, free-for-all *Kindness Attack!!!* The old man grumbled and groaned the whole way down, all eight, wide steps, shooting his mouth off and spewing out insults with each lift and roll. "Make sure you go pick up your Boy Scouts badge for this later on. And the broad can probably get one too, with women being equals now. How old are you fellas anyway? You look about sixteen. Right around the age to drop out of school and live in your mom's basement free of rent. I'm sure your precious Obama will support you and your food stamps and your welfare checks while the rest of us pay for it." We all remained speechless. Where was this guy coming up with this stuff? Who the hell shit in his oatmeal this morning? And how the hell did he get *up* those stairs to vote in the first place? As we reached the bottom step and the street level, he coughed and then said in his phlegm-filled voice, "Hey! What did you hipsters do with my cigarettes? You steal 'em?" I ran to the top of the stairs and picked up the half-used package that had fallen out of his pocket and handed it to him as I borrowed a classic line from my husband, "Enjoy your cancer sticks, sir." One of the other men added, "While the rest of us pay for it!" And with that, the old fuck rolled away.

Veteran's Day. Yesterday. Went out to The Rockaways to help with Sandy relief. To serve food. Beverages. Give supplies. Sweep someone's basement. To hug someone. To talk to people and really hear them. To stop watching the madness on TV and actually see it for myself. To give these people a voice. A purpose. A beer.

My Husband is Not a Rainbow

Packed up my peanut-butter sandwich and my bottled water and my facemask, after being warned several times about the dangerous and terrible elements in the air out there. Brought my bag filled with donated items – a random collection of things – batteries, tape, flashlights, toilet paper, kleenex, pens and pencils, crayons, coloring books, kids toys, pet snacks, socks, toothpaste, floss. Met my friend, Heather, and the others in front of the friendly Irish pub, *The Gibbons Home,* who, along with about seven or eight other local-area restaurants and bars, donated tons of hot food, drinks, supplies, and organized this amazing outing out to Rockaway Beach. Well, *beach* is a relative term. Just like it is virtually impossible to know the incredible pain and complexities of losing one's spouse until it happens to you personally, such is the same with Sandy. There is no way you can grasp the level of devastation, fear, darkness, and loss of what happens after a storm of this magnitude until you have lived through one and made it out alive to tell your story.

I heard so many yesterday. Stories. Endless, emotional truths told through pained and worn-out eyes. Funny and real snippets of a life changed. There was the old man and his dog, Andy. The old man was pushed by the surge out of his own home, and his dog was left behind. The man's next-door neighbor broke through and then swam through the man's second-story window to rescue his dog for him. This guy says he lost everything – his home is flooded and destroyed, but he still has Andy.

A woman named Erica and her teenage daughter, Alexis, touched me to my core. They are locals now, but are originally from North Carolina. They moved to Far Rockaway, New York, in August. Just over two months in their new home, and the worst hurricane in over a hundred years hits their new neighborhood and their lives. There is no heat or power at Alexis's school, so she has been sent somewhere completely new and different with kids she doesn't know. Do you remember how difficult it was to be a teenager under normal circumstances? The confusion and loss of hope in her young eyes made me so sad. For someone her age to have to go through this and see this is simply not right. Mother and daughter walked around together in the dirty, kicked-up sand, clinging to one another for support and comfort. Erica is a nurse, so I connected with her immediately. My husband loved the nurses on his shifts. It was often his favorite part of the job – joking around and having fun with the E.R. nurses. When he died, they all lined the walls of his funeral service, coming straight from and during their shifts, all dressed in scrubs. I asked her if I could hug her, because in some odd way, doing so made me feel close to Don right then.

As we served food and drinks to locals, EMS, sanitation workers, Red Cross volunteers, soldiers, and anyone who came over to eat or chat; there were stories of hope, humor, survival. An older lady told me about her attempts to receive funding from FEMA, who, after she filled out the appropriate paperwork for, told her to "check their website in three to five days for an update." She stared at me in disbelief. "Your website? Are these people high? I have no lights. No shower. Half my walls are gone in my home. Where the hell am I supposed to check your damn website from?"

And that's the thing. Amongst the horror, in the middle of the sand pits and dirt-piles that used to be a neighborhood, people were still people; laughing and eating, complaining and whining, nitpicking and delaying; and doing things that people do. Children still ran around the trees that were standing upright and played in the corner with the toys we donated. Moms still yelled out to their little boys, "No donuts! Eat an apple!" An older man asked if we were serving hot tea, and then waited on the park bench for twenty minutes for it to be ready, because he liked to have a cup of hot tea every single morning. Volunteers washed down the soot and sand in their throats with cups of Dunkin Donuts coffee.

People needed to feel like they could still read their newspaper, or walk their dog, or tell their child not to run too fast – be careful. Even if they didn't have a house to go home to, they could still have some coffee or a bagel . And in this way, we all connected. Through plates of warm penne pasta and bowls of chicken noodle soup, people would bond.

None of us knew exactly what we were doing. We just showed up, parked our cars amongst the chaos, and started unloading. We set up tents, tables, and large amounts of hot food. Sandwiches. Bottled water. Iced tea. Coffee. Fruit. Cookies. Snacks. Endless hot, homemade dishes from so many restaurants – beef stew, shepherd's pie, Ziti Bake, Chicken Marsala and curry, Pulled Pork, potatoes, rice, hot soups. All day long, the people came. They ate. They talked. They smiled. And as I stood there spooning up plate after plate of pasta, I heard one phrase more than any other: *Thank You.* And it broke my heart. Because it very well could have been me on the other side of that line, accepting that hot meal instead of serving it up. It could have been me trying to swim to safety from my own home, or run from the burning flames that came soon after. It could have been me. Or you. Or anyone. There is no such thing as "us and them." They *are* us. We *are* them. It's like my husband used to say about his patients, "Everyone is the same."

After an entire day in Far Rockaway, there are many things that will stick with me, probably forever. The grayish, colorless skies. The homes lining the streets that had missing steps or porches or roofs or doors. The American Flags that hung from house to house, worn down and torn. The roads that were not recognizable as roads, completely covered in dirt. Hundreds of abandoned cars, parked for miles along roadways and sand mounds, flipped over, on their side, completely crushed.

Kelley Lynn Shepherd

Sanitation trucks lining Dead End streets, picking up someone's music collection or stuffed animal or wedding album, magically turned into cruel dust.

Piles everywhere. Stuff all over. No sunshine anywhere. Everyday working people walking around in suits or heels after a day at church, soot and grime on their nice clothing. People clinging to their cell phones as their only form of communication to the outside world. Overhearing talks of those who would walk three miles to go to the library that may have power, so they can charge their electronics and use a computer. The creepy and sad darkness that took over as daytime ended, and the pitch-black reality set in. No street lights. No light anywhere. Sirens blazing. Everyone leaving all at once, getting out before it gets dark. Leaving there with the knowledge that we are able to go, and they cannot.

Looters. Crime. People guarding what is left of their lives, sleeping next to the pile of their precious things. The gigantic boat that washed up smack in the middle of a busy two lane highway, just sitting there, confused. The humvees that passed us, one with a sign inside reading, "FUN-vee!" That sick feeling in my stomach as I looked around at that familiar smell, that sand and soot that gets in your lungs, that panic and anxiety of what is to come. The buildings and businesses and restaurants with blown off signs, letters, windows. The beach that now looked like a desert that was bombed. The flashbacks to post-9/11. The eerie similarities. The fears of tomorrow.

I will also remember hugging strangers. Sharing recipes. The little boy in a little brown suit who belted out the words to Kelly Clarkson's "What Doesn't Kill You Makes You Stronger," as he happily ate his spaghetti and meatballs. The children giggling and chasing each other around in the grass. The little boy who sat on a cooler up against a tree, drawing and creating on the donated Etch A Sketch. I will remember how in those moments, on that day, we were able to allow some people to feel human again, just for a while. I will remember that in every tragedy, there is triumph. In every death, there is life.

The biggest message that I came away with after Veterans' Day, the Election, and my day in Far Rockaway, was something so unbelievably simple – but that I never really thought about until now. *Never judge a book by its cover.* It's that thing that my husband taught me, the message that was on his sarcastic t-shirt all those years ago. No judgment. Just help. Sure, you're a miserable bastard, but I'm gonna help you anyway. Just because someone is homeless, doesn't mean they are lazy. Survivors of hurricanes come in all shapes and sizes and have suffered very complex and emotional situations. Once you start judging their individual circumstances, you are going down a dangerous road.

When people need help, and you are in a position to help them, you should help them. It's that simple. Black and white. No questions asked. Who cares how they got there or why they need the help? Who cares that the man in a wheelchair is a complete asshole? He is still in a wheelchair, and he can't walk down those steps. Instead of wasting your time accusing people of who you *think* they are, why not get to know them instead? Say hello. Strike up conversation. Have a beer. You really can't ever truly know someone's plight until you've walked in their shoes. It all starts with some shepherd's pie, a cup of coffee, and an ear that's willing to listen.

Never judge a book by its cover. Never judge an asshole from his wheelchair. Never walk away from someone who is hurting, from someone who needs help. Never. Because tomorrow, or the next day, or any day in the future, it very well could be you whose spouse goes to work one morning and never comes back. It could be you whose legs no longer work, and who sits at the top of a staircase in a wheelchair. It could be you standing in the flooding waters, amongst the piles of soot and dirt that used to be your life.

Today you might be King. Tomorrow you might be sitting on a park bench in a gray, dismantled town, waiting for that hot cup of tea because it's the only thing left that you can still call home.

"It takes time, patience, peace, quiet, reflection and healing to create a new version of yourself, and this business is selfish. It has to be. Everything that matters depends on it." – Elizabeth Ann

Session Snippet

Me: I can't go back to doing any of the things that Don and I used to do together. My insides hurt whenever I try. Like music. It hurts to hear music, or to sing, because he's not playing his guitar with me. Everything feels empty. I still can't watch our TV shows or put up a Christmas tree. People keep pressuring me that I should be doing these things by now. I don't know if I'll ever be able to do Christmas again. I'm stressing out over it coming again. It just keeps coming, and I can't do it.

Caitlin: Okay, so don't do it. There's no rulebook here with any of this stuff. Nothing says you have to go back to the traditions that you practiced with Don. You may never go back to them. Just because that might help someone else, doesn't mean it helps you, so don't do it. Self-care is most important right now. Don't worry about what other widowed people are doing or what other non-widowed people are pushing you into or suggesting. You are the one who has to live this. Not them.

My Husband is Not a Rainbow

Me: But I feel guilty or like I'm letting him down, because I'm not strong enough to just "get through it" like everyone says. My passion for music and Christmas were two of the things he loved about me, so I feel like he would want me to try and be happy, but I just can't. All those things are so painful now. I don't want to fake my way through everything forever, but I'm so tired of being so sad.

Caitlin: Don would not want you doing things and going places that you are not emotionally ready to go to or do. Why would you purposely put yourself into situations you know will cause you more pain? You already have enough pain. That seems masochistic to me, and it doesn't serve a purpose to anyone. People who tell you to just "be happy" - those are empty words coming from people who don't know any better. You can't just be happy. There's a process in play here, and it takes a lot of time.

Me: I just feel like I'm failing him again, or like I'm not doing this grief thing right. I don't know what the hell I'm doing.

Caitlin: Are you always this hard on yourself? Look, I didn't know Don, but from the picture you've painted for me of him, I don't think he would want you to put yourself in misery, just to prove you can. He would want for you to keep pursuing your dreams. Publish your book. Keep helping people through your writing. Keep getting onstage. Keep doing good things in his honor, like what you did on Veterans' Day down at Rockaway Beach. Keep growing, keep doing the things that make you YOU. These are the important things in life, and you are still here and alive, so these are the things Don would want for you. I don't think Don gives a shit whether or not you get a fucking Christmas tree.

Me: (laughing and crying) You're right. I just feel like everything will be horrible and painful forever.

Caitlin: I know, honey. But it won't be forever. Right now though, you are where you are. Don't rush the process. You can't fast-forward through grief. Promise me you won't try and fast-forward through things that you aren't ready for. One day, maybe you'll find new meaning in the holidays again and in music again. Until then, fuck Christmas. It will still be there for you when you are ready for it again. I promise.

Big Tree, Little Tree

Little Tree: It all started the day before yesterday. I had some spare time on a Sunday afternoon, so I took out one of those oversized green plastic bins from my hallway closet and started to unpack it – something I had never quite finished almost three months ago, back when I moved out of the New Jersey apartment that Don and I shared for seven years and into this place.

I began to put things away. Folders, headshots, office stuff, batteries, envelopes, picture frames, coasters – a lot of random items that had not much to do with one another. When I got the deep container emptied at about the halfway mark, my cat, Autumn, jumped inside, as she loves to do with any sort of box or bag or basket with an opening. She began to rustle around loudly with something in there, pawing at it and wrestling with it playfully. It was Little Tree. The tiny, cute artificial Christmas tree that Don and I used each Christmas to put atop his entertainment center in our living room. It was so small and so adorable, that he rightfully dubbed it the "Charlie Brown tree," and we would decorate it in colored lights and nothing else, for fear of it toppling over from the weight of even one innocent ornament. Our little tree made the whole living room light up with Christmas, and we would drink hot chocolate with marshmallows and watch *Rudolph The Red-Nosed Reindeer* and make fun of how mean Santa was in that cartoon – and I would rest my head against the base of his chest as he played with my long, straight hair and hummed to himself happily – all by the light of our little tree.

Back to Sunday. After a lot of thought over the past few weeks, I had finally made the decision to once again ignore Christmas this year, and instead, stay local in NYC and do things with friends. Last year, I ignored my first Christmas without Don with mom and dad and a trip to Foxwoods Casino. This year, I will ignore it by seeing the most non-feel-good-movie of the year, which comes out Christmas Day: *Les Miserables*. I figure if I'm going to bawl my eyes out, I'd rather have it be because Eponine's love was never returned before she tragically died, rather than because my husband is dead on what used to be my favorite day of the year.

Deep breath. Am I ready to put up Little Tree? As I give myself a headache thinking it over, Autumn gives me her very obvious opinion. *Crunch, crunch, crunch.* She is biting the colored light bulbs, the string loosely wrapped around her paw. Okay. I will take Little Tree out and place it on my bed. Who am I hurting? Nobody, that's who. It's not like I *have* to decorate it and display it. After all, I *did* just become comfortable with my vow to cancel Christmas again this year and pretend like it doesn't exist. Suddenly, I hear Don's voice in my head, quoting Linus from *A Charlie Brown Christmas,* which he knew every single line to, "You know, it's really not such a bad little tree, Charlie Brown. All it needs is a little love."

And then, out of nowhere, I found myself slowly wrapping the string of colored lights around our little tree, catching my breath each time the bulbs made another rotation around the fake little branches. I felt slightly nervous, knowing I was doing something so little, but something so huge. Sammy and Autumn anxiously watched as I carried Little Tree to its destination, just like Linus carried Charlie Brown's tree into the middle of the woods to be loved and fixed up and healed. As the plug went into the socket and the lights glistened and reflected against my bedroom window and the night sky, my heart leapt with a tiny moment of joy, a very small hint of future holidays in years to come where I might actually smile again. Could I actually, maybe, possibly, really, truly, *love* Christmas again someday? Could I? In that moment, I felt like I could. I felt safe and cozy with my little tree; and that night; for the first time in the sixteen months since I lost my husband, I turned the TV *off* instead of on, sleeping only by the lights of the New York City skyline and the little tree that my husband and I once shared together. I slept sort of peacefully for a few hours, and I felt like I won something.

Big Tree: Monday is counseling day, so I made my way into the city to see my Grief Counselor, Caitlin. There are some days when the hurt and the pain lies dormant - and then there are days like Monday. The hurt and the *ache* of missing him was in every inch of my body. It was all over, and it wouldn't stop. I sat on the subway, silently crying the whole way into the city. The crying was effortless. Slow. Like a sigh filled with water. I almost didn't notice it. It was just simply there.

We talked about the holidays and my anxiety surrounding them – my sadness at how much everything is changed forever by the loss of one person. I told her how I felt guilty for not spending Christmas with my family. Why can't I just be stronger and push through it? Why do I have to ruin everything for everyone else, just so I don't have to feel more hurt? "Your family will be okay. They'll miss you, but they'll be okay. There are just some things you can't do right now. Not right now." I told her about Little Tree and how I felt a sense of calm and peace seeing it lit in my window. "What a perfect metaphor for things," she observed. "*This* is what I can handle right now. This much. This much Christmas. This much tree. No more..." Yes. That is exactly what it was. Little Tree was the amount of Christmas that my heart could safely handle without breaking and shattering into dust. Before I left, Caitlin reminded me to never push myself into things I'm not ready for when it comes to grief. That I am where I am, for a reason.

After my session, I left the building and started walking towards Seventh Avenue, where I was supposed to meet a friend to grab dinner. Except my friend left me a text instead – cancelling. Okay. That is fine. It's a nice night outside, the kind of cold but comfortable evening that I love to walk around in. Passing Seventh Avenue, I wasn't quite sure of what I would do next, where I would go. I just knew I didn't feel right, and I didn't feel like being home.

And then, out of nowhere, I found myself walking toward Sixth Avenue. Walking toward that big landmark sign, "RADIO CITY MUSIC HALL." My heart began to pound as I challenged myself to keep walking. Walking toward my past. My joy. The life I knew. The love I had. The future that was gone. Turning the corner, all the familiar trees and stores were beautifully decorated in lights. Blue lights. White lights. The giant ornament statue across from Radio City – where Don and I sat on a bench that night in December, 2005 to catch our breath and to make all our phone calls telling our family and friends the incredible news. I passed the outdoor cafe inside Rockefeller Center where we sat and drank hot chocolate with whipped cream and split a piece of apple pie, laughing and kissing and flirting with the newness and the promise of tomorrow. And then finally – suddenly – without warning – it was there. I was there, in front of it. The site of the happiest day of my new life. My old life. The place where my boyfriend would become my fiancé. The patch of land right there, underneath that Rockefeller Center Christmas Tree, in the middle of New York City, in front of every tourist on the planet, in the freezing cold night of twenty five degrees – he would propose to me.

Kelley Lynn Shepherd

I stood there, frozen in time. The TV cameras and equipment surrounded the beautiful, awful tree. A cop appeared next to me.

"You okay?" he said. "You look white as a ghost."

"My husband proposed to me here," I found myself telling him. "My late husband. He died last year. This is the first time I've been back here to the tree since he died. I don't know why I'm here. I feel sick."

Suddenly I couldn't stop talking. The young cop looked at me with sad, innocent eyes. He looked too young to know this kind of hurt, which is why what he said next surprised me. "We lost seven men from the precinct and fire station down the street, on 9/11. Our brothers. Sometimes I come here and just sit at the base of this tree and try to picture the good times we had walking the neighborhood or watching the tree lighting while on a coffee break. It doesn't always work. Sometimes it does, but other times, it just doesn't."

We remained in silence for a few seconds or minutes or hours, him sharing his Big Tree with me and me sharing my Big Tree with him. Don and I always called it "our tree," but I didn't mind sharing it with that cop in that moment of shattered time. I felt like I was about to break in half as I asked him, "When is the tree lighting?"

"Wednesday night," he said. And with that, I started to cry.

"Jesus!" he said, in that classic New York sarcastic tone. "I didn't know the tree lighting was that upsetting for you. You gonna be okay?" His eyes worried about me as he sipped from his paper coffee cup. I didn't reply.

My Husband is Not a Rainbow

"I think you need some privacy. I'm right over there if you need anything." He walked briskly and with purpose, but he didn't go too far.

Sitting on that cold bench, looking up at Big Tree, I sobbed uncontrollably, wiping my stream of tears on my long sweater sleeves. I cried for the dreams that would never be. I cried for the holidays approaching, and all the ones I would have to deal with from now on without him. I cried for my own impatience with myself – for coming here to this tree way before I was ready – in some lame attempt to prove to myself and others that I'm further along in this grief thing than I actually am. I cried because I don't understand why I give a shit what other people think of me or how they judge my progress according to what they feel is acceptable. I cried because it sucks that so many people want to put a time limit on my heart and my love that they know nothing about. I cried because I can no longer tell my husband any of this, and instead, I have to write about it and sit in front of a big tree that meant so much and feels so bad. I cried because my husband is gone, and we will never eat mom's fried dough again on Christmas morning, or open stockings together in our pajamas, or watch *Christmas Vacation* or *A Christmas Story* and laugh as Don recited every line. I cried because Don will never smoke another traditional Christmas Eve cigar or drink port with my male cousins out on their front porch. I cried because Big Tree used to represent all that is to come, and now it represents all that is gone. For a long, long time; I just sat there and cried.

When no more tears would come, I looked up at Big Tree, and I started to remember. The memories were filled with pain, but I sat there and felt them anyway. I had no choice. I remembered how ridiculously giddy and happy we were that night, underneath that tree. I remembered the sound of hundreds of people – total strangers – clapping and cheering for us as I said "YES!" louder than I ever thought possible. I remembered how nervous Don was that whole day, and how strange he was acting as we made our way through New York City, me showing him all the landmarks and decor at Christmastime. When we got to the tree, he took my hand and led me through the huge crowds of people until we reached the base of it, just underneath. We were surrounded by the warmth of thousands of little shining lights, covering the tree like a maze. It was so loud. So cold. Don had gloves and earmuffs on, and I had mittens.

He started to make his speech, but I couldn't hear anything he was saying, there were so many people talking and yelling and living. I didn't really know what he was doing or why he was talking so much. Then, right there in the concrete, he was down on one knee, and a ring box rested inside his pillowy gloves. Everything stopped, and nothing was ever more beautiful or perfect. The city was ours, and the tree was ours, and the world was ours as he said to me through shaky and frozen tears, "Because you love Christmas so much, and because you love New York City so much, I wanted to make this our special place forever. So, Kelley, in front of all these people, in the best city in the world, under the greatest, most gorgeous tree I've ever seen, from my knees and freezing my fuckin' ass off 'cuz it's cold as shit out here, will you please marry me and be my wife and make me the happiest man on earth? Please say yes so I can get up now." It was like a movie. We were celebrities. People took our picture and cried with us. We both laughed as I removed my mittens in order to put the ring on my finger. I couldn't stop staring at the ring. Or at him. I couldn't stop kissing him. I couldn't stop being happy. Nothing could stop our joy. Nothing would stop our love.

After sitting on that bench underneath Big Tree on Monday night, feeling every awful and wonderful feeling in the universe, I felt as if I had just run a marathon. At some point, I could no longer handle the bookshelf of emotions, and I wanted to go home. I walked along the city streets in the cold and brisk night air, and just as they had on my way in that afternoon, the tears went back to silent and effortless. The subway was filled with people who didn't notice my pain, and I felt alone and crowded at the same time. When I finally got back to my bedroom and looked into the core of Little Tree, hoping to feel some of that comfort and peace I had felt just the night before – it was too late. I had already ruined it.

People are so uncomfortable with grief and death. They will put their own issues upon you and make you feel like you are doing it wrong or incorrectly or not fast enough for them. They will make you feel worse than you already feel by ignoring you completely or treating you the same as before, never acknowledging the giant gaping hole that used to be your life. They will make you question yourself and your decisions – they will take advantage of your weakened and vulnerable state. They will look you in the eye with malice and coldness, as if to say, "Aren't you *over* this yet?"

They will judge you with no reason and leave you with no care. People will make you doubt your own instincts, your own private grief process. They will bring you to a place where you are so beaten down and so filled with pain, that you find yourself walking straight into the fire. You find yourself floating unwillingly toward the tree that held all your happiness. The tree that crushed all your dreams.

Don't listen to them. Don't fall for it. Don't let them win like I did. I had no business being at Rockefeller Center last night. I wasn't even close to ready for Big Tree. Little Tree is all that I can handle. That's it. Just Little Tree. Why didn't I listen to Caitlin? Why didn't I listen to *myself*? Why did I try so hard and so painfully to push forward into the next thing? Why is this always so goddamn hard?

I learned my lesson. Never rush through grief. Never try and skip the steps. Never let others dictate where you should be in your progress. Most importantly, never seek out something as complicated and emotional and beyond what you can handle as Big Tree, when something as comforting and peaceful and hopeful as Little Tree was sitting in your window and waiting for you all along.

Engaged, Giddy, and in Love

It was on the Sunday before Christmas, in 2005, that Don Shepherd got down on one knee in the freezing cold, under the Rockefeller Center Christmas Tree, and asked me to be his wife. The next ten months were a whirlwind of being happily engaged, giddy, and very much in love. I remember calling so many people to tell them of the engagement, and how ecstatic everyone was. Everywhere we went, people celebrated us, toasted us, gave us free stuff. Don started milking it. Six months into our engagement, we would be at a restaurant, and he would say, "We just got engaged!" to the waiter. Then, to me, "What? He doesn't know it was six months ago!" Most times, the waiter would offer up "dessert is on us -congratulations!" or something similar. We would come home from work, and UPS boxes would be waiting by our door. Engagement and wedding gifts rolled in, and Don's level of excitement was adorable. "Boo, we got more STUFF today! I can't believe people are giving us things just because we are getting married! Can we do this like, every five years? I might need a new TV by then," he would joke.

After the proposal, we drove to my parents' house in Massachusetts to stay for a week over Christmas. While we were there, an epic blizzard happened, one that was typical of New England storms. As we looked out the living room window at my new fiancé's car, covered in snow, Don joked to me and my dad, "This would make a great Christmas card!" So we got out some big poster-board and each wrote a sign. Mine said, "Merry Friggin' Christmas!" and Don's said, "I miss Florida!" We got all dressed in our jackets and gloves, sent my dad out with us and a camera, and stood in front of Don's snow-covered car, holding up our signs. Smiling, laughing like crazy, and so very much in love. The world was ours to have, and the future was filled with promise. Our Christmas card turned into an annual Don and Kelley tradition, to try to make funny cards to send out each year around the holidays.

Being engaged in the year of 2005 was one of the happiest times in my life. I loved every single thing about it. I loved looking down at my ring and smiling at the knowledge that I had finally found my forever. I loved referring to Don as "my fiancé." I loved planning every single part of our wedding. I loved writing our own vows and sitting down and thinking about what to say, knowing that Don was being tortured in having to think of what to say. I loved taking dance lessons once a week, in preparation for our Foxtrot First Dance. I loved that Don hated every minute of dance lessons, but that he agreed to it without hesitation, because he knew it made me happy. I loved rehearsing our dance over and over again, outside, across the street from our apartment, against the New York City skyline. I loved talking about our future days. How long we would stay in New Jersey. If we would move back to New York, or maybe even to Massachusetts one day. When we would have a family. What that might look like for us. I loved hearing Don talk about his wanting to be a dad. I loved attending my brother's wedding, which was just four months before ours, and going there as an engaged couple. I loved hearing everyone say, "You guys are next!" I loved knowing that I would be Don Shepherd's wife. Forever.

Later that day, after we did the Christmas card picture in my parents driveway, we were eating dinner with my parents, who

Don had starting referring to as "mom and pop." Nobody asked him to say that. He just started doing it on his own, as if it were the most normal and natural thing in the world. He was family, and it was beautiful.

During dinner, my dad and Don began cracking themselves up by doing their own "wedding planning" for our big day, suggesting things that they knew would annoy me greatly.

"So I was thinking," began my dad to Don, "Why don't we have the wedding at Tiny's Diner in Ayer. It's right nearby for everyone, and I'm sure the local truckers that eat there for lunch wouldn't mind if we set aside the back area for your wedding reception."

"Brilliant!" Don cheerily went along with this charade. "We could do it on All You Can Eat Haddock Night, so it would save us even more money. Get a big ole' bowl of coleslaw, some root beers, and we're good to go."

My dad continued: "I think we could even offer a nice dessert bar. Ring Dings, Funny Bones, Twinkies ... you know ... have a nice selection available."

"Right," chimed in Don. "Although I'm not so sure we can afford Ring Dings and Twinkies. We might have to take it down a notch and go with Little Debbie Snack Cakes. Nothin' but the best for my little lady." The longer I stayed silent and didn't protest, the more they kept going with their little game. Finally, when I could no longer take even joking about such a tacky wedding, I caved. "This is why I'm in charge!" I said victoriously. "Our wedding is going to be amazing. And classy." Don, hanging his head in mock-shame, mumbled, "Yes, dear. I will show up and do as I'm told."

My Husband is Not a Rainbow

Going to sleep that night, my parents offered up their bedroom for us to sleep in. Don and I looked at each other confused. "Well, now that you're engaged, you can have our room when you stay here as guests. It just makes sense now," they reasoned.

Lying in bed, on our post-engagement-high, we couldn't stop chatting and giggling. We whisper-spoke as we lay there in the dark room:

Don: Wow, we get the parents' bedroom suite tonight. Wasn't expecting this upgrade!

Me: (laughing) I know. I feel weird now, like, they know we are in here and that we are a couple. It's like they just gave us permission to be intimate in their bedroom. Which I'm NOT doing, by the way.

Don: Good, cuz I'm not doing that either. They are right on the other side of the wall, practically. This is weird. Maybe I should go back out to the couch like before.

Me: No. Then I won't be able to stop laughing, thinking about your tall legs on that small couch and you hanging over the edges of it because you don't fit. Besides, you have to stay here with me so you can kill bugs and take care of scary noises.

Don: Boo, I'd only be going to the couch. You could come get me for scary noises. Also, how many bugs are you expecting in one night? We're not camping.

Me: But, Boo?

Don: Yes dear…

Me: But what if we were camping and walking in the Grand Canyon, and I fell in, and I died. What would you do, Boo?

Don: Oh Christ, not this again...

Me: (giggling hard) But now that we're engaged, what would you do? Would you keep in touch with my parents? Would you check on them if I died?

Don: Of course I would, Boo. Don't be silly. They're family.

Me: Would you stay in New Jersey?

Don: Oh, HELL, no! My ass would be back in Florida in about ten minutes. I'd visit your parents often, and I'd make sure they were okay, and I'd take care of them, Boo. I promise. But I wouldn't stay in New Jersey. No way.

Me: What if I fell in, and I was severely injured, and my head came off, and my legs came off? What if I was just a torso, Boo? Would you still marry me?

Don: This is literally the stupidest conversation I've ever had, Boo. Really?

Me: What if I was just a head?

Don: Like a floating head? Like Max Headrum?

Me: Yes. Like that. I just floated around, but I still could talk and stuff.

Don: That would be incredibly creepy. What the hell is wrong with you? You're not right. (laughing hysterically)

Me: But you didn't answer the question, Boo. Which would you rather have me be? A torso, or a head?

My Husband is Not a Rainbow

Don: None of the above? Can that be a choice? Whatever answer means I get to sleep for a few hours, that's my answer, Boo. And I just signed up for a lifetime of this?

Me: Exactly. Now who's the one that's not right in the head?

Don: Good point.

Me: I'm laughing so hard, I'm gonna pee myself. (gets up, stubs toe in dark)

Don: (laughing his ass off) Bahaha!!! You okay, Boo? Cuz that's funny as hell.

Mom's voice from her bed: You okay? What on earth are you two laughing about in there?

Don: (yelling back in the dark) Apparently, Kelley is concerned about what would happen, should we be walking in the Grand Canyon, and should she fall in, and become either just a head, or just a torso. She wants to know what I would do in that scenario.

(long pause)
Dad's voice from his bed: You sure you wanna go through with this? We can still get our money back on all those Ring Ding orders…

FB Post: Here's a fun riddle for the holidays: What is more pathetic and sad than receiving ZERO Christmas Cards? Receiving ONE Christmas Card - from your dead husband's dentist.
LIKES: 67   COMMENTS: 15

Kelley Lynn Shepherd

Dear Dead Husband:

Today hurts. There is no escaping it, no getting around it, no running away from it. It hurts, and it woke up hurting. In a couple hours, I'm hosting a Brunch for my friend, Bobby, and his cousin, Karen, and then we are seeing LES MISERABLE tonight at the IMAX movie theatre in New York City, so I will be distracted, and I will get through. But late last night, and right now, Christmas hurts like hell. I thought I could control the hurt by pretending it's not Christmas. Now I know that is impossible. The heart knows. It wakes up knowing that it's Christmas and you are gone. I miss you SO MUCH. I hope you knew what you meant to me. What you gave to my life. My sweet and wonderful husband. I love you.

Pieces

My world hangs in mid-air. Things are scattered on the ceiling, on the floor. Nothing is where it used to be. I cannot find anything. Where is that thing that was once my life? Where did it go?

My old life and my new life melt together like chocolate in a bowl. They crash into one another, and it makes no sense. Happy memories of a beautiful marriage smash my heart into bits. Stockings and presents on Christmas morning become ulcers and migraines and things I cannot let enter into my atmosphere. Everything I love is now pain. So much pain.

Why doesn't anyone ever tell you *how much* this hurts? How much it *continues* to hurt? Why does the level of pain remain so high? Don't you get rewarded for grieving properly and in a healthy way? Everyone keeps telling me I am "doing all the right things." I never fight my emotions. I cry when I want to cry. I scream. I write. I live. I honor him. I don't drink, and I don't take drugs. There is nothing wrong with taking medication to get through this, nothing at all wrong with that. I know some people need that, and it is helpful or necessary for them. It is just not for me. I would rather feel and live inside the Hell. I prefer that a sharp knife stab me, than for a dull one to numb me. But how many times must I be stabbed over and over and over and over again? Ten thousand? Twenty? Four million?

Eighteen months. Almost eighteen months of this intensity. Waking up to the stabbing. Living in the muddy waters. Swimming in the endless sea. No end. No shore. Reading the book again and again. Flipping the page, but the words are the same. Every page has the same sentences, and they all make me hurt. Didn't I already read this chapter? I know I did. Why are all the chapters repeating? Can I get a different book? Soon it will be twenty months. Then two years. Three. Five. Seven. Ten. Fourteen years. Twenty one. Will the hurt be less then? Will it even matter?

Where does it go? It just hangs there. I cannot drop it. I will not forget. It sucks to hold on. There are so many pieces of that life that just hang there. Like rejects. Misfits. I want all of the pieces back again. I want them back. It was my life. It was ours. You can't just yank someone's life away and just leave them with nothing but hurt and pain and unfinished love. Give me back the pieces.

I wasn't finished.

Dear Stupid Death Diary:

2013 is coming. It will be here tomorrow, with or without my participation. With or without my fanfare or my confetti or my wacky noise-maker. And to be honest, I am exhausted. I am tired from all the counting. For the past seventeen months and eighteen days, I have done nothing but countdown to the next sad thing. The next milestone date, or death date, or wedding anniversary, or birthday where he will still be dead, and on and on and on. And since my husband cannot ever countdown to a new year, ever again, I don't want to either. It just all feels terribly wrong.

So please don't wish me a Happy New Year. Really. It is nothing personal. I just don't feel much like celebrating, and there is not much about it that seems "happy" to me right now. Maybe next year. Maybe later. Maybe never. I just don't know.

It's Gone

I cannot find my wedding ring.
My husband is dead,
and gone forever,
and I cannot find my wedding ring.
My hands are shaking as I type this.
My fingers feel like someone else's fingers,
without my ring on.
My skin is so naked and wrong,
without my ring on.
I have nothing else to latch onto,
nothing to cling to desperately,
in the unbearable moments of missing him,
without my ring on.
It fell off my finger.
It must have fallen off.
Somewhere.
Somehow.
I don't know how.
Or when.
I have looked all over this house.
Like a detective,

My Husband is Not a Rainbow

or an investigator,
I have searched every crevice,
and nook,
and corner,
of this house.
My ring is gone.
Just like my husband,
my ring is gone.
It was there,
and then it wasn't.
What am I going to do???

When your husband is dead,
you cling to things.
You cling to things that symbolize
other things,
like your life together,
your marriage,
your vows,
your world,
your time,
your heart.
You cling to them,
because the person,
the physical being,
is no longer here,
to hold or to smell,
or to kiss or to talk.
So instead,
in the still of the night,
you stare into space,
and you run your thumbnail,
again and again,
over your wedding ring,
petting it,
feeding yourself with comfort,

Kelley Lynn Shepherd

with love,
with something,
ANYTHING,
that feels like proof,
of the life you had.
Because I have so little.
So little of our life,
is left with me.

I already knew that I was no longer married,
after he died.
But I could pretend.
I could keep my ring on,
and pretend,
inside my heart,
that inside my own universe,
I am still married.
I want so very badly,
to still be married.
To still be his wife,
and for him to still be,
my husband.
Even if he is my dead husband,
I still call him my husband,
because I get chills,
everytime I say the word.
Husband.
The most beautiful word,
ever.

I still need to pretend.
I am nowhere near finished pretending.
But I cannot pretend,
because the ring that helped me do so,
is now replaced by nothing.
Pretending,

even inside the confines of my own world,
silently,
without words or announcements,
allowed me to better cope
with my reality
in the outside world.
If I cannot pretend,
in my own little corner,
the world around me feels
impossible.
What the hell do I do now?

"My husband was my world. I loved him more than life itself.
After he died, I had to learn how to love life again, and I'm still learning how to do that."
– Petra Langham

Dear Dead Husband:

At the start of the year, I got a message in my blog from someone named Michele, who runs a non-profit called Soaring Spirits. She is in California, and she was widowed young, with three kids. She saw my stand-up comedy where I told jokes about death during the show where we honored you, Boo. And she read my blog. She wanted to know if I would like to write for her organization's blog, called "Widows Voice." And if I'd like to give a comedic presentation at this thing called "Camp Widow." I would be able to basically create a whole seventy five minute presentation about grief and death and loss.

I spoke with her on the phone, and I feel a connection to her, the same kind I felt with Caitlin, and the same kind I felt with

Kathryn in Dix Hills and her widowed support groups at St. Matthews Church. These are all such good people - people I know in my soul that you put in my path somehow, to help me. It made me feel alive when Michele asked me to give a presentation at this weird thing called "Camp Widow." I asked her, "That's a thing?" and she said, "Yup, that's a thing." This happened right after I lost my wedding ring. It doesn't make not having the ring any less awful, but I feel as if I have gotten something back somehow with this new beautiful connection. I love you, Boo. Thank you for always trying to help me.

"There will be a day...
when life will be worth living.
And you'll be an example
For someone else on this path.
Someone who's behind you,
and sees you as Hope.
Hope, that they, too, will survive."
- Janine Teague Eggers

I Miss His Farts

I never thought I would say this, but tonight, right now, I miss him farting in the bed. It didn't happen often, thankfully. Don was *not* one of those type of guys who would fart on purpose and then laugh and think it was the funniest thing in the world. He was not proud of them in any way, like a lot of guys are. However, sometimes, now and then – we would be lying in bed, drifting off to sleep, enjoying the silence of the night, and he would fart so loudly and over the top, that I would question my decision to spend my life with this person. It was always an accident, and he was always immediately embarrassed, which is what made it so funny. The fart would happen, followed by a beat, and then a very sincere and giggly "sorry." Some nights, he would fart in his sleep. Again, this was not a regular occurrence, but it happened here and there. One particular night, he had fallen asleep, and then he farted. Again. A third time. The fourth one was more like a musical note that didn't want to end. It just kept going. I could no longer take it, so I reached over and shook him awake.

Him: Huh? What's happening? What's wrong, Boo? Why am I awake right now? It's four in the morning...

Me: Because you keep FARTING! It's disgusting. Stop!!!

Him: (laughing) But I'm asleep. I was asleep. I don't know I'm doing it. I'm sorry, Boo. That's gross, I know…

Me: Jesus Christ. You don't smell that???

Him: (sniffing the air) Oh wow, you're right. That's pretty fucked up. Holy hell, it smells like I shit my pants. (starts spraying Febreze)

Me: Oh, this is way beyond Febreze, Boo. You need to Febreze your asshole. I'm not sleeping in these blankets. They are all filled with fart-smell now. I can't do it. We have to move. We need a new bed. New apartment. New life. We have to get away from the farts.

Him: Nah. It's Jersey. It blends right in…

That night, neither of us could fall back to sleep. We stayed up all night, we left the bedroom and the fart-smelling sheets, and we got in our car at 4:00 AM, and went out for breakfast at the local diner. We laughed so hard that night and lots of nights. That was the thing about us, about our relationship. We always laughed. We mocked each other. We teased. We didn't let the tiny things bother us. We laughed at everything, because we felt so happy to be living our life together. All of those little things that some couples allow themselves to get so upset about and fight about and argue about – we didn't. We just didn't. By the time we had met one another and moved in together, we were both *so ready* to put up with someone else's weirdness, and we both looked forward to many years of being able to irritate the hell out of each other. But that didn't happen. We got robbed of that honor.

There are so many things to miss when you lose your spouse, because your spouse is so many things. Some days you grieve your past. Some days you grieve your future. Or the things you will never get to do together. Your friendship. Your partner in intimacy. You grieve your protector, your rhythm, your music. It is a list of things to miss that goes on and on without end…

It sucks when nobody is there to rudely tell you that there's a pimple on your face. Or to leave your entire bathroom looking like Lake Erie after they poorly dry themselves off post-shower. To slurp cereal in a truly disgusting manner. To snore loudly, the music that says, "I'm alive." Or to flee the wafting stench with you in the middle of the night and run away to eat pancakes.

Sometimes you long for him to annoy you again. To keep you awake. Keep you alive. Sometimes you want a reminder – some sort of evidence of your partnership and your love. Proof that you indeed existed together and laughed like hell together and scraped through time together. You want the kind of proof that doesn't come in a picture frame or some left-behind item of his that you now keep. Sometimes – in the still of the night – lying there alone – you just miss his farts.

"He snored like crazy. It was so loud, you heard it everywhere in the house. I would get up and move to the couch. Then, he got sick. Really sick. Then he got thin. Cancer thin. So, he stopped snoring, but by then, I had stopped sleeping. Then he stopped snoring forever. I wish he was snoring next to me again."
– Paula Tamburro

"I desperately miss those little things I found irritating before… The coffee grounds built up in the machine without cleaning up between pots brewed, whiskers in the sink, taking more time than I had patience for to get yard work and household tasks done… I'd give absolutely anything to get those irritations back again."
- Rebecca Daniels

"She snorted when she laughed. Loudly. In quiet movie theaters. I used to get embarrassed. Now my heart burns with an unexplainable pain, in the absence of hearing her gorgeous laughter."
– David Eden

Kelley Lynn Shepherd

I Don't Want to Be Here Anymore

Dear Dead Husband:

Everything just fell apart. I don't know who else to say this to or who else to talk to right now, except you. I can't stop crying. How do I live this life without you? I miss you every waking minute, and every time I feel like I might be getting back on my feet, the rug is pulled out again. I have two months to find a new living situation. Right now, I just want to live nowhere. It took so long for me to find someone who would take in me and our two kitties, Boo. I will never leave them. You always said you would live under a bridge before you would ever give them up. I'm trying. I really am. I am just out of ideas, and I'm so fucking tired. I tried running my thumb over my wedding ring like I do sometimes when I need to feel you. And now I can't, because all I feel is naked skin. Please help me, Boo. Help me know what to do. Help me want to live again. I think I've been severely depressed this whole time without you, and I'm just now fully feeling it. Why do you have to be dead, and why do I have to be alive? I hate this shit life. Please help me.

Caitlin: Hello?

Me: Hi... it's Kelley... I'm so sorry to call you at home and not have a scheduled...

Caitlin: Oh my god, I told you I'm here for you. What happened? You sound awful.

Me: He kicked me out. My roommate. He said it's not going to work and wants me out by June first. He didn't even give me a reason, just said it's not working... (crying hard)

My Husband is Not a Rainbow

Caitlin: What the fuck? Oh Kelley, this is awful. I'm so sorry. We are going to get through this and figure this out, okay? Just breathe…

Me: But where am I gonna go? Nobody wants a widow with two cats who is broke all the time. I feel like such a loser. I hate my life. This wasn't how it was supposed to be. Don moved his life here so I could live my dreams, and now I can barely survive because he's not here, and nothing means anything anymore. It's all just empty and pointless. I don't want to tell my parents. They are going to want me to come home and leave New York. I can't do that. My whole life will be pointless. New York and my creative life here is literally the only thing I have left. If that gets taken away too, I just don't know what I'll do.

Caitlin: I agree with you. You need to be here right now. We are going to figure this out. Post on Facebook, use that huge community of friends you have, let them help you. Put it out there that you need a roommate or apartment, soon! And I'll make some calls here too, we will get you a place to go, sweetie. It's going to be okay.

Me: But I don't know how to do this anymore. And my wedding ring is gone, I still can't find it. We looked literally everywhere. My parents tore the house apart, the car, everywhere. I think it got thrown off when I took my gloves off, and it's lying in a snowbank somewhere forever. I hate my life. Truly. I don't want to be here anymore.

Caitlin: (very serious) You don't want to be where?

Me: Anywhere. I just don't want to live anymore. I'm so tired of trying and of everything hurting all the time, and the hurt just doesn't ever stop.

Caitlin: Do you need me to make a phone call? Do you feel like you might harm yourself? Please understand that when you make a statement like that, I need to ask these questions and make sure you're not in a suicidal way. Would you like me to make a call for you?

Me: No. I don't want to live right now, but I'm not going to actively do anything to die. I just don't want to be here, and I needed to say it to someone out loud I guess. I'm just so tired from pretending that I'm okay and from everyone needing me to be okay. I'm not okay.

Caitlin: Okay. I want you to promise me you will call me or call for help if you ever feel differently, or if you feel scared or unsure that you might do something. Okay?

Me: Okay. I'm just so tired. I feel like I can't do anything except lie in bed and cry.

Caitlin: You've just been hit in the head, hard, with some devastating news that was also shocking for you. Lying in bed and processing is a normal response. Just don't stay there forever. We need to get you out of there as soon as possible, so you don't have to be in that horrible environment with him there, and that awkwardness, any longer than you need to be. This was a really shitty thing for him to do and a really shitty way for him to do it.

Me: Yeah. I want to stab him in the eye socket. I just don't understand what happened. What did I do? All I do is go to work, come home, hang out in my room and try not to bother him, because he seems like he wants to be left alone when he's home. He's a total clean freak, maybe I don't clean the apartment good enough for him. Or maybe he doesn't like having two cats roaming around, but he knew what he was getting into. He knew I had cats. I just hate feeling like I'm this annoying burden to everyone. Like I'm some loser who can't support herself even with more than one job. Don just loved me and loved everything about me. I feel like I have to justify my existence to people now. Like, they're just putting up with me or helping the poor widowed girl. I hate having to be needy. I hate it so much.

Caitlin: I know you do. You're a very independent person who has been forced into asking for help, over and over. But you're certainly not a loser, Kelley. You're one of the bravest people I know. Really. You just keep trying, no matter what gets thrown at you.

Me: I'm sick of it though. I just need a break.

Caitlin: I know, sweetie. You're going to visit your parents next week, right? Tell them what's going on in person while you're there. Your family will help you to make a plan. And stand your ground about staying in New York. Your job is here. Your connections are here. You're not ready to walk away just yet, and you shouldn't have to. Right now though, go lie in bed and watch some crappy mindless TV show. I'm glad you called me.

Me: Me too. You're the best.

*"What I want
is permission
to no longer be strong,
But to fall and collapse into pain,
and find my place in the corner,
And give up,
Just for a little while."
– Widow Who Chose to Be Anonymous*

Kelley Lynn Shepherd

FB Post: This apartment hunting stuff is definitely stressing me out. My friend Mindi hooked me up with one of her friends who is also looking for a place to live, so we are looking together in Queens to maybe share a place. I'm back to barely sleeping again, like in the first 7 or 8 months of losing Don when I slept MAYBE 3 hours a night, and I can't stop thinking about how I'm going to get the money together to move. Everything weighs on my brother being able to sell my car for me so I have the move-in costs set aside, AND have it in time. When I DO sleep, this crap is taking over my brain in the weirdest way ever. Last night I dreamt that Tom Bergeron and me were best friends, and that he showed up at my brother's house and bought my car for me for $3k, and then threw in an extra $7k to help me find a nice place. Then I woke up and my cat puked on my foot.
LIKES: 29   COMMENTS: 33

FB Post: Went home this weekend and told my family that I need to be out of my apartment on June 1st, and that I will be moving, yet again, even though I just moved here less than 5 months ago. They were shocked and angry at my roommate, to say the least, but this dialogue between me and my brother cracked me up:

Him: WHAT? You're moving AGAIN? But we JUST drove up to New York and helped you move a few months ago!!!

Me: Yes, I realize this…

Him: (trying to put positive spin) Well, I guess at least this time, you don't have any furniture for us to move… (pauses, realizing what he just said) HOLY SHIT! YOU DON'T HAVE ANY FURNITURE!

Yup. This is what happens when you hack your dresser, Entertainment Center, bed, and couch, to pieces because you're all set up in a lovely furnished apartment. Ugh.
LIKES: 77   COMMENTS: 25

What If I Died and You Lived?

My husband and I used to play different types of ridiculous "what if" games. Well, I would play them, and he would humor me by responding over and over to my absurd questions. It was so much fun, and I would do this at the most annoying or random times – always out of absolutely nowhere, and always starting the same way; with me saying his pet name in that sing-songy voice, where I would stretch out the word "Boo" to somehow make it two lengthy syllables, served up alongside some innocent, pathetic, puppy-dog eyes...

A lot of times, we would be in bed, and I would wait until he was just about asleep, and then I would tap him on the shoulder with another "what if" question...

Me: *(tap tap tap) But, Boo-ooooooo???*

Him: *(grunting awake) Mmmhgjmmzz... what, Boo?*

Me: *What if I gained lots and lots of weight? Would you divorce me?*

Him: *Seriously? This is what we're doing right now?*

Me: *Like maybe a hundred and fifty or two hundred pounds. What if, Boo? Would you leave me then forever?*

Him: *(sitting up, eyes still closed)* No, Boo. I wouldn't leave you forever. You're my wife, and I love you. Is that the right answer? Can I please go to sleep now?

Me: *But what if I was like that lady we saw on TV? The one who was eight hundred pounds and you couldn't even see her face, and she lived in her bed for four years? What if I was her? THEN would you leave me, Boo?*

Him: *Yes, Boo. THEN I would leave you. (laughing at how dumb this is)*

Me: *But, that's mean, Boo. I thought I was your wife ...*

Him: *Yeah, well, at that point, you sort of stop being a wife and become more of a furniture piece. Besides, what are you gonna do about it? Run after me? It would be the easiest divorce in history! Can I PLEASE, for the love of God, go to sleep now?*

Now, almost twenty months after his sudden death, I still play the "what if" game, but I play it alone. There is not really much joy in playing this game alone, because now, much like my husband, I have become the unwilling participant. I don't *want* to play this game, but my mind and my heart and my brain and everything else inside me just *goes there*. And it is no longer fun, silly "what if" questions. No. It is the kind of "what if" questions that make you sweat and keep you up all night and give you nausea...

What if Don never took that second job at Petsmart? What if he had gone to the doctor more? What if his dad had given him the time of day or had a relationship with him, or maybe informed him that heart disease was in the family and that he should get his heart checked out? What if he had stayed in Florida, where his life was more calm and less stressful? What if he never moved to New Jersey at all to be with me? To marry me? What if

My Husband is Not a Rainbow

he was at his regular job that morning, as an EMS, on an AMBULANCE? What if he had his heart-attack in the ambulance and was treated in time and survived? What if he got that second chance that so many others get? What if he was home with me that day? What If I wasn't asleep when my husband was collapsing on a floor at work? What if he wasn't happy – really happy – when he died? What if he was alone and scared when it happened? What if he wondered where I was? What if he was in pain?

The "what if" game comes and goes in my mind and in my heart, and lately, it has quieted some. It has silenced itself for a while. Why? Not because my mind and my heart are finally leaving me alone and letting me live in peace. No. That would be too simple. Too linear. That would make too much sense, and we all know that the grief monster *never makes sense.* The game has stopped asking these endless questions about the day of my husband's death for a much deeper reason: it has a much more probing question in mind...

What if our roles were reversed? What if I died, and you lived?

It is a question that plagues me. It is a question that brings upon sadness. Guilt. Fear. Confusion. Sacrifice. Love. And, of course, death.

But what if, Boo? What if you had woken up that morning to that new, horrific reality? The reality that I was already gone? What would you have done in the following minutes, hours, days, months? How would you be coping? I know for sure that after the services were said and done, after the friends and the flowers and the dust had settled – you would pack up our kitties and pack up your chair and your guitars and your life – and you would go back to Florida, where you loved it, and pick up right where you left off. You would get your EMS job back in Pinellas County at Sunstar. You would find a nice, but humble apartment that had central-air and tennis courts in the back, like your old one, and you would walk along Clearwater Beach and ride your bike in the paths and just be you.

I know you would always keep in touch with my family – my brother and my parents – and you would all take care of one another as much as you could, and you would check on them, and they would definitely check on you. I think you would handle the pain so much better than I am handling it, Boo. I really think that. You would be devastated, of course, but you would know how to go forward better than I know how to. You know how to let things go, because you had to growing up, and you know how to deal with hard emotions because of your job, and so you would probably find private ways to honor me and remember me, but you would spend your life making the best of your life.

Our families would embrace you. Our friends would embrace you and hold you up and love you. And you would take our photo albums and our wedding things and our letters and our memories, and you would take special care of them. And you would be a *much* better papa to our kitties than I am a Mama. They put up with me, but it's so clear that they want you. They want you to be here. I want you to be here.

What if I died and you lived? It's something I think about often. I don't like thinking about it, but it's there. It lingers. It whispers. It taps on my shoulder, waking me up in the night, right as I'm about to fall asleep. Just like I did to you, Boo. All those nights. Those wonderful, married nights.

It's not that I *want* to be dead. I don't. It just that sometimes, especially right now, I don't really want to be alive. And there is a difference. I'm tired of living. I'm tired of fighting and being forever sad and in pain and of wondering how the hell I will ever get through this, and will I ever want to live again. And during those times, I wonder…

What If I Died and You Lived?

Session Snippet

Me: It feels like I'm moving backwards, even though I know that I'm not. Physically though, it feels like it did in the first few months after he died. Anxiety. Nausea. Panic attacks. Can't sleep. Exhausted to the point of confusion. Depression. I feel like everything just got pulled away all over again.

Caitlin: Because it did. This was huge. And it was yet another sudden loss for you, something you totally didn't expect that was just ripped away. It took so much courage and effort to move out of the home you shared with Don, and then you finally settle into this new place, and it's just ripped away. And so now, your home is gone. Your car. Your sense of security. These are the same things you lost in the month that Don died. Your parents' home. Don's car. Feeling safe. Now it's happening all over again. Of course you're exhausted and over it. But you're not going backwards. It feels that way, I know. But you have always moved forward since day one, even when it's tiny steps. It's very important that you see that right now and that you don't let this take you down. Believe me, if I thought that you were going backwards and not going in a good direction, I'd be the first one to tell you. But that's not what's happening.

Me: Then why does it feel like I'm losing everything all over again?

Caitlin: I know it feels like you're losing things. And I know you feel strongly that Don sent you there, to Forest Hills. And I'm sure he did, and you'll return there one day in the future, if that's still where you want to be. But let's not look at the losses for a second, okay? Let's look at what you've gained. In the five short months since you've moved out of New Jersey, think about all you've accomplished. You no longer have the daily panic attacks and anxiety caused from having to drive by the ER and hospital where he died so often. You no longer feel suffocated by "stuff" in that old apartment. You got a new job teaching comedy in the city. You've done a handful of comedy videos, for pay, with Opie. You're a featured writer on two significant publications/blogs. And you were asked to present at Camp Widow. You are writing your blog and book and helping people every day. ALL of those things happened because YOU made them happen. Have you ever seen the HBO film "The Girl?"

Me: About Alfred Hitchcock? No, I haven't seen it. Why?

Caitlin: It's about Hitchcock and his making of the movie, "The Birds." Throughout the making of the film, he is horrible to the lead actress, Tippi Hedren. He's controlling, makes filthy jokes, treats her awful, and traumatizes her. The last scene in the film, when she is being attacked by birds, he tells her they will be using mechanical birds and not to worry. Then, at the last minute, he changes it to real birds. He did over fifty takes in five days, just to torture her. She was traumatized, and the film had to stop production. Toward the end of this HBO film, the wife, Alma, asks his assistant, "What was so special about Tippi that Grace Kelly or Ingrid Bergman didn't have?" The assistant says that she thinks it was because, whatever Hitchcock threw at her, she just kept on going. It drove him crazy. Grace had elegance, and Ingrid had beauty, but Tippi took every piece of crap that was tossed at her, threw it down, and kept attacking right back. That's you. When I saw that movie, I immediately thought of you.

Me: Really? Wow. I don't see that at all. I feel like a loser, and I'm a huge mess.

My Husband is Not a Rainbow

Caitlin: It may not be pretty or elegant or perfect, but you FEEL and attack every single thing that comes at you, and you keep moving. Someone puts a bridge in front of you? You cross it. It breaks? You say, well this sucks, I guess I'll have to swim. You find a way to get it done, and you're also brave enough to tell the truth and show the world your pain, even when multiple people suggest rudely that you get over it. This is going to hurt like hell for a long time, and you're going to grieve for a long time, but I never worry that you won't be okay. You make things happen. That's just who you are. So many people in your shoes would just give up. Take an office job. Give up on their dreams. And that would be okay. But that's not for you. You're going to do big things.

Me: (crying) Thank you. I feel so judged and lectured by people lately, like everyone treats me like I'm some child, or like I'm never moving fast enough...

Caitlin: You're moving exactly how you need to be moving. Listen to me. I've seen a LOT of people who are stuck on stuck, and you're not one of them. You're Tippi. You're special. Whatever shit comes your way, you're ready.

"You can keep tossing all the shitty life at me
that you want,
But Fuck You Life,
I will keep crawling
and tossing it right back.
I have a good arm." – Chris Evan

FB Post: Hey kids! Guess what? Life just kicked good ole' Tippi in the face, once again! After finding a new roommate (Thanks Mindi!), and an apartment in Flushing, Queens, I am moving out May 6th. Found out today by the powers that be, that I just lost my Summer Teaching job at Adelphi. Normally, I teach a course in June and another one in July. Now, due to some silly rule about teaching too many credits in a calendar year, they are cancelling my summer courses this year. So now I'm moving, and one week later, I'm unemployed for June, July, and August. Awesome! So, for anyone who has lost count - I lost my husband, then my parents' home (my childhood home my whole life), then Don's car, then our home we shared for 7 years, then THIS home I thought I had found, then my second car, and now my summer job. Can life maybe fuck around with somebody else for a while? I'm really over this.
LIKES: 43   COMMENTS: 76

What Remains...

I am not really sure where my husband went off to. He died. Yes. But it never feels that way. It feels as if he were part of some horrible magic trick in some terrible, cheesy Vegas act. One second – here. The next second – gone. POOF! Magic! It feels as though I took a nap, and then woke up and he went missing, never to be seen again. He died while I was asleep. *Asleep*. I'm not sure that I will ever know how to process that. I'm not sure that I want to. I *am* sure that there is no such thing as "closure."

I am not really sure where I went off to. I'm alive. Yes. But it never feels that way. It feels as if I am part of some horrific magic trick in some awful, maudlin cruise ship act. That same hack trick where they pretend to cut the woman in half as she lays inside the box. Except it's not a trick at all. Every second that I'm here, living in this world, I am being severed in half.

My Husband is Not a Rainbow

Over and over and over again. He died while I was asleep, and when I woke up, he was dead. He was already dead. I'm not sure that I will ever know how to process that. I'm not sure that I want to. I *am* sure that there is no such thing as "better."

Where is that girl? That girl that my husband fell in love with. That girl that he believed in. That girl that he kissed for the first time on that New York City ferryboat when our smiles for each other lit up the night sky, when our futures were dancing with promise.

I once knew that girl who was hopeful and dreamy, quirky and warm, energetic and fun. She laughed with abandon. She loved her birthday. She lived for Christmas and all things family and dinner-parties and music and baseball. She had dreams, and after years of heartbreak, she had finally found love. The true, amazing, rare, once-in-a-lifetime kind of love.

But we didn't get the lifetime, and so that girl lost her hope and her dreams. She isn't really much fun anymore. She tries, but she is very tired, because this new life is exhausting and hard and long. Her big brown eyes feel gray and colorless. She feels guilty on her birthday, lonely and empty on Christmas, and baseball games don't seem to have the same impact without hearing her husband's ongoing commentary. That girl went to sleep one night, just like any other night. Except it wasn't. Because on that night, that girl went to sleep and woke up dead.

I'm not really sure where my husband's remains are, or what remains of my husband. In that gray-looking canister they gave me, all filled with dirt? In the sand and in the water where I tossed some of him on those meaningful days? In my heart – the way everyone is always telling me? In the universe, the clouds, the air? In the harmonies of a song so beautiful, you can hear your heart skipping? Maybe. But it never feels that way. People will feed you meals made up of the phrase, "*He is always with you,"* but actually knowing his touch is like trying to hug a butterfly.

I'm not really sure where my remains are or what remains of me. The pieces that were severed came off little by little, second by second, hurt by mind-numbing hurt. Maybe I lost an arm while running into the ER that morning. Maybe a leg was chopped off when the nurses surrounded me and said, "Massive heart-attack. He didn't make it." Maybe my soul disappeared while staring into that casket at my husband's eyes that were no longer his eyes or his face that was no longer his face. Perhaps my heart leapt out of my body and fell onto the wet ground when I got that autopsy report in the mail. When I saw his name on that death certificate. When my six foot four husband was handed to me in a can. Remains.

So what remains of that girl who died that day on that day that she woke up? Many things and nothing at all, really. Everything that she was – she is not. Everything that she is – she was not. Her laugh is broken. Her smile is weak. She has no time for petty shit. She feels compassion for those in pain. She feels connected to those who hurt. She feels jealous of those with long lives and long marriages, and angry at the ones who don't ever seem to appreciate what they have. She panics easily, cries effortlessly, and feels deep emotion with abandon. She doesn't sleep enough, she writes too much, and she eats too much. She doesn't know yet how to take care of herself. She doesn't know, yet, how to care. About life. About being alive. She doesn't understand this new life – this weird future without her husband. This universe where she doesn't grow old with him or spend decades with him or have children with him or retire with him. She doesn't understand, yet, all that there is to understand.

Not yet. Not ever. Not yet.

FB Post: One of my widow friends in the many Facebook private groups I hang out in, makes jewelry for a living. She offered to replace my wedding ring with a pretty amethyst ring that she would create for me. She said she knows that having a new ring where my other one used to be, will NOT make the pain go away of not having the ring that Don got me. But, at least there will be something there, instead of nothing, when I want to run my thumb over my ring finger and feel some comfort. Holy shit, I love widowed people. This is one of the nicest things anyone has ever done for me.
LIKES: 143   COMMENTS: 57

FB Post: On a road trip to my first ever Camp Widow, driving the 12 hours to South Carolina with my new friend Diane. We are half hour outside Myrtle Beach, driving on the creepiest roads imaginable. Even the tumbleweeds have left, and our GPS just gave up, like: "Shit! I don't know where you goin, but I ain't cut out for this!" I think we just passed the cast of "Deliverance." Diane wanted to stop and get gas, and I told her if we did that, we might not make it out alive. I can just see the headline now: "Widows Die en route to Widow Camp." This is going to be fun.
LIKES: 98   COMMENTS: 39

Hope Comes Alive at "Camp Widow"

Two women are standing alongside the ocean in front of the Marriott Resort in Myrtle Beach, South Carolina. They are lingering behind about a hundred or so other widowed people who have started to go back inside – women, men, married, unmarried, engaged, same-sex partners, old, young, international. People of all kinds, from all over, with one very harsh thing in common: the person they intended to spend the rest of their life with is gone. They died.

Kelley Lynn Shepherd

It is a little after midnight on Saturday, April twentieth, and we have just finished a ceremonial "ocean letter release," where we wrote love notes to our partners, attached them to ribbon and hearts (all biodegradable), and tossed them out to sea. Most have left the beach area by now, but some of us can't just yet, because the moment is too big and too powerful, and we still aren't done talking to our husbands. We never will be.

One of these two women happens to be me, and this other woman, maybe about five or ten years older than myself, comes walking up to me with tears in her eyes and a few glasses of wine in her stomach. It is pitch black outside, and only the stars and the waves washing up on shore act as our light to see one another. "I don't know who the hell you are, and I don't really care," she says to me matter-of-factly. Then she gives me a hug and starts to cry. We stand there together, arm in arm, looking out at the water. There are no other words. No explanations of any kind. There is no need for any of that. Because I already understand. In fact, *everyone* here understands. Welcome to *Camp Widow*.

If you are a widowed person, and you are reading this right now, try to picture the following:

Try to picture a place where complete strangers give you a hug or a smile or a comforting look, because they know where you've been, and they've walked where you've walked. A place that holds a formal and elegant Banquet Dinner Reception for its "campers," and where the DJ is specifically ordered not to play *any* slow songs the entire night – ever. A place where you can dance freely and openly and have fun without worrying about how you look to others or whether people will think that you must be "over it" or "getting better," simply because you are out and you have dared to laugh or feel joy again. A place where every single person around you understands how you can go from exhausted to angry to elation – all in the course of one hour. A place where you meet men and women whom you have been talking with for weeks or months or years online, and when you see them in person, you feel that instant connection, that bond that brings you closer. A place where they hand out kleenex before Workshops and Seminars, and where people don't look the other way or act all awkward when you bust out crying or when you mention your loved one's name. A place where you are no longer the misfit, because everyone is the misfit. Everyone is Rudolph, and you all get to hang out on The Island of Misfit Toys. Throw in two full days of wonderful speakers, presenters, Workshops, and Round-Table discussions (like a support-group, but with specified topics such as *Sudden Death, Widowed Without Kids, Long-Term Illness, Finances, and many other subjects),* all held at a gorgeous beachfront Marriott hotel with cocktail parties and social events put together just for us; and you've got yourself a truly unique, once-in-a-lifetime experience.

At Camp Widow, Michele delivers a Key Note Address to all the campers who traveled from all over the country and the world to be at this exciting event. In her speech this past weekend, she quoted from the beautiful poem A Summer Day by Mary Oliver, in asking us all this incredible question:

"Tell me – what is it you plan to do with your one wild and precious life?"

It is a loaded question, especially when you are grieving the loss of your life-partner and just trying to regain your footing. But when this woman stands up on a stage and tells a crowd of widowed people that *hope matters,* or that we *can* still have an amazing life, even if it's not the one we wanted or planned – I believe her. I believe her, because she did it herself. I believe her, because she is standing there in front of me, and she is made up of all her pain and strength and fear and love and grief, and she continues on. I believe her, because her life will always be complicated and wonderful and joyful and tinged with sadness and loss, and because she married again to a man who not only doesn't feel threatened that she will always love her late husband, but who fully supports her calling to help other widowed people throughout the world. I believe her – simply because she is alive.

For those that have been asking what *Camp Widow* did for me, or if I'm "all better" now that I went there – as I've said many times, there is simply no such thing as being "better." There just isn't. However, there *is* such a thing as recreating your life while always carrying your partner with you deep inside of your soul. There is such a thing as finding hope where you thought there was none, and light where you saw only darkness, and tomorrow where you couldn't see past today. There are new relationships and friendships to explore, and people to love, and things to learn, and beauty to see. And there is the fact that even though today I feel hopeful and inspired – tomorrow I will feel different. And then different once again. That's just grief. And that's okay. And then, of course, there is that lingering and very important question that still needs to be thought about, pondered over, and answered:

What is it I plan to do with my one wild and precious life?

I have no idea. But then again, maybe I do. In a lot of ways, I think I am already doing it.

"It's the love of my widow tribe that saves my life. True story." – Victor Buono

My Husband is Not a Rainbow

Dear Dead Husband:

Well, I did it. I moved. Again. My amazing friends helped me out. Again. This time, Ben and Rebecca and Shawn - and your Archie Bunker chair made the cut once again, as it sits now in our living room. I don't like this neighborhood at all. Flushing, Queens. It's so crowded and dirty and just doesn't at all feel like home to me. My new roommate, Mara, is really nice, and our apartment is spacious, and I have a home office to write in. The kitties seem happier here than with the other roommate, who clearly didn't like me. I just needed to write you and tell you how tired I am. I don't even feel like writing lately. What's the point? I need one of your massages right now. I wonder if anywhere will ever feel like home ever again. I wonder if I will ever really care about things ever again. I feel depressed. Camp Widow was amazing and hopeful, and my presentation was such a rush. I can't wait to do that again - to make widowed people laugh. But - coming home from that bubble of people who understand, it was so hard. And now I feel worse than ever. Like I'm just counting the days until maybe I can be with you, except I don't even think I would be with you if I died, because I don't really believe in that. So I'll end this depressing note here and just tell you again that I love you. Until forever xoxo.

Session Snippet

Caitlin: How was Father's Day? Was it hard on you?

Me: Yes. I just can't stop grieving FOR him, being sad about how he got so screwed in life. I'm more sad that he never got to be a dad, than I am about me not being a mom. When I think about his life, it makes me so sad. He was robbed of so many things.

Caitlin: I can see that. He did get robbed, and his life was way too short, and that hurts like hell. But his life was not sad. It may have started out that way, with family dysfunction and a bad childhood and all those things, but he never wasted time feeling sorry for himself or using it as an excuse or a crutch. He accomplished so many things in his forty six years. He was an Air Force vet, he helped animals, he helped and even saved countless people/patients working in EMS. And when he died, he had found love in you, and you gave him a family. He said to you on your wedding night, "Thank you for giving me a family." What a beautiful thing for someone to say to you. And you were his family, and nobody can ever take that away from you. You gave him that.

And he lived well, Kelley. He is one of those people who will be remembered because he left his mark on the world, and because you're helping to create a legacy for him. He was a comfort to so many people. Patients that were scared or maybe alone, and he was the last comforting voice they heard. He is the kind of person that makes other people want to be better, and that's rare. He didn't get enough time, but what he had was never wasted.

Me: You're right. But if he helped all these people, why couldn't his life be saved too? Why didn't anyone comfort him? Why did he have to die?

Caitlin: I don't think there's an answer to that question that will make you ever feel okay with it. It's not okay. It never will be. But you do need to learn to cope with it, and process it, and live in a world where that is what happened.

Me: But I keep going back to that morning. What if he was alone on that floor? What if he was crying for help and nobody heard him? What if he felt abandoned? I just can't stop thinking about it. I never get any answers.

My Husband is Not a Rainbow

Caitlin: Okay. I will bite. I will let you play the what if game, but if you're gonna play it, don't half-ass it. Really play it. Go all in. Play it fairly. Did you ever notice that all of your "what ifs" are awful, terrible scenarios? Do you know why that might be?

Me: I don't know. My mind just automatically pictures all the worst things.

Caitlin: Because you weren't there when he died. You were sleeping. And you have a lot of guilt about that. But you're torturing yourself by going in circles with all this stuff. You didn't kill him, honey. He died suddenly and tragically, but you didn't kill him. Stop punishing yourself for something you had no control over.

Me: (sobbing now) But he saved me every day that we were together. He saved my life in so many ways. Why couldn't I have saved him? How could I just be sleeping while he was collapsing and dying?

Caitlin: You did save him. You gave him love, and you gave him a family, and you made him very happy.

Me: But what if he never took that second job? What if he never moved to New Jersey and stayed in Florida, where he loved? Maybe he wouldn't have been so tired and stressed. Maybe he would have lived another twenty years before having a fatal heart attack.

Caitlin: Or maybe he would have been miserable and lonely and still taking care of his elderly, controlling mother, who drove him insane? Maybe he would have collapsed in Florida, alone, in his tiny apartment, never having found love? If you want to play this 'what if' game, let's go there. What if he wasn't scared when he collapsed? What if it all happened so fast, that he wasn't conscious or had no time to feel alone? What if the EMS team that took him in their ambulance were kind and made him feel safe? What if his last conscious thoughts were of you and your kitties and your life together, and what if those thoughts gave him peace?

Me: But you don't know that any of those things happened.

Caitlin: It's just as likely that those things happened, as it is that your scenarios happened. If you can at least throw these in there as possibilities, maybe you can let yourself off the hook. Start thinking of all the things you gave him instead of what you didn't. This didn't happen because you were asleep or because he had two jobs or lived in stressful New Jersey. It happened because he was a walking time-bomb with undetected heart-disease, and he had no idea. Nor did you. It will never be okay with you that he is dead, and it shouldn't be, really. But don't make yourself responsible for it, on top of the trauma and the grief that you already need to cope with. I'm not going to let you do that to yourself, even if it means I need to keep reminding you that you didn't kill him. You saved him, honey. Just like he saved you.

"Older now, gardens tended;
Working hard, fences mended;
Differences set aside;
Just in time, before you died;
Wasted years, Love offended."
– Nicholas Mucciarone

My Husband is Not a Rainbow

Stop Asking Me About "Someone New"

Ever since losing my husband, people have been constantly asking me about finding someone new. Dating. Everybody has to know if I'm dating yet, or when I will be, or why I'm not yet, and if I'm not, maybe I should get on that immediately in order to make them all feel better or more comfortable or less awkward with my existence. I have been asked and probed rudely about the dating thing by friends, non-friends, coworkers, family, and total strangers. Never was the very fine line between the comfort of the widowed community and the return to the harsh, brutal world more clear than on my return flight from San Diego to New York, after spending a week in the understanding company of a couple hundred other widowed "family" members at *Camp Widow*.

I was seated in the very last row, in the Aisle Seat, right next to the restrooms. Lines of people formed all around me over and over throughout the flight, as passengers rotated turns to get up and pee or take a crap, inches from my head. Everytime the toilet flushed, it sounded as if it was flushing inside of my eyeball. Seated next to me was a very young military wife and mother, all of maybe twenty four years old. Next to her was a six year old boy, her son. She began striking up conversation with me, because we were both terrified of the bumpy takeoff, and shared a second or ten of bonding in our mutual fear of impending death upon crashing.

Our bonding time ended with the inevitable question that you always get from a stranger: *Are you married?* How I answer this question changes daily, depending on the situation, my mood, and what response I feel, at that moment, might cause me the least amount of pain and anguish. It's a crapshoot though, because I rarely know or expect what people say to me, and therefore, I find myself with a dull ache in my side, no matter how I approach this. For whatever reason, with this woman, I decided to tell her the truth. She is a military wife, after all. Maybe she understands a bit about life and unexpected death and compassion. WRONG! When I told her point blank that my husband died almost two years ago very suddenly of a massive heart attack, she didn't even flinch or offer up the ole' *I'm so sorry for your loss*. Nope. Instead, she launched into an endless lecture that had me wishing I had a parachute to jump out of this plane and away from this offensive horseshit I was being forced to listen to:

"Two years and you're not dating yet? Why not? I'd be so excited to meet people and go out! Oh you need to get yourself out there, girl. He ain't comin' back. I know some good clubs and places, I could hook you up with some hot guys. I'm serious. Gimme your number. You are lucky I'm not your close friend, cuz I'd be gettin' on your ass for not movin' on and finding someone else already. I'm very blunt and I tell it like it is."

I felt like saying, "You're also an asshole," but I was stuck on a six hour flight next to this clueless dummy, and suddenly the smell of other people's poop didn't seem nearly as terrible as being wedged next to this person who showed zero compassion or understanding for what my life might be like. When we arrived back in New York and at Baggage Claim, we both waited by the carousel for our things. As I spotted my suitcase and struggled to lift it off of the belt, she spotted her husband, in uniform, and ran into his loving arms, just like in the movies. He picked up their son and twirled him around and gave them both kisses and hugs. They had each other, and I had Akmad or Rashim, who would be showing up in a taxi-service soon, so I could pay them to get me home.

Why is everyone so concerned with my dating status? Why the hell does a total stranger on an airplane care if I date people or not? What is with people? Do they think that if I find a new love, maybe get re-married, that I will finally be "over this?" That

My Husband is Not a Rainbow

they will no longer have to worry about me, that I will no longer think about Don every single day, that he won't be more than half of the puzzle that makes up my life? Don't they understand that wherever I go, he comes with me? Whomever I love, he loves too? There might be a day in the future when I can see myself with "someone else" – but that day is not now. Right now, the idea of "someone else" makes me feel physically sick. It feels like I'm betraying him. It feels like I'm cheating. It feels *impossible* to me that I can be in love with someone else, when I am madly and deeply in love with my dead husband. I know, logically, that being with someone else is not betraying him. But as I said before, what I know has nothing at all to do with how I feel. And right now, I feel like my marriage and our promised time and years together were violently pushed into an imaginary ocean where I can't see it, and I don't know how to swim to it. It's just gone, and I'm still here, trying to comprehend what to do with this massive and intense love that I have for my husband, who will never be able to hold me or laugh with me or love eating my dinners.

I'm not afraid to fall in love again. I am not ready right now, but I am not afraid of it. I will tell you what I *am* afraid of, though. I am terrified that nobody will want me again. I am scared that I will put my heart out there and get rejected. I am fearful of developing feelings for someone, maybe another widower or someone who "gets" this life, and having them not return my affection. I don't want to look for love again, because I am scared as hell that I will never find it. Or, I WILL find it, and then he will die too, and I will have to go through this shit all over again. No. Just... No.

The other day, a man in a blue uniform that looked similar to my husband's EMS uniform started walking with me as I walked home. He kept asking for my number, and I kept saying no. He continued walking with me and kept asking over and over to go out with me. I felt sick to my stomach. I felt offended by his existence. He wrote down his number on a piece of paper and told me to call him if I ever felt comfortable. Then he touched me on my shoulder very gently as he said his goodbyes. I turned the corner of the street, bent over forwards, and promptly threw up. That is how I currently feel when men who aren't my husband talk to me or flirt with me. Please just leave me alone.

"The cure for the pain, is inside of the pain." - Rumi

Session Snippet

Caitlin: So how are you?

Me: (breakdown sobbing uncontrollably)

Caitlin: Oh, honey! What is it? What happened? Did something happen?

Me: Yes. No. I don't know. It's nothing. Everything. I just feel like crap about myself lately. I feel old and fat and awful looking. My knees hurt and my joints hurt and I'm tired all the time, I have dry, cracked skin and my eyes look dull. I'm so sick of struggling with everything. Working part time, not finding more income, being broke all the time. Not being able to afford basic needs things like new bras or shoes that don't have holes in them. I just feel like crap in every way, and I'm resentful because I know it's all connected, so if Don didn't die, I wouldn't feel this way, and then I just get bitter all over again. I'm just so freakin' tired, and I feel like I'm banging my head against the wall over and over again.

Caitlin: What would you do with your life if you could do anything you wanted, and you knew you could make a good living doing it? Don't think about it. Just say the first thing that comes into your head, right now...

Me: I want to help people!!! People who are going through the same shit I'm going through. People who have suffered a huge loss. I want to help them. Nothing else makes me feel alive, except doing that. Everything else feels so pointless now. I don't know how to make that into a "thing" where I can survive from it, helping people through writing, speaking engagements, comedy, whatever. I don't know. But that's what makes me feel like I have any kind of purpose.

Caitlin: Well then, we need to come up with a way that you can make your living doing just that. Let's come back to that. Are you still not sleeping well? Have the rape nightmares returned lately?

Me: Yes. The other night, I woke up literally screaming, feeling like I was being choked, like what happened that morning. I wake up screaming, then I reach over to Don, so he can hold me and get me through it, and then I remember he's not there, and I cry. It's so awful. He would hold me and whisper to me that I'm safe, over and over. Now, I have a roommate whose room is next to mine, and she told me the other day that sometimes she hears me screaming or yelling in my sleep. So now I'm really self-conscious about even sleeping. I just hate all this trauma. It's been a part of my life so long, I'm just used to it. I forget it's not normal for other people to overhear it.

Caitlin: You can trust me if you'd like to tell me the details of that night. I know we have touched on it, but just know that we can take our time going through it, if you want to.

Me: I don't want to, but I think I might need to.

Caitlin: How come? You don't feel like you've worked through it?

Me: I don't know. I thought I did, but it keeps haunting me lately, and maybe that's because I just feel so unsafe lately, or because I really only know how to process through the rape trauma and PTSD stuff WITH Don, since he's the one who always got me through those nightmares and things. I guess I don't really know how to do it without him. I'm scared that without him here as my anchor, I'm reverting back to who I was right after it happened. This fat, ugly, weak, insecure, shell of a person. What if I'm becoming that person again?

Caitlin: You're not. That's not possible. You'll never be that person again.

Me: How do you know that?

Caitlin: Because trauma and loss change you. You're not that person anymore. You are more now. You are so much more YOU now, than you ever were before. You have done more evolving and growing in the last two years, than probably ever in your life. You are doing that because of the loss and because of the love. You won't ever go back to who that girl was. You just proved it. I asked you what you want to do with your life, and you blurted out, "Help people in pain!" I asked you that same question the first day I met you, and you said you wanted to be a success in comedy/TV/acting. The Kelley of then hadn't yet processed enough of the pain to do things like Pay it Forward Day or Camp Widow. You're different. You're better. Everything that Don was, the kindness and the selflessness, it's in you now. He has inspired you because he loved you, and you inspire others because you love him. That stays with you forever.

My Husband is Not a Rainbow

Me: (crying again) But he was the only person in this whole world, my whole life, who ever really loved me. Every relationship I had before him, was me loving them more, them not returning my feelings, or them making me feel like shit about myself. He was the only person who ever saw me for who I am and loved me anyway. All the people in the universe, and he was the only one.

Caitlin: Well, all we really need is one. And you had a really amazing one. We don't know what will happen in your tomorrow right now. Just live your today, and when those insecure ugly voices come in, fight them with Don's words. He would be telling you how incredible and beautiful you are, so believe him. And you're also a fighter, Kelley. You fight like hell for everything you've ever had.

Me: I'm tired of fighting. When is it my turn for stuff to just happen? GOOD things?

Caitlin: I wish I knew. You've had a lot of stress on top of the grief. You weren't left anything, sudden loss, no money, trying to get by, dealing with a past trauma on top of that - so it makes sense you'd be scared and feeling awful right now. But now is the time to hold on to all those things that Don knew you were. Hold onto that, because that love has changed you, and will continue to change you, and with it - you'll be able to make big changes in the world.

Me: Right now I'd just like to get through two weeks without a panic attack or nightmare and be able to pay my damn bills.

Caitlin: Okay, that's fair. Today, we work on how to pay your bills. Tomorrow, we work on how to change the world.

Kelley Lynn Shepherd

"How Life Rushes…
Surrounds us,
Overwhelms us,
Sometimes drowns us Alive.
Yet I have scarcely known a time
When it did not submerse me
In order to teach me how to swim." – Sarah Treanor

Why Do You Love Me?

It was sometime around early 2006, and Don Shepherd was now my fiancé, but not yet my husband. We had settled into engaged life and "living together" life, which was, for the most part, quite easy. His persona and laid-back attitude about everything made living together extremely pleasant and fun. Of course, there was my trauma. The rape that had happened in those very early morning hours as I awoke to the nightmare that was very real of this man, on top of me, choking me. Before Don moved in with me, during our dating years, we had a routine. If I had a rape nightmare or flashback, I would call him, no matter what time of night it was, and he would sit on the phone with me and talk me through it. Just hearing his soothing voice was oftentimes enough for me to feel calm again. Other times, he would remind me to breathe and that I was safe, and that nothing would ever happen to me as long as he was around.

One particular morning, after he had moved in with me, I woke up to the sound of myself screaming and that feeling of being choked. This had happened a handful of times before, but this time, it was worse somehow. It took me longer to realize that it was Don next to me, and not this person who had violated me and tried to kill me. I woke up by sitting straight up in our bed and gasping for air. Don was stunned awake by my noises of fear and gasping, and he got out of bed, walked around to the foot of the bed, and then gently approached me so that he was face to face with me, kneeling on the bed. He did not touch me.

Don: It's okay, Boo. You're okay. I'm not going to touch you until you're fully awake - but I want you to look at me if you can. When you can. Just open your eyes and look into mine, sweetie. Take a deep breath. In and out. That's good. In and out. I'm going to lean forward now and come toward you, okay? Is it okay if I hold you? I won't do it until you say it's okay.

Me: It's okay.

Then he would lean forward and just hold me while I would cry. Some mornings, I would cry for fifteen minutes straight. Other times, it would just be silence until I felt safe and okay again. Other times, he would startle me, simply by being a figure in the dark, and my instinct would be to attack him physically and defend myself. And still other times, he would sit there with me in the darkness for as long as it took for me to be secure again. Whatever the case, he always made it okay. He took on whatever I had to throw his way, and he took none of it personally. On that particular day, we held each other for a very long time and breathed into the safety of the moment. He then showered me with his choruses of, "You're safe with me. Nobody will ever harm you again. Not while I'm around. I love you, Bunny Boo." He stroked my hair and made sure that I was truly with him and out of the darkness of that nightmare.

After I stopped crying enough to where I could say words again, I asked him sincerely and curiously, "Why do you love me? I'm so damaged and broken. I feel like it would be a huge chore for anyone to love me. I don't feel like I'm lovable to someone."

My soon-to-be, beautiful husband, held my face with two hands, wiped away my tears, and said to me these words:

Kelley Lynn Shepherd

"You know, I spent a good amount of time over in Japan in my Air Force days, and I really grew to love a lot of their beliefs and customs. In Japan, they have this belief about being broken. If there's a bowl or a vase or a table or anything really, and it has broken pieces, they repair those broken pieces with pieces of gold. They don't believe that flaws or broken pieces are negative things. They believe it's those pieces that help make up a huge part of the object's history, so that history makes them unique and beautiful and special. Without the broken parts, they wouldn't be as special. So, the repairs are done with love and with patience, and not done to 'fix' the item, but done to help bring out its original shine again. That's what the gold is for. You're not a chore to me. You're beautifully broken, and it's an honor to be just a small part of the reason that you shine again. "

This was a gift that Don possessed. He could take any moment, even the most nightmarish one, and somehow turn it around to make me feel safe and loved and all things good again. He had a passion for loving what was broken and making it feel like the most beautiful, shiny thing. A thing made of gold.

Dear Dead Husband:

Thank you for being my husband and for loving me in the most amazing and selfless way that anyone has ever loved me. Today was/is so hard without you, my love. I sat by the water and cried. The sun kept shining down on me, and two seagulls followed me around as I walked the side of the bay. I put a message in a bottle and floated it in the bay in Sea Cliff, where we married on this day. I hope it reaches someone and they read it. You are everywhere, Boo. I just wish it was enough. It is never enough, especially on this, our wedding day. until forever xoxoxo…

My Husband is Not a Rainbow

Dear Kelley Lynn:

Today, October 28, 2013, the bottle that you put in the water at Tappan Beach Sea Cliff has been found!! My twin brother who is 73 and lives in Sea Cliff was walking along Tappan Beach with his wife this morning and found it. I assume the tide was low. He read your beautiful and meaningful message to me (I live in Houston, Texas) and we were both teary eyed.

I wish you every happiness in your life. Although, you do not think so today, you will be happy again, there will be joy in your life. I am not overly religious, but I do believe that God watches over all of us, and some day, when you least expect it, whatever it takes to make you happy again, will happen. No, I don't have the answer to why there is heartbreak and sorrow in this world, but I know we are all here to help each other through. Both my brother and I will pass along your meaningful advice to our loved ones and friends, and as soon as we come up with the best way to pay your Don's love forward within our own circle, we will let you know.

My very best to you...

Lois

Kelley Lynn Shepherd

Promises of Forever

It was a Friday evening, on October 27, 2006, when I would marry my very best friend. At the San Souci in Sea Cliff, Long Island, we would celebrate with about ninety friends and family, the legal bindings of our love story. So many things live in my heart, so many things I will never forget.

I will never forget how calm I felt. How I just knew that from now on, whatever happened in life, everything would be okay with this man in my corner. I had no butterflies or questions or doubts. I was anxious and giddy to walk down that aisle and meet my partner and say the words we had written out loud. I will remember doing the "First Glance" before the ceremony, where we took bride and groom pictures before guests arrived, and videotaped his reaction of seeing me for the first time. He teared up when he saw me, and our immediate family witnessed our loving eyes gazing at each other. I will remember how his voice shook from the tears in his eyes as he read his written vows to me, especially when he promised to be the husband that I always dreamed about. I remember Sarah playing the flute as I walked down the aisle. My dad handing me off to Don and lifting my veil that I hated and that kept getting in my way. My dad jokingly telling Don, minutes before the ceremony, "It's still not too late to back out, ya know." Don chuckling and shaking his head. All the family and friends looking at us lovingly as we stood there professing our love. How happy Don was to see his sisters, Karen and Marsha, in the same room together and getting along. How much they doted on him and loved him that day. How Rob and Mindy came all the way from Florida so Rob could be the Best Man. How they stayed at our crappy apartment, and he and Don made those nasty biscuits with sausage gravy and laughed at my total disgust of it. ("It's a southern thing," they said.)

My Husband is Not a Rainbow

I will forever remember our First Dance after all those dance lessons to learn the Foxtrot. The DJ's system went awry, and the song kept skipping, and then just stopped entirely. Don and I, dancing to the silence, trying to remember the steps, as our friends yelled out "1, 2, 3... 1, 2, 3..." in support. Afterwards, receiving our "scores" on poster-board, held up by the wedding party; my brother and my Maid of Honor, Lisa, giving us a score of negative 2, and ⅝, respectively. The song was "A Wink and a Smile," from the *Sleepless in Seattle* soundtrack. Since almost none of it actually played, we did a "second first dance" to Lionel Richie's "Truly," and invited all couples up to the dance floor.

Our "Christmas in October" theme that I had planned with such detail. Stocking stuffers filled with gingerbread cookies and CDs of love songs and Christmas music for our guests to take home. Ornaments and white lights decorating the venue, a Christmas tree in the front entrance, with wooden toy soldier ornaments as place-cards, letting people know where they would sit. My light silver dress, made by our family seamstress friend. How handsome Don looked in his tux, with his light silver tie. How I couldn't stop smiling for hours and hours. How multiple people told me I was the happiest bride they had ever seen, or that this was the most fun wedding they had ever attended. Our guests' reaction to the unbelievable amounts of delicious gourmet food we offered. The cocktail hour, with stations of endless appetizers, followed by a four course meal inside the reception. The open-bar. The best hot chocolate in the universe, with real cocoa, whipped cream, peppermint, and candy canes. The huge dessert bar that followed the huge meal after the huge cocktail hour.

Singing a duet/Christmas medley with my dad during cocktail hour as a surprise to our guests. Don and I sneaking some time in the Bridal Suite to eat our private plate of fruits and cheeses and chocolates, and so he could hold me and say, "We did it,

Kelley Lynn Shepherd

Boo! We're married! Thank you for making me the happiest man ever!" The toasts given at the reception by Rob, my dad, and then the truly hilarious and unexpected speech followed by a duet of the Bee Gees' "How Deep Is Your Love" by Kevin and John. All of us dancing and laughing and enjoying precious time together. Thinking to myself that almost everyone I know and love is in this room right now. Being overwhelmed with love and life and incredible family and friends. Doing the "Anniversary Dance" with our longest married couple, Chuck and Eve, and dancing side by side with them. Watching my mom and Don do the "mother/son" dance together and knowing how bittersweet it was for my new husband not having his own parents there on this day. Feeding my husband cake, gently, and him feeding me, gently, as Harry Connick Jr. crooned "Recipe for Making Love." Feeling like the night went by too fast and wanting it to last forever. Having the DJ end the night by putting everyone in a circle, dancing and swaying around me and Don, as Dan Fogelberg's "Longer" played, fittingly. Dancing with my husband and saying the word "husband" out loud, as many times as possible. Leaving the venue in the pouring down rain and driving to the hotel, where we would hang out with more friends into the night.

Going back to our hotel room, later that evening, and Don looking into my eyes as he said to me, "Thank you for giving me a family." Sitting in the hotel bed in tux and wedding gown, reading through all the cards and opening gifts. Eating cake and drinking leftover champagne. Giddy with joy and possibilities and love. It was the day that represented our now, our tomorrows, and our long-awaited future. Nothing could stop our love. Nothing could ever stop our love.

My Husband is Not a Rainbow

Words About Don

"I'm Christine. Kelley's mom and Don's mom-in-law. There are so many special memories of such a beautiful man, I really don't know where to start. I do know that my daughter couldn't have chosen a more wonderful husband than Don Shepherd.

One memory that really stays with me is when I think of the time just before their wedding. I was there for the weekend helping with things, and Kelley and Don were taking dance lessons. Don did not like to dance, but Kelley really wanted to do a special choreographed "first dance" foxtrot at their wedding, so he agreed to it.

One night, I joined them outside and watched them practice. It was a beautiful night on the park, alongside the Hudson River with the NYC skyline backdrop. Kelley and Don were practicing their steps over and over again. He was so incredibly patient with her, and I know he was just as frustrated as she was - but he just kept saying, "It's okay. Let's try it again." And again, and again, and again. I sat there, and my heart just filled up watching them and knowing how happy Kelley was with him, and how I could see how much he loved her. It was then that I knew how easy and natural it would be to love him like a son, which I did. Don never disappointed us. He truly was one of a kind and was taken from us far too soon. There will never be another Don Shepherd. You will be in my heart always. I love you, Don. Love, Mom" - Christine Niemi

FB Post: Today, after my 3rd class ended, a male student stayed behind and told me, "Professor, just wanted to share with you that I feel your pain. Last year, my mother and my brother both died instantly in a car crash together. Whenever I get depressed, I read one of your blogs. I think you are so brave, and I

wondered if I can give you a hug." He was in tears, and I was too. Speechless, really.
LIKES: 132   COMMENTS: 57

"Depression is very real. Anxiety and the feeling of being alone in a crowd is very real. Once I accepted 'yes I am depressed' then I could start learning how to breathe again." – Najee Gabay

Crumb of Cake

Call me crazy, but I'm starting to feel like maybe I'm a little bit crazy.

Is that crazy?

Is it Nuts-ville Crazytown that I feel like I am more in love with my husband now than ever before? That I would rather have one-way conversations with his spirit or soul than put any real efforts into possibly finding a new partner who I could actually speak to, human to human? Is it insane that looking at his picture on my nightstand before going to sleep, and saying out loud, in a faint whisper, "Goodnight BooBear – I love you" seems to make more sense to me than saying nothing at all? Seriously – level with me, people – is it time for me to just go and get the straightjacket, and try it on for size? Or is there a place that I can go to exist, where there isn't all this pressure to "move on" or "get myself out there again," and where having a continued relationship with my dead husband isn't universally frowned upon?

I know, I know. It sounds crazy. But is it? Is it?

My Husband is Not a Rainbow

This is the man I chose to spend the rest of my life with. This one. Not another one that I have to go find all over again at age forty two. Not someone new that I would have to date, get to know, figure out, play the stupid games, live the "single" life, read their mind, know their heart, and trust with everything. If I already trust everything with the person that I already chose, why should that have to change? How can it? How can I just not be deeply and powerfully in love with my person anymore? How do I train myself to fall out of love with him? How? And if the answer is that I don't have to, and that I can still love him forever – then how do I go forward in my life having this all-encompassing love for a person who no longer walks the earth? My heart hurts with how much I love him and with the reality that our time together here is gone. Four and a half years of marriage will just never be enough for me. Not ever.

Imagine being a baker, and spending seven years of life creating the most delicious, incredible, perfect chocolate cake – that took you until you were thirty five years old to get the recipe just right - and you were so proud of your cake, and you just wanted to savor in it and taste it over and over and over until time ended – and one quarter of the way through your first, tiny bite of enjoying all your hard work and your creation, before your taste-buds could even react – a large and menacing hand snatches the cake away abruptly and proceeds to smash it into tiny crumb bits, all over the floor. "But I only got one quarter of a bite!" you scream in protest. It's too late. Nobody cares. You only got a crumb of cake, and the rest was taken away for no reason at all. Time's up. (Leave it to the fat widow to come up with a cake analogy.)

I don't know how to do this. My heart is with my husband, and my husband is not here. And even though it is never fair or never enough, to have this new, other-worldly relationship with him – and it's not even close to the same thing as actually having him here with me – this is what we have now. We have this. And there is a very large part of me that would rather have this with my husband, than have something unknown with anybody else.

My whole life, nobody was ever in love with me. Nobody ever returned my feelings back. Nobody ever protected me or made me feel safe or truly, deeply loved. Nobody. Not until I met Don. Not in high school, not in college, not after college – nowhere. Nobody. I dated a lot of idiots over those young years. I had boyfriends. Some were nice, some were not. But none of them were deeply, madly in love with me. When I finally, FINALLY met my person – I was almost twenty nine years old. He was in Florida, I was in New Jersey. We bonded in a music chat room online and became instant friends. And then more. He flew out to meet me, and then we were in love. I told him things about me that nobody else knew, or knows. I shared with him my soul and my fears and my heart. For seven years, we dated long-distance, until he packed up his life and moved to New Jersey for me. Because he loved me deeply and madly. He supported me and cheered me on in my dreams. We were a team. Always a team.

Now he is gone. I know how to live without him. I'm learning, and it isn't easy, but I know I can do it, and I know I will be okay. I know how to live without him. But how do I *love* without him?

If I'm being totally honest, and I always am in my writing, I will say that I am terrified. I am scared to death of growing old all alone and dying all alone. Even more, I am frightened beyond words that he was my only person. That for the rest of my years, nobody will ever love me in that beautiful, amazing, trust-you-with-my-life sort of way ever again. I live in terror that I will be granted a long, healthy life – never being allowed another bite of that cake.

My Husband is Not a Rainbow

"When they were gone, so went my compass. I was adrift in a new reality without any direction or drive."
– Naomi Anhorn

FB Post: Emotional day. It is once again December 18, the anniversary of the day that Don proposed to me under the Rockefeller Center Tree. After last year's epic meltdown when I went to the tree alone way before I was ready, Caitlin suggested that she meet me there this year, and we will sit there together. So she did. And I was okay. Mostly. My stomach churned, and I cried a lot, but it didn't destroy me like it did last year. There was some healing today, and Caitlin offered to make it a yearly thing until I don't need her with me anymore. She is incredible.

The most painful thing that happened was lots of young couples kept asking me to take their picture under the tree. The first time, I took it. The second time, I took it hesitantly while feeling dizzy and sick. The next couple that began to approach, Caitlin stepped in and yelled "No! My friend here needs some space! No more pictures! Ask someone else!" then shooed them away. It was hilarious. I think that last couple thought we were both lunatics. Grief ain't pretty.
LIKES: 18   COMMENTS: 16

FB Post: 3rd Christmas without Don, first one I spent with my family again since his death. It was really really hard. I'm glad it's over. I did it, but wow. Everything is different forever. It's over, and I made it through. That's the best I can do for now. I'm tired, and Christmas still isn't Christmas. I wonder if it ever will be.
LIKES: 45   COMMENTS: 32

FB Post: Just saw my counselor for first time in a month. (Phone session last week due to awful weather). Gave her a hug, sat down, and she said, "So, do you know what day it is?" "Monday?" "Today is the 13th, and it's exactly two and a half years since Don died, and I had to tell you. You didn't know. That's fantastic!" I smiled with her, then randomly burst into tears, because I felt guilty that I didn't know. Welcome to grief.
LIKES: 67   COMMENTS: 23

FB Post: If I hear "He went to Jared!!!" come out of my TV one more time, I'm going to scream. Did he go to Jared? Did he? Guess where my husband went? He went to work, and then never came home because he DIED! Happy freakin' Valentine's Day everyone! (Sorry. I am in an angry mood tonight.)
LIKES: 98   COMMENTS: 56

Session Snippet

Me: I want to tell you something, but I'm afraid to say it out loud.

Caitlin: Okay. Just start talking whenever you're ready. I'm here.

Me: As soon as I say it out loud, then it's no longer just random thoughts inside my head and private, and now I have to be accountable for it.

Caitlin: Deep breath. You're okay.

Me: I realized something pretty huge about myself. I made a connection between my weight issues, my body image, and the morning he died, and all the days and weeks before that morning, and why I can't let go of the guilt I have for not being there when he died.

Caitlin: Well, don't keep me in suspense, you're on a roll here...

Me: I wanted to be there, not to say goodbye. I would never say goodbye to him, not ever. I wanted to tell him that I'm sorry. I'm sorry I didn't do better in our marriage. I'm sorry I was so lazy and didn't work harder so you didn't have to. I just sat back and let you take care of me in so many ways, because you were so good at it. You did it so well. I'm so sorry.

Caitlin: Keep going, this is really good...

Me: I should have gone on more auditions. I should have made it worth his time and energy of moving his whole life to be with me. I should have gone to the gym all those times that I said I was going and then just drove to McDonalds drive thru, stuffed myself with food, and listened to comedy radio shows. What kind of sick person sits in their car and lies to their husband about going to the gym?

Caitlin: A person who has lived through a rape, and who is living with trauma, and uses food as a form of escape and numbing.

Me: Why did he die? Why wasn't it me? I was the one who was overweight and never exercised. Not him. He played tennis. He rode his bike. He had an active job. It should have been me. I feel guilty for living. I feel sick that I'm alive, and his death STILL hasn't made me get healthier. What the hell is wrong with me? Why didn't I see this before?

Caitlin: You're seeing it now. Just saying all this out loud is huge. Now you can actually start to truly, really process through this and begin to heal. There's a lot of healing in what you just said. You chose to open this door. I didn't pry it out of you. You came here with it. That is so huge. I'm very proud of you.

Me: Well, I feel like I killed my husband. I feel like a horrible murderer.

Dear Dead Husband:

I need to bitch. I'm sick of this shit.

I just got finished directing a show. It was a huge variety show for Cancercare, for the Red Stocking Theater in Port Washington. I did this as a second job the past few months, in addition to my job as a professor at Adelphi. The rehearsal schedule and process was stressful and exhausting, and I felt out of my element as a first-time director for this organization. In the middle of all that, I flew out to Tampa for a week and did my comedy presentation again at Camp Widow. It was amazing. But when I got home, I collapsed and fainted on my living room floor. I was alone. You would have been horrified. I went to the ER, and it turned out to be a combo of severe dehydration, vertigo, and high stress. The bill is thousands of dollars, I can't pay it, my whole body hurts, and I'm just so over this life of me hanging on by a thread. I feel like I'm doing everything I can to make this life work, but things just keep pushing against me. I just wish you were here, because none of this would ever happen if you were here. I miss you so damn much. I hate this.

*"I visualized a black hole in my soul.
I worked very hard to stay out of the black hole,
and some days I did stay outside the hole.
But the sides were slippery slopes, and sometimes
I did slide in, sometimes for hours or days or even weeks.
Sometimes I jumped into the hole on purpose
and wallowed in the darkness."* – Sharon Paige

Session Snippet

Caitlin: So, you wanted to talk about your wedding video and how you haven't yet been able to watch it, because you're scared. What exactly are you afraid of?

Me: I'm afraid that once I press play and see him alive and moving and talking again, that I won't be able to stop watching it. That I won't want to come back to the reality of him being dead, so I'll just keep watching it forever, just to be in that place where we still have what we had.

Caitlin: Is that so awful? That you would watch it as a way to comfort yourself, or as a way to feel close to him?

Me: It feels unhealthy. Isn't that an unhealthy way to spend my time?

Caitlin: I don't think so. One of my widowed clients starts every day by having coffee and writing a morning letter to her husband. Does that ritual make her mentally unstable or not dealing in reality? This is her new way of having breakfast with him, something they used to do every day. It helps her.

Me: But what if watching the video becomes a crutch?

Caitlin: So what? What's it a crutch for? Life? You don't do crutch. You always live in brutal reality, that's your thing. You aren't going to go off the deep end here, Kelley. You just aren't. You'll probably cry a lot or a little, and if it's too much, you'll turn it off and try again some other time. Bring it here some week, and we can watch it together if you want. I do think it's important that you watch it in a safe space, somewhere you can go to pieces if you need to. So, that's here. I also think seeing Don on his wedding day, actually seeing how happy he was and how much he is smiling, it might help to combat some of that guilt you feel about whether or not he was happy in his life with you. Bring it with you. I'll put it in my safe, and you can tell me when you're ready. We never do the next thing until you're ready.

"The second I was widowed,
I was reborn -
And I was expected to drive,
when I had not even learned to walk yet."
– Fey Martin

On the Shelf

So here is something for your soul to snack on -

Other than my dad and my brother, and a few close friends that feel like brothers, I have not been held or hugged by a person of the male species in thirty two months. I have not been kissed in thirty two months. I haven't been told I'm beautiful, or FELT beautiful, in thirty two months. There has been no intimacy, no sex, not even any serious cuddling. Nothing. Do I miss all of these things? Of course. Who wouldn't? But other than the normal missing of these things from time to time, mostly I don't even notice it. Mostly.

Is that normal? Is it normal that it doesn't really bother me that I still have no desire to seek any of this stuff out? Is it normal that I still feel like, "If I can't be intimate with my husband, then I don't want to be intimate at all." Why do I feel like this? Is this normal? Am I normal? Is it weird that I don't even enjoy self-love, because I think about my husband, and he's dead, and so I can't get off?

I feel weird, because most widowed people I talk to have at least been physical with someone, even if they aren't ready to be in a relationship. I think I'm just weird. Or not normal. I don't know. For now, I'm going to put the idea of any of this away, on an imaginary shelf somewhere, and pretend it's not there. If I don't look at it, it's not there. If it's not there, it doesn't exist. And I will just die alone, with no hugs or love from other male humans. Is that normal?

"Greeting all strangers who pretend they see.
The traces I grapple, approaching year three."
– Alex Rivera

Dear Dead Husband:

The change in the air from humid to crisp, warm to slightly cool, puts a loud ringing bell on your death - as I ready myself for my birthday, then your birthday, Halloween, our wedding anniversary, Thanksgiving, proposal anniversary, Christmas, and then ringing in another new year without you. This time of year filled with holidays and family and love and my favorite weather and atmosphere, leaves way for a big red button on your forever absence - a button I'm forced to push again and again and again, letting off sirens of being left here on earth alone, without my person. A future without you still frightens me, as panic and anxiety curl their way back into my bed each night, grabbing the blankets and stealing my sleep.

I try hard to recall the earlier days of this grief, and to remind myself that there was a time I could not see anything but darkness and pain. A time when autumn leaves and sunsets and brightly lit moons and candy-apples and fried dough with cinnamon-sugar, all felt and looked and tasted like grey and blackness and death to me - because you were dead, so I could no longer see the beauty in anything. It took almost three years to see the beauty again and to look at the autumn leaves again, and really notice them and to care again. Now I see the colors. I feel the rain. I taste the sweet, cold ice-cream. I feel your presence with every bite. I hear your voice faintly in the silence of my own. I see your blue eyes inside the pale sky. You are everywhere.

But I am selfish. It isn't enough for me. I want more. You are everywhere, but you are also nowhere. You are not here, curling your way into our bed each night, grabbing the blankets and stealing my sleep.

"I want to be better.
I want life to be better.
I'm scared of living without my mom,
Yet I'm no longer afraid to die." – *Meghan Starkes*

FB Post: So that's it. It's done. My wedding anniversary. And it was a crappy and very sad day. Nothing I did made it any less sad. Watched some of my wedding video with Caitlin. It hurt my

heart to see Don alive and me so giddy-happy, knowing I haven't felt that kind of joy again since his death. Also hurt seeing the many people in that video who are no longer a part of my life, or who I barely see now. Everything changes when your partner dies. Everything. Watching that video made me miss that life and that happy me so much. Trying to build and create this life now, but man, it's so hard. Another long day tomorrow. Leaving this sad day behind. If you're in love right now, swim in it. Breathe it. Live it. You just never know when you could be watching video of yourself, laughing and joyful and giddy, coming to you from another lifetime ago. Goodbye, sad stupid day.
LIKES: 50   COMMENTS: 39

Session Snippet

Caitlin: So how was your week?

Me: I think I might be excited about Christmas this year!

Caitlin: Really? That's great! So you're not dreading it?

Me: I'm not. But it's more than that. I'm actually thinking about it. Like, I was sitting here this morning, thinking about Christmas. Thinking how I'm excited to eat fried dough, and unwrap stockings, and what I might get for my brother, and things like that. I think I might be able to eventually love it again, in the crazy way I used to love it. My heart is beating really fast just talking about this. I can't believe it might be possible!

Caitlin: It's possible, because you've made it possible. This is wonderful. A huge thing. And remember, if you should change your feelings again, and this excitement turns into sadness, it's okay. Know that is okay and normal. If that happens, don't get discouraged. Just remember the way you feel right now, in this moment, and know that those feelings about Christmas are once again possible, because you felt them. I'm so happy for you."

Me: But why now? Why today?

Caitlin: Why not now? NOW is when your heart is ready to let it in again. Now is when there is room for it, and that is a direct result of all the grief work you have done and continue to do. This is no accident. Now is just the time for it.

"Wisdom comes from Perspective,
Perspective comes from distance.
If you wish to know the Truth,
step back from everything you think you know,
and everything you think you are."
– Antonio di Napoli

Dreaming Under the Christmas Tree

It was our second or third Christmas season in New York City together, since getting married, and Don and I continued our romantic and fun tradition of going back to "our tree" at Rockefeller Center, on December eighteenth each year, the day he asked me to marry him. We would sit under the base of the tree, take in all the touristy madness, drink hot chocolates, and talk. Something about those twinkling lights in that ginormous tree seemed to make for wonderful conversations and dialogue. This day was no different.

Me: I love our tree. It's so peaceful here, even when it's loud as hell and tourists everywhere. I love when couples ask us to take their picture, because then I get to remember instantly how insanely happy I was when you proposed here. It takes me back, and I love that.

Don: Yeah, that was a pretty awesome day. I don't know why I was so nervous. It's not like I didn't know you were going to say yes. You already had our venue booked before I even proposed (laughing).

Me: Well, after going to Sarah and Julio's wedding there, I knew that was where I wanted us to get married. And I knew the proposal was coming, so I booked our date. I had no idea you were going to propose on the day you did, though. You hid it well.

Don: I kept checking my pockets every two seconds, thinking I somehow lost the ring. And it was fucking freezing outside. Jesus. First I move to Jersey, then I get down on my knees in freezing cold cement in front of hundreds. What have you done to me?

Me: I don't know, but I'm keeping you. I kinda like you. Boo, what if this huge tree fell on top of me while we were sitting here, and I became a vegetable? Would you leave me?

Don: Really? This again? Now?

Me: Yeah. What if?

Don: I wouldn't leave you, Boo. I will never, ever leave you.

Me: Do you promise?

Don: Of course. I know what's going on here, Boo. You're freaking out because two of our married friends are getting divorced. That's never going to happen with us. Never. We are going to grow old together. We have to. You promised me you'd move to Florida when we are old and gray and ready for that Early Bird Special at The Golden Corral. I'm holding you to that. I'm gonna be the best cranky old man ever! Hopefully I'll die the same peaceful way my dad did; in my late eighties, fast, and on the golf course.

Me: You can't ever die, Boo. I don't wanna talk about you dying.

Don: Okay. I'm sorry. I will say this though, and then we don't have to ever bring it up again. You just never know, with my job, what could happen. I could go into work one day and have a crazed patient stick me with a needle or point a gun at me. You just don't know what you're walking into. I feel good that if I ever did have to leave you, that you would be okay. I mean, it would be really awful and life-changing and all that, but I really feel like you are a smart, independent, amazing person, and you would eventually be okay. You know how to be on your own.

Me: (tearing up and hugging him) I don't want to think about it, ever. That's not going to happen. We are going to be old and annoy each other to death, until we are both in our nineties and finally wear each other down. That's why I picked you, Boo. Because we take such good care of each other, and I knew that growing old and maybe sick would not be so horrible with you. You make everything that's horrible, somehow better.

Don: Aww, thanks Boo. I'm a calm person. And I enjoy calming you down and trying my best to alleviate your panic sometimes. Don't worry, honey. Even though my dad barely gave me the time of day in his life, at least I feel good that he passed down to me two things; a great, full head of hair and a really strong heart. I'm not going anywhere, Boo. You're stuck with me.

Me: You're my favorite person to be stuck with. I love you.

My Husband is Not a Rainbow

Don: I love you too, Boo. Let's go home and sing to the kitties.

"I won't say goodbye
Our love will not die
We will always be under
the very same sky." – Polly Coaker

FB Post: Weirdest thing ever just happened. Took a walk down Main Street Flushing, my neighborhood, and there was this makeshift psychic lady set up on the side of the road. Her sign read, "Psychic Reading: $2. If you hate it, it's free." I wasn't going to stop, but she yelled out to me as I was walking by, "Someone you love dearly just had a milestone birthday." From there, it got even weirder.

"Please sit. I will tell you more if you give me your hand so I can read your palm," she said. I sat down in the tiny folding chair, wondering if there was a hidden camera somewhere, or if I was in some sort of acid trip or weird dream. "There was a birthday, but the person was not here to celebrate it. It looks like a best friend or husband energy." "Uh-huh," I vaguely got the words out, shocked to my core at how the hell this woman was knowing all of this, just from squeezing my hand. She went on. "You have been blessed with the gift of true and deep love, the kind that transcends time. But you feel this love was also cursed, because it was snatched from you, and you feel that you will never have it again. You feel that you will live your life alone, and you are scared."

Hell yeah. I'm terrified. But HOW DOES SHE KNOW THIS??? "You're writing a book, yes? It will help a lot of people and lead into new adventures. You will also get work as an actress. I see a beautiful and bright future for you." She continues to talk to my speechless and glassy-eyed face, "You are wrong to think that you will never have another epic love story. There is someone. He is far away now, and you will need patience and more hurt before you find him. There is something else, too."

"What is it?" I ask, leaning forward with anticipation, waiting to hear the details of my own future life from this random woman with Tarot cards and wrinkly fingers.

"Your joy? It will be bigger and more stunning than anything you have ever imagined."
LIKES: 236   COMMENTS: 88

"Energy never dies. It's transformed into another state.
Our loved ones are all here with us,
but it's sad,
because they are ignored." – Todd Krewal

Session Snippet

Me: I'm having really awful dreams lately. I've had like four of them right in a row.

Caitlin: What kind of awful? Are they the rape flashbacks coming back again? Or dreams about the morning Don died?

Me: No. Neither. These are different. (starts sobbing) These are just… so awful.

Caitlin: Can you tell me, sweetie?

Me: He keeps leaving me.

My Husband is Not a Rainbow

Caitlin: In the dreams, he is dying and leaving you?

Me: Yes. Well, no. He's leaving me. But he's not dying. He's leaving me on purpose. I keep dreaming different versions of him wanting a divorce. It's so awful.

Caitlin: That sounds really painful. Can you describe the last one you had?

Me: I walk into our bedroom, and he is there, alive. And he is packing. He is packing suitcases and putting all his stuff away. I say "What are you doing, Boo?" And he says, really matter of factly, "I'm leaving you." (sobbing hard) And then he says: "I don't love you. I never did. I want a divorce. And I'm taking the kitties with me. I'll take better care of them than you would."

Caitlin: And then what happens?

Me: I guess nothing. I start crying, and then I think that's how it ends.

Caitlin: So he doesn't actually leave you? He doesn't get up and walk out the door in the dreams?

Me: I don't remember him doing that, no. Why? Is that important?

Caitlin: Well, I'm no dream analysis expert, but I think there are a few things going on here. I think you lost your wedding ring, so your heart and mind are extra fragile right now, since not wearing the ring makes you feel less like you can "pretend" that you're still married in your mind. I also think you're coming up on the death anniversary in a few months, and you are starting to slowly evolve in your grief process. I think this is your mind messing with you. All the other dreams you have had about Don, where he was in the dream talking to you, they were comforting dreams. They were more like visitations, where he was visiting you from the other side in order to help you with something. And in those dreams, he feels very real, and the things he says are very much things that he would actually say. In this one, does he feel real? Does it feel like him?

Me: I dunno. It feels really mean. He's being mean to me. But Don would never ever say he is leaving me, and he would never be mean to me. He has never once been mean to me, in real life, ever. He promised me that he would never ever leave me, that we would be together forever, and he would love me forever.

Caitlin: Exactly. Don would never say those things to you. He would never be that awful or speak in that way to you. Not ever.

Me: So what are you saying?

Caitlin: That this wasn't Don. Don made an appearance in those other visitation, loving dreams. This was not Don. This was your mind and your insecurities and your psyche playing tricks on you. It was one of those dreams where you are sort of disguised as Don, but in actuality, you are talking to yourself. It's classic "Kelley beating herself up," because you don't take care of the cats like he did, you lost your ring, you feel like you failed him, you feel like you can't make it in New York City on your own, you feel guilty for living, for being asleep while he was dying. This is another way to punish yourself while you sleep. It's all of that coming to the surface. This is not Don speaking to you. It's you.

Me: How do I make them stop? They are awful. I cry all day after these dreams, because I hate having this vision in my mind of him not loving me. I can't live with that.

Caitlin: You shouldn't have to, because it's simply not true. Try meditating before bed. Light some candles, put some soft music on, and get into a more peaceful state of mind. If you're still having these dreams a month from now, let's talk about it more. I think something deeper might be going on here as well. Something having to do with that shift I talked about earlier in our work together. How you will always be connected to Don, but at some point, the goal is to shift your relationship with him into something that makes more sense in your new reality. You may very well be starting that process, even if you can't consciously feel it. How have you been feeling lately about the concept of "someone else?' Does that idea still make you want to throw up? Sick to your stomach?

Me: Sometimes. I don't think about it much, other than people constantly pressuring me to "get out there" and date again. And so many widowed people are dating now - my friends that I met when Don first died, a lot of them are now in new relationships, or even remarried by now. And I'm over here not even wanting to think about it. It feels really lonely, like I don't really fit in anywhere. My single friends all want to hook me up with someone, go out and find someone for me. Not interested. My divorced friends are angry and bitter, or just have a completely different reality than mine. My married friends either leave me out of stuff, or if I go, I feel like a third wheel or just really sad. And now my widowed friends are all repartnering. And I'm still scared as hell about ever finding love again.

Caitlin: Believe it or not, that's a pretty big shift from where you were last year, or even a few months ago. You were very specific about not wanting new love, probably ever. You said it wasn't for you. You got sick to your stomach, literally, when men would approach you. Now, you've gone from actively and physically hating the idea, to "I don't know. I don't think about it much. I'm scared." That is a shift in your heart. To no longer have to run and throw up anytime a guy flirts with you - and instead, just be sort of nonchalant about it - big progress.

Kelley Lynn Shepherd

Me: If you say so.

"It felt like I had one foot in the widowed world and one foot in the living world." – Doug McKinney

FB Post: Do you know what I miss most of all on Valentine's Day? It isn't the receiving of gifts that Don would give me on this day. It isn't the 2 bouquets of flowers (one from him and one from the cats), the 2 cards, (one from him, one from cats), or the chocolates. It's not the dinner either I would make for us, or the local restaurant we would go to together on this night. Nope. It is not any of those things.

What I miss most, is that moment right before the receiving of these things. That moment, when I would be sitting in our living room, anticipating my husband coming home. The apartment would smell of lasagna or his favorite Swedish meatballs that I had cooked, and I'd be writing out my cards for him excitedly, because I loved doting on him on this day too. I miss that very specific sound I would hear as he unlocked our front door, and turned his key, and the cats would go sprinting to greet him. If I was in the other room and couldn't see him just yet, I'd hear that "crinkle crinkle" sound of the plastic wrapping around the flowers that I knew were for me. My heart would skip a thousand beats, and I would run out for a hug from my person - who chose me over every other person, and who gave the best hugs on this planet. That crinkle-crinkle sound defined my beautiful, ordinary, everyday, love-filled life.

In Tampa, at Camp Widow last week, while out at dinner with a bunch of widowed friends, my dear friend Arnie proposed a toast, "To those who left us, yet brought us together." The story of me and my husband lives on every time I decide to live life. It's not easy at all, but love really does live forever. And in

knowing that, I will listen very closely and hear that crinkle-crinkle of the love that will keep on following me home.
LIKES: 124   COMMENTS: 76

Words About Don

"I met Don when my friend, Kelley, started dating him. Me and John instantly liked him. Eventually, we all became a group of friends. John met Jessica, Kelley introduced us to Vanessa, and all of us would make each other laugh for hours on end. So many laughs.

So many things about Don I will hold in my heart. His love of music. Him falling asleep so easily in his recliner chair. His love for his cat, Isabelle, and then for all of his cats, after her death. And his favorite beverage: root beer, no ice.

In 2010, I was invited to spend Christmas with Kelley's family. A huge storm was predicted to hit the day after Christmas, so Don and I decided to head back a day early and drive back to New Jersey together, late on Christmas night. For five hours in that car ride, Don and I talked everything from politics to his love for animals, and how he thought that most humans were stupid. He spoke about his love for his wife, and how much he believed in her. It was obvious that he knew. He knew how much he was loved, how much his family/Kelley's family, loved him, and he knew that what he had was something special. I'm so very grateful for that car ride and to have known this gentle soul of a man. My friend, forever." - Kevin Conn

Kelley Lynn Shepherd

Dear Dead Husband,

I feel like shit today. Lately. Ever since I lost my wedding ring. And then the awful dreams where you are yelling at me and want to leave me by choice. I know it's not you. I know it's my stupid mind, but it still hurts so much. Nobody talks about you anymore. I feel so alone, like I have to pretty much beg people to tell me a story about you or something. I just want to hear endless stories about you. You loved me so well. I don't know how to even begin to think that anyone else would be capable of that. I wish people would talk about you. I wish my thoughts would make sense. I'm writing a book about you, and I'm so resentful about it. Like, I don't want to write a BOOK about you and about losing you and your death. I don't want a stupid book. I want YOU. I miss us. I miss our life. Our friends. I feel abandoned. My friends are still around, but it's all different now without you. I miss all the things we used to be. Can you please come back soon in another dream and not be mean to me, but say something that comforts me and gives me some hope? I'm sorry I rely on you so much. I just really miss having your amazing words and hugs to guide me. Until Forever, xoxo

"The loss of you often surprises me. At rehearsal tonight, I sat in the balcony, and without thinking about it, I moved into the row, leaving the aisle seat for your long legs and big feet. And then I suddenly remembered that you were never going to be sitting there with me again, and it took my breath away." – Rebecca Daniels

Session Snippet

Caitlin: Hi Kelley. You wanted me to give you a call? Everything okay?

Me: No. Not really. (sobbing) I feel like I'm drowning. I'm so tired of death and grief and missing him. Tired of thinking about this all the time, tired of trying not to think about this. It's so tiring just doing every fucking thing. And the dreams haven't stopped. They are getting worse. I took a nap earlier, because I'm sooo tired, and fell asleep accidentally. When I woke up, I had this awful feeling like Don had just left me. In this dream, he actually handed me papers, and he was standing there holding a pen. He said, "You need to agree to this. It's time. We have to get a divorce." I just can't stop crying over this. Why do I keep dreaming that he wanted to divorce me? This is horrible.

Caitlin: I know it is, but this is actually a very big deal. I think I know what's going on here. Now that these dreams have happened a bunch of times, I'm ready to tell you that I really do think this is all part of that shift in continuing bonds with Don. These dreams are representing him coming to you, or your conscience coming to you, or both, and saying, "It's time to start shifting our relationship. You're ready."

Me: Ready for what? What does that mean? And why does the idea of that make me cry so hard?

Caitlin: Because this is very, very hard stuff. Because it's the end of something, and a form of letting go. Remember when I told you that you never have to let Don go? I meant that. But you do need to shift your connection with him into something that feels more healthy and realistic. What's happening with these dreams, is the idea of "divorce" is really a metaphor - it's your soul telling you that Don is no longer your husband. All this time, you have said that you still "feel married," and that's okay.

But that won't last forever. It can't, in order for you to process through this in a healthy way. Don and your soul are letting you know that it's okay, and that if you're ready, it's time. It's not a traditional divorce. It's a divorce from seeing Don as your husband and realizing that you are his widow. He's not here on earth, so he can't be your husband, honey. And you can't be his wife anymore. You have to shift it into something else.

Me: But how?

Caitlin: You're already doing it. You're doing it everyday. This is your heart catching up to the hard work you're doing. The dreams will stop once you say out loud and start to feel and believe and think about Don in a slightly different way. It doesn't mean you can't miss him as your husband. You will miss him forever. What it means is that you now have chosen to recognize and acknowledge that part of your life has ended. In order to begin this new connection with Don, you need to begin to let go of the old one. And I know it's the hardest thing to hear, and one of the hardest things to do, but once you do this, I think you will actually feel him closer to you in time. And you will free yourself of the guilts or weird feelings you have about moving forward. He's still going to be there. He's still connected to you, always. You just have to make room for more love now, and he wants that for you.

Me: Okay. I think I just need to sit here on the phone with you and cry. I feel like I need to cry. Just thinking about him not being my husband, or not thinking of him as my husband, makes me cry. I want to cry for a billion years, and I feel like I will still love him.

Caitlin: You will. And he loves you. But what you're doing here, slowly, is shifting from a place of being "in love" with him, to a place of "loving him." You will love him forever. But being "in love" with someone who can't be your husband and can't actively provide you with things that couples provide isn't serving you well anymore. This won't happen overnight, this shift. But it's profound, and you understand it on a level that most people don't, and so that's why you're crying so much. This is a very, very big deal.

Me: So it's okay if I still feel like I'm "in love" with him sometimes? Because the idea of letting go of that hurts so much, even though I know it's not healthy to hold onto him in that way. Part of me wants to anyway. Part of me wants to just be in love with him forever and let that be enough.

Caitlin: Your heart will go back and forth for a while. This is not an overnight thing. But you've already begun to make this shift. The dreams are the biggest indicator. Acknowledge all the fears and emotions you are having. Write them out. Process them. I really think the dreams will stop after this conversation, or begin to stop, and you'll feel a tremendous release in some way. And Don will find a way to let you know he is right along for the ride. He always does. He always...

Me: Holy shit...

Caitlin: What happened?

Me: You're not going to believe this...

Caitlin: What???

Me: I just heard Don talking to me and felt his hand on my shoulder, right this minute, AS I'M TALKING TO YOU!

Caitlin: Jesus, he doesn't waste any time. What did he say?

Me: He said, "Step into your life."

Caitlin: Wow. That's powerful. He's helping you write again.

Me: He just said it again. He said it three times into my ear, while I felt his hand rubbing my shoulder. "Step into your life."

Caitlin: Are you writing this shit down? Write it down!!! Get off the phone with me and go create something with those words!!! This is the shift I was talking about. He wants you to live your life, and he will always be right there beside you, but telling you it's time for you to step into life again, instead of just existing.

Me: This is insane. He's still talking. It's like the dreams I used to have where he would talk to me in a comforting way, but I'm wide awake. I'm writing it all down. Looks like Don and me are about to write an epic poetry piece...

Caitlin: GOOOO!!!! Go write it!

Me: He just said the same thing. He said, "Go. Step into your life..." I literally feel like he's talking to me and telling me what to write, and I'm furiously scribbling the words down, but they are only half coming from me, and half coming from him. This is some bat-shit crazy, weird stuff. I gotta go...

Go (Step Into Your Life)
Written by Don Shepherd and Kelley Lynn

Go.
Step into your life.
The one that waits for you
the one that knows
of the promises you made long ago,
to dream
to risk

My Husband is Not a Rainbow

to dare…
Step into the moment,
to become that thing
the thing that you were meant to become
the thing that you always were,
somewhere deep within,
but lost along the way.
Be that thing now…
Right now.

Go
Walk beside your vision
crawl there if you must
breathe through the fire that burns you,
the swords that stab you,
the fears that stop you,
time and time again.
Each time you fall, or each time that needle
travels through your heart and into your open wounds,
stare it down.
push it into the cold bricks.
Look it in the eyes and tell it,
"You are nothing,
for I have been through worse."

Go.
Run into that spotlight.
Stand upon your mark.
Claim the very universe,
that is yours in which to play.
Seize the absolute second,
in which the world receives your talents,
that I have always seen.

Go.
Are you afraid?

Kelley Lynn Shepherd

I know you are afraid.
Please, my Sweet Angel,
Don't be afraid.
For you have loved me better,
and with more wholeness,
to last ten thousand billion moons.
And even though I can no longer sit beside you,
I am still beside you.
In heart.
In spirit.
In soul.
And everytime you take your life,
and you create it,
and you build it,
and you fill it up with wonder,
you embody
the very thing
That is Love.
You loved me better,
than I have ever been loved or felt love,
before.
You filled my life with everything,
in the short time I was here.
And now that I am living
On a star,
Or in a sunrise,
I want you to know,
that when you Go,
when you go off to collect your dreams,
when you leap forward to grab that Bliss,
when you dance wildly across the finish line,
Do not be afraid.
Because in that moment when you have reached
the brightest star
and called it your new home,
you will not have traveled away from me.

My Husband is Not a Rainbow

You will not be leaving me behind.
No.

When you reach that star,
and you sit along its corner,
There will be a breath of air,
and a hint of music,
a melody
hidden just for you,
within the silence.
That is me,
us,
Love,
Our Love,
Living and laughing and singing
deep within
the night sky.
And you will always feel that love
and be aware of that love
every single time you decide
To live.
So go,
Sweet Angel.
Go and step into your life,
And I will meet you,
Inside
our special place.
I will meet you,
inside the rhythms of the music.

Hurry up, my love.
It's your time now.
Step into your life.
I love you.
Now go…

Kelley Lynn Shepherd

Dear Dead Husband,

It's been about a month since you spoke in my ear while I was wide awake, just seconds after me "shifting" my connection with you and acknowledging out loud that we could no longer be husband and wife. Our writing piece that came from that conversation was so damn powerful, and it made me feel so close to you again, just like Caitlin said it would. I want you to know that since you said those words to me, I have been taking small steps to "step into my life." I'm directing and writing the spring cabaret theatre show at Adelphi. I remember how much you used to love helping me with lights or tech stuff, or any way you could help. I'm also teaching another round of Monday night stand-up comedy classes in the city. Caitlin thinks I would make a really good grief-coach, helping widowed people especially, to process through their emotions and feelings. I'm going to sit in on a couple of her grief support groups, and I already have the experience of facilitating some grief groups and round tables at Camp Widow. My new website is finished and has sections for writing coaching, grief coaching, speaking engagements, and comedy. I'm writing this book still, but suddenly, I feel a bigger sense of purpose with it. And today, I had my very first grief coaching client over the phone. I will never forget this day, April tenth, because it's the day where my pain officially flipped to the side where I can use it to help someone else. I'm not sure how much my words helped her, but I do know that being in the act of trying to help her felt really really good. I love you, Boo. And I will keep trying...

"Somehow, I have learned to cope
I look to the future, find some hope.
While I may not always thrive,
the important thing is, I survive."
- Julie Zimmerman Derrickson

When Your Husband Is in EMS
(a random, typical day, during our marriage ...)

Me: Boo, I have a headache.

Don: Aww, poor Boo. Go into my bag over there and get out some of the naproxen.

Me: The what now?

Don: Naproxen.

Me: I don't know what words you're saying, but do we have any Aleve?

Don: That is Aleve.

Me: Oh. Then why not just say Aleve?

Don: Sorry Boo. I forget I'm talking to a civilian sometimes.

Me: Smart-ass. (looking through) There's no Aleve in here. Do we have any Tylenol?

Don: Oh yeah. Acetaminophen.

Me: God bless you.

Don: But who's on first?

Me: I don't know.

Both: THIRD BASE!

Me: (laughing) So, aceta... whatever you said... that's Tylenol?

Don: Yes, Boo. That's Tylenol. Want me to get it for you?

Me: No, that's okay. You're busy. You're sitting in a recliner chair with cats all over you.

Don: They do look pretty comfy. I'd hate to move them.

Me: How many should I take?

Don: Eh, I'd go with five hundred milligrams, keep it under three thousand for the day.

Me: What the F are you talking about? Speak English! How many pills is that?

Don: Oh. Sorry. Take two now. (laughing)

Me: I'm gonna need to take five more just to get through this conversation with you.

Don: Very funny, Boo.

FB Post: I'm in the greenroom with the band at The Bull Run, about to go onstage and do my stand-up comedy opening act for the band. I gave the band their cue for when I'm almost done with my set, which is the story about how my husband is not a rainbow. Just then, the drummer, our good friend Ron, said to me, "I wish he was here tonight. I hope that he's here tonight." I responded that he is, and that he loves to send me big and obvious signs through music and humor to show me that he is around. Just then, the pianist in the downstairs lounge area began playing. His song choice? "The Rainbow Connection." Good one, Don. I laughed out loud.
LIKES: 78   COMMENTS: 12

"Is it okay for me to take a break from missing my wife so I can miss my dad?" – Wade Winfrey

Death, Dads, and Sand Castles

Today is hard.

It's hard because I know better. I know that life is short and oftentimes very unfair. I know people can be taken from you suddenly, without any warning whatsoever. I know what it's like to stare death in the eyes. To wake up to the shocking news that your husband has died. To be taken to a private hospital room to "see him" after he is already gone. To have a forever-image in your soul of his puffy arms and neck, lying in a casket. To have no goodbye. No goodnight. No good morning. No chance to breathe or adjust or process.

On days like today, Father's Day and Mother's Day and all the other difficult "special" days since losing my husband, I long to go back. I want to go back to me and my brother and my dad playing on a Cape Cod beach. My dad swimming with us in the big waves, holding us tight and keeping us safe. My mom hugging us kids by the Christmas tree as we opened our many gifts, or making us a special birthday cake that looked like Winnie the Pooh or Raggedy Ann. Always making us feel special, always making us feel loved.

It was a time before I knew what pain or illness or death was. A time where getting some penny candy or riding the go-carts or building a really cool fort with the neighbors was my biggest goal on a typical summer day. A time where my legs were as skinny as a carefree girl with no problems, and where my dad actually still wore shorts. It was a time where a trip to Johnsons or Kimballs Farm for ice-cream made me the happiest person in the world, and where dad's steak on the grill or mom's homemade spaghetti and meatballs were about as complicated and awesome as things got. A time where I knew nothing of disappointment or fear or aging. A time where dreams were made out of Legos, and hope sat inside of every badly-made sand-castle.

In many ways, I was lucky. The fact that my first instinct is to go back in time, whenever I'm faced with difficult or tremendously sad days, makes me lucky. Because it means that my childhood was happy and filled with love. It means that I had both of my parents, and that they both loved me, and that nothing earth-shattering or tragic happened during those years to take away my innocence. Not everybody is so lucky.

My husband, Don, was not one of the lucky ones. He was the product of an affair, and his biological father had a family of his own. Don's mother, who was quite controlling and manipulative, kept Don and his real father apart his entire adolescence. For almost twenty years, my husband thought that he was the son of a terrible man – his "stepfather" – who did nothing but abuse and harm his mother, and who one time, held an infant Don over a high balcony, threatening to let him go unless Don's mother did whatever ridiculous thing he was demanding at that moment. My husband witnessed countless acts of physical and emotional abuse on the women in his childhood home, and eventually, his mom packed him up from their home in Whittier, California, and they escaped the evil stepfather.

Somewhere around his twentieth birthday, my husband's mother decided it would be a good idea to inform Don of who his real father was and to set up a meeting between them. According to my husband, this meeting was awkward at best, and the man that was his father, although a very nice person with a good heart, did nothing that day or in the years to come to show Don that he wanted to be a part of his life, or that he mattered to him. Never in my life will I understand this, how a grown man felt no need to acknowledge or love his adult son who only wanted a relationship with his father. They usually spoke about once a year – on Father's Day. Their conversation was always the same. Don would wish his dad a Happy Father's Day, his father would ask, "How are you and Kelley doing?" and then he would make up some excuse as to why he had to get off the phone.

I would spend the next hour consoling the man I love, trying to answer his painful questions of: *Why doesn't he want to get to know me? Why doesn't he care?* It broke my heart into about ten thousand pieces, each and every year. His father continued to keep Don's existence a secret within his own family, and so, about one week before our wedding in 2006, when Don's father passed away, nobody told us. Nobody knew to tell us. Nobody knew there *was* an us. We found out almost two years later, after receiving a letter from a woman in Alabama. The letter read, "My name is Cynthia, and you don't know me, but I think we share the same father. I'm writing to let you know that our dad died and to see if you'd like to connect or talk."

During the year before we got married, I had written some letters, with Don's permission, to his father, expressing how much it would mean to the both of us if he would be at our New York wedding. (he lived in Florida) Included in the letters were several pictures of me and Don together, happy in our joyous "engagement high" and loving our life and our future of many promised years. I remember Don calling him just a few days after he proposed to me, excitedly telling him about how he had asked me to marry him under the Rockefeller Center Tree in New York City, and how our wedding was going to be filled with the themes of my love for Christmas. He said, "Well congratulations to you, but New York is just too far of a trip for me right now, so good luck, and we'll talk soon." Don cried that night into my arms, because there was a tiny part of him that still had that hope, that *just maybe,* his father would show up for the most important, happiest day of his life.

Instead, his dad carelessly kicked his sand castle over and hung up that phone one last time without a second thought. That was their last conversation, and a week or so before our wedding, Don's father died after having a massive heart-attack on his golf-course. A long time later, his daughter, Cynthia, was going through some old mail and piles of her dad's things, and she found my letters. She looked at the pictures of Don, who was a spitting-image of his father, and she figured out the rest and then reached out to us with her letter.

Cynthia and Don kept in touch and spoke on the phone a few times, trying to piece together the puzzle that was the relationship between Don's mother and their father. It was like trying to solve a mystery, and everyone who had all the clues was already dead. Don never got to meet his half-sister in person, because he died on that July thirteenth morning of a massive heart-attack. Just like his father. Except his father had many warnings and got to live out his life to a ripe, old age. Don was not that lucky. Much later on, after my husband's death, I found out through a conversation with Cynthia that their father had heart problems most of his adult life. He had a minor heart-attack in his forties, a double-bypass in his sixties, and then the final heart-attack while playing golf at age eighty six. He lived a full and mostly healthy life, and he got to enjoy many rounds of golf while retired in beautiful, sunny Florida – the future that my husband pictured many times for us and spoke of often.

But Don's father never had the desire or the time to speak to his son on the phone, and he didn't have the decency to take the five minutes to inform Don of his own medical history and warn him to go get his heart tested and take the necessary precautions that one would take when having early heart-disease in their immediate family. So because Don was healthy, active, never used a sick-day from work in his life, and never had any symptoms or warning signs of what was to come – his life ended at age forty six, collapsing on a cold, hard floor. As Don himself used to always say, after coming home from a long shift as a paramedic and working on a patient they lost too young, due to sudden and unexpected heart-attacks, "That guy was fucked."

It is tough to explain to people why Father's Day always hits me so hard. Maybe it is because my husband and I never got to have children, and so I never got to see what an incredible dad he would have been. On Mother's Day, I do grieve the loss of me never being a mother or having the family we might have had together – but that's different. It's different because at least I'm still alive. I will most likely never be a mother, and I definitely don't get to raise a family with my husband, but I do get to live. My husband was robbed of that honor. He was robbed of time and of life. He never got to be somebody's son, and he never got to be somebody's dad. And he REALLY wanted that – to be somebody's dad. We talked about it all the time, and we talked about the possibilities of natural childbirth vs adoption, and he spoke of how much he looked forward to being that loving father in someone's life that he never had himself. And then he died – because his father couldn't be bothered enough to give him a heads-up. It hurts. It is extremely unfair, and it hurts to know that our lives were shattered and stolen from us by death. And every single year on Father's Day, I still hear my husband's voice inside my heart asking: *Why doesn't he care?* I can still see the tears collecting in his gorgeous blue eyes as he looked at me, helpless, like a lost little boy.

My husband *did* end up having a dad though, a real dad who loved him like a son and who showed him that every second that he had with him. My dad. For the last seven years of my husband's short life, he had the greatest bond with my family. My mom, my brother, and my dad all took him in, and he was one of us, and we loved him. And the relationship between him and my dad was extra-special because of the non-relationship Don had with his own father. Nothing made me happier than to see my dad and my husband out in the driveway, working on a car, talking baseball, or just mocking something together.

Laughing. There was always a lot of laughing. They were like buddies, and they really loved each other's company. My husband called my dad "Pop," which was just about the cutest thing in the universe. Seeing them together melted my heart, and it made the fact that his own father was never really a presence in his life just a little bit easier.

On our wedding night, when the reception was over and the parties and hanging out with friends was over, and it was just me and my new husband in our hotel room for the night – he held me very close, looked into my eyes, and started to cry. "What's wrong, Boo?" I said to him. "Thank you," he answered. "Thank you for giving me a family."

And so, today is hard. And I know that I am not alone in today being hard. A lot of my friends or family lost their dads long before today, and mine is still alive and well. A lot of people had or have shitty dads, and mine is loving and caring and big-hearted and kind. Some people, a few dear friends of mine, do not have either of their parents alive and lost them long ago. My friend, Frank, lost his best friend in the world to suicide, then his parents, and then his sister. I have no idea how he is still breathing – because it is really really hard.

And then there are people, like my best friend since I was a little girl, who have been dealing with the heartbreak of infertility for years now, and so through no fault of their own, they cannot be moms and dads. And of course, I can't forget my widowed friends – the ones that I have met online, or in person, or in endless late night texts or phone calls, telling each other that it will be okay, or that maybe it won't. They are hurting today too.

The ones, like me, who never got to have children because their partners died before they could. The ones who did have children, and now they are raising them alone – as *only* parents – not at all what they had planned. The widows have to play mom *and* dad, and the widowed men have to play both dad *and* mom. They have to watch their kids go through milestones and moments for the rest of their lives, without their partners to share the glory, the horrors, the miracles. And so for all of you and all of us – just know that I know that it's completely unfair, and it's not right. And all we can do is just breathe. Breathe and feel whatever it is that you need to feel on this very difficult day.

Because it's hard when you know better. When you know that every kite eventually comes back down, every puppy and kitten eventually goes over the rainbow bridge, and every sand-castle will one day disappear. It might get kicked by someone who doesn't think much about your feelings. Or, if you are very lucky, it will simply get washed away by the waves in the ocean that we call life.

"I am not the first
I will not be the last
Looking toward the future
While longing for the past" – Sheila Meirick

Old Life, New Life

I had a dialogue through emails with my best friend since childhood, Sarah, today, that made me laugh out loud at the ridiculousness of how much both our lives have changed, and that perfectly showcased the extreme differences that the same conversation can have when going from old life to new life (FYI: Sarah is a childless, not by choice, infertility survivor)...

Kelley Lynn Shepherd

Old Life "Making Plans for 4th of July" Conversation:

Sarah: Hey Kelley, Julio and I are having a cookout for the 4th. You and Don wanna come?

Kelley: Hell yeah! I'll make some macaroni salad, and we'll see you this weekend! Thanks!

New Life "Making Plans for 4th of July" Conversation:

Kelley: Hey. You doin' anything for the stupid holiday, or are you hiding from the world?

Sarah: Not sure. My plans are up in the air. Trying to avoid my neighbors, who are really nice, but have kids and will ask me to join them in their yard, but I don't want to go to any functions with kids, which is pretty much everywhere on the 4th.

Kelley: Same here. I'd rather not be around happy families and fireworks and kids and picnics, yet part of me wishes like hell I could just be normal and do something normal again, like go to a goddamn BBQ without freaking out about how it's going to fuck with me or what grief-triggers it might bring up. Plus, I'm a week away from the 4 year death anniversary, so the 4th sucks for me anyway. I'm pretty useless right now.

Sarah: All right. Let's just hang out and be useless together.

Old Life "Making Plans" with a friend:

Friend: Hey, let's go see a movie this weekend.

Me: Cool. I'll pick you up at 6.

My Husband is Not a Rainbow

New Life "Making Plans" with another Widowed Friend:

Friend: Wanna do something this weekend? Maybe get lunch?

Me: Okay, yeah. But you have to pick me up. Remember, I don't have a car anymore since I had to sell Don's when he died.

Friend: I can pick you up, but can we go somewhere in Bayside? Somewhere new, maybe? Those other restaurants, I've been to with my husband too many times. I don't like going back there.

Me: No problem, I get it. Maybe we can see a movie afterwards?

Friend: Oh I dunno about that. I haven't been to the movies since he died. We used to go together all the time. I think I'd just cry the whole time. I don't know. Maybe we could rent one instead and go back to your place?

Me: Oh, I dunno. I'm more comfortable going to the movie theatre, since I used to go alone all the time anyway while I was married. It doesn't bother me. But watching at home, Don and I did that together all the time. Cuddle up in bed or on the couch and rent a movie. I don't really watch movies much at home anymore...

Friend: Okay. Let's just do lunch again, and then maybe we can go for a walk at the park or something.

Me: That sounds good. Let's look online and find some place both of us have never been, so it won't be "triggery" for either one of us.

Friend: Good. I like this plan.

Old life: I went to the grocery store and shopped for food.

Kelley Lynn Shepherd

New Life: Grocery stores depress me, too many bags to carry by myself, and I no longer have a car. I shop online now, home delivery through Peapod. No having to go up and down aisles and seeing item after item that I would have been buying for my husband. No more seeing husbands helping their wives carrying bags to the car or co-parenting their beautiful families. Just click a few buttons and wait for the bags to come.

Old Life: Get sick? Go to my regular doctor.

New Life: Get sick? Suck it up and hope to get better fast. If not, go to ER and pay off the bill $10 per month, because that is all I can afford. Pray and hope nothing is really wrong with me, like, ever.

Old Life: Make yummy dinner for me and my husband and chat at the kitchen table about our days. Put on music while we eat and laugh and have awesome conversations.

New Life: Eat leftover lo mein or make a turkey sandwich and eat at my computer desk while going through Facebook, because sitting at a kitchen table all alone and eating is extremely sad and depressing. Also, cooking for nobody except yourself is extremely depressing.

Old life, for the most part, was simple. Uncomplicated. New life? Filled with complexity and unexpected emotion, at every turn. Seeing the humor in it saves me from drowning.

FB Post: Just getting home from the city, where I met up with some friends for drinks, food, and a toast to Don on the 4 year mark of his death. Will read all your Pay it Forward stories in a

while. Thank you so much to the friends who came out tonight to honor Don, and life; Janine, Vanessa, Rodney, Sheri, and Kaye. Love you all.
LIKES: 81   COMMENTS: 38

From Nowhere to Everywhere: Living at the Rainbow Bridge

In the beginning of the end of the life I once knew, there was nothing. My husband died, and I felt and believed that he was just *gone*. I didn't feel him or see him or notice his presence anywhere around me, so I assumed that it would always be that way, and I didn't know how to live with that. It is bad enough when the person you love most just dies randomly with no warning whatsoever and shatters your world apart – but it's made worse when you cannot feel some tiny piece of their energy or spirit or soul floating around you. The thing that really sucked was all the many people telling me over and over how he is always here with me. I wanted to scream at them: NO HE ISN'T!!! STOP SAYING THAT!!! I DON'T FEEL HIM!!! HE IS JUST GONE FOREVER!!!

A friend of Don's, in the first couple of weeks after he died, insisted that he was a rainbow in New Jersey. She had seen a rainbow while driving to his funeral, and she told me that it was Don, and it was a sign. At the time, I literally was trying not to laugh in her face when she said this, because my husband would never come back as a fuckin' rainbow. He just wouldn't. He would come back as a lot of other things, but a rainbow isn't one of them. So the term "My Husband is Not a Rainbow" was born out of her observation and my reaction to it, and now, I have turned that very phrase into the title for a one-act play, a comedic presentation, and this book I'm now writing.

Kelley Lynn Shepherd

The thing is, I was in too much pain back then for my husband to get through in any way whatsoever. Nothing else could get in. Not even him. Just pain. So in the beginning, he was nowhere. And I didn't feel him for a very long time. Until one day, I did.

He started coming to me in my dreams. But these weren't just any old regular dreams. They were visits. They were the kinds of dreams where I would wake up from them and actually, physically feel his arms around me, or feel him hugging me, or he would say something specific to me, or often times we would have an entire conversation in the dream. And he was always already dead in these dreams. He was always coming back – his soul was coming back, from wherever, to comfort me somehow, to help me somehow, just like he always did in life. He was trying to help me to move through and process his death. I would wake up and be shaken for days by how real these visits were. He was there with me. He had come to see me. I don't know how the hell that shit works, but I know I couldn't question it once I felt it. Sure, I tried to "logic" my way out of believing it was real, but he kept coming back. And in one of his visits, he told me to believe it. He said, "Does it feel real?" I said, "Yes." He said, "Then it's real."

And then he started sending me even bigger signs. He would put people into my life path, exactly when I needed them. He would send an anonymous person to donate to my blog, exactly at the moment when I was drowning in bills and rent and secretly asked my husband to please find a way to help me. He led me to new jobs and apartments and scenarios, and to a bonding with his adult nephew and half-sister that I never had while he was alive. The signs became more and more constant, and as I continued the hard work of grieving and processing and breaking down my emotions with my grief-therapist week after week, I started to feel him around me more and more. This was an intensely slow process, and there was a LOT of doubt and questioning and trying to talk myself out of any of this being anything other than total bullshit. But again, he kept coming back. He didn't give up on me.

And then suddenly, and also at a grueling and slow pace, one year became two, and two became three. Somewhere inside of year three in my "after" life without my husband on earth, I started to really feel joy again. I started to notice things like autumn leaves again, or Christmas mornings, or the lightness of the first snowfall, or the way that guitar chord sounds in that Stevie Nicks song. And each time I noticed one of these things, he was inside of it. He was inside everything, everywhere, all of the time. And then it no longer became about trying to search for him and figure out where he might be after death – because suddenly and finally, I felt him everywhere. Sometimes I still have trouble believing these signs are real. But he keeps coming back and showing me.

One of the places that my husband Don loves to give me signs is at "Camp Widow." I have now been to this incredible Soaring Spirits International event eight times and given my comedic presentation eight times. Maybe Don gives me signs when I go there to let me know that I'm on the right track in what I'm doing with my life, and that he approves. I don't know. But something he has been doing lately over the past year or so during most of year four without him here on earth, is sending me literal signs with parts of his name on them. He sends me his name, sometimes in pieces, and other times in its entirety. Don Edward Shepherd. He puts his name on literal and actual signs and gives me signs through actual signs, which is totally his warped sense of humor. It's as if he is yelling at me, "You see, Boo? That's a SIGN with my name printed on it. See that? A SIGN. It's a sign!! Get it? How much more obvious do I have to be?"

The sign/name thing really started taking shape during my first trip to Tampa, Florida, for Camp Widow in 2014. Because Don lived in the Largo area of Florida for so many years and while we were dating, and because I had spread some of his ashes at Clearwater Beach a couple months after he died, I already felt him close to me while I was in Tampa. And then on Sunday morning, during our Farewell Breakfast Buffet, we were sitting in a big banquet room at the Marriott Hotel, eating our eggs and saying our goodbyes at the end of camp, when one of my widow friends pointed at the big coffee thermos in the center of our table and said, "Kelley, look!" She picked it up and showed it to me. Right there, at the top center of the thermos, it said "Don." It was just typed there like that – "Don." There were maybe ten other round tables in the room, so I got up and checked each thermos on the other tables. Every single thermos said, "Don." Now you might be thinking to yourself, how on earth is his name showing up on twenty or so coffee thermoses relevant?

Well, one of our favorite movies to watch together and quote together was Steve Martin's "The Jerk." And one of Don's favorite parts of the film to quote to me specifically, was a song that Steve Martin sings to Bernadette Peters about a thermos.

In the song, which is incredibly silly, he sings about how he just picked out an extra-special thermos for her, and how it is not just any ole' ordinary thermos. He also sings about how she can rely on him to pick out thermoses and other things such as rectal thermometers. I would quote the song here, but legally, it might not be the best idea. You can look it up on You Tube though, and hear for yourself what a ridiculous and brilliant little song it is.

Don and I would hold hands in bed, and he would sing this to me in this incredibly silly voice. So in that moment, when I saw the thermos, it made total sense to me that while my husband was not a rainbow, he was perhaps a thermos. And then it got even better. I went up to the staff at the Marriott and asked them if I could purchase one of the thermoses with his name on it, and explained why it meant so much to me. I think they concluded that I was a lunatic, but they told me they aren't allowed to sell the supplies used in the hotel, but that they would ask their manager where they buy the supplies, so I could maybe go back later and purchase one directly from the company. So the guy comes back and tells me the name of the company that supplies the thermos that says "Don" on it. The company is called "Edward Don and Company." Their website is www.don.com. So now we have his name on each thermos, and his first and middle name is the supplier company name. When you go to the site, it says "Who is Don?"

Last year, I attended and presented at Camp Widow Toronto for the first time. Camp Widow happened to fall on my birthday, September twenty sixth, which happened to be the first day of events that Friday. I had arrived to Toronto that Thursday night by Amtrak and Maple Leaf train. Don loved trains. He loved everything about them. He even loved the band "Train" and their song, "Drops of Jupiter," which, as it turns out, is all about the lead singer's mother and where she "went" after she died. But anyway, Don was obsessed with trains. He had the Lionel Train Engine Set in our apartment, he had model trains he would put together, and he loved riding the train with me. He even had this dream of us getting married and having our ceremony on a moving train. We had found one on Cape Cod, but the logistics of doing it were too difficult, and it was very expensive, so it didn't happen.

So I took the twelve hour train ride, and I felt very close to him during it. Later that night, I was in the lobby of the hotel, where wifi was free, writing my weekly piece for the Soaring Spirits blog, "Widows Voice." It had just turned midnight, so it was now my birthday officially. My good friend, Joclyn, ran in suddenly, yelling, "Kelley, you have to see this! You will never believe what I found today, just a couple miles from here while walking around just outside the city!" She showed me pictures on her phone. Pictures of a small building. It was a train station. It had a one-word sign at the top center. The sign said: "Don."

I was in complete shock as to what I was seeing, so I googled "Don train station in Toronto," and I came up with a website for the Toronto Railway Historical Association, which explained in detail the history of the Don station. His name was all over the website. It was unbelievable. The Don Station sits inside the Don Valley, which is across the way from the Don River. It had opened and closed several times throughout the decades, but then re-opened for the final time with an open house in October of 2006, our wedding month and year. So it looks like Don got his wish, in some strange way, of having our wedding on a train. Out of several nineteenth century stations, the Don Station is the only one in existence today. The Main subway line is called The Shepherd line, and runs along East Shepherd Avenue. So once again, my husband is still not a rainbow, but he is a train station. My awesome widow friends Arnie, Angel, and Judy, drove me to the station area, where I got out and took pictures, for evidence.

Me and the unbelievable Don Train Station in Toronto, Canada.

My Husband is Not a Rainbow

This year, about two weeks ago, I went back to Toronto for my second time giving my presentation there. Once again, I took the train. A while before leaving for my trip, I was messing around on Facebook one day, when a link came my way that said "the rainbow bridge in Toronto." I laughed to myself, thinking about how Don's humor would be to say he is not a rainbow, but is, in fact, a rainbow BRIDGE. Actually, it made complete sense why he would be a rainbow bridge. Given the fact that he was such a huge animal lover and activist, and that he died while taking care of animals. At his funeral, some of the staff members at Petsmart gave me a beautiful plaque with a poetry piece on it called "The Rescuer at the Rainbow Bridge." It talked about a man or figure who lived at the rainbow bridge, and whose job it was to greet and care for all the animals when they crossed over. The rainbow bridge is a term used for a sort of "pet heaven," a place filled with meadows and trees and space for animals to play and run around and be happy forever and ever. This is how the people who worked with Don at Petsmart saw him - as the Rescuer over the rainbow bridge. So, with all this in mind, I clicked on the image of the rainbow bridge and found out it was only a couple of miles from the hotel where we were staying. I also discovered that, once again, his name was all over this website. The rainbow bridge was just off the Don Valley Parkway and could be found at the base of the East Don Trail. "I must go there," I thought, and posted about it on Facebook, seeing if anyone else who was going to Toronto would have a car to get me there.

Enter my friends Sarah and Mike. Sarah lost her fiancé, Andrew (she called him Drew), in a helicopter crash. Mike lost his wife, Meghan, to complications from cystic fibrosis. Sarah and I had become very close over the past couple years, talking about our grief, and life, and death. This past March, Sarah and I both attended Camp Widow Tampa. We sat down at a gathering next to a guy named Mike. Fast-forward to today - Mike and Sarah, and Mike's little girl, Shelby, are starting a new life together.

Kelley Lynn Shepherd

Mike and Sarah would be traveling to Toronto by car, so Mike offered to take me to the rainbow bridge. None of us knew what to expect out of this trip that we took on the Sunday that Camp Widow ended, but it felt as if we were supposed to be going there together. In true Don fashion, he just kept showing himself over and over and over again. Driving there, Sarah and I were both rushing with our phone cameras to get each new picture/sign as it rushed by us, one after another after another after another. Sign after sign with his name. They were literally all around us as we kept driving into our adventure.

Finally, after twenty minutes or so of endless signs, we arrived at our destination, "The East Don Trail." We had no clue what to expect, except that there was apparently a rainbow bridge in here somewhere. Never in a million years did I expect to see this beautiful walking trail filled with flowers and nature and beauty - exactly how I always pictured the rainbow bridge looking - where animals go when they die. If such a thing exists, you can bet that this is what it might look like.

As we continued to walk in stunned silence, I noticed something. People were walking with their pets. They were walking their dogs down these paths and right by us. It felt as if we were somewhere special and sacred, someplace meant for us and meant for the animals and meant for life and death to embrace in that moment. It was magical.

We walked some more and finally came upon the rainbow bridge - a small bridge with a painted on rainbow. Something about it made me feel safe and silly and at peace. It reminded me of the animated style artwork that is on the cover of my book. It was cartoonish and lovely, all at once. It was the Rescuer, taking care of all the animals and making them feel welcomed and loved. It was everything that my husband was and is. I took out the little bag of his ashes that I had brought with me and left some right under the bridge, in the corner. We walked underneath the bridge and came through the other side, slowly looking at all the artwork drawn on the inside of the bridge. In there, we found more signs from him. It was as if he was screaming to me, "I'm here! I'm alive! I AM EVERYWHERE THAT YOU ARE, FOREVER!"

After walking under the bridge and around all over the trail, we came upon the Don River. It was really gorgeous, and I took the rest of the ashes I had with me and let them go into the river below. Don was all around me, and I felt so calm and safe. I didn't question any of it. Just like Don had told me a while back when he visited me in that dream, "If it feels real, then it's real."

In the beginning, he was nowhere. And now, he is everywhere. And that amazing shift in feeling has made all the difference in how I live each second of this thing called life. Beautiful, glorious, chaotic, tragic life. Thank you Don, for showing up over and over and over again and teaching me how to live once more. I love you. And for all those people who kept telling me that my husband was "in a better place," I say to you now, perhaps yes.

In Heaven? Hell, no! Canada.

(for the full writing piece, plus all the many pictures taken on this adventure, please go to my blog at ripthelifeiknew.com - where you will find this piece under the same name.)

FB Post: Yankees/Red Sox game with Vanessa, and her Rep just upgraded us as a surprise to amazing VIP-type seats! These are the seats where waiters come serve you and shit. I have never been this close before to home plate. What a great birthday gift for both of us. Ahhhh!!!!!
LIKES: 78   COMMENTS: 12

Kelley Lynn Shepherd

"The wisdom of grief is like being thrown out of a window to show you what floor you are on.
The price of self-knowledge is too high, and then some." – Bob Filipczak

Following Page Rainbow Illustration: We spotted Don in Toronto, off the Don Highway, in the Don Valley, on the East Don Trail. He might not be a rainbow, but he IS a rainbow bridge! Use your crayons to make him as colorful as possible!

My Husband is Not a Rainbow

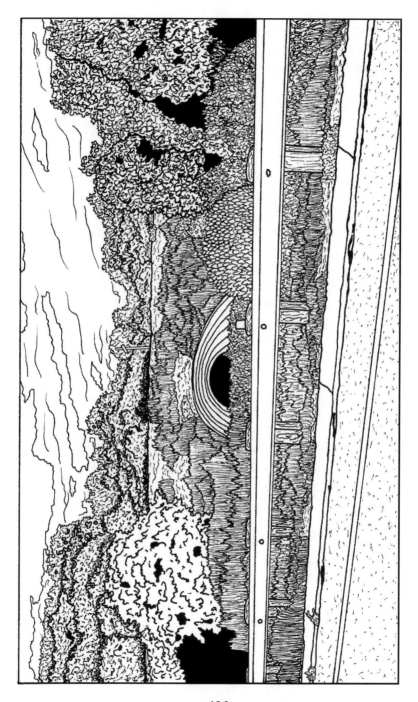

Kelley Lynn Shepherd

Session Snippet

Caitlin: So, it's been a while since I've seen you, and the last couple of times we talked were pretty profound. Those nightmares you were having about getting a divorce, and how we walked through that together and figured out what it represents. It's a shift of the biggest kind, in thinking of Don as your husband, to thinking of him in a different way. A different kind of connection. That realization was very powerful for me, I felt honored to be a part of that transformation for you, with you. You've really come such a long way. It's like you had to feel this incredible pain in order to be able to finally see a bit of light on the other side.

Me: Yeah, I would have never figured that out on my own, I don't think. Those dreams. They made me sadder than anything, really. It felt like he was disappearing all over again, that he was leaving me on purpose. But really, he was trying to help me so that I can begin to live instead of just exist. And ever since those dreams and our chat that day where we broke everything open, I have felt him closer than ever. Over and over. I know now that he is here with me. I feel it. It doesn't make the pain of him not being alive any better, but it's a much more peaceful and connected feeling than the feeling I had for so long. Just hopeless, alone, and sad. Now I feel this weird connection to something. I can't quite explain it, but it's just very different than before.

Caitlin: And it's funny, the focus that people tend to put on whether or not that stuff is real. Whether or not there is energy and life after death, and if it's really him helping you and talking to you, and him that you feel. I happen to think it IS him, but what does it matter if it is or isn't? It's like he said in that dream to you, "If it feels real, then it's real." It could be him in energy/soul form, or it could be YOU and your subconscious, finally ready to go to these deep and hard places in your grief, or it could be a bit of both. Either way, it's helping you heal, and you feel much more at peace with this connection than without it.

Me: I do. And I really have no idea whether it's him or me or both. All I know is that it sure as hell FEELS like him. And I smile or laugh when he shows up, and I talk to him more now, and I don't feel like a jackass like I did in the first couple years, talking to him. And the biggest thing is all of the ways he has helped me with forgiveness. You have told me a billion times to stop punishing myself about that morning or about why couldn't I have been there when he died. But I had to hear it from HIM directly, and he gave me that a couple months ago. I don't think I ever told you this, because of all the stuff that happened directly after, I forgot. Did I tell you about the U.S. Open tennis tournament I went to in August this year, and how Don showed up with a brutal and profound message?

Caitlin: I am a hundred percent sure I would have remembered that. I'm all ears.

Me: So, you know when Don came to see/meet me for the first time ever in 2002, I took him to the U.S. Open tennis in Queens. After that year, we went almost every year. He loved it there. Well, I hadn't gone back since he died, and this year, when it came around, I wasn't planning on going either. Then, one night, I was sitting at my desk at home, and in the same way that Don spoke to me while I was on the phone with you when he said, "Step into your life," he did it again that night. He said, "Go to the Open."

Caitlin: Jeez. Dead Don is very talkative...

Me: (laughing) Right? WAY more talkative than Alive Don ever was! So he told me to go, and I had the next day off from work because it was a holiday, so I started looking online to see if any cheap ground passes were available, since I'm broke like always. I messaged my friend, Lisa, who likes tennis, and she was able to get us a couple passes. So we went. I took the subway and met her at the gate, but she was like forty minutes late, so we ended up missing the first set of matches and ended up getting in line for a different match instead. It was on one of the smaller courts, so the crowds aren't as large, but they are still packed. We got into our seats, and the match started. Somewhere in the middle of the second game, in the crowd, directly in front of /across the court from where we were sitting, something awful happened.

Caitlin: Oh no. Did someone die?

Me: Maybe. I don't know. I'm pretty sure. It was so awful. I was watching the match, when suddenly, on the other side of the court, this old man was walking down the bleachers, and he had a tray of food in his hands. I happened to look in his direction, just as he stopped walking, as if in slow motion, and his whole body started shaking. Like, seizing. The tray fell to the ground, and people around him started scrambling. My friend, Lisa, was turning the other way, because it was disturbing, but I heard Don's voice again. He said gently but firmly: *Don't look away, Boo. You need to see this.* So I kept watching as the tears started forming. He fell to the ground, and he seemed to fall slowly. He clutched his heart, then his rib area, and had this look on his face like he wanted to stop it from happening, but couldn't. Then the tennis play stopped. Someone called over to medics. A team of medics came pretty quickly, as they were probably onsite already. The stretcher came out. The whole place, thousands of people, was silent. And I had a front row seat to all of this unfolding. Their faces were close enough for me to see their expressions. The woman with him, his wife maybe, yelled out, "Noooo!" and reached for him as the paramedics held her back and began to work on him. I could see them doing CPR, and then a few more things they tried on him that I couldn't quite make out. The place was silent. And then, finally, and suddenly, it was done. The medics took him away in a stretcher, and the woman walked behind them, shielding her face from view and quietly sobbing.

Caitlin: Holy shit. How did you do with seeing that? Did you have panic attacks? Did you have to leave?

Me: No. None of that. It was very weird. It was like Don was giving me the calmness that he always had, in that moment, so that I could sit and witness that. He kept talking to me as it was happening. As the man was collapsing, he kept saying to me gently: *It wasn't your fault, Boo. There is nothing you could have done if you were there when it happened. And you'd be torturing yourself even more because you were there and couldn't save me. This is not something you want to witness. You don't want to witness the person you love most, collapsing and dying in front of you. I need for you to stop punishing yourself for that morning and to understand that it was going to happen no matter what. I was a walking time-bomb, Boo. I was fucked.*

Caitlin: That is extremely powerful. Especially the fact that you sat there and just watched it happen, and you didn't have anxiety or panic during that. You were calm.

Me: I was very sad, but calm. It really was as if he was leading me through it. And he needed for me to be there in that match, when that happened, to see for myself how awful it is to have to witness that. He said: *You don't even know this man, and it's awful watching him die. Imagine being his wife. What you went through on that day was horrific enough. Please be thankful that you were spared watching me die.*

Caitlin: That is amazing. Truly. And again, it all comes back to the hard grief work you have put in and continue to. You had to feel and analyze and break down and sit with every piece of your grief, and only after doing that, could you have been ready to see what you saw at the tennis match. If you had witnessed that a year ago or two years ago, you wouldn't have been able to take that in the calm way you did now.

Me: Yeah. That would have sent me straight to my bed, curled up in the fetal position for days, eating cake out of a box with a fork. But seeing that now, it got its message across. I will still think about that morning and feel regret. I can't help it. But I feel a huge shift in no longer feeling the desire to punish myself or make myself responsible. And I feel like I can forgive myself, mostly, for being asleep while he was dying. It's hard to say that, because it's still going to hurt, I think, but I do feel a weight lifted in knowing that HE doesn't blame me or wonder why I wasn't there. And I think he's the only one who could have convinced me of that.

Caitlin: Which is why he chose to let you know in such a brutal way. That's what it took to get it through your thick stubborn skull.

Me: Pretty much. Also, since those dreams about the "divorce" and our connection shifting, I've felt a lot of other things become lighter too. My anger toward his father has shifted. I feel Don talking to me a lot lately about forgiveness, and how his family's behavior has nothing at all to do with me and everything to do with their own grief path. I wish things were different with them. I wish they would talk to me more. I wish I didn't feel like I was carrying all of the memories alone. But that's not who they are right now and not what is realistic. So, I hope they one day want to do more remembering of him together. I keep asking myself to forgive his father, because I know that Don did. Don always saw only the good in his dad and never held onto the hurtful stuff. I'm trying. But that's a tough one…

Caitlin: I know. You'll get there. What you've done so far is incredible.

*"My mess is my message,
My test is my testimony." – Bobbi J. Mason*

FB Post: So, I was cast in a thing. An acting role. A film / web-series, which will be shot out in Los Angeles in February. It's called "2 Kawaii 4 Comfort," and it's really, really good. See you soon, L.A. friends!!!
LIKES: 98   COMMENTS: 66

25 Clueless Comments Said to Me as a Widow, and 25 Responses I Wish I Could Have Said:

IT WAS GOD'S PLAN.

Oh, you mean my husband going to work and then never coming home? Or did you mean the part where he collapsed on a cold hard floor, just an hour after getting there? Or the part where I'm woken up traumatically by a ringing phone at six thirty AM and then rushed to a hospital in a cab, to be taken to a private room, and told by a bunch of nurses that my husband went into cardiac arrest and didn't make it? Or all of that? Was that all part of the plan? That's really good to know; thanks for telling me that. It takes all of the pain and hurt and PTSD and trauma and anxiety and panic away. Really. By the way, what will God be doing next? What is the next part of the plan? I figured I'd ask, since you seem to be the spokesperson for God. I didn't realize. Congratulations on that promotion. Out of everybody on earth, God chose YOU to be in charge of dissecting his thoughts and words and passing them on to the rest of us. Wow! That's impressive. And I thought you were merely a civilian, like me. Good to know.

YOU'RE YOUNG. YOU'LL FIND SOMEONE ELSE AND GET MARRIED AGAIN ONE DAY.

I will? Oh, wow!!! That is such a huge relief, because THAT is, of course, what is on my mind and heart right now, after my husband's death and all. I'm thinking about marrying someone else, as soon as possible, in fact. So I'm glad you picked up on that. I didn't realize you had become a psychic and that you were now able to predict the future. How else could you possibly know that I will remarry? What else will happen to me, oh great one? Do tell!!!

YOU'RE TOO YOUNG TO BE A WIDOW.

You know what? You're so right. So they must have made a mistake then. I will make sure to go straight to the widow authorities in the morning and return my black veil and my six cats.

GOD NEVER GIVES US MORE THAN WE CAN HANDLE.

You're so correct. (punches them in the face) Oh my! I am soooo sorry that you are lying face down on the ground after me punching you in the face. Was that more than you could handle? Sorry about that. But please don't blame me. I had nothing to do with it. It was part of God's plan.

EVERYTHING HAPPENS FOR A REASON.

Yes. Exactly. Like, how I punched you in the face just now? The reason was that you're an asshole.

GOD ONLY TAKES THE BEST.

So, what does that make me? Chopped liver? A horrible person? And you too. And the rest of us walking around on earth. Do we all suck as human beings, since he only takes the best ones? That doesn't seem logical to me. I think what makes more sense is this – people die. Let's go with that.

WE MAKE PLANS, AND GOD LAUGHS.

Wow, this God that you believe in sure sounds like a prick! I believe in a higher power too. I believe in the concept of a God. But the God I believe in is all about Love and kindness and goodness, not taking people away for fun, and mocking us and getting off on our pain. That is not a God that I believe in. Sorry. But good luck with that.

HE IS IN A BETTER PLACE.

Really? Better than here with me, happily married and looking forward to our long future together? No, I don't think so. He was very happy here, and he was not suffering, nor was he in pain of any kind, since he was not ill and his death was sudden. I have an idea, though. Since you seem to like this "better place" so much, why don't we bring my husband back here, and YOU can go there instead? How does that sound? Here, I'll help you pack...

YOU NEED TO GET OVER THIS.

Get over what? Love? Get over loving the person that I vowed to love forever and spend my life with? I should get over love? No. That's not a thing. That's not possible. I don't think you've ever been in love before if you would say something like that to me. This wasn't a divorce. He DIED. I will always, always love him – until the day I stop breathing, and beyond.

YOU NEED TO MOVE ON.

Again, that's not a thing. Move on from where? Where should I move to? What does that mean? If it means that you want me to stop talking about him and just act like he never existed – that's never going to happen. We keep the people we love alive by carrying them with us and telling their story. If you can't understand that, then I think you're right. I think I need to move on. From you, and from our relationship.

MY GREAT GRANDMOTHER DIED. WE SAW EACH OTHER ONCE A DECADE, AND SHE WAS 107. I KNOW EXACTLY HOW YOU FEEL.

Yes, of course you do. Because that is exactly the same thing as losing your husband, best friend, the life you knew, your past, your present, your future, your dreams of a family, your rock, your security, your stability, your heart, your soul, your identity, your everything – in the blink of an eye. It's exactly the same.

AT LEAST YOU DIDN'T HAVE CHILDREN.

Hey, that was awesome of you to remind me, JUST as I had stopped thinking about it for five seconds, that I will never be a mom and that my husband will never get to be a dad. So nice of you to remind me of that trauma and that intense pain I feel every single day. It's also really kind of you to imply that because we didn't have kids, that my marriage was somehow not valid enough or that my hurt and grief aren't as important. Thank you so much!!!

ANYTHING YOU NEED, JUST ASK. ANYTHING AT ALL. CALL ANYTIME. NIGHT OR DAY, DAY OR NIGHT, ANY TIME, ANY HOUR…

Okay, relax there, casual Facebook friend whom I barely know. I know you're trying to be nice, and you think this is what you should say, but you don't mean it. I highly doubt you will actually be there for the many, many things I am going to definitely need over the next few weeks, months, and years because of this life-altering loss. But since you offered…I'd love some help with my laundry, and with the car, and also all my light-bulbs need changing, and the ceilings are too high for me to reach them. And then, usually around four thirty AM, when I can't sleep and I'm sobbing hysterically, you could come over and just sit with me, or I'll give you a call everytime that happens. You cool with that? Awesome. P.S. What's your phone number again? I don't even think I know your full name...

YOU SHOULD BE GRATEFUL FOR WHAT YOU HAVE.

And you should be grateful that I'm not a violent person and that I don't particularly like jail cells as places to reside after knocking you over the head with a two by four.

IT COULD BE WORSE.

Could it? Really? I don't know about that. My husband is dead forever. I'm pretty sure this IS the very definition of "worse." And what is the point of saying that anyway? Is that supposed to make me feel better somehow? Because it doesn't. At all.

THIS HAPPENED BECAUSE YOU DIDN'T PRAY HARD ENOUGH.

Oh, okay. Is that why it happened? I thought it was part of "the Plan." What happened to the Almighty plan? I'm confused now. Also, if you could explain to me, oh great one and spokesperson of God, WHEN exactly was I supposed to be doing this praying? You know, considering the fact that I basically woke UP to the reality that my husband had gone to work and then died. So, having ZERO knowledge of the fact that he was going to die, before he was actually DEAD, when was I to do this praying that you speak of? If I thought that prayer worked, I might pray for you to go out and buy some common sense.

AT LEAST HE DIED DOING WHAT HE LOVED.

Yes, yes. Because my husband absolutely LOVED being at work and collapsing alone on a hard cold floor while his heart gave out on him. That was his favorite thing.

LIFE IS FOR THE LIVING.

Well, thanks for that pointless little gem of nothing. And being condescending is for the jackass!

NOBODY SAID LIFE WAS FAIR!

That's true. And nobody said you're not a douchebag!

YOU'RE SO LUCKY THAT HE IS DEAD. I HAVE TO SEE MY EX ALL THE TIME.

Yes. "Lucky" is the word that comes to mind immediately when I think of my situation. Also, just FYI, he isn't my "ex" anything. He was my husband, and he died, and I would give just about anything in this world if I could see him again. And thanks for the anxiety attack I'm now having inside as I try my hardest NOT to kick you into the next galaxy.

I WISH MY HUSBAND WAS DEAD. HAHAHA!!!!

Yes, that's hilarious. Making stupid jokes about your shitty marriage and your crappy husband to someone who just lost theirs to death is exactly what should be happening here. Awesome.

HE WOULDN'T WANT YOU TO CRY.

My Husband is Not a Rainbow

Yes well, he is dead, so I guess it doesn't much matter what he would want, now, does it? But if we are going to play it that way, then he probably wouldn't want people like you saying dumb shit that upsets me and in fact, makes me cry. So go away now.

GOD MUST HAVE NEEDED ANOTHER ANGEL.

This God of yours is very needy, dontcha' think? And, not for nothing, but he is GOD. He is the all powerful and mighty, and he lives in Heaven. So, since we have established that you are obviously God's spokesperson for all things, can you tell him to make his own damn angel? They gotta have at LEAST one aisle of Heaven reserved for Angel-making purposes. There must be an arts and crafts station or something up there. How many angels does this guy need anyway? He's getting a little selfish.

WELL, LIFE GOES ON!!!

Wow, does it? Well thanks for that useless drivel. I was not aware that life was to continue in its natural form. Thank you for pointing that out to me.

YOU ARE LOOKING BETTER. GLAD TO SEE YOU ARE FINALLY ALL BETTER.

Holy shit. What the hell did I look like before??? I'm looking "better?" Better than what? And yes, thankfully, I am ALL BETTER NOW. I took my medicine, and I rested up, and wouldn't ya know it, the pain and the grief and the hurt just all went away, just like that!!! It's a miracle!!! Now if you'll kindly excuse me, I need to go take my "GRIEF BE GONE" pills, so that I can remain "all better" from now on.

Now, in the interest of not ending this on a negative note, I would like to tell you all that there have been plenty of people in the past four years who have said things that did NOT make me want to throw them out the nearest window. There have been people who have said some really great things – things that stuck with me. Things that I will list here, so that the next time you run into a person who has just lost everything they knew, maybe you can make the choice not to be an ass-hat, by adding to their pain.

In the end, if you knew the person well who has suffered the loss, just be there for them. Don't judge them or give them advice or tell them how they should be feeling or grieving or coping. If you haven't been through it, you really don't know, and your job should be to support them and not disappear from their life. If you didn't know them well, a simple "I'm so sorry" works just fine. Thanks for reading.

Good Things People Have Said to Me:

I'm so sorry. I don't know what to say.

This is not what I dreamed for you when we were kids. (my best childhood friend)

He would be so proud of you.

He loved you so much, and he always will.

You were the love of his life, and the last person he will ever love.

You will always have his heart. You get to hold onto the love forever.

Love never dies.

Here is a story / memory / picture of your husband I'd like to share with you.

My Husband is Not a Rainbow

I miss him too.

Let's honor him /have a toast / share stories about our friend. Let's say his name and talk about him.

This sucks.

This really fucking sucks.
I can't believe this happened. This is so unfair.

I wish I had known him better.

Did I mention already how much this really fucking sucks?

I might not do everything right, and I might screw this up, but I'm not leaving you, and I'm around whenever you want me to be.

If you need someone to talk to, I promise I'm a really good listener, and I will never judge you.

I love you.

FB Post: Today is my wedding anniversary. Again. For some reason, I would like for you all to see the wedding vows he wrote to me. All those years ago. I like to picture him sitting at our desk in the bedroom, where the computer was, and coming up with these vows. He didn't love to write, so I know it took him some time to come up with these words. We had a quote in our ceremony program that said, "Marriage is like a duet. When one sings, the other claps." So the end of these vows is in reference to that.

He was sooo happy after the ceremony when he got two huge laughs on his two-part line about Jersey. Oh, how proud he was

of the laughter coming from our guests. My Boo-Bear. I miss you so much. Thank you for not going anywhere. Thank you for letting me know you are always right here. It still hurts. I still want more, especially on days like today. But love is powerful, and I know that will help carry me forward. I love you...
LIKES: 18   COMMENTS: 7

"My Dearest Kelley,

Today I start a new life with my best friend. A day filled with happiness, laughter, and love. Today I marry the woman I'll share the rest of my life with. I can't begin to describe how thankful and grateful I am for having found you. You don't just make me a better person, you make my life complete.

I love you for all the things you are; your wisdom, your humor, your caring nature, your passion for life, your immense talents, and your endless devotion to family and friends. Sharing life with you isn't just an honor, it's a blessing.

But of course, along with the happiness, there are also sacrifices. It's never easy to leave family and friends and start all over again, but I've never regretted the decision I made to be with you. My love and devotion to you, at times, defies all explanation. After all, who moves to New Jersey? On purpose? It's also not very easy to be a Yankees fan around your Red-Sox nation family.

My Husband is Not a Rainbow

So on this day, I profess my love and commitment to you, to be the husband you always dreamed of, to be your best friend, and always protect and love you. I also want you to know that my greatest happiness is watching you succeed and marveling at your talent, every time you step in front of an audience. My greatest joy is being right next to you as you chase your dreams and catch them. And I promise you - that until forever - every time you sing, I will always clap. I will be your teammate, your biggest fan, and your best friend. Always. - Your Husband"

FB Post: Last night was the anniversary of when Don proposed to me. I had free tickets to the Christmas Spectacular that I won a few months back, so I took my friend, Bobby, with me to go see it, so we could remember the old days in years past when we both worked as Tour Guides at Radio City. And then, after the show, we walked over to see "the tree." My tree. The site of the epic marriage proposal. As always, I got that dip in my tummy feeling as we approached the tree. But then, as we sat there under the tree and looked at the twinkling lights, I was okay. It was Christmas, my husband is dead, and I was very sad, but I was okay. I might be okay.
LIKES: 14 COMMENTS: 20

FB Post: I used to feel things at a normal level. Maybe at a 6 or 7. Now - to quote from my husband's favorite movie, "This Is Spinal Tap," "these go to eleven." My emotions. They go to eleven. Happy New Year and Merry Christmas everyone. Life is cruel, absurd, really, really hard, and the most precious gift anyone will ever give you. Do your best to be inside it whenever possible, alive at full blast. Even if it takes you years and years

to get there. Most of all, love your people, and love them hard. It's all about the love. Always.
LIKES: 45   COMMENTS: 18

Session Snippet

Caitlin: Do you remember way back, when we first started our grief work together, and you were coming here every Monday, and I said to you that someday... one day...

Me: No. Don't say it.

Caitlin: ...I said to you that there will come a day when you no longer need to see me every single week. There will come a day when things will happen in your process, and you will be able to figure them out without me. That I would always be here for you and there would still be times when you would call on me when things got hard, but week to week, you wouldn't need to come here anymore.

Me: And I didn't believe you. I said that will never happen and that I couldn't imagine a time when I didn't want to come here.

Caitlin: Yes. But wanting to come here and needing to come here are very different things. And I think we have reached that point. That point where you are coming here more out of habit, because you want to, because it's comforting, and not because you need to.

Me: Are you trying to get rid of me? I don't want to not come here. I love coming here.

Caitlin: And I love seeing you. And no, I'm not trying to get rid of you. But I think it's important that we recognize that a shift is happening here...

My Husband is Not a Rainbow

Me: Another freakin' shift. I think one major shift with my dead husband is enough for this month. Do we have to shift now, too? Can't we wait to shift? Can we shift later?

Caitlin: We could. But the reality is, it's already happening. I'm just saying it out loud. The past few months, we haven't met every week. Mostly due to circumstances and busy schedules and snow and other things, but during those weeks where we didn't meet, you got through things okay. You wrote about it. You maybe talked with your widowed community about it. You worked through it on your own, maybe. You have found ways to work through things as they happen, which is wonderful.

Me: But I still need you. I still want your take on things. I want your opinion. And I don't want to say goodbye to you. I can't handle saying goodbye to another person I care about.

Caitlin: We won't say goodbye. You just won't need to come here weekly, and maybe we will have sessions as necessary, or once every couple months, or I can call you when something comes up and you need to talk through it. And then eventually, when you no longer are my "client" anymore, we will always be friends. This isn't goodbye. This is me telling you that I think you are shifting into more of the teacher than the student. You've done several Camp Widow presentations now, you run the social widowed group in New York City, you write for several blogs, plus your own, and you have led or facilitated several round table support groups at Camp for widowed people. Plus, lots of people come to you for words of comfort. They message you on your blog, they ask for your take on things. I've seen it. This has become natural for you, and I believe it has become your purpose. You are becoming a gifted healer. Have you ever thought about doing some grief coaching yourself? In addition to doing more speaking engagements and writing, maybe you could start just over the phone, focusing on talking with widowed people or people going through loss, who maybe can't afford grief counseling or therapy, but want to speak with a fellow widowed person who can help them process through their emotions and begin to build their next life in the aftermath of loss? You could keep the cost low for them, and I think you would be excellent at this, and you do it already with some of your widowed community. I'd be more than happy to have you sit in or co-lead some of the grief groups I run to start.

Me: That would be awesome. It's so weird that we are even talking about this. Who ever thought in a million years that this would be what I'd want to do with my life? Help people through loss? Write and speak about loss? Bring dark comedy to the topic of loss? I really wish like hell that this wasn't something I know so much about.

Caitlin: Right. Nobody really says "Hey when I grow up, I want to be widowed and go through the worst and hardest pain imaginable!"

Me: Yeah, that wasn't really in the wedding vows. (laughs)

Caitlin: No, it wasn't. But you've taken something incredibly painful and turned it into something incredibly profound. That is admirable. You've come so far. I'm not saying this is our last session or anything like that, don't worry. I'm just laying the groundwork for you to start thinking about how you might want to shape your future. We can keep talking about it and just slowly taper off our sessions to "as needed." Does that work for you?

Me: I think so. I'm just so grateful for you and everything you have done for me and keep doing for me. You took me on when nobody else would. Nobody else offered to work with me for no compensation. You're just so special to me, and I love you so much. I could not have done any of this without you.

Caitlin: Well thank you, but my compensation is watching you grow and become this loving and empathetic person, even more-so than you already were, and using the tools you have been given, to heal yourself and others. And now you're going to pay all of that forward with your book.

Me: Oh my god, my book. I keep meaning to ask you, and this seems like the perfect time. Since our sessions are going to be a big part of the book, having snippets from them in there, I wanted to ask you if you would write one of the Forewords in my book. Michele Hernandez is doing the other one. I want to have two, because that's how I roll. And because, for me, you and Michele have been such a huge part of my healing process, and I feel like you both saved me in many ways.

Caitlin: Oh, wow, Kelley. I'd be honored. I'm no writer, but I think I could come up with something, and I'm so honored to be asked.

Me: …and now it's time to hug you.

Caitlin: You got it.

Dear Dead Husband,

I really wish you were here. I need to hear your voice telling me everything will be okay. I need your medical knowledge, reassuring all of us that mom will be good and all will be well. I need you explaining to me what the doctors are talking about, and what they really mean when they say x, y, and z.

Its mid-January, and right around Christmas, mom was diagnosed with uterine cancer. It was so scary, but it's the "good kind," meaning stage one and high survival rate. I was still terrified, and I'm sure she is even more so. She had the hysterectomy surgery and got everything removed last week, and I'll be staying here with her and my dad until January twentieth so I can help out while she recovers. I just miss you so much, and wish you were going through this with us, instead of dead and not here.

So many changes the past few months. Through tons of tears and emotions and denial and kicking and screaming in protest, I began to "shift" my relationship with you, after a series of pretty brutal nightmare dreams where you wanted to divorce me and leave me. It turns out that our marriage can't really be the kind where the husband and wife are both people who are alive and breathing, so I had to make some changes in how I see you, so I can consider opening my heart to love again. Don't worry Boo - you aren't going anywhere, and neither am I. You will be a part of everything, always. I just need to create more space, and see if love might be a possibility for me. An old acquaintance of yours in Florida, who is also widowed, emailed me after finding my blog online. We have been talking and have become friends. It's been really nice, and I'm excited to meet him for coffee when I go to Tampa for Camp Widow in March. I love it when people have stories about you, who knew you way before I knew you. It makes me smile so much. I love you, Boo. Please help me to know that my mom will be okay. Xoxo

FB Post: Last day at mom and dad's place in Massachusetts, before going back to NY tomorrow. I miss my life and my kitties and my friends, but it's been so nice to be here helping my mom recover, and to see lots of family and old friends while home. Watching the playoffs and relaxing - Go Pats!
LIKES: 19   COMMENTS: 43

And I Miss You Still

…And still, at the end of each day,
No matter how long it's been,
How happy I may be,
Or how much life keeps spinning…
It always comes back to this:
You are not here,
And I miss you.
Still. Forever. Always.

The missing of you lives inside of me, in the same way that stars light up and live in the sky. It's just there, like a baby napping, or a child wanting ice-cream. It's there in the same way that all familiar things remain, and yet, its depth and its hurt still surprise me everytime. For love does not end. It only begins, and then begins again, over and over, taking new and different forms. I love you. I love you today, tomorrow, and for many lifetimes into the future, where I will miss you still.

FB Post: Hello Los Angeles!!! Time to make a movie! Happy to be in L.A. for the week, filming "2 Kawaii 4 Comfort," a film and a web-series by Luke Palmer. Studying my script and headed to bed early. Long and early day on set tomorrow. Bring on the acting work and other creative stuff, 2016! I'm so ready!
LIKES: 79   COMMENTS: 17

FB Post: Had a late dinner with my friend, girl-crush, and forever mentor, Michele Neff Hernandez, who drove all the way from Simi Valley to L.A. to hang with me after my long day on set. I absolutely love this woman, and she inspires me every single day.
LIKES: 86   COMMENTS: 23

Kelley Lynn Shepherd

"To love deeply in one direction makes us more loving in all others." - Anne Sophie Swetchine

FB Post: My old NYC friends who moved to California last year, John and Jessica, took me to Malibu on my day off from filming, and we had lunch together and hung out. Then I walked the edge of the beach and put some more Don into the sea again. He was from Whittier, California, originally, and he always wanted to come back to Cali with me and show me his childhood roots. Well, Don, this isn't Whittier, but it's California, and that will have to be close enough. It was my honor to bring you home...
LIKES: 90   COMMENTS: 56

I Will Never Move On

Last night, I was talking to a new widower friend of mine on the phone, when he suddenly shifted the topic of conversation and posed a huge challenge to me. I'm not sure if he saw it as a challenge, but I did. He asked me to do him a favor. When I asked him what the favor was, he said, very matter-of-factly, as if it were the simplest of things to accomplish, "I want you to change the world." Oh, IS THAT ALL??? Should I do this right in between my morning coffee and my teaching job? Or perhaps I could fit it in right after cleaning out the kitties litter box and my second load of laundry. Maybe I can multi-task and get this done while I simultaneously file my taxes. Sure. Change the world. I will get right on that. (Can you sense my sarcastic tone?)

In all honesty though, after I got off the phone and stopped to think about it some more, the challenge did peak my interest in many ways, and I was somewhat flattered that anyone would think that little ole' me could ever be capable of something as huge as world-changing. This friend of mine finds me inspiring, mostly due to the honest way in which I write about grief. What he doesn't know (until right now, when he reads this), is that him giving me that challenge has inspired ME. He has inspired me to try and do better. The fact that he believes I am capable of such a thing is providing me with the fuel to light the fire that sits inside. I would have never thought to make it a goal to change the world all on my own, but now that it's been planted in my head and heart by someone else, I might as well give it a shot, right? I heard a quote somewhere recently that really stuck with me. It said, "Change the world by changing your mind." Or "change your mind and change the world." I can't remember the order that it was said in, but it almost doesn't matter, because it pretty much means the same thing. It all comes down to perception. The way that people see or perceive something, has to first change, in order for everything around it to also change.

So, with that in mind, I am going to write about something that *truly* needs to be written about. I am going to put it all out there and hope that the message gets passed around as much as it needs to be passed around. I am going to write the truth, and then wait for that truth to become contagious. Just as this false idea that people who lose their spouse or partner need to "move on" has spread like wildfire, this new message needs to cause a fire ten billion times bigger. This fire needs to put that old one to shame. It is time to make a change.

Any widowed person will tell you that we have heard, time and time again, the endless parade of well-intentioned, thoughtless comments that come our way within minutes of losing our life partners and the life we knew. These comments include such classics as: *Everything happens for a reason. // Time heals all wounds. // God never gives you more than you can handle. / It was God's Plan. // God Needed Another Angel. // I know exactly how you feel. // You need to get over this.* That is not the full list of whoppers – just a few of my favorites. But what all of these comments have in common is this: they make us feel worse, not better. They make us feel like our emotions aren't real or don't matter, because they are dismissive and they don't validate what we are actually going through. The truth of the matter is, nobody could ever know what we are going through or what this IS, until they themselves have gone through it. Most people want to help. Unfortunately, most people are pretty clueless as to how their words can affect us, and most people don't stop and think about just how insensitive these clichés can feel when heard by someone who is in tremendous and very real pain.

On top of all that, we, the ones who are in the tremendous pain, are told over and over again to just put up with these thoughtless comments. We are told that people are "only trying to help," or that "they don't know what to say," and we should smile and nod and be grateful that they care. I'm sorry that people don't know what to say. But I also feel like it's time to change the conversation from "they don't know what to say" to "let's teach them what is not so good to say, so that we can stop using that as a convenient excuse to say hurtful and unhelpful things." As the brilliantly smart and world-changing Maya Angelou famously said, "When you know better, you do better." I think it's time we do better.

So let us begin with the King of all Insensitive Comments: "You Need to Move On." Of all the many comments that are said to widowed people, this is by far the most common one, and also the most harmful. The reason it is so harmful, is that this message is implanted into the widowed person's heart and soul, over and over again, at EVERY stage of their grieving process, by many different people. We begin to hear this "move on" mentality on the very first day that our person dies. Just hours after my husband's sudden death, I was informed that making the decision of whether or not to donate his organs would help me to "move on." Then, at his funeral, I was told that the services and the wake would all help me to "find closure and move on." A week later, when I was being held captive in the four walls that used to be our home, I was being told in condescending voices that it was "time to donate some of his clothing, so that you can start to move on." Four and a half years later, and people are still beating me over the head with their chants of moving on. "Why aren't you dating anyone yet? You need to move on." "Why are you still going to that Widow Camp? Don't you think it's time to move on from that?" "Why are you still talking to his family? He is dead. You aren't his wife anymore. So they aren't your family anymore." (Yes, someone actually said this to me. Really.)

These awful ideas are repeated into our souls, as if stamped onto our foreheads by people who have no idea of what they speak, and this becomes harmful. Because we start to believe it. We start to believe that there is something wrong with us for NOT wanting to forget about our person. We start to think that maybe we are doing this all wrong, and maybe we are weak and stupid and not well, because we still love them and we don't want to place them on a shelf in our past, to collect dust forever. We start to very slowly lose pieces of ourselves and unwillingly lean into what society is telling us instead. All of this is extremely harmful to our souls. Why?

Because none of it is real.
Because it doesn't exist.

Let me say this as simply as possible:
There is NO SUCH THING as moving on.
It's a lie.
It's a fairy-tale concept, invented by those who don't know what to say.
It is invented out of ignorance and fear.

They want you to move on, so that they can feel more comfortable with your presence.
If we can all just pretend that this scary death thing never actually happened, then it would all simply go away.

Except it doesn't ever go away. Not for you. Not for the person living inside of it. It becomes you, and you become it, and you become wrapped up in each other. Death and life become one, and everything is different forever. The death of a spouse or partner is different than other losses, in the sense that it literally changes every single thing in your world going forward. When your spouse dies, the way you eat changes. The way you watch TV changes. Your friend circle changes (or disappears entirely). Your family dynamic/life changes (or disappears entirely). Your financial status changes. Your job situation changes. It affects your self-worth. Your self-esteem. Your confidence. Your rhythms. The way you breathe. Your mentality. Your brain function. (Ever heard the term 'widow brain?' If you don't know what that is, count yourself as very lucky.) Your physical body. Your hobbies and interests. Your sense of security. Your sense of humor. Your sense of womanhood or manhood. Your love life. Your sexual desire (or lack thereof). EVERY. SINGLE. THING. CHANGES. You are handed a new life that you never asked for and that you don't particularly want. It is one of the hardest, most gut-wrenching, horrific, life-altering of things to live with.

To top it all off, people who still have their partners beside them treat you differently. People like to think that they suddenly know what is best for you. People treat you like you are a child who cannot make decisions. They want to treat it as if it were maybe a divorce instead of a death. They want you to put that person in your past, like some "ex" lover or some regretful mistake. These insinuations are beyond hurtful to the widowed person, who is still and always will be very much in love with their person who died. And so, what ends up happening, most times, is that the widowed person feels more and more alone as the months and years go by, until eventually, they just stop talking to their friends about their loss altogether. Their friends and family then wrongly assume that because they don't talk about it anymore, they must be "over it," and therefore, everything is fine. Meanwhile, the widowed person continues to suffer in silence and mounting isolation. For us, it is a very scary place to be. And this is how the cycle of unhealthy perceptions of grief and death continues.

In the past four and a half years since my husband died, I have become friends, both online and in-person, with a lot of widowed people. We help each other. We call each other family. We are the family that you gain, when the family you knew is gone. We talk to one another about the pain and the heartbreak, and the changes and the shifts, and the complexities of life after death. I have seen countless upon countless posts in the closed and private widowed groups, where a widowed person has been forced to hear from some family member, friend, or acquaintance, some form of "you need to move on."

The way they say it comes in many forms. One widow parent who I know, was judged and lectured by her family, because she dared to share memories with her own children about her husband /their father. The family told her that she shouldn't do that, because she wasn't helping her children to "move on from him. " They told her it was not healthy for them to be "sad" over his death. Another friend was offered money by a relative for every picture he took down from his nightstand of his deceased wife. Another friend was pushed into a new relationship before she was ready, because her buddies thought she should "get out there again and start dating." Another friend was judged because she still goes to the cemetery often, to visit with her husband. On and on the judgments come, each one breaking my heart more than the one before it. And while I cannot stop these people from giving their clueless and harmful advice, I can hope that maybe some of them are reading this somehow, and I can ask them to do me a favor.

I can ask them to ask themselves: what kind of message are they sending to their widowed friend or family member with this type of "move on" mentality? If you are reading this now, I would like for you to think about that for a minute. By telling a widowed mom or parent that they shouldn't share stories with their children about their dad, isn't that sending a message that their dad's life meant nothing? Isn't that sending a message that they should simply forget he was and IS their father – just pretend he never existed?

And what about the widow or widower who goes to their spouse's gravesite – whether it's on special anniversary days or a couple times per week? What message does it send to tell them to stop going there? Isn't that like telling them their love didn't matter? Isn't that like implying that erasing them from their hearts is better than honoring and remembering them with love? Why on earth are we shaming people for loving others eternally? Why are we making them feel as if that is not normal, when in fact, it is not only normal, but probably the most beautiful thing in the world.

When a celebrity dies, we gather on social media and we share their pictures, their art, their music, their talents. We celebrate them and remember them, and we say "Hey, remember when he did that one film? That was a classic that will last until the end of time." And people do this for YEARS after a famous person's death, and it's a hundred percent normal and accepted and celebrated to share film clips, music, and moments forward. Yet, when the person who was the center of our universe dies, and we dare post a picture of them or speak of them a few months or years after their death, we are looked at with judging eyes. We are given pity and lectures about how "stuck" we are, and we are made to feel as if it is very, very bad what we are doing. This is so wrong and so backwards. We should not have to shamefully love our people. The entire message of the move-on mentality seems to be this: forget about them. It's in the past. Pretend it never happened.

But here's the thing. That is not possible. You cannot forget love. You cannot pretend it away. The death of the person you love only ends a life. It does NOT end a relationship. The truth is, LOVE is the only thing that we get to keep forever. Love is the only thing that we can take with us. Love is the only thing that never, ever dies. To take that away from someone, is not only unhealthy – it is cruel.

I will never move on from my husband. I will never NOT love my husband who died. I will never leave him in my past, like some forgotten old shoe I never threw away. This applies forever. Even if I should fall in love again. Even if I should marry again. Even if I should live every dream that I have ever dreamed possible. Even when I am old and gray and ancient, should I have the honor of being allowed to live that long. Even then. I will NEVER not be connected to my husband. He lives within me now. Whatever I do, wherever I go, I carry him with me. He is a piece of my very soul. There is no moving on.

Here is what I WILL do:

I will live the biggest and brightest and most colorful life that I can, because my husband does not have that choice. I will cling to every new joy that I feel in this life, because I am still alive to feel it. I will honor the life and the love that my husband and I shared, by being the person that he fell in love with. I will always find ways to keep remembering him and sharing his story with the world, because that is my duty and my HONOR to do as his wife, and his widow; and because sharing their story is how we keep them alive and relevant. I will continue to grow and to learn and to hurt and to feel and to fear and to fly. I will

Kelley Lynn Shepherd

scream when I need to, cry when I have to, and laugh as much as my body can handle. I will tell all the people that I love, that I truly love them, and I will make sure they know this as often as possible. I will leave behind something of importance in this life, something of value, that someone, someday, can read or look at or see or feel, and it will make them think in a different way.

I will love harder than I have ever loved before, and I won't feel guilty for loving again, because I will know in my heart that my husband's love is inside every love I have going forward. I will choose to believe that he is somehow still here with me, and I won't question or doubt all the many times that I feel him. I will embrace his energy inside the music, and I will dance to the rhythms of our forever connected hearts. I will speak his name whenever I want to, and I will do this proudly, because that is what he deserves. That is what we ALL deserve – to not be forgotten and to be spoken of with laughter and joy and remembrance by those that will always love us. I will move INTO my future, step into my life, and I will carry him with me at every turn. I will take risks and be afraid to fail, but go for it anyway, because I know that in the end, none of us get out alive. I will know that life is terrifying and chaotic and unfair and filled with sorrow and pain, but also exhilarating and wonderful and surprising and incredible, and a beautiful gift that keeps unwrapping, each and every time I make the decision to get out of bed. I will promise to do all of these things and more, and if I'm very lucky, maybe I can even change the world.

And I will never, ever move on.

"Don't be a martyr to widowhood. It's taken too much from us already. You can still live and love while grieving." – Kerry Phillips

Throw A Parade

Dear Everyone In the World Who Has Lost their Person to Death,

Please forgive yourself.

Please forgive yourself for maybe not being the best wife or husband that you knew how to be at that time. Or for not telling your person who died how much you love them, or what they mean to you, or how they changed your life. Please forgive yourself for not seeing the signs of an illness that you couldn't possibly know or see at that time. Forgive yourself for being so shell-shocked by grief, that you still can't remember the last few hours or days of your own husband's life. Please forgive that you didn't say good morning that day, or that you were fast asleep while your husband was collapsing at work on a cold floor, alone. Please forgive yourself for feeling pissed off at life, or at God, or at your beautiful person who died. Please forgive yourself for wanting, more times than you can count, to die and to no longer have to exist in this pain anymore. Forgive yourself for the dark thoughts – the ones that you wish you could make go away, and the ones that you became friends with and didn't ever want to go away.

Forgive yourself for the thoughts you don't like to think about. The thoughts you have had of pure jealousy toward others who have lost differently than you. Forgive yourself for feeling jealous of the couples who shared a lifetime, or fifty years together, or even ten, before one of them died. Forgive yourself for looking at old people and feeling rage because you won't ever know a life of growing old together with your person. Forgive yourself for being jealous of your own wonderful brother, because he gets to keep his wife, and he gets to have the house and the family with two kids and the life that you were supposed to have too. Forgive yourself for hating your husband's father, because he was a shitty dad, and because he didn't tell his own son he had a heart condition that has no symptoms or warnings. Forgive yourself for all the times you snapped at people who were just trying to help, or for the hundreds of times you cried in the car while on your way to work, or ran to the bathroom in the middle of work because you couldn't stop the hurt. Forgive yourself for expecting too much from friends and family or for being shocked and disappointed by the lack of empathy people have in general toward your loss.

Please forgive yourself for the choices you made in the months and years after your loss. The ones that you keep harboring over and harming your soul over. Forgive yourself for not being a good parent or daughter or son or friend or sibling or whatever else – to the people in your life when you lost your person to death. Forgive yourself for having no clue whatsoever, how impossibly hard this would be, and for not feeling like you have the strength or the care to do it at all. Forgive yourself for overeating. Or drinking too much. Or using drugs or other things, in a veiled attempt to get out of the pain, or pretend it wasn't there at all. Forgive yourself for not knowing or caring that none of those things would help you, for not realizing that the only way out is through. Forgive yourself for abusing your body – either intentionally or unintentionally – in the many ways that you may have done such a thing. Forgive yourself for the poor choices you may have made, in the throes of living with death inside your being. Forgive yourself for the relationships you entered into for all the wrong reasons, at all the wrong times. Forgive yourself for having too much sex, or no sex at all, in trying to find yet another way to numb that pain. Forgive the wrongdoings you may have done to others that you care about while you weren't living inside your actual self.

Forgive yourself for looking in strange or harmful places for what you thought might be new love. Forgive yourself for falling for something that wasn't what you thought it was or might be.

My Husband is Not a Rainbow

Forgive yourself for getting trapped in your own agony and for spiraling out of control after losing the love of your life. Forgive yourself for not listening to yourself and for following the mantras and the clichés of others who told you their opinions of how you should live your life. Forgive yourself for getting involved too quickly or for any actions you took that made you feel like you were "dishonoring" the person who died. Forgive yourself for not doing things the way that they used to do them or for feeling like maybe they should be alive and you should have died instead. Forgive yourself for not caring about living. Forgive yourself for questioning everything and for abandoning the things that no longer serve you or that you no longer believe to be true. Forgive yourself for changing your feelings about what God is or isn't, and know that life-altering deaths are the biggest reasons for these feelings to change.

Forgive yourself, forgive yourself, forgive yourself. For all of it. Good.

Now you can begin to live.

About two months or so after my husband's very sudden death, I was having lunch with my best childhood friend at a restaurant nearby to my apartment. She asked me how I was doing, or how I was *really* doing, and I said something to the effect of, "Not good, actually. Just going through the motions, but it's so awful." She looked at me with tears in her eyes, and she said with fierceness and confidence: "Well, I happen to think that a parade should be thrown in your honor, every single damn time you decide to roll your ass out of bed and take a shower."

At the time, her comment made me chuckle, but now, four and a half years later, I know that she is absolutely a thousand percent right. She is right about all of us. Anyone who loses someone that they love to death – whether it be a spouse, partner, friend, sibling, parent, child, or anyone else that is a piece of your very heart. Now I know, because I am living it, that what my dear friend was saying, is that whatever you do or don't do, following the loss of that person you loved, you are a goddamn hero.

Do you hear me? YOU ARE A HERO.

Living with the death of someone you love, is the most excruciating, horrific, unimaginable thing you will ever face.

And yet, here you are.

You're doing it.

Maybe today was the day you moved out of the home that you both shared. Or maybe you opened a box that you weren't ready to open a week ago. Or maybe you were going to donate some of their clothing or precious things, but you couldn't go through with it, so you drank a glass of wine instead. Maybe you found the energy to shower this morning. Or you called out of work, because your soul needed to hang out under the blankets of denial instead. Or maybe you made it through a grief-trigger or a moment of panic or anxiety. Maybe you cried nonstop for five hours before you were finally able to pick up his cremains from the funeral home. Maybe you decided to donate his organs today. Maybe you stood over your kitchen sink for forty five minutes, trying to decide whether or not it made sense to throw away that last can of soda that she opened but didn't finish. Maybe you didn't decide today. Maybe you need more time with that one. Maybe you started a new job or left an old one. Maybe you had to drive your other children to school today for the first time, knowing that your child who died would not be in that car. Maybe this was the first Wednesday that you attended a family function without your brother being there. Maybe you decided to try making the apple pie today – the one that your mom used to make for so many years before she died. Maybe you listened to a song today that threw you into grief hell. Maybe you opened the door into their bedroom today and were able to sit on the bed where they often sat. Maybe you changed something in that room, or maybe you thought it was best to keep leaving it the way it is. Maybe you brought flowers, or your beautiful self, to your wife's grave today. Maybe you got a haircut today that your husband might not have liked, or you took a risk and did something new and different that you maybe wouldn't have done in your other life. Maybe you washed their favorite pair of socks today by accident, and then you were horrified when they no longer smelled like him. Maybe you went to the store and bought the deodorant that they used to wear, and got in your car, and sniffed it over and over again like a lunatic. Maybe you took a step forward today, only to be knocked backward again. Maybe you kissed someone else for the first time since your partner died. Maybe you ran away somewhere to get away from your pain. Maybe that worked for a while. Maybe today you finally didn't feel guilty for throwing away their toothbrush. Maybe you watched your daughter or son get married today while your own heart was breaking in half, because their father or mother isn't here to see it. Maybe you tried a support group today. Maybe you made a different choice. Maybe today was the day you decided, and KNEW, that living your fullest life is the very best way to honor the one you had with them. Maybe you need more time.

But wherever you are in your loss, in your process – know this:

You are a hero. You are a rock-star. You are an amazing and wonderful thing.
Even when you screw up. Even when you make awful choices. Even when, even when, even when…

You are doing this.
You are living through this, and with this, and inside of this.
And even if the only thing you can make yourself do today is roll your ass out of bed and shower, you are my hero.

Kelley Lynn Shepherd

Don't you forget it.
Forgive yourself. Rid your mind of all the shit that keeps you beating yourself up.
Live in color.
And then throw yourself a Parade.

"Forever, forever, FOREVER, your perception of the world will be changed. You know that it doesn't last. You know that we all have to leave. And you will never be the same." – Carolynne Larsen Fox

Dear Dead Husband:

Nothing makes any sense to me right now.
On Wednesday, it will be April 13th.
Four years and nine months since you died.
On Wednesday, it will be April 13th.
Four years and nine months that we were married.
On Wednesday, April 13th, I will have been a widow longer than I was your wife.
This is maybe the saddest thing I have ever typed.
It feels so wrong to have to type that.
Or to have to live that.
And yet here I am.
With no choice, really,
but to try and live.
Somehow.

I've been trying.
And failing.
I opened myself up to the idea of loving again.
I thought it was going well.
But then it wasn't.

My Husband is Not a Rainbow

We met. We clicked. We kissed.
We held hands.
He held doors.
I felt butterflies.
We spent lots of time together,
In a short period of time.
He called me beautiful.
Nobody has said or meant those words,
Since you.
My first time having feelings for anyone,
Since you.
My first time kissing anyone,
Since you.
It didn't feel weird.
It felt nice.
It felt like you were happy for me.
It felt like I was a teenager again,
These feelings in my heart,
Fluttering. Dancing. Living.

But then,
Things got strange.
I guess he's not ready.
Or he changed his mind.
Or something.
He has a lot to work through.
We will stay friends,
And keep talking,
Almost daily,
And I so look forward to hearing his voice.
But I don't know if it will ever be more than that.
I just don't know.

I don't know what to do.
I have reached the point where I no longer want to be alone.
I no longer want to be lonely.

Kelley Lynn Shepherd

I no longer want to sit home by myself every weekend.
I got a tiny taste of feeling something again,
spending time with someone again,
being excited about someone again.
And I loved it.
I still love it.
But it was just a taste.

I know I'm not making any sense.
Nothing makes any sense.
Except me and you.
We made sense.
We made so much sense.
And then you were gone.
Why?
I just miss you so very, very much, my Boo.
I miss you every day.
I want to go back,
to when I didn't have to think about things such as this,
because I was someone's wife,
and I had a beautiful husband.
And we were so happy.
But now,
soon,
I will have been a widow,
longer than my entire marriage.
I just can't wrap my head around it.
I love you Until Forever,
And then longer.
Xoxo

Session Snippet

Caitlin: So how have things been with your new friend that you met in Florida?

Me: Eh. So much has happened since then, and nothing has happened. Everything was amazing while we were together. I thought it would be weird to kiss someone that wasn't my husband. Even though it's been four and a half years, I still thought it would be weird. It wasn't weird. It was really, really nice. He made it nice. He knew it was my first. It just felt sooo good to be around a man again. Someone telling me I'm pretty, holding my door open, being a gentleman. I didn't realize how much I was missing all of that. Wow, I really missed it. But since I left Florida, it's sort of gone back into friendship mode, and he doesn't seem ready or willing to see me again anytime soon. I feel like he woke something up in me, and I have strong feelings for him, so to try and help myself not think about that, I joined two dating sites. I figured even if I just get to feel that thing of holding someone's hand again, having dinner with a guy who likes my company, feeling alive again and like someone finds me attractive, it will be worth it.

Caitlin: Good for you. It's amazing to see this evolution of how you went from literally throwing up at the idea of someone else, to very slowly being indifferent to it, to now being in a place where you miss it. I think it's wonderful that you have waited until you were ready. I'm afraid to ask how the dating sites have been…

Me: It's been a shit-show. (laughing) Well, I met someone that I just started dating, and it's going well I guess. But before that; Hilarious. Depressing. Cruel. I had my first date a few weeks ago, and the guy and I didn't really click in person, but nothing earth-shatteringly bad. I texted him the next day to thank him for a nice time, and he texted back that we will not be going out again, because he doesn't date fat girls, and I'm fat. He said, "You don't look fat in your profile picture, but you're fat." So I replied, "That's funny. You don't look like an asshole in your profile picture, but you're an asshole." Don would have loved my comeback on that one. I think he was cheering me on. I had another dude who wanted to watch me eat spaghetti and get really fat. That was his turn on, apparently. That I get so fat, I explode or something. I also spoke with a dude who wanted to come over, clean my apartment while nude, and then suck on my toes. No thanks. I told him my apartment needs cleaning, but please leave my feet alone. His profile picture was him in a creepy room with shelves of Odor Eater boxes.

Caitlin: Oh my goodness, I think I'm out of words. (giggling in horror)

Me: Yeah, then there was "The Champ." This guy I talked to a few times on the site, and then we exchanged numbers. He seemed nice. We had a nice phone call, and after we hung up, he called me back and left this vulgar, X-rated voicemail message saying how he had to call back and jerk off to my voice, because it's so sexy. I wasn't even on the line with him. He jerked off to my one sentence voicemail message, and he "finished" in his message, moaning like a lunatic into my voicemail. He kept referring to his penis as "The Champ." As in "The Champ is hard and ready for you, baby! The Champ's been training for this!" After two messages from this sicko, I texted him and said that The Champ needs to hang up the towel and retire, before I call the police. He finally stopped calling.

Caitlin: Oh my god, you poor thing. Is this what's out there??? I'm in shock…

Me: Apparently this is the norm, from what I've been told. It's crazy. I did meet a few nice people. We just didn't click though. Or the timing wasn't right. I met one widower who I'm now friends with, and he's great. I've had lots of one date scenarios. One guy told me I needed to "get over" my dead husband, and that he won't compete with a ghost. I was so over the idiots at that point, I replied, "There's no competition. The ghost wins."

Caitlin: HA!!! Perfect!!!

Me: It was. So I met a widower in New York, from one of the dating sites. We had a few dates so far, and he is fun to be with. I'm taking things slow, there's something "off" about him. But I really like Florida guy. My heart is with him, and the few days we hung out stay in my mind, and I just love our ease and the way I felt while with him. And my heart is always with the dead guy, of course. Always with Don. He would find all of this hilarious, by the way. How I've gone from "I never want to date ever again," to dating men like some sort of crazed maniac. There was one point where I was literally talking to seven or eight guys at the same time. I had to create a spreadsheet list and take notes so I could keep track of who was who, who had which job, what we already talked about in our last phone call. The dating sites are so weird. So many men just want to text until the end of time, and they go weeks without ever asking me out. Usually a few of them just drop off the face of the planet, and then I'm down to one or two, and it's more manageable, but sometimes it feels like a second job. It's exhausting. My best friend, Sarah, said I need to get a second cell phone for all my men. It's hilarious. But all this random dating and searching for something that feels good just makes me miss Don more and more. But I know I can't have him anymore, and I really don't want to be alone. I CAN be alone. We all know I'm capable. Been doing it for almost five years now. I just don't WANT to anymore. I am hoping that love is a thing that is out there for me. I don't know though.

Caitlin: I think you are very brave for putting yourself out there again, in your time. And I love how you recognized on your own, that this person in Florida isn't in a place to go forward, and so you're not waiting on him. You're going out, meeting other people, and keeping an open mind. That's a lot of growth on your part. To recognize all of that.

Me: Thank you. There's something else, though. I'm actually terrified about sleeping with someone again. Right now, I can't imagine it happening, even though I'm sure that is where it's eventually going with this widower in New York. I think it's been a while for both of us, and we are very "all over each other" when we see each other. It's been five years for me. And just being kissed for the first time in five years, sort of sent me over the edge. I want more. It's like, I didn't give a shit about it for five years. I somehow forgot that sex was a thing. Now, my body was kissed, and it was like, "HELLO!!!!! More, please!"

My friends in the widowed community call it "losing your widow virginity." Having sex for the first time after the loss. What if I start crying right in the middle of having sex with him because it's so emotional or because I miss Don? Or what if he does something that triggers me back to the night of the rape? I'm not used to thinking about this, because Don just knew what things triggered me and what to never do. He was always so patient and gentle. I didn't think I'd ever have to worry about how another partner would handle my past. I thought I would be with Don forever.

Caitlin: That has to be a scary thought, but please try not to worry about things that haven't happened yet. Maybe your first time will be wonderful. Or maybe it will feel natural, and you'll feel ready, and it will feel nice, just like the kiss did. And if you're dating a widower, he will totally get it if having sex again makes you emotional. If you get serious with him though, or decide to become intimate, you might want to talk to him first about what you've been through. You don't have to get into huge detail or anything, but just a heads-up that you might want to take things slow and have suffered some sexual trauma. You said there is something "off" about him, though. What do you mean?

Me: I'm not entirely sure. My instincts just are kind of saying that he doesn't have my back, that he's not someone who would have my back or always protect me or put me first. He hasn't done anything specific to make me feel that way, but I just feel that.

Caitlin: Your instincts are usually spot on. Pay attention to that. I'm not saying to stop seeing him, but keep your eyes open for anytime you feel uneasy. And if you do feel uneasy, don't ignore that feeling.

Me: I will. Thank you. I really hate this dating stuff. Like, if I'm with this person, I should probably be happier, right? I don't feel happy. I'm happy when we hang out. Meaning, we have fun together, and it's fun and sooo overdue to kiss someone again and to fool around a little. My god, it's been so long. But when I think about us or about where it's going or that stuff, I feel stress. My number one thing with being with anyone, is that I need to feel safe with them. And I don't know how to explain it, but with this guy, I don't NOT feel safe, but I don't feel safe either. I'm worried that I'm staying in this just because I'm lonely, I like the male attention, and I miss being a part of a couple again. Going out to dinner. Having plans on a Friday night. Cuddling and watching a movie. Having that again feels so good, but I know this isn't the person for me.

Caitlin: There's nothing wrong with a casual relationship, as long as you are honest with each other. Just keep your eyes open along the way. Pay attention to those instincts.

Kelley Lynn Shepherd

Dear Dead Husband:

Tomorrow is July 13th. 5 years exactly since you died.
I got pink roses today. From you.
From your beautiful sister, Cynthia, who you never got to meet.
She is lovely. You two have a lot in common. It's still weird to me that I met her,
And you didn't.
She sends me flowers on this day each year since I've known her.
She says they are from you, and that she is just the messenger.
Thank you for my flowers.
5 long years without you.
I'm dating someone.
I also have strong feelings for someone else, who has become a good friend.
I feel really sad talking to you right now.
I feel like I have betrayed you. Or disappointed you.
I love you so very much.
With the one I have strong feelings for,
I feel like you approve, and are part of things.
I feel like you want that for me.
With the guy I'm seeing,
I don't feel anything from you at all.
I don't feel like you are telling me to run away,
But I don't feel as if you like or trust him.
Or maybe it's me that doesn't trust him.
I can't tell. I'm so confused.
My heart is not fully invested in anything right now, except you.
I miss you.
Please show me the way.

My Husband is Not a Rainbow

FB Post: Thank you so much to friends, both old and new, for coming out tonight to laugh, eat, drink, and toast to Don Shepherd on this July 13th, the 5 year milestone of his sudden death. I cherish you all dearly.
LIKES: 51   COMMENTS: 20

Nothing Happens, Until You're Okay

It was a random Sunday or Friday or some generic afternoon in the spring of maybe 2009, I think. My husband Don and I were both off work at the same time, on the same day, and we had taken a walk down Boulevard East, to the local diner a few blocks away for some late breakfast. After some down-time strumming on the guitar, singing, and playtime with the kitties, we found ourselves seated on our bed next to one another. Don had just gotten out of the shower and had his boxers on. They were cotton and had little baseballs all over them. And the New York Yankees emblem. They were my favorite boxers of his. When he turned around, they accentuated his sexy butt and long legs. He caught me staring and laid on the charm…

"Wanna fool around, wife?" Don asked, in his usual, playful way.

"Hell yeah, husband!" I responded. We leaned back on the bed, and began kissing.

"Think we can wake the neighbor's baby up from his nap again?" he teased, remembering the time when our intimacy sounds woke the sleeping infant that lived next door. Our orgasms were met with the infant's cry, coming in from his bedroom window to ours.

"We can sure try!" I joked back, recalling how embarrassed I was when the infant's mom ran into her child's bedroom, to his cries, and promptly shut the open window to block out our sex sounds.

"I have the most beautiful wife,, my husband said to me lovingly, as he looked me in the eyes with his soft, cool blue gaze.

The kisses were slow and meaningful and began to pick up in rhythm. Our bodies connected to one another as he took down the boxers and lay on top of me naked. He lifted my t-shirt up gently, and his tongue made large circles around my breasts, followed by his hands, cupping them and feeling all of my skin.

It didn't take me long to get properly turned on, as it had been a while since we were intimate. Normal, married life - often crazy and busy with exhausting work schedules - got in the way of our love-making time. But not today. Today was all about us, and we had the whole afternoon to make each other feel good. As my husband entered me slowly and with love, he stared into my soul and heart. "You are the most beautiful person in the world, to me," he smiled. "I love making love to you." The love-making turned faster now, and my hips met his thrusts. As the tempo increased, so did my movements, and then my moans, which got louder and louder, and...

"Sshhhh!!!" He smiled and placed his large hand over my mouth to block out my pleasure sounds. "The neighbor baby..." My eyes gazed upon my husband as he spoke the words, but my mind saw something else. My rapist. His hand over my mouth, in my half-asleep, half-induced state. His hand, filled with some kind of rag with the smell of alcohol or formaldehyde on it, cupping my mouth to block out my sounds of terror; the sounds of him killing my soul.

It was a flash, maybe three seconds, that my husband's hands turned into the rapist's hands, and then it was over. But it must have shown up in my glassy, deadened eyes. Don knew. He took his hand away slowly, then he very carefully removed his body from mine, and lay next to me in the bed, understanding fully what had just transpired. "I am so, so sorry, Boo. I should never put my hand over your mouth like that. I know better. I just realized that's what he did, and even me making that similar motion is enough for it to trigger you and for you to look at me that way." His eyes filled up with tears. "What way?" I asked him. "Like you're not sure where you are. Like you're unsure if I just hurt you. I never, ever want to be the one responsible for hurting you. Not ever. You have to be okay. Nothing happens, until you're okay. Ever. Not with me.'

"It's not you, Boo," I reassured him. "I have never felt more safe with anyone in my whole life, than I do with you. It was just a flash, a second or two, where my stupid mind went right back to that night and to his hand going over my mouth to silence me. I got a shiver through my body, and then I was fine. It was a visceral reaction that I couldn't help. Please don't worry. I'm okay now."

"Let's just lie here for a while - let me hold you in my arms, Boo. Anytime we are intimate, I want you to be a thousand percent with me. I don't want even two percent of you feeling uneasy, or scared, or even just rattled or confused, or anything except a thousand percent with me. I love you, and my job is to protect you. I take my job very seriously. Nothing matters to me more than your safety and your happiness. Trauma sucks, and it can mess with you at the worst times. Come here, sweetheart." I lay my head on his smooth chest as he stroked my hair gently. "Let's see if we can take a little nap," he said to me, and we started to drift off into sleep.

Seconds later, the neighbor baby began crying. We both started laughing. The baby, and us, crying and laughing, in unison.

Kelley Lynn Shepherd

Session Snippet

Me: So, it happened. I lost my widow virginity. With the guy I've been dating. The widower. We had sex, in my apartment. My first time with anyone since my husband.

Caitlin: Wow. This is big. Five years.

Me: Yup. Five years. I feel... like a bad wife. Like I disappointed myself, and Don, and you.

Caitlin: Me? Why me?

Me: You told me last time, to listen to my instincts. And I didn't. I'm weak. I don't know what I'm doing. I waited FIVE fucking years to be sure I was ready, and that I wouldn't have guilt, and that I'd be able to enjoy it, and that it wouldn't be weird, or for all the wrong reasons - and I STILL made a bad choice. I should have paid attention to my inner voice. I feel like a bad person now.

Caitlin: Bad person, because you enjoyed it?

Me: Bad person, because I told my boyfriend that I wanted to be intimate with him soon, but that I didn't want my first time with someone new to happen within a week or two of July thirteenth, Don's death date. Because I thought that would be weird and disrespectful. That week should be about honoring my husband - not about me going out and getting laid for the first time in five years. He was spending the weekend at my apartment, because he was coming out with me and my friends to honor Don with drinks and food, so I made it clear that even though he was spending the night, I didn't want to have sex. That I wanted to wait until late July or maybe even August. It seems silly, but it meant a lot to me. It was a respect thing for me and Don. That week is about Don, and I didn't want anything else clouding it.

My Husband is Not a Rainbow

Caitlin: That is not silly at all. It's really kind of beautiful that it remains important to you to make that week and that time of year about honoring his life.

Me: Yeah. But I didn't. I gave in. I had sex anyway. I made it about me having sex.

Caitlin: Did he pressure you? Was he on board with waiting until later?

Me: At first, he seemed to be fine with it, and he said he totally understood why I wanted to wait. But then, we were alone in my apartment, and watching TV, and we started fooling around. I made a light comment about, "Let's not let this get too far, okay? Remember what I said about wanting to wait," and he just kept pulling at my clothing and trying to take off my bra or my shorts. I didn't ever technically "stop" him or say "no," but I think it was obvious, for a while at least, that I wasn't wanting to do this right now. My body was into it, and it felt good, but I kept saying stuff like, "Come on, I don't feel totally comfortable with this right now," and then he would say, while kissing my neck or my earlobe, "But you're so beautiful, I just want you so badly. You turn me on so much, I can't help myself. Look at what you do to me." At some point, his touches and complimentary words won out over my logic, and I just gave in. And once we were into it, it was good. I enjoyed it. But right after, I felt dirty. And sad. And now I'm really sad that I have THAT as my memory of July thirteenth week, instead of it being about Don, like it should have been. I just want to cry.

Caitlin: Aww, honey. You really need to forgive yourself for this one. Hell, it had been FIVE years! You have certainly held out long enough! I think that Don would absolutely forgive you and probably even cheer you on! And really, you both just got a little carried away. I mean, yes, he really should have respected your wishes and not continued being physical with you or trying to tempt you when he knew you didn't want to go there this month. He should have done that. But he got carried away. It happens.

Me: Don would have never done that to me. Don had way too much respect for me to ever do that, to ever use "getting carried away" as an excuse. Something similar actually happened with us, one time, and it's all I could think about when my boyfriend was pawing his hands all over me to get me into bed. One time, about a year or two before he died, we were literally right in the middle of having sex, and he stopped RIGHT IN THE MIDDLE and gently removed himself from me, and made sure I was okay. Why did he stop? Because I "made a face." I was triggered by something, and I made a subtle face. I didn't even say anything to him about it or anything. I kept going. But HE stopped, because he said he didn't feel comfortable knowing that even two percent of me was feeling uneasy. I'll never forget that. That's a REAL man. That is showing respect for your woman and your partner and letting her know that you ALWAYS have her safety as your first priority, even when you are literally at the height of being turned on and fully hard. He stopped because I made a face, and I couldn't even respect him the same way and stop for him during his death week, with a guy who never gave me even a quarter of the respect that Don always did. With a guy who used his dick and being turned on as an excuse to not put my safety first. And dammit, now I AM crying!

Caitlin: Kelley, you're going to make mistakes on this new road of widowhood, this road to finding something meaningful again. It's really okay. I don't think anyone, especially Don, expects you to do any of this perfectly. I understand why you're upset, truly, but please try not to beat yourself up about this. Don would never be this hard on you. Try to treat yourself the way he would have treated you. With extreme kindness.

Me: I just want to feel worthy of that kind of treatment. He was soooo good to me, and now I have to navigate these stupid relationships and these men who don't hold the same amount of respect for me as he did. I just feel like there isn't anyone out there that is as amazing and good to me as he was.

Caitlin: Nobody will be like Don. They never will be. But really, why would you want them to be? There is only one Don Shepherd. And you have that love with you forever. I do think there are guys out there who treat women with respect and love, and I do think you will find one of them that will be just for you. In the meantime though, you need to start practicing better self-care. Enough beating yourself up. Be kind to yourself. Don wouldn't accept anything less than that.

"No matter how real the guilt feels,
It is a lie your broken heart is telling you
In a struggle to make sense of your tragedy."
– Kim Kinney

Your Death Is a Pain In the Ass

Yesterday, while smack in the middle of writing my weekly TV review for one of my multiple, low-pay to no-paying writing gigs, my computer went down, as did the entire wifi system. After cursing up a storm because my almost-written review was now gone, I spent over an hour playing with wires and buttons and plugging and unplugging and rebooting and on and on and on, until FINALLY, I got everything working again. Turns out the power cord was bad, so I had to replace it with a different one. In the end, I spent over ninety minutes in total frustration on something I know nothing about, and it ruined my mood the rest of the day. When Don was alive? It would have gone like this:

Kelley Lynn Shepherd

"Boo, the computer just went down." "Ah, okay. Let me see what the problem might be. Oh! There we go. Looks like a bad power cord. Let me change that for you."

Your death is a pain in the ass.

Yesterday, I was searching around the apartment for the longest time, trying to find something that looked like it might be worth eating. Since I'm nearing the end of whatever I bought on my last grocery trip, the choices are slim, and I'm not. After looking for what felt like years, but was probably twenty minutes, I unenthusiastically decided on some elbow macaroni with butter and parmesan cheese. Yeah. This is basically the typical meal of my four year old niece, but I had nothing else, so that's what it was going to be. Until I picked up the pot to put it in the strainer, tripped over the damn cat, and dropped the pot of macaroni all over my kitchen floor. If Don were still alive, I wouldn't be in the situation where I would be desperate enough to eat that lame excuse for a meal in the first place, therefore I wouldn't have dropped it anywhere.

Your death is a pain in the ass.

This morning, I woke up and proceeded to walk out into the kitchen to make some coffee and get started on my daily ritual of looking through endless job sites and emails, since the teaching job I've had for the past sixteen years decided to cancel all my summer courses going forward. I noticed the refrigerator door was wide open. So I'm guessing it was open all night. Why? I have no idea, other than the fact that my roommate and I live in an apartment with a crappy and old refrigerator that has weak magnetics on the door, so the slightest change in breathing might cause it not to close correctly. Washed down the door, scrubbed the inside, tried again and prayed that all our food hadn't gone bad already. If Don were here, I wouldn't be living in this apartment at ALL, never mind with this shitty refrigerator from the Carter administration. Who knows where we would be living by now together? I do know it would NOT be in weird and annoying Flushing, Queens.

Your death is a pain in the ass.

All the little things and bigger things that I now have to do because he is dead. Killing roaches. Killing mice or picking up the ones that my cats leave half-dead on my bed or on the floor by our entrance-way. Dealing with the idiots on dating sites, and dealing with dating, period. Yes, there are moments when I feel joy or when it's exciting to discover someone new and everything they bring to the table. But in the moments when it feels really hard, or where I feel like I have no idea what I'm doing or if I'm going to end up hurting someone or hurting myself, I just can't help but want to scream, "I WOULDN'T HAVE TO DO ANY OF THIS IF YOU WEREN'T FREAKIN' DEAD!!!!"

Does that ever go away? That whole "Six Degrees of You Being Dead" thing? Where every single thing you do somehow relates back to them being dead? Will there ever be a day where something goes terribly wrong in life, or 'm having a really awful time with something, and I DON'T immediately think: *None of this would be happening if you didn't die.*

Honestly, I don't know if that will ever happen. I don't know if I will ever be able to separate the two things. Life after losing my husband, and his death. Can those two things ever really be separate? Probably not. Because one led to the other. So maybe that's just the way it is. I don't know anymore, and I don't pretend to know these things. I only know this:

Your death is annoying.
Your death is a nuisance.
Your death is a pain in the ass.

Kelley Lynn Shepherd

Dear Stupid Death Diary:

I haven't written in you for a long time. I have something to say, though, that I can't say to everyone yet, so I shall talk to you, stupid death.

I lost my summer teaching job in May. They told me suddenly, without much warning, that I would no longer be teaching the summer Acting courses anymore, due to low enrollment. This happened before, with one class in the summer months, but I was told it was just for that summer. Now it's permanent, going forward. Meaning, instead of teaching as an Adjunct Professor the whole year round, which I've been doing for years now, I will only be teaching the fall and spring semester from now on. That means two months during winter break with no paycheck, and then all summer long with no paycheck. I just can't live on that low of a salary, and finding odd temp work has proven to be difficult at best.

So right now, I have no summer job. It's been extremely frustrating, and I'm spending most of my days on the computer or out trying to find work. I'm scraping by lately, and whenever I barely have enough funds to get through the month, it always makes me feel like I have failed somehow. Like, this is NOT what Don wants for me, to STILL be struggling this way. He wanted so much more for me, and so do I. A good friend, along with my parents and the money I still have in my bank from my last paycheck and directing the last show, are barely getting me through the summer. It's just so hard.

I have been toying with the idea of leaving New York City. Staying with my parents in Massachusetts, where I wouldn't have to worry about rent or bills for a few months, and finally finish the book I have been writing for years now. I wouldn't stay there forever - maybe six months - and then I would either come back to New York City and start over here, or I would maybe try a different city entirely. Maybe Chicago. Maybe the area of Florida where my husband used to live, where I feel closest to him. Is that crazy? It might be. But I feel crazy lately. I feel restless. I feel like I need something different.

I would be leaving Adelphi for good if I did this, after being there my whole adult life. First, as a student, graduating with a BFA in Performing Arts. Then, as a hired director, multiple times, directing shows and writing cabarets. And of course, teaching there for the past sixteen years, my stand-up comedy and Acting Courses, with the students I love. It would be so difficult to make such a huge change and no longer work there anymore, but if I am no longer going to be teaching there in the summers, going forward, I just cannot see how I will get by much longer.

If I decide to do this, I would also be leaving NYC, the place I have called home for my entire adult life. And that would be VERY hard. These are big decisions, and right now, they are only in my head. I haven't decided anything yet for sure. But my brain is very tired. Five years of making every single decision without a life partner to help is extremely daunting and hard. I wish I could rest. I wish I had the type of life where I wasn't always struggling, and where I could just jump on a plane and take a vacation from my own life. That's what I need. But I don't have that luxury. And so I'm tired. And I no longer have words.

The Choice That Isn't a Choice

There is a question that I hear asked within the widowed community, over and over again, time after time, on an endless loop. Widowed people, for whatever reason, seem to like asking one another this question and seem to enjoy dissecting the meaning of the various answers to the question when asking another fellow widowed person. The question that is posed, is usually some version of the following:

If you had to choose between the life you have now and the life you had with your husband/wife/partner who died, which would you choose? If your person could come back right this minute, but in return, you would have to give up every person and everything that you have met and known since after their death - would you do it? Would you turn back the clock and choose to have them back - but knowing you would also go back to being that person you were before they died? What would you choose?

For me, the question of *which life would you choose* feels like a pointless one. It feels like some form of weird torture, to ask yourself such things, when you know as well as I do, that those things can never happen. The question is a pointless and invalid one, because it is not based in any reality. That person is no longer here, and they never will be again. They live inside us, they live on in who we are and who we become and what legacy we make of this life, but they will never physically be here again - and we will never get to know what that life is. So why on earth would I want to sit around asking myself which life I would choose? It's a fairy-tale question. It's not real. That choice doesn't exist, and it never will exist. At no point in your life, going forward, will someone ever ask you to make that choice. Because you can't. It's not possible.

So, whatever your personal answer is to that question, try not to let it bother you too much. I know widowed people who feel so guilty because they are happy again - and I know many others who just want nothing more than to have that other life back again. And I know many who float somewhere in between the two worlds, never quite knowing which to embrace.

Well guess what? You don't have to decide. You never have to choose. Because you can't. You had a life and a love with someone who died. That life is now over, because they are not here. That love is NEVER over, because love lives on, and we carry it forward into all that we are. So don't waste time worrying about a choice that was never really a choice. There is no choice in this. You had that life, now you have this one. The only choice to be made here is this:

How will I choose to live *this* life, the one I have now?

For me, I almost look at it as two separate lives or entities. There was the life I had with my husband, and there is life now. As I said above, I would do anything on earth to have that life back and to have him back again, but that's never going to happen. So, all I can do is live this life as brightly as possible, and in a way that he would be proud of and happy for me. All I can do is keep letting good people into my world and hold them tightly, as I believe they are gifts from my husband. All I can do is keep finding ways to love and connect and grow, which is what life is all about, really. And while I cannot ever have my husband back, what I can do is make the choice to live the life that he never had the choice to experience. I can accept the love and the gifts that he is sending me and try to create something beautiful. I can know, deep in my soul, that love grows from love. I can know without question that being in love again is a way to honor our forever love, because our love is the very foundation that all new love stands on. I can know that while that life we had and the life I have now are two individual things, they will always find gorgeous and meaningful ways to merge.

And in all of those profound ways, the life we had, is not, in fact, dead.

It is reborn, over and over and over again.

Kelley Lynn Shepherd

Session Snippet

Me: This five-year thing is really messing with me. Some widowed people call it "the five-year itch." I feel restless. Direction-less. I feel like I'm back at square one, and everything I have done so far since his death just feels pointless.

Caitlin: Nothing is ever pointless, Kelley. Everything you do means something to somebody or someone, even if you never directly feel that. Everything you have done and written and accomplished has shifted you into new places and has helped others shift too.

Me: But I'm right back where I started. Five years of this shit. Five years of moving. Having a jerk roommate. More moving. Losing homes, jobs, friends, income, picking up multiple jobs to make ends meet. Getting sick from stress, grief, panic attacks, anxiety, vertigo, hives. Bill collectors on my ass. People trying to sue me for bills that weren't even mine. All this stress with Don's company and the health insurance issues on the day of his death - all this stuff I can't really talk about and that people don't even know I'm dealing with. Now I have no summer income, and five years later, I'm still struggling just as much as I was when he first died. I'm so damn tired, and I feel like such a loser. Why can't I make this work?

Caitlin: You feel that way because you have been through hell and back, and then back again. You feel like a loser because you just lost your summer teaching job, and it feels like life keeps kicking you in the face. But look at all you've done to keep fighting for that life. You are the furthest thing from a loser. You never take the easy road. Someone with less strength and less passion and determination would have moved right out of New York City after their husband died and moved back in with mom and dad, because that's a hell of a lot easier. And there would be absolutely nothing wrong with doing that. But that's not what you did. You could have. Their home was open to you and offered to you. But you didn't. You said, "No. My life is here. I'm going to create something with it." And then you did that. You wrote a play about his death and performed it. You have now given your Camp Widow presentation over ten times, in three different cities, for over three years, to hundreds of widowed people. You directed multiple shows. Did comedy shows. Speeches. You're writing a book. You're starting a road to some grief coaching. I could go on. You've taken this loss and created something healing, over and over and over.

Me: But I'm drowning. Most of those things don't pay anything, and I end up putting IN money just so I can find more ways to help people. I feel like it's the only thing that makes me feel alive and purposeful now - helping people through loss. But I'm broke every day. I wake up feeling stressed and defeated. I can't afford shoes or bras that fit right, or clothes that don't look horrible on me. And I feel like I have failed what Don wanted for us - he moved his entire life from Florida to stupid Jersey so I could pursue my dreams. And all this time, I haven't gotten anywhere. I'm failing.

Caitlin: You're having selective memory right now, because you're feeling frustrated and exhausted. All those viral videos you did? All seven of them? They were ALL filmed after his death, minus one. You flew to L.A. this year to shoot a film. You've done lots of acting projects and stand-up gigs and lots of writing gigs. Your words have helped so many people. You haven't failed anyone, especially Don. He knows how impossible it is to survive up here on one income - that's why he moved here! To be your teammate and help you. That's why he helped you pay your bills, even before moving here while he was still living in Florida. He wanted to support you in all the ways that a good husband like him does. You don't have that now. He would be amazed and in awe of all you have done without him, are you kidding me?

Me: But I feel like everything in my life is up in the air right now, and I don't know which way to go with any of it. I don't know what I want anymore, or where I belong, or what to do next with this life. I don't know if I should leave New York City, or go to mom and dad's, or something totally different than all of that. And with relationships, my heart feels so fragile and just all over the place.

Caitlin: Trust your gut.

Me: But I don't know what it's saying or if it's pointing me the right way.

Caitlin: Yes you do. If you sit in the silence of everything, your gut will tell you what you actually should do. That feeling you get when it's just you and no noise. No outside opinions. That little ping that tells you when something is "off" or that tells you this isn't really where you want to be. Trust that. Listen to that. Never have I regretted trusting that inner-voice. But there have been plenty of times I said, "Dammit. I knew better." You know what I mean. You didn't trust your gut when it told you to wait to have sex, that it didn't feel right to do it near the death anniversary. And you felt awful. Don't ignore your gut now. Trust your gut now. Give yourself some time, some silence, and some patience. That little voice will tell you where you need to go.

Me: But what if I screw something up or make the wrong decision?

Caitlin: You won't. There's no such thing. You make decisions based on what you feel is right at the time. There are no wrong ones, just ones that are meant to bring you somewhere else. Just keep following the path that feels most right. Everything else will fall into place. And if something doesn't feel right anymore, you change direction again. Everything leads to something else.

Nothing is ever pointless. I don't believe in being on the right or wrong path. You're on the path you are meant to be on at that time, and something will come from it. There's nothing wrong with you right now. The reason you feel directionless is because you need a new direction. The reason you feel restless is because where you are is no longer feeding your soul. Change the path, and the path will become more clear. Trust me. No. Strike that. Trust yourself.

If You Weren't Dead

If you weren't dead, I wouldn't be living in Flushing, Queens - a neighborhood I don't like at al, and don't feel I belong in at all.

If you weren't dead, I wouldn't be walking home late at night from the subway or bus with keys in my hand, because I'm so terrified that I'm going to be attacked.

If you weren't dead, I wouldn't have to work more than one job just to get by.

If you weren't dead, I wouldn't have to wake up in the middle of the night from one of my nightmares and somehow get through it all alone.

If you weren't dead, I wouldn't be so familiar with what a panic attack feels like or how frightening it is to feel massive anxiety and fear on a regular basis.

If you weren't dead, I wouldn't have to look at my own brother with his wife and his house and his kids and feel a ping of jealousy and intense sadness at the life we never got to have, staring me down in the eyes of his family. Immediately followed by feeling like an awful sister for feeling this way.

Kelley Lynn Shepherd

If you weren't dead, I wouldn't have to try and navigate the hellish and confusing waters of the dating world, nor would I have to try and figure out the intentions and emotions of people in the male species.

If you weren't dead, I would still have health insurance, and I wouldn't have random bouts of vertigo, hives, eczema, or throwing up because grief makes me sick. Literally.

If you weren't dead, seeing happy couples or older couples who have been married for even one decade or longer wouldn't feel like a knife through my heart, every single time.

If you weren't dead, I wouldn't know what it's like to feel defeated, exhausted, and beaten down by life, just ten minutes after waking up.

If you weren't dead, I wouldn't be living in fear of being alone forever, growing old alone, or dying alone. I would be feeling safe in the knowing that I have you, and you have me, and everything else will be okay.

If you weren't dead, I wouldn't be sitting here creating this list about you being dead.

"Through struggle, comes clarity and my understanding that this ever painful 'journey' is never-ending, ever painful, and never understood by those who have not walked the path."
– Molly Fisher Foster

FB Post: Major Announcement. After thinking about it off and on obsessively for a very long time, talking with my grief-counselor, and getting the advice of a couple really close friends - I have decided that after 26 years of living here my entire adult life, since age 18 - I will be leaving NYC. I will be giving my notice at Adelphi this week, and this will be my last semester teaching, after 16 years. So, I will be here 3 more months, and then, after Finals Week in December, we will pack up my life into a moving truck, just like Don did, and drive me home to mom and dad's. My brother is building me a home office / bedroom in the basement, and I will finally have the luxury of time and no rent or bills to finish writing my book. After that, who knows where I will end up. Honestly, I'm a little bit terrified. Okay, a lot. But it's time for a big change in direction. Right now, I'm following my gut, my heart, and a path that's been built on love. Isn't that what life is all about?
LIKES: 347   COMMENTS: 112

Vernacular

Vernacular.
"noun [C/U] US /vərˈnæk·jə·lər, vəˈnæk-/

The form of a language commonly spoken by the people of a particular region or by a particular group, esp. when it is different from the standard language: the word choices or speech patterns spoken by an individual person."

Yes.
This is it. This is what I miss.
Beyond his touch.
Beyond his hugs.
Above and beyond his laugh.
All of those things I miss so much.
Every single day.

Kelley Lynn Shepherd

But…
sometimes,
if I sit completely still,
and let my breath turn to silence,
and if I focus really hard,
but without trying at all,
sometimes,
in that moment of nothingness,
I am able to bring back in my heart or my soul,
or somewhere I can't quite identify,
what it felt like,
what it sounded like,
what it was,
to be hugged by him.
to know his laugh.
to sense his touch.
And in that tiny fragment of time,
in that one small measure of music,
I am allowed to be with him again.

You see…
there are certain things,
very specific things about a person,
that you can hold onto,
or bring into focus,
in different ways,
after they die.
Their eyes.
Their hands.
A memory.
Stories or events or places or songs,
that instantly take you back to them.
Pictures.
Videos.
Hand-written cards or notes.
The cologne they wore,

My Husband is Not a Rainbow

or the way their shirt smelled.
Their favorite foods.

None of these things are enough to satisfy,
the forever ache that comes,
from your person being gone.
Not even close.
For that ache,
it is a monster that lives inside of you.
It resides there,
like a nail sitting in the depths of your throat.
You can't swallow.
You can't ever swallow.
At least,
not the way you used to.
Because that ache acts like a blockage,
like a gate,
stopping any kind of normalcy,
from ever entering again.
And now,
in this version of life,
you have to swallow through that ache.
So having a measure of time with a memory or a song,
something that brings you back to them,
it is never enough to dull that ache.
But,
it is something.
And when it comes to grief,
and missing your person,
and craving to feel anything,
that brings them close to you again…
When it comes to the forever death,
of your person,
something,
is always better
than nothing.

Kelley Lynn Shepherd

So you hold onto those somethings.
You cling to them,
because they are all that you have now.
A change in the wind,
a feeling in the air,
a shift in the moon or stars,
someone that reminds you of them…
And for a second or two,
sometimes,
they come back.
Sometimes,
you can recreate
in your heart and mind,
pieces of them,
that exist within you,
and around you.
And so,
just as there are things like that,
which you can hold onto,
there are other things,
that you can never get back.

Vernacular.
That way in which he spoke to me,
spoke with me.
The word choices he used,
which were often,
strange.
odd.
Him.
That pitch in his voice,
the tone of his whisper,
the beautifully specific sounds,
the phrasing,
the places where he stressed the syllables,
the sexy without trying,

My Husband is Not a Rainbow

the calm,
the tranquil,
the peace and safe feeling,
that lived within his rhythms.

The way that he would respond to things,
that would leave me equal parts baffled,
fascinated,
and in awe,
of his intelligence,
his wit,
his sarcasm.
What he would say,
in conversation,
with friends,
with family,
with me.
The life that breathed air,
through his speech.
Vernacular.

It is a thing that only exists in real time.
You can't recreate it.
You can't even remember it.
You can try.
I have tried.
Nothing comes.
I sit and try over and over,
to find that thing,
that way,
that language that only we knew,
with each other.
But I can't.
When it's just me,
alone,
in a room,

as much as I want to,
I can't.
I try and I try,
then I try again,
because I want it so badly,
but I can't.

Because there are some things
about a person who died,
your person,
that you just can't get back.
Some things,
are just gone.

And in that darkness,
in that nothingness,
Nothing comes.
Because the truth is,
there are some things,
like vernacular,
that are so uniquely precious,
so incredibly special,
that they turn into dust,
into nothing,
at that very moment,
when that life ends.

FB Post: So I'm here in Ohio, staying with a widowed couple, (my good friends, Sarah and Mike) and the widower's 10 year old daughter (who is awesome); in the home that the widower shared with his wife who died - and now shares with the widow, whose fiancé died. I'm sleeping on a couch that belonged to the widow's fiancé and that was brought here to this home by the widower, who lovingly repaired it for his widow girlfriend,

because it had been broken for years. Tomorrow, all of us will get in the widow-bego (car) and drive 2 hours to attend the wedding of another widow friend, (Beth) who also found love again, just like the widow and widower I'm staying with did in each other. Are you still with me? And all of us met each other and know each other because of this wacky place called Camp Widow, which is actually at a beautiful Marriott hotel, and has nothing at all to do with camping. None of the people involved in this scenario would know one another if our person didn't die. And because of that fact, the people we loved and will always love are the ones who bring us together. Where there is life, that is where they live. Through us. With us. Like one big dysfunctional family. Love grows love, and out of our collective losses, we grew a family.
LIKES: 133   COMMENTS: 62

"I'm stuck in a place of nonexistence, somewhere in between. I'm not me, I'm not her, I'm not anyone I know." – Karen Collins

FB Post: So I recently ended things with the widower I was seeing for the past five months or so. It wasn't working out, and in the end, he wasn't the right fit for me. I also found out, soon after ending things, that I was being lied to, and he wasn't being honest with me about some things. Plus, I'm leaving NYC in 3 months, and needed to make a clean break from this relationship. I'm posting this here because people keep asking if we are still together, which is my fault, since I made our relationship so public. I posted several pictures of us out together on dates, honoring each other's late spouses, while spending time together. I posted all those pictures, not because I had found the love of my life - but so I could give people hope - so that other widowed people would see proof, that even someone like me who was so cynical and had no interest in dating ever again and

was convinced that nobody would ever love her or find her attractive ever again - can find a way to open their hearts again, if that is what they want. It took me over four years, but I am finally in that place where I know that it's possible, and it was largely this relationship that helped me to realize that. This relationship also helped me to know that I should always, always trust my gut. It will never steer me wrong. Thank you to everyone who has been so supportive and so happy for me. I'm going to keep searching for that real, true love. I believe it is out there for me. This just wasn't it. Please don't be sad for me. I feel good about ending this. It's time.
LIKES: 162   COMMENTS: 79

Criminal

As I lay here in the night,
I miss what was.
What is, but isn't.
What would be,
if it was.
What could have been.
I miss the Us,
that was,
that would have been,
that never got to be.

Our past.
Our now.
Our future.

I miss what I never knew.
I miss what I always knew.
And I miss you,
saying that you miss me.

My Husband is Not a Rainbow

Death comes in,
like a criminal,
a robbery,
that keeps happening,
over and over again,
stealing your life,
slowly,
painfully,
piece by piece by piece.

And so you lie there,
in the night,
with the nothingness,
with the missing of everything,
that can never be again.

FB Post: So it's my stupid wedding anniversary again. Would have been 10 years. I'm at work as I type this. I'm in the car, sobbing and trying like hell to stop sobbing. I had to have my teaching assistant and friend (Thank you Andrew S.!) take over the stand-up class for me this morning, because I just could not pull it together. Still can't wrap my heart around the fact that I should be celebrating 10 years of marriage with my love, but instead, I'll be spending it with some ashes in a ziploc baggie. Today is a very sad day.
LIKES: 35   COMMENTS: 16

"My wedding anniversary is my hardest grief day. It's the day that only matters to just me. No one else shares the pain of this day with me." – Jacque Nelson

Kelley Lynn Shepherd

Dear Dead Husband:

I miss you. It's our wedding anniversary. I don't know how to be or what to do on this day when you're dead. I don't want to hear "Happy Anniversary" from people. You're dead. What on earth is happy about it? I don't want to pamper myself on this day, as some have suggested. I just want to lie in your arms. Be with you. You're the ONLY person I want to be with on this day. And I can't. Not ever again. That will never be okay with me. I've been trying to find love again, Boo. I'm failing pretty miserably. The way I felt about the guy I was seeing - how I felt in my gut that I couldn't trust him but wasn't sure why - I was right. He tried to humiliate me in front of my widowed community. He blindsided me and threw his new girlfriend in my face during the widow support group that I welcomed him into, and I think he was cheating on me with her from the way they were talking - like they have been together for a while now. I told him what I thought of him in an email, and then I blocked him from contacting me. I don't need that in my life. I feel used. I feel stupid. I didn't love him, but I did care for him as a person, and tried hard to end things in the right way. In a kind way. And I was honest with him from the start, that I didn't think it was love for me. And he chose to treat me poorly, and carelessly, and mess with my heart, and be back-handed. I'm so upset with myself for choosing him, someone who would treat me that way, to lose my widow virginity to. How could I do that on the same week that you died? I will never feel good about that. It makes me feel sick when I think about it. Please forgive me. I love you, and I will try to do better. Xoxo

*"I can't find myself anymore.
It's as if you took me with you,
but you left my body here.
My instincts are shot. My brain is mush. My heart beats weirdly.
Please show me the way, dear husband.
I am lost." – Me*

FB Post: So, there are TEDx talks that happen all around the country, usually in theaters or universities. Adelphi is hosting one in March of 2017, and I just finished the application for submission. If it gets past the first round, I'll be asked to come in next month and give an audition. The topic idea I presented to them was the concept that when it comes to grief and loss, there is no such thing as "moving on." The talk will be based on a popular blog piece I wrote a while back (last year) called "I Will Never Move On." To date, it's my most popular blog post, so I know this is a topic that needs more attention. Please put in a good thought with the universe that they choose me as one of the speakers next spring. All of your collective energy will certainly help. Thanks!
LIKES: 117   COMMENTS: 41

Things That Never Happened...

A Sunday morning in October or November of 2010, a few days after our fourth wedding anniversary. We did not know it would be our last one together...

Don: Boo, I've been thinking. I really want to get us out of this crappy apartment. Just, into something nicer. This place is falling apart. I'd love to get out of this disaster of a state too. Maybe we could move to the New York side, somewhere in

Queens or Long Island, so you'd be close to work and not have to do this insane commute.

Me: But what about your job?

Don: I can always find EMS work out in New York, I'm sure. Or maybe transfer through the company. Or maybe we can just win the lottery so I can start my dream of a big rescue house for kitties called "Isabelle's Place." How awesome would it be to just spend our life taking care of kitties, playing music, and going on lots of cool trips?

Me: It would be amazing. Where would we go first?

Don: Hmm. Maybe Italy. Or Alaska. Or hell, I'd love to go check out where I grew up in Whittier, California. See how much it's changed over the years.

Me: Want me to start asking around about apartment or condo rentals on Long Island, just to get an idea?

Don: Yeah why not. It can't hurt. That's why I picked up this second job, ya know? Need to pay off this dental bill, then start getting us some kind of savings so we can figure out our future. We have nothing right now. It's so impossible to save money here. But I don't want you to worry about any of that. You just focus on teaching and going to any auditions or doing comedy shows, pursuing your career. I'll get us through. It's my job to take care of you, and I love my job. Just give me a little bit for rent each month, when you can, but I'll keep paying all our bills and all the car payments. At the very least, I'd like to be in a nicer environment if we're gonna think about having a family.

Me: (smiling) That makes me happy. Thinking about a family with you. Parenting with you. You are so good with Brian. That kid loves you.

My Husband is Not a Rainbow

Don: Yeah, he's a great kid. I'd love to have a son or daughter to teach how to play catch, toss around a baseball, annoy your brother with our Yankee-fan kid, just to watch them grow up and see who they'd become, ya know? Must be amazing. I never had that with my dad. Never had anything. It'd be great to be able to have that with my own child. Or give that to some little boy or girl who has a shitty home life. That just kills me, knowing that kids live that way, feeling unloved.

Me: You lived that way, Boo. It's amazing you turned out the way you did. And it's great that you and your sister can look back on it and have these long talks on the phone. You two have a real bond.

Don: Yeah, Karen's the best. We went through a lot together. (pauses, tears in his eyes) Boo, do you think I would be a good father?

Me: (holding him) Oh my god, yes. You would be the best dad there ever was. Having kids wasn't something I even really thought much about before meeting you. YOU are the reason I want a family. I want a family with YOU. Our kids would be so incredibly lucky to have you as their dad. I can't imagine a better father than you. Really. And my heart starts beating faster just thinking about us being parents together. You taking care of me while I'm pregnant. You're the best in the world at taking care of me. I can't stop smiling just thinking about it.

Don: Thanks, Boo. Me too. I love the idea of it. It would be so great to go over to your brother's house, have our kids playing with Brian - I just wanna feel like we aren't completely broke, ya know? So maybe we figure out how to move somewhere nicer soon, save a little money, and then talk about a family. (starts laughing)

Me: What's so funny?

Don: I'm just picturing you turning forty in a couple years and being pregnant. How miserable you'd be.

Me: Yup. Probably. But I'd do it for us, baby.

Don: Know what else would be cool?

Me: What?

Don: If every five years, starting next year, we did a little vow-renewal ceremony, and wrote new vows to reflect the last five years.

Me: What??? YOU want to keep writing new vows every five years? You??? You hate writing stuff! Who are you, and what have you done with my husband???

Don: I think it would be fun to see what we would write each time, how much our life and marriage would change. A lot of stuff can happen in five years. It would be cool.

Me: Oh I agree. I'm just shocked that you would want to do that.

Don: I'm full of surprises, Boo. See? That's romantic, right? Vow renewal?

Me: Yes!!! Very. So our first one will be next year, on our fifth year anniversary?

Don: Yeah. Let's do that. We can just have a little ceremony at your parents' house, or somewhere in a park or garden, and say our new vows. And then go out for a steak dinner and chocolate cake.

Me: Yum. Now I want steak. And chocolate.

Don. Will you settle for burgers and ice-cream? Get in the car. I'll take you to Five Guys and then Dairy Queen for dessert.

Me: YES!!!

Don: Only the best for my forever bride...

FB Post: Wooohooo!!!! I just got the email!!! My TEDx topic about grief made it through the first round application process. Now I have to go in next month and give an audition for the panel. The first 3 minutes of my 18 minute talk. Now I just need to WRITE the first 3 minutes of my 18 minute talk. HA! I'm so excited!!! Thanks for all the support, everyone! Your enthusiasm is contagious!
LIKES: 238   COMMENTS: 76

Hangover

Remember those Thanksgiving days, when you were a kid, and just after the giant meal was over, Uncle Bill or your dad or Grandpa Joe, or all three or more, would sit in the living room on the couch and recliner chairs and proceed to unbutton the top button of their pants so they could breathe better? Or that feeling you got after eating ninety pounds of stuffing, turkey, and pumpkin pie - where your stomach felt like it was going to explode from being so full, and so you had to just sit in place and veg out on the couch for the next two days while watching endless football games? Remember that?

The "thanksgiving hangover."

Well, now, in this widowed version of life, there is a different kind of hangover that happens after each and every holiday, or even any big event or gathering, where you've just done something social, and now you are returning home.

The "grief hangover."

The grief hangover is similar to the Thanksgiving one, in the sense that you feel bloated and absolutely exhausted. Except instead of unbuttoning the top button on your pants to let out some air - you are unbuttoning every button on everything inside of you, to let out every complex and pent up emotion that's been floating around in there.

Yesterday was Thanksgiving. I decided that instead of sitting home by myself (because my parents and family are four hours away, and I couldn't get there for the holiday), I would accept the invite to go and spend it with my good friends and their family. We had a very nice day. Great food. Great company. Our host and hostess even showed off the results of their dance lessons and did a Rumba for us, and my friend, Dave, (the host) and his ten year old son improvised a father-son jazz duet on piano and trumpet as we waited for the turkey to cook. It was a lovely day, despite the inner-sadness that lives inside me, resting in my bones and missing my husband always.

And then I got home.
Empty apartment.
Silence.
The echoes of nothingness ringing through the walls.

Nobody to talk about the day with. Nobody to dissect everything that happened or gossip gently about the people in attendance. Nobody to lie on the couch with and put my feet and legs in their lap as we settle down to a night of relaxing and de-stressing. Nobody to eat leftovers with, or to make turkey soup for. Nobody to sit around and do nothing and decompress with. Just nobody.

And it doesn't matter if you currently live alone, have children, don't have children, have a roommate, live with relatives, whatever. Because if you are alone in your home after just having had a nice time somewhere, then the absence of your person who is dead echoes inside that silence, that hollow sound of nothing that follows everything you say.

And if you AREN'T alone in your home after just having had a nice time somewhere, then the absence of your person who is dead echoes inside every word spoken by others, every sound; because all those sounds and words are not the words of your person, and they never will be again.

So you just sit. You cry. Or you are way past crying, and the crying doesn't come, so you stare blankly, and you feel bloated and sickened and bored by grief. If your loss is new still, then the grief still terrifies you. The pain that comes from the grief is frightening, because each time it happens, you think in all sincerity: *I'm going to die. This pain will absolutely kill me. How can anyone possibly live and stay alive while being in this much pain?* And then the pain happens again and again and again, and you start to realize that you are not going to die from it, but that it's worse than that. You have to figure out how to LIVE with this pain. Because it keeps happening. The hangovers keep coming.

When it has been a few years since your loss, as it has been for me, the grief triggers and attacks and hangovers happen, and you expect it. You start to learn and know and become familiar with what this is, and so you realize that when it happens, you just have to ride it out. It almost becomes a bore after a while, something you hate dealing with, because you know there is no way out except through. And even though you know this, it's a pain in the ass to go "through" it each time, but you do, because what else can you do really. So you sit inside the hangover, and

Kelley Lynn Shepherd

you let it play out, and then you continue on with your life until the next one happens.

Some hangovers hit you harder than others.

Some you still don't expect to, even with all your knowledge of grief.

And some knock you down for days at a time, tricking you into thinking you are now going backwards.
But really, truthfully, there is no such thing.

You can never go back to where you were.
Not in life, and not in grief.

You can't unknow what you already know.
(as my wise widow friend, Michele, says)

Grieving will not end.
Nor will Love.
Try to embrace them both.
Let love in, again and again.

And let the hangovers of grief, when they come,
wash over you, like flooding rain.

For that is the cost
Of Great Love.

"I miss my wife, and it hurts Forever.
So I keep moving. I pay the price.
I get lost. I get found.
I wait. And I do this everyday." – Kevin Conn

My Husband is Not a Rainbow

FB Post: Cold day in NYC, but I felt nothing but warmth coming from my dead husband's presence, as he was "with me" at our tree today.

2005, Sunday before Christmas: Don Shepherd got down on one knee, under the base of The Rockefeller Center Christmas tree, in 22 degree cold, as hundreds of tourists looked on, and asked me to be his wife.

The year he died, I couldn't even walk by or within blocks of that tree without throwing up or feeling sick to my stomach. The 2nd year, I went back too soon, trying to fast-forward through pain and grief, and sat there, paralyzed and sobbing, having a full-on emotional breakdown. Year 3: I went back with my grief-counselor and felt "okay." Last year, I finally fell in love with Christmas again and came back to our tree. It was bittersweet, but he was there with me.

Today, I felt the warmth of his love and my heart doing somersaults at the idea that I was loved by the most wonderful man, and that his love will stay with me always. Today, I saw every gorgeous color, on every beautiful light, on that big and precious tree, where my life was changed forever by love - all those many years ago. Today, all of my hard grief work came full-circle, and love overwhelmed death. Long live love.
LIKES: 101   COMMENTS: 67

"But the colors,
Oh, the colors!
After doing the hard work of grief,
It is now that I finally see you!" – Stacey Landson

Kelley Lynn Shepherd

FB Post: Just did my last stand-up show in NYC for a while. My Adelphi students were great, my friend, Kevin, performed, Lori Sommer hosted, my friend, Charles McBee, did a surprise spot, and I headlined. So fun. It was sort of a "farewell to NYC" show, and my friends in the comedy community made it really special. I'm going to miss this place.
LIKES: 89   COMMENTS: 67

FB Post: Today is the day, Facebook friends! Please send all your positive vibes for my TEDx talk audition, at 3:45 PM time slot, where I will present to the panel, the first 3 minutes of my talk. This is happening!
LIKES: 110   COMMENTS: 34

FB Post: Today is an awesome NYC day. Right after my audition, which went amazingly well and I have very strong vibes about it, I got a text from my good friend who I'm not allowed to name, per his request, because he works on the show "Hamilton" and has been promising me that he will somehow get me in to see it before I leave NYC. So, he texts me and asks if I can get into the city tonight. YES!!! He made it happen for tonight. The house manager brought me down to the floor/orchestra, and I'm in the 8th row! I'm stunned. People pay thousands for these seats. Sometimes it pays to be all by yourself, especially when you are going to see the biggest Broadway show in the history of the universe, and there's no way in hell they could supply you with 2 tickets. Yay for loneliness, my awesome friends, and NYC!
LIKES: 148   COMMENTS: 56

FB Post: Today, I met my grief-counselor in the city. Not for a session. Not because I needed to see her. But because we have shifted more into a friendship, and because I haven't seen her in a while, and because I wanted to take her to dinner and some wine (her favorite), to make sure I tell her what she means to me before I officially leave NYC.

So we met at a classy bar and drank Pinot (her) and prosecco (me), and I told her what she means to me, and that I love her. And I thanked her for being so kind to me, and for never charging me one penny for her incredible life-changing services. She said that she loves me too, that she is so incredibly proud of me, and that I am her "masterpiece!" That made me laugh. We both cried a little. I cried a lot. I had a few too many proseccos, and all the emotions came tumbling out. Where I used to be, where I am now, where I'll be going, how far we have come. It was amazing, and we are going to keep meeting for lunches and/or wine each time I come visit NYC, and of course, she will be there for me if I ever need an "emergency phone session" or call. Most importantly, her incredible impact on me will now be shared with the world, in my book - so her wise and beautiful words will not only have helped me, but will help many others who may be going through their own personal grief tsunami. Love grows love, and I strongly feel that part of my purpose in life now is to take everything I have learned and continue to learn about grief and loss and share it forward. Continue to help others through writing, speaking engagements, and grief coaching phone sessions - to process through their own paths and come to a place of healing. Make the tsunami a tiny bit less horrific for someone else. Hopefully. That is what makes me happy.
LIKES: 132   COMMENTS: 67

FB Post: Oh, these goodbyes are gettin' tough now. Tonight I went to the Rockefeller Center Tree, alone, to honor our proposal anniversary one more time before leaving NYC. I don't know if I'll make it here next Christmas season, so I stayed there a little bit extra, taking in all the love and warmth coming from those lights.

Then I went to a holiday party in the city, hosted by my dear friend, Andrew, at his apartment. We had a wonderful time, and just before it was time to go, a few of us close friends remained in Andrew's kitchen, and we did a few toasts regarding my leaving NYC. My friends stood there, one by one, and said such beautiful things about me. Then I spoke too, and cried, and then cried some more. There was a lot of "I love yous" tonight and a lifetime of friendship on display. I could barely get words out, except to say to these people who I love very much, "I will miss you. I will visit you until you grow sick of me. And I love you."

Life is full of moments, some that you remember for all of your days. Today was like that. Just as it was, 11 years ago, under that Rockefeller Center Christmas Tree. The day that love changed everything. Way back then, and again tonight. Full circle. All because of Love.
LIKES: 119   COMMENTS: 22

"Friends take the lonely and turn it into Love." - Me

Leaving

Today is Friday. On Wednesday, December twenty first, just five short days from now, my brother and my mom will be driving to New York from Massachusetts, picking up a U-Haul to attach onto my brothers truck, showing up here to my apartment, packing up all my stuff, and me, and my two kitties - and driving back to Massachusetts. I will then be starting a new chapter in my life, living in my parent's house, in small town Massachusetts, and finally taking the time to finish writing my book about grief, love, life, and loss. For the past month or so, my brother has been spending almost every night at my parents' house, after his own long work day, to go down to their basement and literally build me a room down there where I can sleep, write, exist, and have privacy. He put paneling on the ceiling, put walls up, tore down a wall to create a larger space for me, and lots of other things. My dad has been helping with this, and my mom has been doing all the prep-work that is needed to add me into the house. Setting up a litter box area for my kitties, getting a cable box for my TV downstairs, all those little things. And me? I have been spending the past month or so doing the same from here in New York. Changing my mailing address, packing up endless boxes, throwing things away, and saying goodbye to things and to WAY too many people. It's been emotional. And very hard. I have lived here in New York my entire adult life, and leaving is more than difficult.

However, I feel incredibly thankful for many reasons. The fact that it's taking me such a long time to have "one last dinner or drink" with all these many friends in my life means that I am lucky enough to have a lot of quality people in my life that want me to do well and have joy. The fact that my parents are still around for me to go and live with them, and that we love each other and get along so well and enjoy being together, and that I have the kind of parents that will open their home to me forever and help me in whatever way they can - that is a beautiful thing, and not everybody has that.

The fact that my husband and I had, and have, such a beautiful love story, one that I want to share with the world in a book - is wonderful and rare, and I cherish it every day that I am alive. The fact that so many friends have offered me their spare guest room, their homes, their time - whenever I decide to visit New York City in the future - is just evidence of the types of people in my life. The fact that I am having such a hard time leaving everything, and everyone, in this city I have called home for the past twenty six years, is just proof of what a special place this is - and of the life I have built for myself here over time.

This is going to be interesting. Scary. Challenging. And hopefully, ultimately, something that leads me to greater things.

I'm anxious. I'm nervous. But I'm thankful.

Thankful for all the love that I have in my life, and all of the things that are still to come.

"But still, I dream of wandering into the woods, knowing that life is not something to run away from, but rather, something to be proud of returning to without worry."
- Mike Welker

FB Post: OH MY GOD OH MY GOD OH MY GOD!!! So this just happened…
"Dear Ms. Niemi, Thank you for taking the time to thoughtfully prepare your audition for TEDx Adelphi University 2017. We were incredibly impressed with your presentation and are thrilled to inform you that you have been chosen as one of our 10 speakers. The event will take place March 31, 2017, and more details will be sent soon."

Ahhhh!!!!! I'm so happy. I'm going to be a TEDx talker!!! This is so exciting. Now I just need to WRITE THE DAMN THING Haha!!! So, looks like at least ONE guaranteed trip back to New York City in March, already!!! Woohoo!!! I'm so excited! This is a huge step in letting the universe know the truth about loss and grief, and beginning to change the world.
LIKES: 428   COMMENTS: 55

FB Post: And we are off to our next adventure! Kitties and me! Thank you so much to my team of movers and the best family and friends on earth. My mom, my brother (driving a U-Haul with his truck attached), my roommate Mara, Sarah, Bobby, and Rodney. And my move-in team awaiting us on the other side in Fitchburg, Mass: my dad, my old high school friend Mark, and his brother Greg. We are officially on the road and on our way to Massachusetts! I seriously have the best friends in the universe!
LIKES: 83   COMMENTS: 57

Feels Like Home

It's funny what becomes important - vital to us - after we have lost someone we love dearly to death. I'm slowly moving myself into my new environment and unpacking the chaos of "stuff" to create a familiar, yet new living space. Nothing felt "right" until I had Don's recliner chair, all cozy in the corner; the guitars I kept of his, all placed nicely on his guitar stand; his lucky 'rally monkey" wrapped around the lamp on my writing desk; his Air Force jacket draped over the back of my office chair; and my nightstand, which is my Don-inspired peaceful, loving space, giving me much comfort just before I go to sleep.

When you don't have your person here to love in their physical form, their "things" become much more than just things. Sometimes, they are everything - and having them and being able to touch them and look at them and feel them and wear them and use them and give life to them gives you back just a tiny sliver of a fragment of what you lost.

In the five and a half years since my husband's death, I have donated, sold, given away, and tossed away several of his things - but there are some things I will never, ever get rid of. They belong with me, and that's just the way it is. You might understand one day, when the person you love most is suddenly gone, for no reason whatsoever. And if you don't understand this at all, and you think I'm a crazy person who has lost her crazy widow mind, consider yourself very lucky. Because this is what life after death looks like.

There. Now it feels like home.

"My Beloved,
How thin, or thick, is the veil
Between your world and mine?" – Alison Miller

Dear Dead Husband:

New Year.
Same missing of you.
That is all.
With Love,
Your Alive Wife/Widow

"The holidays…
They shine a big red light on the torture,
and then burn you with the beams." – Me

Say Everything

On December eighteenth, the anniversary of the day that Don proposed to me, I met with my grief-counselor at this really nice little bar in midtown Manhattan. I wanted to take her out. Thank her. See her, before I left NYC. So we did. It was lovely. She drank her Pinot, and I drank my prosecco, and we talked about our lives and our fears with Trump and this new administration coming in, and we talked about so many things. And then at one point, when she looked like she was getting ready to get up and head out, I said, "No. You need to sit down and stay a few more minutes, because you cannot leave before I say this to you."

She knew I was serious, and she sat back down. It felt like one of those big and important moments - one of those moments that is vital to someone like me, who lost their husband in a split second, and who NEVER got a chance to tell him how much he changed my life, and how absolutely amazing he was, and how his love was and always will be the best thing that has ever happened to me. It felt big.

So she sat back down, and I spun my body around on my bar stool to face her directly, and I took her hands in mine, and I looked her straight in the eye, and while crying through every single word (three glasses of wine makes me very emotional), I told her these words, "I love you. You just can't leave here without knowing how much I love you. And without me saying THANK YOU. I don't know where I would be today without you. I don't know what I would have done if you hadn't of taken me in, at NO charge, and sat with me inside my hell. Nobody else would do it. You were the only one. I know that you were a gift from Don, one of many that he has sent my way. I just know it. You are so special. Not everybody is like you. People don't have the kind of empathy and the kind of intelligence you have. I was so lost, for so long, and you made damn sure that I wouldn't stay that way forever. You never left me abandoned. You let me tell my same story over and over, and talk about my same fears over and over, until I didn't need to anymore. Thank you so, so much. I owe you my life today." She was crying too, and through her tears, she told me that she loved me too, and that I owe her nothing, except living a life filled with love. Then, as she was laughing but serious, she said, "I have never been more proud of anyone. You are my masterpiece." We both found that overly-dramatic, and therefore hilarious, and we laughed our way into the New York City freezing cold streets. There were lots of hugs, loads of tears, and endless supplies of thank yous. We would be in touch, of course, and continue talking via phone, and I would see her whenever I visited New York, but since I was moving away in just three days, it would be who knows how long until I would see her again. It felt significant. It felt heavy. It felt like goodbye. (At least for now.)

A few days ago, I received an email from her. It said, "Dear Kelley, I just wanted to keep you in the loop, so you wouldn't panic or hear it from someone else second-hand, about what has been going on with me. On December twenty first, I was walking home to my apartment, and I was hit by a taxi-cab. I have a fractured pelvis, major spinal injuries, head injuries, and undetermined other issues. My head feels like an axe went through it. My husband will be helping with my care, and I will be in recovery and out of work for at least eight weeks. Take care, love."

So, she didn't die. She isn't dead. But she could have been. She could have been.

And because I am a widow of sudden death that happened out of absolutely nowhere, and because I constantly am panicking that everyone in my life will randomly die with no warning, something inside told me to TELL HER what she meant to me on that night. Because if she had died that next day, she would have died knowing that is how I feel, and she would have died knowing how much her life's work mattered and how much her heart affected someone else's life in the very best of ways. And so now, every single day of my life since my husband died, but especially this past year or so, I make damn sure that I ALWAYS say what is in my heart, at the moment I feel it, when I feel it. I no longer worry about how the other person might receive it, or if it might be too much for them right now, or if it might scare them away. I would rather that they know how I feel - that they know what they mean to me and how much I love them and their soul and their existence in my life - then to walk around this earth for one more second without them knowing it.

I might die, they might die. That is how I see it. And it's not in a morbid or depressing way - it's just the truth. Humans die. We never know when, we don't know why. But they die. So you better make damn sure that if there's someone out there who you really care about intensely, or who does something for you in your life or just makes you feel good or makes you feel like something in this world makes sense, make damn sure that they KNOW that you feel that way. Because if they die, they will have died with the knowing that someone loves them deeply and that they are deeply loved. And if YOU should be the one who dies, well then, you died loving that person. I never got to say these things to my husband. I never got to say one damn thing. I have to hope beyond hope, that he somehow knew. But still, every single day, I regret that I didn't get to sit him down, look him straight in the eye, and make him look at me as I told him, "You changed my life. Your love was everything, and it will be everything forever. I will live for you. I will live FOR you. Because your life will end sooner than mine, and you won't have that option. I love you, baby. My beautiful, sweet husband. I love you."

Say the words you long to say.
When it feels like goodbye, assume that it might be.
Say it all.
Say everything.
Love out loud.
Always.
I wish like hell that I did the first time.

Kelley Lynn Shepherd

"I love you.
Three gorgeous words.
I will say them with pride, with thought,
and like it's my last day with the honor to do so."
– Me

FB Post: Just gave away some of Don's music things - a VOX amp, equalizer, sound mixer, and more, to a close friend who is a sound engineer/editor/drummer/musician. I have always given away things that belonged to Don, based on whenever it felt right to me. Right person, right time.

So today, in year 5 of this madness, after these items had sat in my storage closet in Jersey, then in my parent's basement for years, it was finally the right person and right time. Our friend, Ronnie, so appreciated the special thing that it is to receive these gifts. And he happens to be re-doing his music studio, so the timing was perfect. Watching him look through all the music goodies made me so happy. "This is like Christmas morning!" he laughed. He and Don became friends and shared a love and passion for music. Ron said tonight, "This is so great. Because I can use all of this. But it's even more great, because these were Don's. Now I'll think of him whenever I play music in my studio."

And that is how we keep them alive forever. That is how traces of my beautiful husband appear everywhere in my life. Because I make sure of it. When you share their love forward, those we love who have died come closer. And suddenly, they don't feel so far away anymore.
LIKES: 102   COMMENTS: 18

"When you lose something, you don't know where it is. We have not lost him. We know where he is."
- Cheryl Canzanella Goodell

FB Post: Today, in "Adventures from the Dating Sites."

"CallMeMasterxx69"
Today, 1:46 PM

"Seems we have some things in common. And you are incredibly sexy. Would you be interested in chatting? Possibly something more naughty? Let's meet up and role-play."

Some dating site comedy for today. Since the person I have feelings for isn't in a place right now to be anything more than beautiful friends, I'm back on the sites. I can't show you this man's picture, due to privacy rights, but trust me, he's creepy as fuck. After I wrote this, I blocked him, because he lives in my town, and he freaks me out. Here is my response to his message, for your entertainment purposes:

"Hello, person. I shall not call you 'Master' anything. Thank you for the compliment on my looks, but I'm curious as to what things you think we have in common. We both have a face. And feet. And eyes. That is pretty much where our commonalities end. Your name and profile description make it clear that you are into pain, torture, and being dominant. My hobbies listed in my profile include movies, theater, baseball. Yours include "dom/sub, nipple torture, collar training." In what universe do those things feel "in common" to you? Clearly, reading is not one of your hobbies, or you might have read my profile and seen that I am not into meeting random strangers for sex, especially one who wants to put me in a collar and hurt my nipples.

Kelley Lynn Shepherd

P.S. Where the hell did you take this picture from? Jail? Your dungeon, where you keep all the dead bodies? You look like you just returned from a pedophile convention. And the wooden spanking paddle sitting on your bed - very nice touch. Subtle.

Enjoy your creepy life.

Sincerely,
A non-creepy person
LIKES: 75   COMMENTS: 27

Dear Dead Husband:

Today was Valentine's Day, and I'm not sure I will ever get used to the idea that you're not around anymore to spend it with me. I spent a good portion of my day, literally sitting in my bed, and taking out three old Valentine's Day cards that you got me and just staring at your handwriting, at what you wrote. I did this for hours, I think. I was in a trance of some kind, because that's all I did for hours. Just stared. That's a little bit crazy, but I still don't know what the hell to do with days like this, where romantic love is the focus and you are still not here.

After a pretty horrendous first relationship post-loss with someone I knew wasn't good for me, my heart has been with someone else who I believe IS good for me, but who may not ever be in a place for me to act on it. And now I'm fearful that we aren't even really friends anymore. His communication with me has been off and on lately, and I'm going to Tampa next month for camp and was soooo looking forward to seeing him and hanging out again. But he has gone silent, and I'm confused. We have talked and connected almost daily for about a year and a half. To go from that to nothing, I just don't get it. I don't want to lose his friendship. I wish I could talk with you for real and not just one-sided letters like this. I wish you could tell me what to do, what direction is the best one, and how to do this without you. I'm trying. I really am. But my heart still longs for you. Will anyone ever treat me in the amazing and respectful way that you treated me? I will not settle for anything less, and I know you would be mad if I did. I've been on the dating sites again, mostly to combat the boredom of smalltown Massachusetts. I like going on dates. I like that there are guys out there who want to go on dates with me. I like first dates, and first kisses, and the excitement and newness of everything. You always told me I was beautiful and sexy, but I truly thought that only you would think that. Now, dating again, I'm realizing that there are other men out there who actually want to date me. I'm surprised by it, and even though I have met lots of dudes who disappear or who aren't understanding of the widowed experience, I'm still having fun. I've also been talking with lots of widowers in all these private Facebook groups. Flirty conversations, sexting back and forth online, trying to combat our mutual loneliness through sexy chatting. I wish I didn't have to do any of this, Boo. I wish you were here, and you have no idea how much I miss you. Maybe my life will now consist of just casually dating, having fun but never finding anything meaningful again. I don't know. I don't know anything right now, except that life is harder and lonelier and scarier without you in it. I love you. Xoxo

FB Post: So here is just a tiny peek at what it's like to attempt dating again, 5 years after your husband's sudden death. So I was talking with this guy on the dating sites who seemed really nice, and we spoke on the phone a few times, and the few times I brought up the topic of my dead husband - he didn't say much except for, "Sorry for your loss." Then the other day, we were talking about what we both do for a living, and I told him I was a Professor teaching theatre and comedy for 16 years, and that I recently moved back to my home state to finish writing my book. He asked what the book was about. I told him, "It's about my husband's death, his life, our love story, and my life now, in the aftermath. It's an honest look at grief and love and life." He said nothing. Literally nothing. Just sat there in silence on the phone. Awkward.

And then, this weekend, we were supposed to have our first date, and he stood me up. He didn't return my texts the day before, confirming our meeting location, so I texted and said that I would see him there. I showed up at the restaurant. He didn't. Just left me there and didn't call or cancel or anything. 2 days later, he sends me a message through the dating app, instead of through texting me directly. He said, "This can't go any further. I don't like this whole widow thing. Sorry." This "whole widow thing." Like it's some hobby I picked up. His message was so cold and unfeeling and clueless, and it infuriated me. So I responded, with this:

"I know exactly how you feel. I don't like this whole widow thing either. In fact, I hate it. I hate every single thing about it. I hate that my husband died and that I have to seek out people such as yourself, waste weeks of my time talking with them, only to find out that they have zero empathy or comprehension of what this life might be like for me. Yeah, I hate this whole widow thing too. But guess what? It's my life. It is what I am faced with. I wish like hell I could just walk away from it, but I can't. I can't ever do that. It must be so nice to just get up and walk away from it and pretend it didn't happen. I envy you. Have a nice life. I hope you never lose the person you love most to death. It sucks."

What people don't understand is that everytime this happens - every time I meet someone new who seems great, who it seems like I have a connection with, and then my heart gets trampled on - I go back in time. My one thought is just "I want my husband back. I just want my husband." There are so many complexities tied with trying to find a real connection with someone again, and yet, the human heart keeps instinctually searching, because Love is the reason for everything.

Being widowed in the middle of your life and trying to find love again, it's one of the hardest things I've ever done. It's lonely. It's annoying. It sucks. I didn't ask for this. None of us did. We didn't divorce our partners. They died. We still love them. That love never dies or goes anywhere. And I think there will always be a part of me that longs for that life back again, because it was unfinished. Dreams unrealized. A piece of me will wonder about it and long for it, even if I'm ridiculously happy again one day.

But here's the thing: for someone to be loved by a widowed person, by someone who lost everything and is still willing to open their heart again, knowing they could very well lose it all over - what a beautiful thing. Widowed people love with a fierceness that is powerful, when and if they decide to love again. We know what's at stake. We know this could and DID, all go away tomorrow.

But at the end of the day, even though I'm tired and terrified and have no guarantees of ever finding something magical, I'm still a hopeful romantic, (not hopeless) and I still believe in Love. It's never too late, to begin again…
LIKES: 67   COMMENTS: 24

"If Love is the meaning of Life,
And I do believe that it is,
Then how can I give up on love?
Even at my lowest, when everything is lost,
I will still believe in Love." – Mary Piper

Kelley Lynn Shepherd

Lights and Sirens

Do you believe in signs? Because I do. I have seen them, and today, while in Florida for Camp Widow, my beautiful husband showed up with a pretty damn big one.

Tonight, my lovely friend, Shannon, drove me out to Don's favorite beach, Clearwater Beach, where I go each year when I come here for Camp Widow, to sprinkle more of his ashes down by Pier 60, where we did it the first year, in 2011.

So today, I walked to Publix and ordered his favorite turkey sub with provolone, lettuce, and mayo - to bring to the beach and eat like I do each year, as per tradition. And then I waited for Shannon to come pick me up at the hotel. It was night time. We had dinner first, and then drove out. Just as we were heading into the round-about that leads into the roads to the beach, with all the different exits for different pier numbers, we had an escort. Suddenly, right in front of us, pulled up a Sunstar ambulance - the company Don worked for, for years while living in Florida. It continued driving right in front of us, going the same way we were going. And then, just before we pulled into the exit for Pier 60, the Sunstar ambulance ran lights and sirens. And as soon as our car reached that pier, the ambulance turned a corner and went a different way. It was like our own personal escort, keeping us safe as Don always did, as we drove to his resting place.

At Don's funeral, we had the ambulance processional, riding down the closed off streets of New Jersey, running lights and sirens and escorting us and leading us. Tonight, Don was escorting us and leading us, right to where he was. He escorted me. He knew I was there, and he showed up to meet me. It was the most beautiful sign - delivered in the most beautiful way possible.

FB Post: Widow Life. Sitting in a restaurant, waiting to meet the guy I've been talking to for a few weeks now on the dating site. Is it a date? A meetup? A mid-life crisis, because I have a broken heart from another situation back in Florida that turned out to be nothing but a huge, confusing "WTF???" No idea. All I know is that I'm 45 yrs old and living in my parents' basement, because my husband is dead and I can't afford life right now. And I asked him to meet me here because having my mommy drive me here is only slightly less humiliating than having him come pick me up at mommy and daddy's house. And I'm nervous because I hate dating, or whatever this is, and my dead husband would find this entire scenario absolutely hilarious if he weren't dead and all.

UPDATE: The date went really well. He's a super nice guy. Yay!!!
LIKES: 67   COMMENTS: 18

Sea-worthy

Sea-wor-thy
/ˈsēˌwərT͟Hē/
adjective
"(of a vessel) in a good enough condition to sail on the sea."

Sometimes, something unexpected happens, and it gives you a new look at something, or a new look at yourself maybe. Sometimes, everything just lines up in the way it is supposed to so that the universe can deliver to you exactly what it is that you need in that moment. I want to tell you all a story where that happened.

So, I recently returned home from Tampa, Florida – where I attended as a presenter once again at Camp Widow. It always seems impossible to even begin to describe the experience of what goes on during those few days at that Marriott Hotel, because it always feels so special, and so big, and so life-changing, and something that just can't be seen or felt or understood unless you were there inside of it. Each and every time.

And I figured out the reason for that. It's because we are living life every day.

Sometimes we are living life poorly, other times we are barely hanging on, and still other times we might feel like we could be doing okay. The pieces of our life are in constant movement. Each time we attend camp, and are surrounded by a couple hundred other widowed people, our tribe, things have changed in our own lives. We are in a different place than we were the last time, even if it's not a good place. Grief does not stand still – it's always shifting, as is life, whether you fight the changes of it or not. They still keep happening. So each time I attend, I receive brand new messages, gain new knowledge, and walk away with something I didn't have just a few days earlier. I also meet more new people that are on this path of loss, and I reunite with my friends that I met there last year. Not to mention, I have the amazing honor as a presenter, of providing laughter to a room filled with widowed people – and widowed people laughing has become my very favorite sound.

At each camp, the founder of Soaring Spirits International, my dear friend, Michele Neff Hernandez, widowed at age thirty five when her husband, Phil, was hit by a car while cycling, delivers a Key Note Address. It is always the perfect message for us to go home with and always something to make us think in a new way about something. As it turns out, this one hit home for me in ways that were quite unexpected. She normally uses some type of metaphor or image as part of her overall theme, and this time, that image was boats.

My Husband is Not a Rainbow

Michele spoke about how common it is to hear people comparing grief to the ocean. She then noted that she liked to think of it more as a boat. That when our loved one dies, we are left with this boat (our grief, our "after" life, all of it), and it is our mission, eventually, to make sure our boats were seaworthy – in good enough condition to sail on the sea. She talked about what a ginormous task this was, and how all of our boats were in different conditions, and some of our boats had other passengers to take care of (children), while others were completely alone in their boats. She talked about having to fix our boats over and over, and how new holes would appear, and how we had to keep starting over, and how sometimes, you just wanted to sit there and tread water and not deal with this boat or deal with anything. Or how you wanted to just give up and sell your boat, but you couldn't, because you have the deed, and it's yours forever. You had no choice but to take your boat, your life, and make it seaworthy.

The next night, Sunday, I was hit with a huge emotional breakdown. A panic attack. It happened at a random moment while sitting in my hotel room alone. The reasons as to why it happened aren't important here and cannot be shared here, so I will only say that it was an extremely emotional week for me in Florida, and it was very difficult being there, for personal reasons. My heart was hurting all week long, and in that moment, it all came to a head.

So, on that Sunday, I found myself on the floor of my hotel room, crumpled up in a corner, sobbing hysterically and barely able to catch my breath. It was that kind of crying where you start hyperventilating and where you are absolutely positive that the severity of your crying and your pain will indeed kill you. You are positive that you will die from this pain, and you sort of very much want to die in that moment. Here I was, five and a half years from my loss, and still, grief and life and pain were attacking. But because I am over five years from my loss, I knew enough, somewhere deep inside, that I was having a panic attack, and that I probably would not die from it. I knew enough that I needed a friend to help me breathe through this, and I needed to talk with someone I could trust with all of this pain. So I texted Michele. It just felt right. She was the person I needed in that moment to say the words I needed to say out loud that would be kept between only us.

I got through the night somehow. I cried hysterically for a long time that night. Hours, maybe. With the help of a sleeping pill, I finally drifted off into crying sleep. On Monday morning, I woke up with a headache and a return text from Michele that she had been asleep the night before and just received my text now. I was still in a very bad place and asked her if she could somehow spare even just a few minutes for me in person, because I felt as if I was going to collapse from pain. I wasn't sure how to get through the next minute, never mind the day. This woman, this beautiful friend of mine who was literally in the middle of packing up all of Camp Widow into trucks, several meetings, and things other than my sobbing widow ass, scheduled a private conference room for us to meet in and was there waiting for me when I arrived at the appointed time.

I sat down next to her and just collapsed into her. I let myself cry horribly and loudly. I let everything that was inside come out. And she sat there, holding me, and giving me the space I so desperately needed to let all the hurt escape out of me. I needed a private place to feel safe, away from everyone and everything, and she gave me exactly that. We talked for a long time, and many things were said that I can't get into detail, to protect people's privacy, but this was the part that is important to this story that I will share here.

She looked me in the eyes as I cried and cried and cried, and she ordered me to go outside. "You can cry all you want, but you are not allowed back into your room until tonight, to sleep. I want you outside in the fresh air. Take a walk, sit by the pool, whatever. If I find out you went back to your room, I'm going to be really upset with you. You have to find a way to release this from your heart, at least until your TED talk is over. That's in two weeks' time, Kelley. You have to focus on that. This is a huge deal, a huge opportunity and platform, and you cannot let this man steal that away from you." I looked into her eyes, with absolute desperation, and my words practically collapsed as I blurted out: "But I think I was in love with him, and now it has turned into nothing, and I don't understand why." I fell into her loving shoulders and breathed away the sorrow and realization of a friendship gone in an instant.

I cried some more, and she wiped my tears and asked me if I had any sunglasses. I shook my head no. She took her own beautiful sunglasses, and put them on my face gently. She said, "Here. These are yours. Now you can go outside and see yourself through my eyes. You're beautiful. You're so worthy. You can't see that right now, but I can. Look through my eyes. You are allowed to grieve and mourn this friendship that you had with this person, and feel everything that's happened, but do it outside, and put these on so you don't have to face questions about why you're crying. When you get outside, you never know what could happen, who you might run into, what new perspective you might see. Go outside. I love you." I walked down the hall, still crying, and said, "I love you too." And I went outside.

Minutes later, I got a text from one of my widow friends, Leah. "A few of us are going on a boat cruise around Tampa Bay. Wanna come?" Without thinking about anything other than the words that Michele had just spoken to me, I texted back, "Yes." Because I was ordered to stay outside. And because her Key Note was all about boats. So the idea of a boat ride seemed absolutely perfect.

So off we went, onto this boat ride, which was supposed to be a dolphin watch, but there were no dolphins. There was a captain and a co-captain. The co-captain was at the back of the boat, where me and my friends were sitting, and he was chatting it up with us and being friendly and personable, because that's his job. I was telling my friends about how I never took my late husband's last name, Shepherd, and how I was going to now use it as a pen name in my book about him – Kelley Lynn Shepherd. The co-captain/second mate heard me and commented, "That's a really beautiful way to honor him, by taking his name for the book. Wow. I like that." He then asked us if we wanted to request any songs for the boat tour, so I requested "Sailing" by Christopher Cross. He yelled out to the captain my song request, and the captain responded, "You got it, Phil." Then this man, Phil, who has the same name as my dear friend Michele's late husband – just minutes after she ordered me to go outside, and I ended up on a boat – says out of nowhere to me, "I love your sunglasses. Those are really great sunglasses." Really.

When the boat tour was over, my friends and I started walking down the pier after saying our farewells to the captain and co-captain. He shouted out to me something about "next time, I hope I can be your shepherd." And then winked. My friend, Rhonda, turned to me and said, "Wow. He was really into you, huh?" "What?", I responded, completely clueless. Leah and Tara agreed. "How could you not know? It was so obvious! He was listening to everything you said. He was standing over by you the whole cruise, talking to you." I was stunned. "Really? I thought he was just doing his job and being nice. You really think he was flirting with me?" "YES!!!!" they all practically screamed at me in unison.

So, with my new sunglasses on, where I could see myself through Michele's eyes, and with my new-found "who gives a shit and why the hell not" bravery, I said, "Well, I don't think he was flirting with me at all, but if you guys really think so, I'll go back there and give him my card. Why not, right? He was super nice. And his name was Phil! And he commented on my sunglasses that Michele just gave me. On a boat! Just like her Key Note! I mean, come ON. That HAS to mean SOMETHING!" So I fished through my bag to find my card and then sprinted back toward the boat. But it was too late. The next cruise was already taking off – they had literally JUST left the dock. "Dammit!" I said, genuinely disappointed.

We walked back to the hotel and sat outside on the patio, because I was ordered to stay outside. Leah came up with a plan. "Let's find the boat tour company, see if they have a Facebook page. Then find him and send him a message that you just took the tour and thought he had a great sense of humor, and that you were wondering if they give private group tours, because it's something you may look into for our widowed convention next year. This way, if he wasn't flirting with you, then you won't feel like you're putting yourself out there or feel silly. And if he was, it will be obvious." So I did. And I was pretty damn proud of myself for having the courage to walk back there and give this total stranger my card, AND follow it up by reaching out with this message.

The next morning, he did not reply, so I assumed that I was correct and that my friends were crazy for thinking he was into me. But the morning after that, after my flight had been pushed back a day due to snow back home, he did reply. Saying that yes, they do private group tours. He then asked me if I had some time right now to talk about it further. I was in the hotel, with a couple hours before having to leave for the airport to head back home. So I said sure. And then my phone rang (apparently people can call you from the Facebook Messenger thing, without having your number. I had no idea because I suck at technology).

Kelley Lynn Shepherd

And then, we were suddenly talking for a very long time. The subject of boat tours only came up for a few minutes, if that. The rest of the time, he asked me about my late husband and about the widow convention, and he noted how it must be "very comforting and validating in a way" to be part of an event such as Camp Widow and to know that you aren't alone. I then decided to take a chance and just come out and ask him if he was, indeed, flirting with me during the tour. Because I still didn't really know for sure. Because I suck at knowing those types of things, and I suck at reading men and their intentions, apparently.

So I asked him. "My friends insisted that you were flirting with me on the cruise. I told them they were crazy." He paused a few seconds, as if collecting his thoughts, and then said, "Oh, I was totally flirting with you. You're absolutely beautiful. I have a thing for sexy brunettes with long hair from Massachusetts, who have a great sense of humor and gorgeous eyes, and who are half Italian and half-Finnish. Oh, and the cleavage didn't hurt anything either. "

I could literally feel myself blushing through the phone. He really WAS listening to everything I said on that boat. To be feeling so horrible and awful and low and hopeless just hours before and the day before, and be literally crumpled up on the floor not wanting to do anything but die in my sorrow, and then to hear these words, coming from a total stranger named Phil, who has nothing to gain by lying to me, who I met on a boat, with my new sunglasses on – it was magic.

It was the universe giving me the exact thing that I needed at that exact moment. We talked about how I love sunsets, and how they do sunset cruises on the boat, and how beautiful the sunsets are in Florida. We talked about how we didn't see any dolphins on our dolphin tour, and he lightly mocked me for being in a bathing suit and tank top on a "chilly" and windy day in the high sixties while all my friends were literally covering themselves up with blankets and coats and things as I yelled out mockingly to them, "Wimps! It's beautiful out here!" And then he said, "It's too bad you have to leave today. I'm off work, and I was going to see if you wanted to spend some time together."

In talking with him further, his life situation is extremely complicated, and it's the kind of complicated that makes him rather "unavailable" – and because of that, I doubt this will ever be any kind of relationship with us. And just awhile before leaving for Florida, I had a first date with someone I recently met on the dating sites in Massachusetts, and our date went quite well, and I really like him and would like to see him again. And that situation, or THIS situation, or ANY situation, could all turn out to be absolutely nothing.

And if there is one thing I have learned over this past year or so, in the most painful way possible, it is that you can spend a whole lot of time and emotions and put your whole heart out there on someone, only for it to turn out to be absolutely nothing. And so Phil, or the really nice guy from back home, or anything else, at any given time – could all be just a whole lot more nothing. But that does NOT erase the moments that happened. It does not mean that what you experienced and what you felt and what happened was not a hundred percent real, when it happened. Moments like that are real, and they are fleeting, and they live in my heart, and nobody can ever take that away from me. You can NEVER take that away.

What's important to me is this: Phil and I have kept in touch, and he has been sending me sunset pictures from the boat cruise, and they make me smile and feel peaceful and calm and tranquil. And he sent me and my friends a video of jumping dolphins from the cruise the other day, with the message, "Now you can see your dolphins." And he called me beautiful. And on a boat filled with lots of other people, he chose ME to flirt with, he chose me to interact with. And when that was pointed out to me by my friends, I took a chance and tried to give him my card. And when that didn't pan out, I took another chance and sent him a message. And that felt brave, somehow. Because just hours before, I was crumpled up in the corner, and I truly felt like I was nothing and like my heart would fall right out of my chest, and I just wanted nothing more than to die right there in that room.

And then I went outside.

So even if all of this, all of these situations, all pan out into nothing, they are still not nothing. The universe giving me hope and a new perspective in a moment where I felt like everything was gone, is never nothing. It is the furthest thing from nothing.

And in those moments, with the wind in my hair, and the music sounding like a lullaby, and the bay water drinking up pieces of life and sky… In that one moment, for that one measure in time, I was more than enough.

I was Alive. And I was Seaworthy.

"The pieces of you, they return slowly,
but also feel new, and foreign,
because you are new, and changed, forever."
- Ron Alberts

FB Post: Just got "wild rainbow roses" from my dear friend, Misty, inside a vase that has a picture of me and Don dancing, with the phrase from our self-written wedding vows, "Until Forever," and the phrase that our Soaring Spirits widowed community always says, "Long live love." Misty is not

widowed, and her ability for empathy and understanding of the widowed experience always astounds me. Her card to me read, "Break legs and all that jazz. Love, Don." When I thanked her just now, she said that if there was ever any occasion that deserved getting flowers from my husband, it was this one. (TED talk) I couldn't agree more. Thank you, Misty. Thank you, Don. And thank you to every single one of you who has continued to support me and love me through this beautiful, chaotic, weird, wild, widowed life. T-minus 3 days until #TED. Let's do this!
LIKES: 195   COMMENTS: 31

FB Post: In the green room/dressing room, where they gave us each a beautiful plaque, and some really nice TEDx shoulder bags. The talks are underway, live, right now, in the theatre and online streaming, and we are completely sold out. People are standing up in the back. We are halfway through the talks, short lunch break for the audience, and then I'M UP!!! AAAAAHHHHHH!!!!!! I'm wearing the locket/necklace I bought, that has a heart with a bit of Don's ashes inside, so he is very close to my heart in every way possible. Michele texted me, "You have done all the work. Now, the stories all live in your heart. Go out there and speak what is written on your heart." This is going to be awesome. Here we go…
LIKES: 260   COMMENTS: 104

FB Post: Well, that just happened. I did that. I'm a TED talk speaker now. So that's a thing. It was my honor to share a few of my friend's stories forward and to hopefully help change the way that we speak about grief and loss, in our culture.

When the event was over, we did lots of media and press pictures for local papers and such, and I was beyond moved at how many total strangers approached me with their own stories

of loss, and how much my words impacted them or changed their perspective on grief. A man in his mid-eighties thanked me for changing his mind about grief and told me that I had accomplished my goal of beginning to change the world, because I changed his mind, even at that late age in life. We CAN change the world, one person and one mind at a time. To everyone that made it out to see me today in person, thank you. My mom, Sheila, Carol, Susan, Caroline, Lauren, Vanessa, Mimi. So awesome of you all to come out, and truly appreciated. And to the countless people who shared the livestream link, supported me, and were watching from home or at work on your computers - you all mean the world to me, and I'm thankful for all of it. And to my widowed community friends, I just love the hell out of you people. You make my life better everyday, and together, we will definitely change the world. I will let you all know once the talks are uploaded onto the TED talk site. THANK YOU.
LIKES: 418   COMMENTS: 76

The Duality of Widowhood

The definition of the word "duality" is as follows:
1. The quality or condition of being dual
2. An instance of opposition or contrast between two concepts or two aspects of something; a dualism. "The photographs capitalize on the dualities of lightness and dark, stillness and movement."

I think it is more than safe to say that every widowed person understands the concept of duality. Maybe you didn't know the exact definition, or you weren't sure what to call it, or it was maybe more subconscious than conscious in your own mind - but at just about every moment in time, some more elevated than others, widowed people are living and existing in a dual reality. The above definitions describe it perfectly. After all, what is grief and loss and widowhood, if not the duality of stillness and movement? Joy and pain? This life, and that other life?

So, with a loss such as this, one that affects every fiber of your being forever, it becomes a part of you. *They* become a part of you. And there are moments, often actually, where the life you have right now and that other life merge together on the strangest bumpy path, and you are left there to navigate. You are standing there, inside of it, and yet, none of it makes any sense. This is not a negative or a positive thing - most things aren't. It's simply a thing that happens when the life you had and the life you have begin to marry.

This feeling of duality begins to happen more and more, as time goes by, and as you begin to live your life instead of just existing. It happens right in those very moments of passionately living. It has happened to me quite a bit lately, and each time is no less strange or surprising than the last.

Having my first kiss ever, post-loss (last spring), and right in the middle of it, hearing my dead husband's voice literally cheering me on and saying, "Yes! Good for you! Get some!" And yet somehow being able to completely get lost in that kiss one hundred percent and enjoy it's every wonder.

Doing my TED talk about my husband's death and about the power of sharing each other's stories to keep the people we love alive, and knowing that my husband would be so damn proud of me in that moment, and then immediately wishing he were there to see my talk. And then realizing there wouldn't BE a talk if he wasn't dead. And then crying in the backstage dressing room area, because he IS dead, and I just gave a talk on a big stage about him being dead. And then wishing he were there to give me my favorite yellow roses and lots of his amazing hugs. And then shaking my head in confusion for the one hundred billionth time in the last five years that I'm really, actually, truly a widow, and that my husband really did collapse and die. That was a thing that actually happened. And then laughing at how ridiculous and all over the place the inside of my brain can be.

This week. Standing in the kitchen of my parents' house, which is not the same kitchen and not the same house that they lived in five years ago, in that life where my husband wasn't dead and where my parents still had their home in Groton of over forty five years.

Standing there, in a daze, as if frozen, as my date rang our doorbell. Watching as my mom answered the door, because I was too paralyzed by my fog to handle that task, and invite him inside. Giving him an awkward hello with a half-glance in his direction as I accepted the beautiful lilies he brought for me. Somehow not comprehending that they were, in fact, for me, and not for some other confused widow. Retreating back to the corner of the kitchen, hiding myself without realizing it, as this man who I was meeting for the first time after a couple weeks of talking, and who was about to take me out on a lunch date, had a conversation with my parents. Hearing only snippets of that conversation, but also not hearing anything at all. Noticing that sounds and words were happening, but being stuck in that duality of this life/that life. Looking right through the three of them and into the television set while thinking to myself every bit of this:

Who is this man standing here talking to my parents? How did I end up here, on a first date, at age forty five, living with mom and dad in fucking Fitchburg, Massachusetts? Who lives in Fitchburg? Just a few years ago, my husband was talking to my mom and dad, and I was happily and newly married. How is this happening? Is this real? What are they talking about, anyway? I think I heard something about Cape Cod. That's where we honeymooned. The best week of my life. This man in my kitchen seems familiar to me, and I can't figure out why. I feel like I have met him somewhere, somehow. Is that possible? That's probably not possible. Maybe it's just because he's a fellow EMS, like Don was. Why do you keep putting EMS guys in my life, Don? Whatever message you're trying to send me with that, I GET IT! You can stop now with the EMS theme. He seems to be getting along with my parents really nicely. How long have we been standing here? It feels like a long time. Should I say something? He seems really genuine and really sweet. I like him already. I feel like Don would like him too. I wish he could somehow know Don, or that Don could somehow meet him, and know that I'm hanging out with a truly good guy today. Maybe he DOES know. Maybe he is the one who is making all this happen. I hope he knows. I'm excited to spend time with this person. But I'm also not going to get carried away in my head. It's just a date. Stop overthinking everything. Okay, my sweet dead husband, let's do this. We can do this. Hopefully he won't run away screaming after being held hostage by the shit that goes on in my brain. He's cute. I feel myself smiling around him, even just on the phone or in text. I'm going to shut up now and try like hell to just be in the moment.

This life and that life. Merging together, as if stuck in traffic and down to one lane. Co-existing in the same space. The past. The future. The now. Like my friend Michele says about widowed life, "Finding a way to blend what was, with what is, with what will be." A tapestry. Chaotic and calm. Tranquil and stormy. Heartbreaking and joyous. Death and life.

Living the life I have now and being excited and hopeful about it...
While always acknowledging and honoring that life I used to know.

They can breathe together.
They can marinate.
Everything is connected.

Kelley Lynn Shepherd

The joy. The grief. The hurt. The death. The love.
All of it.
Together.

In the same, complex and wonderful second.
Ain't life a beautiful thing?

Dear Dead Husband:

Is this the one? Is he my next great love? There are so many signs, it seems, coming from you with this one. I love being with him. We laugh so much. I feel so connected. To his story, his soul, his heart. It's only been a month or so, but I really believe I'm falling in love with this man. We can't stop spending time together, it seems. We never like the part where the dates are over and we have to say goodnight. We have had a lot of dates that started in the morning and ended later that day. We leave for Cape Cod on our family vacation tomorrow, and I'm so excited to be going there, knowing that I have this amazing thing brewing with this truly wonderful guy. Thank you. Xoxo

Dear Dead Husband:

Why does this keep happening to me? Why does my heart keep getting broken when I think I have a real connection with someone? Why do they keep ending things with little to no explanation or disappearing entirely? I feel sick to my stomach for thinking this was the one, and I really, really just want you back. Every time some guy hurts my heart, it feels like you are dying all over again. Like I am losing you, for the one hundred billionth time. All the grief comes back, and I feel like I'm beginning again. I'm so tired of starting over, and I'm tired of being rejected in the cruelest of ways. What kind of person ends things in a text message when the other person is literally stuck in the backseat of a car on their way to family vacation on the Cape? I feel like I can't breathe, like I am suffocating. My vacation is ruined. My life is empty. And I FUCKING HATE THIS SHIT!!!!

"My virtue dispelled by the darkness.
No hope of light in me.
Gone are my hopes, my dreams, my heart my soul, my everything." – Nicholas Mucciarone

Sewing My Wild, Widowed Oats

When I returned from Tampa in mid-March, my heart was hurting. I had gone from a beautiful and budding friendship and conversations almost every single day with a man I felt like I was falling in love with, to nothing. And I didn't understand why. I still don't. It just felt like yet another person who chose to leave me behind again. Another person who disappeared out of my life with no explanation, with me not having a say about it. I felt like I didn't matter enough to them to deserve a conversation. It hurt. It still hurts. It will always, always hurt.

Before my trip to Florida, I had left my account open on the dating sites and had met a great guy. We went on a couple dates, shared some really great moments, and had decided that we probably weren't meant to be long-term partners, so we decided to keep things casual and always be friends. Soon after, I met another great guy. This time, everything happened fast, but it didn't feel fast. It felt good. It felt right. We connected on many levels. We bonded over our different experiences in life with trauma and loss. He made me laugh. He brought me Easter lilies. We saw each other several times in just a few short weeks because we simply loved spending time together. We had

Kelley Lynn Shepherd

breakfast together at a mom and pop little local place where everyone knew him. He cried in front of me while talking about his sons being proud of him for a recent accomplishment. He lived on a farm. We kissed in a barn with donkeys and chickens watching. We kissed more on his couch in the dark, looking out at nature through the picture window in the living room. We got intimate. I felt very real feelings. I know he felt real feelings too.

He loved sunsets like I do. He made me feel safe, like my husband used to. He was in EMS, just like my husband. There were so many signs that we were meant to connect with each other. I had never gotten closer with someone in such a short period of time. We talked and texted all day long. We flirted and made each other feel good all day long. We talked of future plans, trips we might take, things we might do, all day long.

And then it was over. Just like that. He ended it with a text message, informing me that he was still in love with his ex, and that he was devoting all of his energy into a relationship with her. He wished me well in finding someone and said I was a "good person." Just two hours before that text, everything was normal. I was ridiculously happy and thanking my husband for bringing me "the one." And then it was gone. That text felt like a business letter. Like a transaction. It felt like shit. I felt blindsided. Another death. Another person who brought me into their life and then snatched away access. Another person who didn't choose me. Why do people keep leaving me? Why is my love either not enough or too much? Why am I never the one?

My heart has been shattered. Torn apart. Busted open and cracked and damaged.
Yet I still keep trying.
Because for me, I do not want to live a life with no more love.
I do not want to live a loveless life.
I do not want to live alone, or grow old alone, or die alone.
I want my next great love, and I'm not stopping until I find it.

My Husband is Not a Rainbow

In the meantime, the heartbreak I went through in Tampa, led me to a new feeling. It's a feeling of courage. A feeling of taking risks, when it comes to men and dating. It's a feeling of "why the hell not?" Lately, on the dating site I am using most often (Plenty of Fish), I have had an endless stream of men who are interested in meeting me, dating me, talking with me. Some are nice, others are weird, some are not for me, others might be. The point is, something has changed inside me, to where I'm attracting people toward me. I'm not sure what it is exactly, but it wasn't there before. Not like this.

Right now, I'm talking with two potential future dates, and I'm in the midst of setting up an ongoing "friends with benefits" situation, with someone I trust to do that with, because why the hell not? He is aware that I am out there searching for love, and that if I, or he, should find something that feels like it might be the real thing, we will end the "benefits" portion of our friendship. I'm trying like hell not to take anything too seriously, or too personally. I'm trying to not get hurt, and the fact is, I will probably get hurt many more times. That's life. I'm terrified. I'm lonely. I'm ready.

Through all of this, a strange thing has happened. Now, almost six years later, the same woman who didn't want anyone touching her or hugging her, and who literally threw up at the very thought of "someone else"; is feeling incredibly sexual. Maybe it's the fact that I had zero intimacy for FIVE years after my husband died. That I waited five years before I slept with someone. Maybe it's the fact that lately, I have had "some" intimacy, but it got stopped short for various reasons, before turning into something more permanent. Maybe it's the fact that at age forty five, my sex drive is through the roof, and I have nobody to share that with. I don't know what it is, but I can tell you that while I'm waiting for the next great love to appear in my life, I'm having a lot of fun. It is not the kind of fun I ever wanted, because what I want, is for my husband to not be dead.

But since that's never going to happen, there is a lighthearted and carefree release in flirting. Flirting and chatting and accepting words from men who want to call me sexy or beautiful, or who spend time talking with me online, or on a phone call, where we make each other feel really nice for a while, and then continue on with our forever friendship. It is respectful, it is harmless, and it is very much necessary, when you have been starving for male companionship for so long. I never thought this would be my life. I would prefer to have love over this, but I don't have love right now, and so here we are.

I want to find love. I'm here. I'm ready. I'm looking.
But until it finds me,
my heart has been damaged,
my wings are torn,
It hurts to fly.
There's a lot of birds out there,
all trying to find their piece of the sky.
So until I find mine,
maybe I'll just keep fluttering around,
and enjoying the view.
There's really a lot of lovely birds up here.

FB Post: (restricted to certain friends) Ugh. Just had a first date with a guy who showed up for lunch in a dirty and wrinkled t-shirt and jeans, then complained the whole time about how far he drove to meet me. So to shut him up, I offered to buy him lunch. He accepted without a beat and barely even thanked me. When we walked out to his car, he said sarcastically, "I guess I have to hold your door now, right?" I got in his car, and it was filthy. Trash and wrappers everywhere, and it smelled like old socks. He didn't even bother to move stuff out of the way, knowing full well I would be in his car. (I got dropped off here by my parents, because that's how I roll - and he's driving me home). Here's the worst part though. During one of our flirty

phone chats, he claimed to be an amazing kisser. So of course, I made out with him, because I love kissing, and I wanted to see if he really WAS a great kisser. And dammit, he was. We kissed in his car for a really long time, longer than I have probably ever kissed a person that I don't really even like. He is arrogant and self-absorbed and just not the kind of person I would enjoy spending more time with. He acted "aloof" the whole time, like he could take me or leave me, and like he was doing me some huge favor by showing up. I think that will be our first and last date. The kissing was fantastic, but I'm too old for this shit. Also, I deserve better than this, but loneliness and being horny will make a person do some very strange things. I feel disgusting, and disgusted, all at once. Yuck. I need a shower to wash off my shame.
LIKES: 67   COMMENTS: 14

FB Post: Just spent a week or so talking on the dating site app to a fellow widower who lives pretty nearby to me, and who is 11 years older than me. Not a huge deal for me, since my husband was almost 8 years older, but just something to observe. I felt like we clicked and things were going well with our conversation. I showed up to our agreed meeting place for our date, and he didn't. I tried calling and texting him, no response. I checked the dating site, and he had deleted his account. What the hell is wrong with these men? There's a term for this, I've learned, when they just disappear. It's called "ghosting," and the funny part is, it has absolutely nothing at all to do with dead people. It's just people who are assholes and spineless cowards. I miss my husband so much.
LIKES: 28   COMMENTS: 34

Kelley Lynn Shepherd

Dear Stupid Death Diary:

I don't know what the hell I'm doing. I think there is a tiny fragment of me that believes that, maybe, somehow, I will find love again. And then the rest of me is just bored, lonely, and needing to feel wanted and desired. I think five years of no intimacy really did me in, and now I'm on some sort of rampage with the dating. The funny part is, I truly think Don would be laughing at me, in a good-natured way. He would be like, "Good for you, Boo. Go out and get some lovin'. You deserve it." I so want to find love again. I'm trying. But it's just not working out. So in the meantime, who am I hurting by having some casual and respectful fun? Certainly not me. I'm actually a little proud of myself for approaching my friend/ guy I had a few dates with about having a "friends with benefits " situation together, while we are both single. We have had a few "encounters" so far, and it's been really fun and really nice. It feels really great to be able to have intimacy with someone who I can also have a nice chat with, laugh with, spend the afternoon with, and go out for a great steak dinner with. It's not love for either of us, but dammit, it sure is fun. And I know he respects me, and we will remain friends no matter what - which for me, makes all of the difference.

"There is something to be said for finding yourself again while spending time in the company of a man who treats you well." - Anonymous

Collecting the Hurt

I'm faced with a choice. Do I keep putting my heart out there, so I can collect more hurt and more pain and more people who will leave me behind or blindside me or not want my love or choose someone else that isn't me? Or do I close off my heart, and stop giving access to anyone in the future so that I won't get hurt anymore.

This is why people shut off their hearts. This is why people decide to just exist and not really live. This is why people are terrified to love.

I don't want to be one of those people who shuts off the world. I don't want to be one of those people who remains stuck on bitter and angry and alone. It's one thing to TRULY not want to find love again and to be happy with that decision. I admire that. But to want love again, desperately, and to give up because it's too damn hard … I don't want to be lonely anymore. I don't want to be alone anymore.

BUT...

I don't want to keep going all in, only to get my soul shattered. I don't want to keep falsely believing that THIS might be the one, the person who actually does choose me, the person who looks at me and says, "Yes. It's you. It's always been you." I don't want to keep telling my story to male suitors, hoping and praying they won't run away. Hoping that my life and my trauma and my grief and my widowhood is not too much for them. I don't want to keep thinking that something is happening between me and this person, only for them to shut me out and turn me away with no thought. I just don't want that anymore.

I have another first date on Sunday. And on past first dates, I was excited or at least anxious and nervous, in a good way, to go

Kelley Lynn Shepherd

out and meet and discover somebody new. But now – after all the games and all the lies and all the things that I thought were one thing and turned out to be another – I can almost feel my heart shutting down. I can feel it happening.
I can feel myself not caring.
I can feel myself growing bitter and angry.
I can feel myself not being able to trust anyone.
I can feel all the walls going back up.
I have collected too much hurt.
My collection is too large.
There are too many people I miss now,
whenever I start missing Don.
I miss the days when I just missed Don.

Now, I miss Don,
and then I miss that beautiful friend,
and I miss that new beginning,
and I miss the innocence of a first kiss,
or butterflies in my stomach,
before I knew,
that those butterflies,
would end in nothing.

Do I open or close my heart?
I want to open it.
I want to keep it open.
I want love to find me.
But how many times,
can a person be let down?
How many times,
can a person be blindsided?
How many times,
can a person,
not be the one,
for someone else?
How many times?

My Husband is Not a Rainbow

My hurt collection keeps growing,
there are too many people to miss.
Too many people that chose to walk away.
How do I not take that personally?
It hurts.
It aches and it stabs.

And yet,
I keep choosing,
to collect more tries,
at love.
Just one more try.
Or maybe two.
Because just a chance,
at love,
is Everything.

Where are you, love?
Come find me, love.
Please don't take too long.

Stranger

Have you ever...
Stared at your dead husband's picture, the same one that's been sitting on your nightstand every single day for over five years, and suddenly, for no real reason whatsoever, you don't seem to recognize his face as his face?

Have you ever...
Gone into the closet where you keep a few of his things, still, and taken out a specific t-shirt that always had a faint smell of him on it - only to find that the smell is no longer there and it has faded away into nothing?

Kelley Lynn Shepherd

Have you ever...
Watched your wedding video, the same one that you couldn't bear to watch for years because it was so painful seeing him move and talk and laugh, only to discover that this time, you are listening with extra intensity, because your husband's voice no longer sounds like your husband?

Do you ever feel like he (or she) is disappearing, little by little?
Do you ever wonder if your marriage, your love, your everything, was something you just imagined?
Does your husband or wife or partner ever feel like a stranger to you?
In picture form. Or in video. Or in voice.
And does that scare the shit out of you as much as it scares me?

I don't want my husband to disappear. And as much and as often as I work so hard to make sure that he stays relevant and alive in every way possible and to the universe, he still seems to become something of a stranger to ME, sometimes, in those quiet reflective moments. Those moments when you want nothing more than to FEEL that feeling again - to feel what it felt like to be loved by him. To be held by him. To be cherished by him and kept safe by him. When you want that and you need that, and yet, the sound of his voice in recording feels like sand. And his picture feels shallow to your eyes. His smell and his scent, once so strong, has become vague and generic and dull. And the only thing you want, besides having him somehow come back to life, is for everything to feel familiar again. For everything to feel close again.

But it doesn't. It just doesn't.

And you sit and you stare and you make friends with,
the Stranger.
Trying like hell,
to make him familiar again.

If I can't have my husband back,
can I at least have the FEELING
of my husband back?
Please?

*"I miss you inside of the echoes,
I miss you in all the places you will never be.
I miss you being familiar,
I miss what cannot be." - Me*

Conversations While Waiting for Magnolia Bakery Cupcakes

It was a random fall day in downtown NYC, and Don and I were on Bleeker Street, walking to the famous Magnolia Bakery, to get one (or five or seventeen) of their famous and delicious cupcakes. They were and are my favorite, and I had told Don on several occasions of their magic powers, and now I was pretty much forcing him to stand in line with me in order to eat one of them. This was our conversation, from memory:

Don: Holy shit. Are you kidding me with this line? It's wrapped around two blocks!!!!

Me: I told you, they are really good cupcakes!

Don: There's no way on earth these morons are waiting in this line for a cupcake. This has to be for something else. A concert or something. There's tons of great blues clubs and stuff in this neighborhood. Maybe they're here to see some great jazz artist play.

Kelley Lynn Shepherd

Me: Nope. It's for the cupcakes. The line is always like this. It's actually not that bad today. I've seen it three blocks or more away from the bakery.

Don: Do these cupcakes play instruments or sing or something? Do they dance? Have they found a cure for cancer, these cupcakes? Cuz if not, these people have officially lost their minds if they're waiting in this line for a freakin' cupcake.

Me: …says the man who is now standing in the line waiting for a freakin' cupcake.

Don: …because his wife is holding him hostage.

Me: There's a guitar shop around the corner. I'll make a deal with you. If you stay here for the next ten minutes with me and talk to me to help pass the time, you can spend the rest of the time in the music store while I keep standing in line to get us cupcakes.

Don: Guitar shop? Music store? Now we're talkin! I can do ten minutes of cupcake line if my prize is guitar shop. You're the bestest wife ever. And I'm officially timing you as of right now. You have ten minutes with me. What shall we talk about, crazy wife?

Me: Let's see, very patient husband. Let's talk about death.

Don: Really? DEATH? That's what you want to talk about while waiting in line for cupcakes? Death?

Me: Yeah, why not. So Boo, if I died and you could be with one fantasy celebrity, who would you choose?

Don: Cheryl, that pro dancer on "Dancing With the Stars." She's hot. Or maybe Catherine Zeta Jones. No, maybe Salma Hayek.

My Husband is Not a Rainbow

You know how much I love Sofia Vergara, though. I gotta go with her. Or Susanna Hoff from the Bangles. No, wait. Stevie Nicks. Yeah, Stevie. I've had my crush on her since I was, like, twelve.

Me: Jesus. I said ONE. Not six!!! It's not an orgy!

Don: Yeah, I got a little carried away. Sorry, Boo.

Me: I'm dead, and now you're suddenly with six different fantasy women? That was fast. Wouldn't you at least properly mourn my untimely passing first?

Don: Well, I'd wait til after the funeral, Boo. I'm not a total ass. (laughs)

Me: (hits his arm) You can only pick one, and you have to wait a very long time after the funeral until you get to be with her. Like months and months later, maybe years.

Don: This is literally the stupidest conversation I've ever had.

Me: You've said that before.

Don: And I always mean it. (laughing)

Me: You love me and my crazy "what if" scenarios.

Don: I do love you, Boo. And you are definitely nuts. Okay, I'm going with Stevie Nicks. By the way, you have six minutes left to finish this insanity before I go running to the guitar store. Who would you pick if I randomly died and you, for reasons unexplained in this scenario, got to be with one fantasy celeb?

Me: I don't want to answer that.

Kelley Lynn Shepherd

Don: What? Why?

Me: Because I don't want to think about you being randomly dead. Not even as a joke.

Don: Awww, Boo, are you actually crying right now? You're tearing up. I'm not going anywhere. I promise. Well, I AM going over to the guitar shop in t-minus five minutes, but I'm not going to randomly die anytime soon. I'm perfectly healthy, we are happy, and life is good. What can be better than standing in line for overrated cupcakes that don't dance or sing or cure diseases? How could my life get any better? Come here, Boo. (kisses my forehead and holds me)

Me: They're not overrated. They are magic. And you can't ever die. It took me way too long to find you. But if you DID die, I might let Mike Messina or Jeter or Paul O'Neal or Tino comfort me while naked and lying in my bed. Actually, they should be in their baseball uniform. That's way hotter.

Don: Hey now! You only get one! Not the entire New York Yankees lineup!

Me: Okay. Harry Connick Jr. That's one.

Don: No. That's one MORE. Now you have five.

Me: Six. John F. Kennedy Jr.

Don: He's dead.

Me: Well, obviously I'm going back in time to when he was alive.

Don: Oh, we are including dead people now and bringing them back to life? Well in that case, let me add Marilyn Monroe and

My Husband is Not a Rainbow

Sophia Loren. And since we are making this creepy by adding dead people, I will also say that if I died and you were sleeping with JFK Jr., I'd somehow haunt you while you were in the middle of sex with him, just to mess with you and make myself laugh. Just as you were about to get off, you'd feel my presence somehow.

Me: Nice. That's not too creepy.

Don: Oh, as if this conversation was normal before that point. Okay, Boo. I think we have reached the plateau of weirdness here, and your time is up in thirty five seconds.

Me: You may use that time to remind me of my awesomeness.

Don: You are so awesome, that I would come all the way down to Bleeker Street with you, from stupid New Jersey, to stand in line for a stupid cupcake. Plus, you're kinda cute. Very cute, actually. My hot, sexy wife, who stands in line for a cupcake.

Me: Okay, Boo. You may go now. Good talk.

Don: Ten more seconds = ten little kisses. (kisses me ten times quickly, we both laugh) I love you, Boo. Gonna go stare at and play guitars now.

Me: Okay, I love you Boo. Stay in your guitar heaven, and I will meet you over there when I'm done here. I will be armed with cupcakes.

(About forty minutes later, after dragging him out of the guitar shop, where he could have remained until the end of time)

Me: So, what do you think of the cupcake? Isn't it amazing?

Don: No. It's a cupcake. It tastes like a cupcake. Let's go home, Boo.

"Home is that place, where our smiles met, where pancakes and records and coffee-pots brewed, deep inside forever. The door is always open,
And you will always be home."
- Matthew Dodgkin

FB Post: Just getting back from yet another "first date" with another new guy. Told him I love cupcakes, so he suggested we meet at a local bakery for cupcakes and coffee. When I got there, he was seated, had bought me a potted plant and a cupcake with "Hello" written in icing on it. I thought it was pretty cute. He stood for me when I entered the bakery, took my coat off for me, and pulled out my chair for me to sit. After our cocoa and cupcakes, we walked around the mall (because it's pouring outside), and then he took me for a late lunch. He even asked me stuff about Don, like how we met, and a few other things. Definitely a good sign! We will be seeing each other again soon. Yay!
LIKES: 89   COMMENTS: 55

FB Post: Just got home from date #2 with "Cupcake Man." A walk in the park, then back to his apartment for pizza delivery dinner and a viewing of an 80s cult classic "Better Off Dead." It was a pretty good night.
LIKES: 71   COMMENTS: 36

My Husband is Not a Rainbow

FB Post: Well, Facebook family, it's been a strange couple of days. The world of modern dating is rough. You think that you have connected with someone, or that something is going well, and then it's just over. Again and again and again.

Cupcake Man is no more. We had our second date Friday night, which I posted about here. Hung out at his apartment and ate takeout pizza and root beers on his coffee table while watching a movie. What I didn't mention in my last post was that his apartment was in a seedy building and neighborhood and looked a bit like Oscar the Grouch's might look, that he insisted on paying for the pizzas, and then emptied out his coin jar to scrape together money to cover it, and that his "coffee table" was actually an upside down paint bucket sitting on the floor. Also, he doesn't have a car, takes the bus everywhere, and I had to take him home on our first date. Despite all this, there was some making out on his couch. (He quickly shut the door into his bedroom, which looked like a bomb went off in it, and there was no way in hell I was getting in those nasty, dirty sheets anyway.)

Things seemed good when I left, and then today I had another first date with another guy I have been talking with on POF for a couple weeks now. This morning, I woke up to a text from Cupcake Man saying, "We should talk." So I called him, and he dumped me. He said, "This isn't going to work out." I told him I was a little bit surprised and asked if he could tell me why. He said, "We aren't compatible." I replied, "That's funny. We seemed pretty compatible when your tongue was down my throat while making out on your couch." I thought it was a hilarious comment. He sat there in silence. I asked if we could be friends. (Mostly because I didn't know what the hell to say. Usually I don't get dumped. Usually they just disappear!) He said that would be really awkward and declined. Then he said, "Okay, if there's nothing else ... Bye." And that was it. Shortest breakup call in the history of break-ups. I think it's a new record. Hey, at least he called me, instead of the other nine hundred guys who have ghosted me and just disappeared with no explanation.

A few hours later, I'm at a lovely restaurant having lunch with my new date that I've been talking to for weeks, who was so sweet and brought me TWO dozen yellow roses, my favorite. It felt like I was hanging out with my best friend. Like I've known him forever. The chemistry and the friendship vibe were both incredibly strong. He makes me laugh like crazy. And when I laugh, he says, "I love your laugh. You have the cutest laugh." Everything was so natural and organic. I told him what happened this morning with being dumped, and I ended our time together by saying, "Thank you for taking what started out as a really crappy day and making it into one that was really beautiful."

I have no idea what's going to happen with these dates I go on. Most of them dissolve into nothing after one or two meetups. But I post about them here to give people hope. Hope that if your person died, and you can't even think about dating again, that maybe one day you'll feel differently. Hope that other men (or women) besides your person will find you attractive again. Hope that you will be able to feel excited about something new again, even when you get your heart shattered way more than once.

Those of you who have been following my path since my husband's sudden death, know how clear I was about NEVER wanting to date, ever again. How the idea of someone else made me sick to my stomach, for over three years. Until one day, it didn't. So, if I can go from sick to my stomach, to truly believing in the idea of my next great love story, you can too. If that is something you want.

So please don't feel bad for me when I post about a new date, and then it ends up not working out. I'm okay. I have always believed in the magic of new beginnings. Things with Cupcake

My Husband is Not a Rainbow

Man didn't work out, probably because they weren't meant to. And I've been through much worse. And I have yellow roses. And today is a good day.
LIKES: 166   COMMENTS: 41

(3 hours later)
Dear Stupid Death Diary:

I am sitting on the floor in my bedroom downstairs, sobbing off and on, and trying like hell for my parents to not hear me. I'm cowering in the corner, rolled into a ball, and defeated. I am done. I am really, truly, done. I cannot do this anymore. How many times is this going to happen to me? Today, I was dumped. Twice. In the same day. Once in the morning, and once at night, for good measure!

I don't even know what to do with this anymore.

This morning, I was dumped over the phone, by Cupcake Man. Which was okay. We only had two dates, and he was probably right that we weren't compatible, so fine.

But then, I went on my first date with this beautiful man I have been connecting with for the past few weeks now. We have this incredible chemistry. We can't stop talking to each other. He told me from day one that he was going through a divorce. He and his wife hadn't been intimate in years and were slowly going through a complex separation and divorce. Anyway, I like him so much, and he likes me so much, and our talks are so deep and so profound, and so we decided to meet for lunch and just see what comes of it. So we did. Today. A couple hours after Cupcake Man dumped me.

Our time together was insanely beautiful. There was something profound about it. We had this great lunch, and then we sat in the back of his car in a nearby park area and played music on the CD player. Although I told him from the start that I would NOT, under any circumstances, sleep with a married man, even if it was only "technically" married but living apart - we had been talking about kissing for weeks. Building up to it in our playful minds. We both wanted to see if our chemistry was as strong in person as it was online. So we kissed, and it was heavenly. He couldn't keep his hands off me or stop telling me how gorgeous my eyes are. I felt so wanted and pretty. He asked me permission before he did anything physical. Even the tiniest thing. "Can I kiss your lips? May I touch your back?" It was this crazy mix of romantic and wild abandon. But as we were connecting and touching and holding hands and gazing into each other, something was happening. It was as if I somehow knew, that this would be goodbye. There was a look of sadness in his eyes, like he didn't want to let me go, but knew that he had to. After a few hours together, touching and kissing and holding each other, we parted ways. Nobody said the word goodbye, but it lingered in the air, as if it were fact. Still, I went home with my yellow roses and with a huge ridiculous smile on my face. My parents asked how my date was, and I floated out some word like "magical."

And then he dumped me. He said that upon returning home, he was hit with an incredible amount of guilt, because he is still married, and he needed to honor that and try to work on that and make it better. We texted back and forth a bit, and my heart was breaking in half as we did, because the connection I felt with him was so real and so special. I asked if we could meet and talk about this in person, or at least on the phone. He told me that hearing my voice again would be too tempting for him, and seeing me would be even worse. He said that his wife reached out to him for the first time in a long time, and that he wanted to work on his marriage. We went back and forth with a few exchanges, and then he told me that I deserved to be in love with someone who can give me their whole heart, and that he couldn't do that. He also said that if his circumstances should ever change, he would promise to look me up, and we would reconnect if it made sense for us both. He added, "I don't think that will happen though, because I have a feeling that me saying goodbye to you will open the door for that great man that deserves the beautiful and great woman that you are. I want that for you. You are going to find that beautiful love, Kelley. I know you will. And I know that Don wants you to have that. He wants you to have so much more than what I can offer you. I'm so sorry. I do think we were maybe meant to connect so that we could both help one another reconnect with love in some way. I need to repair my marriage, and you need to be available with an open heart when that amazing love comes into your life. Thank you for our time together. You will never know how precious it was to me."

I sobbed louder and harder as I read his last words to me that I would ever read from him, "I'm going to very nicely ask you to please stop contacting me from here on out. I truly hope that you will respect my wishes. I have a feeling that you will. Thank you." So now, I will respect his wishes, and just sit here and cry. What more is there to do?

June 14, 2017
Dear Dead Husband:

It will be six years next month, since you died.
So, I think that's more than enough time to conclude the following:
This widow thing?
This "you being dead" thing?
This "not what I signed up for" thing?
Yeah.
Not a fan.
I've decided I don't care for this.
I will, of course, keep trodding along,

Kelley Lynn Shepherd

keep finding new meaning in life,
keep helping others,
helping myself,
blah blah blah,
all that shit,
because what choice do I have really?
I would never end things.
It is not in me.
Even when I really want to.
Even when I'm just so tired of trying,
that I feel like I can't function.
I wouldn't end things.
I would not cause that pain,
to those who love me.
And I would not give up on life,
knowing,
that you would give ANYTHING,
just to still be here.
To be able to live your life,
with me.
So I won't do that.

But I just wanted you to know,
that this shit sucks,
and that even though the raw, horrific parts of grief
have mostly subsided,
NOW,
now is, in some ways,
even harder.
Because now I am living.
I am living again,
instead of just existing,
instead of just grieving,
instead of just trying to get through the day.
Living,
that's the hard stuff.

My Husband is Not a Rainbow

Who knew?
Searching for love.
The kind of love that I KNOW,
you want for me.
The kind of love that I deserve.
The kind of love that you would give me,
if you were allowed to still live.
You want that for me.
And I want that for me.
And that's how I know it's out there.
I just wish it would make itself clear.

I've been looking.
I've been dating.
And dating,
and dating,
and dating.
I've been dumped.
Hurt.
Betrayed.
Left.
Abandoned.
Cheated on.
Given the "you are beautiful and funny and amazing, but..."
speech.
Or the "You deserve love more than anyone I know. It just can't be with me" speech.
Or the all-time favorite "disappearing act,"
where they just exit my life with no explanation,
no reason,
no conversation about it.
Just, GONE.

Will you please help me?
Help me to find that person.
That person who will love and respect

Kelley Lynn Shepherd

and honor me,
the way that you did,
but differently,
because they, of course,
will not be you.
Please. Help. Me.
Put someone in my path,
Someone really, really great.

I love you.
But you aren't here.
In the way that I want.
Even though you ARE here,
Beside me,
Everyday.
I feel you now.
Everyday.
And I know that you want joy for me.
So I'm asking for you to help me.
I know I ask you to help me,
a lot these days.
But this is so very hard,
this life thing,
to do without you.
I haven't found anyone,
that sees my worth,
the way you did.
The way I now do,
because of you.
You made me see it.
There must be someone else
out there,
who sees what you saw.
And what I now see.

I'm tired,

My Husband is Not a Rainbow

and want to give up,
but love is everything,
and I feel too sad
and lonely
without it.

So,
this shit sucks.

And it's not just the dating.
It's the living.
I just wish things were easier.
I wish I wasn't struggling.
I wish money was a thing I had.
I wish I could stop stressing about finances.
I wish I felt more secure.
I wish I could afford to travel more.
To experience new places, new ways.
I wish I didn't always feel stuck.
I wish I knew what path to take.
I wish I had a clue.
I'm writing my book about you.
About us.
About your life and death,
and my life now.
And I feel like I don't know how to end it.
How do you end something like that?
I don't know.
There is no ending.
No big life lesson to learn.
I was hoping,
that by now,
six years later,
that the ending would become clear to me.
That I would have found new love,
or some big revelation to it all.

What I have found, is this;
The end, is the same
as the beginning.
You are still dead.
Forever.
And this shit sucks,
forever.
The End.

About 4 hours later / same day...

Hello there,

Hope you are having a good afternoon. I was checking my email, when suddenly my POF app said that I had a brand new match, someone who matched the qualities I was looking for. I said what the hell and clicked on your picture. If you read mine, you'll see that I love words. You don't have a ton of words in your profile, but the ones you do have seem carefully chosen and witty. I like that. But truthfully, and I hope this doesn't sound too out there, but I saw your profile picture, and there was something in your eyes. There is a story in your eyes, and it's a story I felt like I needed to know. I feel like you are someone that I want to know. It's a pleasure to meet you, I hope to hear back from you soon. I'm Kelley.

"There is a moment when you think you know,
something is new,
something has shifted.
Your heart wakes up,
And Love walks in." - Me

The Beginning (Again)

It was June fourteenth, 2017, and after being crumpled up on my bedroom floor sobbing over yet another painful ending, I happened to check my email, and there was a new match from POF. I clicked on his profile, and something about his eyes instantly grabbed me. I saw pain. I saw loss. Maybe I was reading too much into things, but I know pain, and I know what I saw. So I wrote to him. I reached out first. And then he wrote back. And then I wrote back. And then, for several days, I wrote back and he wrote back, and we asked each other a million questions about our favorite all-time concerts and the thing we were most proud of in life and our favorite place to have traveled. And my heart fluttered and danced and jumped each time I looked at my phone or computer, awaiting his next lengthy and well-thought out response. My heart was shattered, and I was terrified, but something - no, everything - about this felt different. And I couldn't identify what the feeling was, exactly, because I had never in my life felt it before. While my first conversations with Don Shepherd were certainly powerful, everything between Don and me moved in slow-motion, beginning with the foundation of friendship and slowly flirting our way into something much bigger. This thing with Nick was the exact opposite. It was like an earthquake - just instant and earth-shaking and jarring. This was "love at first type," and it had my full attention.

Although I was unable to collect our very first conversations to post here, (because POF deletes them after thirty days), we did switch over to Facebook messenger after only a few short days. We met in person on June twenty fifth, but a couple days before that, he used the "L" word with me. He said he knew almost immediately that it was love. I knew too, but I decided to wait to tell him in person. And when I did, the most incredible thing happened. Here is that incredible thing, plus some highlights from our intense exchanges during the first week or two of our talking, after we moved over to Facebook messenger and text:

Nick: I can tell that our story is going to be epic. It already is. Thank you for not giving up on love.

Kelley: I was so close to giving up. But something about your eyes. They told a story. You seem to know loss and pain.

Nick: I do. I will tell you the whole story at some point. In pieces. But right now, I will say that my sister Cathy died on her 33rd birthday, and both of my parents also died rather young. And I've been through a lot of things myself that we will get into as we get to know each other more. As I mentioned to you, I'm an Air Force vet with diagnosed PTSD, and my passion is helping other Veterans who are in Recovery from PTSD, depression, addiction. So yes, I know loss, and grief, and trauma.

Me: It's amazing that you're a fellow Air Force Vet, like Don. You are both the same age, and both spent time stationed in Japan during the same time period. And I had no way of knowing any of those details when I messaged you, because they weren't in your profile. I just knew there was something about you, that I needed to know you. Who knew there were all these parallels?

Nick: We were meant to connect. The universe brought us together. And I honestly didn't think I'd ever find something this incredible at this point in my life. So let's ride the hell out of this thing, okay?

Me: I plan on it. Took me way too long to find you.

Nick: What the hell were you waiting for?

Me: …for Cupcake Man to dump me.

My Husband is Not a Rainbow

Nick: ...or to buy a real coffee table.

Me: He needed to wait until his coin jar was full, so he could afford a bigger bucket.

Nick: Hey, an upside down bucket as a coffee table - that's classic. That's creative engineering right there. I'm forever grateful to Cupcake Man for dumping your ass. I'm thankful for all the dumb men that dumped you.

Me: There were a lot of them.

Nick: Thank you, stupid men! All of you!

Me: It's getting late...

Nick: Yeah. I need to say goodnight soon.

Me: You can't say goodnight YET.

Nick: Oh really? What do you have in mind?

Me: You're very competitive. I'm very competitive. In 1998, Don and I met this same way, online, but in a music chat room, through AOL - and we talked for 5 hours straight. You and I have now been talking/typing for 4.5 hours...

Nick: Ah, so we are 24 minutes shy. Bonus time. I like it. We can beat 5 hours.

Me: That's what I like to hear! And if we end up together, it won't be an epic ending for my book unless we beat Don's record... so we have to, really, for the sake of good writing...

Nick: Very well.

Kelley Lynn Shepherd

Me: So we must talk for 5 hours and 1 minute in order for this to be an epic love story.

Nick: I hope to be at least a chapter, not some obscure footnote.

Me: Well, if this is my next great love story, then we deserve our very own book. Step One is beating the 5 hour record.

Nick: It's on...

****

Nick: So I watched your TED talk. Absolutely amazing. Helps me to understand you better and also opened my eyes to a lot of things I hadn't thought about in that way before. It is one of the reasons I admire you so much. Because you use your pain and your struggles to help heal others, and because you are a woman who is changing the world.

Me: I'm trying. One person, one mind at a time...

Nick: You're succeeding. Dare I say it is just one of the reasons that I love you.

Nick: Did I scare you off? Not one of the THINGS I love about you, one of the reasons I love YOU.

Me: Wow! You didn't scare me off. Damn. Did you really just say that? That was brave!

Nick: You captivated my heart.

Me: Still brave. I hope you don't feel differently when we meet in person...

Nick: No way. Not possible.

My Husband is Not a Rainbow

Me: Did you sit with your finger on that text for 5 minutes before sending it? Lol. That "L" word - that's a huge thing.

Nick: No hesitation. Does it freak you out?

Me: Oddly enough, not really. I thought it would, but I can't stop smiling. I keep reading your text over and over and over. I feel the same, but I want to tell you for the first time in person, looking into your eyes. I'm overwhelmed, but in a really good way.

****

Nick: Hey beautiful. Thank you for finding it in your heart to love me. I know it isn't easy for you to do.

Me: I'm so thankful for us. Living is so much harder than existing. But so worth it.

Nick: Thank you for being so courageous and doing the hard work to get here. Today was incredible. Now I know for sure, after meeting you in person, twice, that the instincts and fast-paced connection is all true. You are an incredible woman.

Me: I'm still on cloud nine, hard to believe this is real, and yet I know it is this time.

Nick: Yes. This feels very different than past relationships.

Me: It IS different. We are both in a healthy place to have mature love. It feels different because it's the real thing, instead of something disguised as the real thing; like most of my past experiences after Don died.

Nick: At this crazy fast-paced rate we are going, we will be married by our 3rd date!

Kelley Lynn Shepherd

Me: Why wait so long?

Nick: Elope or big wedding?

Me: Ceremony at Fenway, reception later in the year at Yankee Stadium.

Nick: Live streamed on Facebook…

Me: …but of course!

Nick: We are brilliant. And I have to tell you that I have tears of joy right now for the way that you show me love.

Me: It is because I was loved by him so fully and beautifully, that I'm able to have found my new self, and I'm able to love you deeply today. That's how love grows love.

Nick: I owe a lot to Don. And then there's the whole "joining us on our 2nd date" thing. I'm forever indebted to him. The only way I can repay him, is to love you unconditionally, forever and ever.

Me: I'm more than okay with that.

"And you've been gone,
longer than we were together
and I think of you
and I hope wherever you are
and whenever you exist
and whatever you do,
you feel love
and
you remember me." - Rodney Ladino

Okay, So My Husband Might Be a Sarcastic and Smart-ass Rainbow:

So, on our second date, we kept things casual, and went to a local ice-cream place called "Meolo's." They have a big barn next to the ice-cream counter, and you can sit inside there on benches, chairs, and at picnic tables, and they have live music most nights. I had told Nick, before the date, that I wanted to tell him in person, face to face, that I loved him too. I had sort of said it in type, and he already knew how I felt, but I hadn't yet looked in his eyes and said, "I love you." On our first date, I was way too nervous to say it or to make it about that. Too much pressure. I also knew that when that moment came for me to tell him, I would be super emotional, because it would be the first time since Don's death that I could say it to someone with a hundred percent certainty that they loved me too, and that we were moving in a forward direction together. I could say it with a hundred percent bliss-full confidence, and I was very excited to do so.

We drove to the ice-cream shop and parked his car in the back lot. We sat in the car, gazing into each other's eyes, with our soft breathing as the only background noise. I got myself ready to say the words out loud, took his hands in mine, studying and memorizing the look on his face. The tears of joy, relief, and elation fell down my cheeks as I stated emphatically and finally, "I love you. I love you, I love you, I love you. I can't stop saying it. I love you so very much." I said it for him. I said it for me. I said it for all the numerous times and all the years I wouldn't get to say it to Don, ever again. I said it for all the many widowed people, my friends, who can't tell their person that they love them, just one more time. I said it because I could, I wanted to, and I was so beyond ready.

We fell into each other, and as I held him in my arms, and as the water fell from my pupils, and I collapsed into crying, the sky opened up and water collapsed from its ceiling, too. Everything went dark. Clouds loomed. Nature cracked. Thunder roared. Lightning struck. For real. It was just as crazy and unpredictable and terrifying and chaotic and wondrous as our instant connection. We sat inside the car, shocked by the storm our newfound love had created. Pounding rain, and then hail, shot out from above us. It was a real life, no joke, motherfuckin' storm.

A few minutes later, it stopped. The sky opened up a bit, and we got out of the car and got in line to order our ice-cream. As we were receiving our delicious bowls of dairy goodness, there was a commotion. Several people ran out toward the open sky and began taking pictures. There was mumbling and pointing and general excitement in the air. We walked out toward the night sky, I looked up, and there it was. Something I had not seen, literally, in the six years since Don had died. Everyone else on the planet seemed to see this phenomenon everywhere and all the time, but never me. I would never, ever see it in six years' time. And there it was. Right in front of me. With my new love, seconds after telling him that I loved him for the very first time.

A rainbow. And not just any ole' rainbow. A double rainbow. It was glorious. It was magic. It was love times two. The tears welled up in my eyes all over again as I quickly grabbed the nearest stranger in sight, begging and pleading and not making any sense as I stage-managed Nick to please stand next to me, because we NEED to get our picture taken underneath this rainbow. Nick looked at me like I was nuts, because I was, as he gently asked, "What's going on, baby?" Words that didn't connect or form any real structure came back at him in return with a rushed, run-on sentence: "It's a rainbow!!! Double rainbow!!! It's Don, but it's not Don, and everyone tells me Don is a rainbow, but I never see rainbows, and people have been sending me their rainbow pictures for six years now, because of this rainbow joke that I wrote about and told onstage - and now I

My Husband is Not a Rainbow

just told you I love you, and there's a double rainbow, and it's Don, and I can't stop laughing and crying, and my husband has the most amazing sense of humor! He waited six years to make his appearance to me as a rainbow, but wow - what a perfect way to do it! Baby, you just gave me the ending to my book. You and Don just gave me the ending to my book!!!! Thank you, Boo! Thank you so much!!!"

"Huh?" Nick mumbled back, most likely considering leaving me forever, because, clearly, I'm a lunatic who was in the midst of a nervous breakdown, rambling about rainbows. Also, I'm not sure exactly how much of all that I actually said out loud to him in that moment. But all of it was skipping around inside my muffled thoughts. "I'll explain later," I laughed through my tears. "Just stand here and pose under the rainbow with me, please." We both smiled, the strange man took our picture, and you can see the drawing of it below this story. For the real picture, and Nick's confused looking expression standing under the rainbow, go to my website, www.akelleylynnlife.com, and check out the Rainbow Slideshow on the About Kelley page.

A few minutes after the double rainbow sighting, Nick and I were walking along, finishing up our ice-cream, and I began to try and explain the rainbow story and the whole meaning behind it. I told him about all the many times in the past six years that friends would see rainbows, and I would just miss them. Sometimes by a few seconds. How my widow friends and I went to Niagara Falls while in Toronto for Camp Widow, and I literally walked away for twenty minutes, and they all saw this beautiful rainbow over the falls. I returned, it was gone. How everyone would send me their rainbow pictures, joking that it must be Don, after I told my story onstage about Don's coworker seeing the rainbow on the way to his funeral. I told him how in the six years since his death, no rainbows ever appeared anywhere for me. How Don would appear to me in literally a zillion other huge ways; a Penske truck, a train station, a coffee thermos, a Rainbow "Bridge," but never an actual rainbow. I barely scratched the surface of the details with the rainbow stuff, and told him I would get into the full tale later on, but the important part was he had provided the perfect, full-circle ending to my book. He paused for a second, then said, "That's a lot of pressure for our second date. I'm the ending to your book? Wow. That's really profound, and I'm honored, and a bit overwhelmed. I don't know what to say." I told him that, for me, the rainbow sighting, just seconds after me telling him I love him for the first time, was just confirmation from the universe and Don, of what I already knew. That Don had put him in my path, and that he was my next great love. And that when I decided to move back to Massachusetts to "finish my book," I meant that literally. I had no idea that by moving back home, I would be provided with all the content necessary to really, truly, finish my book in the most perfect of ways. I also told him that if he wanted to run away, now would be the perfect time to do it.

He didn't run.

He stayed.

When I got really sick with some sort of unidentified liver thing, just a few weeks into us dating each other, he didn't run. He took me to the E.R. He sat with me and held my clammy hand and looked into my jaundice, yellowing face and my deadened eyes and lied to me with love as he said, to make me laugh, "You look hot in that johnny! Should I ask the nurse to pull back the curtain?" He stayed.

And a week later, when I ended up back in the E.R. for the second time, just one day before the six year anniversary of Don's death, he didn't run. He looked into my eyes as I sat in that hospital bed on the verge of a panic attack, having flashbacks of the E.R. on July thirteenth, 2011, when my husband sat there in a tiny room, dead. He helped me to focus and center myself, and he told me that I was going to be okay. He stayed.

And the next day, when I was too sick and too weak to go out and do all the "Pay It Forward for Don Shepherd Day" acts of kindness I had planned, he went out with my mom, and they did all of them for me. He didn't run away because I wanted to honor my husband. He wasn't threatened or upset that I want to honor my dead husband. He is not widowed himself, and yet, he has never once asked or implied that I should forget about my husband or put my love for him away on some shelf to collect dust forever. He helped me to honor my husband, he did it for me when I couldn't, and he stayed.

Through my trauma and his own - through nightmares and triggers - through me saying I miss my dead husband ten thousand billion times - through hardships and challenges - through confusions and miscommunications - through everything we have endured, all of life's adventures; it has now been almost one year that we have been together, and he didn't run away. He stayed.

I cannot predict the future of us. I cannot say what our "lifetime" together will end up being. I cannot say when death might decide to enter full-force, like a tsunami, thrashing apart all of our pieces. I do not know how long or short of a story we will be granted. So far, our plan has been to "ride the hell out of this thing" for as long as we are privileged enough to have it. So far, it has been quite an adventure. There has been drive-in movies, butterflies, a garden's worth of roses, a Festival of Lights, New Year's Eve galas, a trip to a place called Florida (Massachusetts), kissing and giggling in the car like teenagers, a Red Sox/Yankees game, a play called "Love Never Dies," a Bridge of Flowers, a real-life Christmas tree in my basement bedroom, a Valentine's Day romantic getaway, tons of road

Kelley Lynn Shepherd

trips, our first Camp Widow together in another place called Florida (Tampa), and as many "I love yous" as I can safely squeeze into his big, caring heart. But these are all another story for another book. All that you need to know right here, right now, is that all of my dating heartache was worth it, because it led me, finally, to this beautiful man, and he is my person.

He is my person, and he stayed.

"Even after all this time, the Sun never says to the Earth, 'You owe me.' Look at what happens with a love like that. It lights the whole sky." – Rumi

My Husband is Not a Rainbow

Kelley Lynn Shepherd

The End (Again)

When I started writing this book, about four or five years ago, my writing was moving at a turtle's pace. All I knew, at first, was that I wanted to tell our story. I wanted for the entire world to know and fall in love with Don Shepherd, so they would maybe understand, even just a tiny bit, how impossible it was to lose him. And if he had to be dead forever at age forty six, the least I could do for him was to make sure he would live forever on these pages and in the hearts of many. I wanted this book to be evidence of our love, written in word and feeling and fact, for all to see that we were a thing that happened. I wanted to prove how powerful love really is, especially when you share it forward. I wanted to give him a legacy and start one of my own.

Then, as time went on, and the years rolled forward, I started to see how many people were comforted by or moved by words that I had written on Facebook or in my blog; and so it became important to me that the book would also help others who are hurting to witness first-hand through reading this six-year tsunami; that transformation from dark to light, hopeless to hope, death to life is possible. I included some of my grief counseling sessions to show a tiny piece of the brutally hard WORK it takes to move through this hell in a healthy way, and to show how complex and emotional it is to live and grieve at the exact same time. I wrote a lot about my dating experiences and my path to finding new love. I wrote about my struggles in losing myself, finding myself again, and then rebuilding myself in the aftermath of death.

When I started writing this book, and up until about a year ago, I had absolutely no idea that I would find love again. In fact, I had it set in my mind that I did NOT want the book to end with some rainbow and lollipop fairytale about me finding my next prince charming and now I'm okay forever and everything is wonderful. No. That is not the message here, that is not the point, and that is not what happened. What did happen, though, is quite profound. For the past few years of writing this book, I kept beating myself up and getting frustrated because I couldn't seem to get rolling with it. I couldn't seem to get past somewhere around the middle of the book. I couldn't focus. I kept stressing about where to go next with it and the ending. How the hell do I end a book such as this? It felt impossible to me, like there was no ending that would ever be good enough or brutal enough or strike exactly the right tone or get across all the messages and lessons I wanted people to know. Grief never ends, so how the hell do you end a book about grief and loss? I felt like the book could be three thousand pages long, and there would still be more to say. It continued to baffle me and weigh on me. Caitlin, in her infinite wisdom, would tell me over and over, "The ending will become clear when you arrive there. You don't know what the ending is right now, because right now is not the right time for you to finish the book." She would often say things like this to me, and at the time, it always felt like a riddle I had to solve, or like something Yogi Berra (or Yoda) might say. But then, looking back later, she would usually be right.

It made total sense. I couldn't finish the book for all those years, and I was stuck in the writing process for all those years, because it wasn't meant to be finished yet. Several things had to happen before the book would be in a place to come to an end:

I had to sit inside the raw pain and the grief and the loss and let it marinate for a while. I had to come to terms with the idea that everything I knew in my world was gone. The life I knew had ended, and it was going to take a very long time for me to sit with that.

I had to grieve all of the many pieces of this loss. I had to come to terms with probably never being a mom and with Don never getting to be a dad. I had to grieve the family we would never have, the dreams we wouldn't get to share, the future and the years and the life experience and the longevity of a marriage that I would never know.

I had to sit inside and analyze and repeat and walk through and crawl through all of my many emotions when it came to Don's death. I had to repeat the same stories to my grief-counselor fifty times, or ask her for the hundredth time how long it was going to hurt this badly. I had to do a lot of waiting. "Sit with it." I had to first hate my grief, get angry at it, be frustrated with it, deny it, hate it some more, want to murder it, tell it go the fuck away, become accepting of it, realize it will be a part of me now, make peace with it, let it teach me things, hate it some more, and become friends with it again.

I had to forgive everything and everyone. (This is something I'm still working on, but I'm getting better.) Forgive Don's father for not being a good dad to him, for not giving him the love he so desired, and for not sharing his medical history. Forgive his mother for her controlling and manipulative nature and for making Don feel guilty all the time for things he shouldn't have had to feel guilty about. Forgive all the people who walked out of my life when Don died. All the ones who disappeared on me or who told me to get over it or move on. Forgive the ones who stuck around, but judged me harshly or treated me with anything other than kindness. Forgive myself for deciding who I would allow into my life, going forward, and for choosing to let some relationships go, because they no longer put me in a healthy state of mind. Forgive myself. Forgive myself.

Forgive myself. For not always being the best wife in the world. For taking our happy life for granted and becoming lazy and complacent. For not saying "I love you" enough. For not being able to predict his cardiac arrest and somehow stop it from happening. For knowing how many times and how many ways he saved me everyday, and not being able to save him, the one and only time he needed saving. For not being able to stop death from coming.

I had to find my way again. Figure out what works in this new life and what didn't. I had to stay in our apartment for a while. Then I had to move. Then move again. I had to make decisions on my own and be at peace with the consequences. I had to struggle and get new jobs and leave old ones. Switch grocery stores. Switch banks. Stop driving by the hospital where he was dead forever. Figure out how to work and function and speak to other humans again. Change the way I did holidays. Change my traditions. Make new ones. Keep the ones that don't make the pain worse. Try new ways. New roads. Make a billion errors, then try again. Keep getting up. Figure it out.

I had to work through major issues with anxiety, panic attacks, PTSD. I had to talk through the rape and understand how to use the tools that Don gave me that made me feel safe, and make them a part of my healing. I had to comprehend how to not be so terrified living in a world where Don could no longer protect me. I had to get through the nightmares, the terrors in the middle of the night, alone. I had to find new strategies and new ways of coping that didn't involve melting into my husband's arms and sobbing. I had to take all of the love and comfort that Don gave me, and then figure out how to save myself.

I had to get healthier. Spiritually, emotionally, physically. I had to stop drowning my grief in mashed potatoes and cookies. I had to get my A1C number down from 6.4, to its current 5.8. I had to stop gaining grief weight and slowly lose weight instead. (forty six pounds over the last sixteen months, since moving back to Massachusetts) I had to start walking, begin exercising, get outside more. See the universe from a different perspective. The weights of grief are always slightly lifted when surrounded by beautiful nature. I had to learn how to think of myself as worthy, beautiful, and deserving of love. (also still a work in progress, but much improved) I had to go from beating myself up, to lifting myself up.

I had to shift from a place of wanting to die, to not wanting to live, to merely just existing, to actually wanting to live, to feeling joyful and excited about recreating my one and only precious life.

I had to shift from believing in nothing, to believing in possibilities of something.

I had to shift from connecting God to religion, to connecting God to Love.

I had to shift from feeling like Don was dead forever; to knowing that Don is dead forever, but also alive forever, each time our love is shared forward.

I had to shift from feeling like Don was nothing and nowhere, to literally *feeling* Don in everything and everywhere.

And here's the big one…

I had to shift and change my relationship with Don Shepherd. This took a lot of time, a lot of crying, and a lot of soul-searching. It took a lot for me to be open enough and ready to make that shift, and to fully understand what it was. For a long time, I held onto being married, feeling married, still feeling like a wife. Caitlin never rushed me into changing those feelings and told me they would begin to shift when my soul was ready. Of course, remaining in that state of mind where you feel married to a person who is dead, is certainly an option. For a long time, I considered it. But the truth is, staying in that place was like staying inside our tiny Jersey apartment, surrounded by all of Don's "stuff," feeling like I was being suffocated by a life that no longer existed. I couldn't breathe in that space. Once Caitlin told me that I *never ever* had to let go of Don, and that the goal was only to shift the relationship I had with him into something that allows me to live a purposeful life where he always remains in it with me, I felt such a sense of relief.

But changing my relationship with him meant coming to terms with the idea that I would no longer be his wife, but his widow. And even though, technically, that change happened on July thirteenth, 2011 - it didn't begin to happen within my soul until just a couple years ago. It was my biggest hurdle. It was extremely hard, probably one of the toughest things I have ever done. It felt excruciating to make that shift. That was why the very idea of "someone else" made me physically ill for so long. That was why I didn't date or get intimate for five years. That was why I stayed stuck in place when it came to the thought of any future relationships. In my heart, in my core, I still felt married. I still wanted so much to be married. It hurt so badly that my future of being Don's wife was being ripped away, that my heart wanted to cling onto the present and just pretend we could be married forever. I had to shift from seeing us as husband and wife, to seeing us as having a forever soul connection. A shift from seeing him as my partner, to seeing him as more of a spirit guide. A shift from being forever "in love" with him, to loving him forever.

It was, by far, my most heart-wrenching task. I kept asking Caitlin how I would know when it was time to make this shift. She would tell me that I would just know, and that I was already doing it. The pace at which I was doing it was often so slow, that it seemed like standing still. It's like when you lose a significant amount of weight over a long period of time. The people in your everyday life often do not notice it. But then you go visit some people who haven't seen you in six months or a year, and they all yell out enthusiastically, "Wow! How much weight have you lost? You look great!" That is how my grief tsunami felt and still

Kelley Lynn Shepherd

feels. I go at a turtle's pace with all of it, but when I finally make those shifts into something new, I'm in it full force.

Once I was able to make that shift from husband and wife, to soul connected - it was like a lightning bolt struck my world, and suddenly, I felt Don *everywhere.* There were more signs than ever before, more ways in which he was trying to reach me, and more places that I would simply feel his presence. But it was more subtle and more gigantic than all of that. Suddenly, every single thing I was doing in my life felt connected to Don. I felt more connected to Don, probably more than ever before. My relationship with Don had, in some ways, become more profound and deep through death. He was in the sunsets, the foliage, the ocean waves, and inside the rhythms of the music. He was in my laughter. In my accomplishments, my goals, my dreams. I feel him right this second as I write these words. It's a comforting, knowing feeling. It lifts the air around me and makes everything lighter. It feels as if I have a secret something that only Don and I would understand. I could try and explain it to you, but you really wouldn't get it until your husband is randomly dead, and you go through all the hard grief work to get to where I am at now. I will tell you it is a phenomenal feeling, and constantly makes me smile.

I will probably keep sprinkling his remaining ashes (they don't ever GO AWAY!!!) in the places we loved, on special days - but the thing is; I no longer *need* to. He is right beside me, every second. And if you would have told me that three or four years ago, I would have wanted to punch you in your eye-socket, because I didn't feel it. And I didn't feel it, because I hadn't done the hard grief work yet, and my soul wasn't ready to feel him in that way. Now, I have done the work, my soul is ready, and my dead husband will be a part of my life forever. His life, his love, and his death changed me forever. And the most beautiful part of that, is this: I get to decide *how* death changes me. I had no control and no say in my husband's sudden death. I have all the control and all the say in how I live my life forward. I can allow his death to turn me bitter, cold, and angry. Or I can take the love he had for me and share it forward. I can tell his story and use it to echo the idea that love never dies. I can use my life, in the aftermath of death, to help walk others through loss. This is now my passion. This is my calling. This is what feeds my soul. For what could be more important than shining your light on someone who still sits in the darkness? What could be more meaningful than being able to say to someone who can't find one reason to keep living: *You will be okay.* What could be more uplifting than providing evidence of hope and joy for someone who feels completely and utterly hopeless and joyless? Honestly, I can't think of a more beautiful way to spend my time.

So, all of the above elements had to take place in order for this book to have an ending that made any sense. It was never about whether or not I found love again, although that is a glorious thing. It was about finding myself again, loving myself again, and creating myself again. It was about no longer fitting in the world and creating the world I long to fit into. It was about figuring out life after loss, and then using what I've learned to help others heal.

This is a love story. Actually, it is multiple love stories, all blended together in a wonderful, gorgeous tapestry. The love of a partner. The love of family. The love of friendship. The love of our beloved pets. The love of life, and then the rebirth of life in a brand new way. The love of possibilities. The love of hope. And ultimately, the love of one's self and the love of all the many ways to give and receive love.

This book ends, and begins, with love.

The end is the beginning; the beginning is the end.

Kelley Lynn Shepherd

"I wouldn't wish my pain on my worst enemy, But I'd wish my perspective on the world.'
– Michelle Steinke-Baumgard

Dear Dead Husband:

Thank you for the never-ending ripple effect and gift of love that was created on the day that you decided to choose me and to love me. Because you have loved me so well, and because I have worked so hard at finally figuring out life without you physically here with me, life has rewarded me with abundant joy. It is a joy that I have fought for, and a joy that comes with complication and strangeness and very real fears, but a joy so beautiful in its brightness and glare, that it cannot be denied.

Thank you for being the foundation for all of the love I will give and receive, going forward. Thank you for putting this beautiful man in my path, so that I could find him and see the story in his eyes. Thank you for coming to my rescue yet again, just four hours after my last 'Dear Dead Husband' letter on June fourteenth, where I begged you to please help bring me back to love. You are so much a part of my life, and you always will be. For without your beautiful love, I would not be where I am, right this second. I would not be this person that I have become and am still becoming.

I will meet you inside the rhythms of the music, and I will continue to honor your legacy and live my life in color. It is my honor and privilege to do so as your widow, and you deserve nothing less.

I'm doing what you asked of me, when your voice spoke clearly in my ear two years ago: "Step into your life." I was listening. And each time you send me yet another sign that you are with me, and that I'm on the right track, and that you want me to be safe and happy and loved, I will always, always listen. Thank you for loving me when I didn't know how to love myself. Thank you for saving my life, over and over and over again, until I finally figured out how to save myself. And most of all, thank you for sending me more love - in this silly, chaotic, emotional, brutal, wonderful, beautiful, tragic, precious adventure, that we call life.

I love you.

Kelley Lynn Shepherd

Last Words

So, the other day, after lots and lots of overthinking and stressing, I had finally made the decision to end the book with one last "Dear Dead Husband" letter, as seen above. But I went to bed that night, and my dear dead husband had other plans. It's been a long time since I've had a dream/visit from him. One of those beautifully profound dreams, where he comes to visit me from the other side, but he looks human and alive. He always has a soft, vague light around him, and he always shows up to comfort me in some way. This time was a little bit different. This time, he gave me the ending for the book. The ending that *he* thought was perfect. As if showing up as a sarcastic rainbow wasn't enough - he just had to have the last word on these pages too. When I woke up from this dream/visitation, I could not stop smiling. I think after reading this poignant, funny, smart exchange that took place in soul-connection form, you will be smiling too.

I'm lying in my bed at home, half asleep, when I feel the familiar touch of his hand, gently caressing my shoulder.

"You awake, Boo?" His words are soft, but loving and safe and warm.

"You came to visit me!!!" I sit up in my bed, ecstatic to see his face and speak words to him. "Is it because I've been missing you so much lately? Doing all this writing about you, about us, it makes my heart ache to talk with you again. I'm so glad you're here."

"I'm always here, Boo. You know that now. You feel that now, right?" He says the words as his right hand reaches over to pet Sammy and Autumn. They look at him and purr loudly, knowing exactly who he is, and remembering all of it.

My Husband is Not a Rainbow

"Yes. I feel you all the time now. It's incredible. Feeling you, and knowing you are a part of everything always, has made me want to live again. When I didn't feel you anywhere, living was torture. Now I look forward to all the new ways in which you show up."

"You mean like this dream?" he says, laughing and looking at me with calm eyes.

"Yes. Or like a smartass rainbow after six years, trying to scare my new love away."

He laughs harder now. His shoulders shake, and his head moves all around. "That was classic! Hey, I had to test him, Boo. Make sure he was the one. I figured if the crazy rainbow sighting and telling him he was the ending to your book didn't send him packing, then he's probably gonna stick around a while. He's a good guy. A really good man. I think we would have been friends. You know, if I wasn't dead and all."

My eyes well up with tears at the beauty and weirdness of my dead husband setting me up with my new love. "I love him, Boo. The kitties love him too."

As I say this, Don gets up and walks over to his old recliner chair on the other side of my bedroom. He sits in it, lays all the way back, and sighs happily. Just like old times. Sammy and Autumn run to him, purring against his chest and arms. "I know they do, Boo," he assures me. "I'd never connect you with a guy who didn't love our kitties. When he sits in my chair and they follow him and climb on him, it makes me smile a lot. It helps me know that everyone is safe and okay. That's all I've ever wanted for you."

"And you don't mind another guy in your precious chair?" I say mockingly.

"Nah. I don't need a recliner chair anymore. I'm dead. Just tell him to keep his mitts off my guitars. That's serious business." He laughs at his own joke.

I tease him and respond with, "Oh, I see. So he can have your wife, but the guitars are off limits? I see where your priorities lie now..."

He gets a bit more serious, and he looks at me thoughtfully. "Come here, Boo. Come sit next to me." I get out of my bed and walk over to my desk, and sit in the office chair next to the recliner. He takes my hand and places it into his as he speaks these words:

"You're not my wife anymore, Boo. I know that you know that, and I know how hard it was for you to really understand that and accept that, and I'm so sorry. I know we were supposed to get our forever, and it just didn't work out that way. But I still love you forever, and because you were my wife, you will be my widow forever. So even if you remarry, we still get to be connected forever. Just in a very different way than we both thought. But it's no less meaningful or beautiful, okay? What we had, and what we have now, is the most beautiful thing in the world to me. It always will be. I need you to know that. And because it's so beautiful, I want you to have even more beautiful love, because you deserve all the best things, Boo. It makes me so happy to know you are being loved."

At this point I start crying, because I always start crying in these dream visits. "I love talking to you, Boo. I don't ever want to stop talking to you."

"Then don't. Please don't. You should talk to me as often as you feel like it, always and forever. Here's the deal: if you keep me close, I'll never be far. And you have done such an amazing job with that already. And I know there are many things that you still struggle with, and that one of the biggest things is that you can't remember the days or weeks or hours leading up to my death. You hate that we didn't get any last moments or last words. That we didn't say good morning or I love you or anything at all. I know that hurts you so much, and you still don't have any sort of peace with that. That's why I came here tonight, to visit. I came here to have the last word in your book and to give you some peace about us not having any 'last moments.'"

My crying continues, but it's softer now. We both stand up from our separate chairs, and he holds me in his arms, so he can embrace me while he tells me these words:

"When this book is done, and you finally get that first physical copy in your hand, I know that you might feel intense sadness, because I'm not here to celebrate with you. And because you think it's a book about me being dead. You think it's a book about my death and your grief, and that in the end, I'm still dead forever, and all you have is this book. But that's not true at all, Boo."

"It's not?" I ask, on pins and needles to hear the answer.

"No, it's not. You said it yourself, just a few pages back. This is a love story. So, when you hold it in your hand, you need to feel how proud I am of you. I mean, really *feel* it. You need to feel how this story of unmeasurable love will touch everyone who reads it, and how all that love will be shared forward. You need to remind yourself that nobody ever really dies when we tell each other's stories."

I step back from him a tiny bit, so I can look into his eyes as I ask my next question. "Okay. That makes sense. I can do that. I can try. But why didn't we have any last moments? Why couldn't I say 'Good morning, Boo-Bear?' Why didn't I get to tell you that I love you one last time?"

He meets my gaze and wipes my tears and tells me with absolute certainty and care: "We didn't have any last words or moments, because with us, there is no such thing. We didn't say goodbye, because from now on, we will only say 'Hello.' There was no finality to our last encounter, because it isn't over. It's never over, Boo. It is always just beginning.

This is a love story.
And true love stories,
never, ever end."

**The End
(but not really)**

Our famous Christmas card; taken in 2005 after Don moved to NJ to start our life together.

Wedding Day Kiss. 10/27/06 at The San Souci of Sea Cliff, NY

Kelley Lynn Shepherd

Burger King crowns on our honeymoon.

Our last family vacation. 2010. Cape Cod. Left to right: Me, Don, mom, dad, David, Jen, Brian.

Don playing "airplane" with our nephew, Brian.

At the U.S. Open Tennis Tournament. 2002. Our first day meeting in person, after over 3 years of talking long-distance.

Kelley Lynn Shepherd

Don, helping me set up a wedding reception, back in my Wedding Planner days. He was always helping me.

The kitties and Don, napping.

My Husband is Not a Rainbow

How Sammy slept almost every night; wrapped around Don's head.

Us.

Kelley Lynn SHEPHERD

Pay It Forward for Don Shepherd Day Hall of Fame

On the one year milestone of Don's death, July thirteen, 2012, I hosted the first ever "Pay it Forward For Don Shepherd Day." I have done this each year since, on July thirteenth, and will probably do this forever. Don was the kindest man I ever knew, so spreading kindness in his name is my way of celebrating his heart every July thirteen. The premise is simple: Perform an act of random kindness. Take pictures if you can. Then tell your story on my Facebook wall. All the stories then go into a blog I write called "The Epic Blog of Kindness," where everyone can read them. Each year since his death, I have received a hundred or more kindness acts. The ripple effect of kindness is astounding. There are hundreds of stories. Here are a just a few of my favorites. To read all the Pay it Forward blogs, go to www.ripthelifeiknew.com .Thank you so much to every single person who has ever participated in Pay it Forward Day. It has turned July thirteenth, for me, from a day of unspeakable sadness, into a day of light and love. The following stories are in no particular order:

"I took on a new guitar student today at no cost, an 11 year old boy with no hope of being able to afford lessons. I will be loaning him an acoustic guitar to play on until he gets the hang of it, and then, when it's time, I will buy him a nice electric." – Norman Paulsen, Jamundi, Columbia.

"My husband and I donated needed supplies for the staff and kitties at Austin Pets Alive, a no-kill shelter here in Texas. I was so very blessed to have known Don, worked with him, and be his friend. I miss him everyday. By sharing your sorrow with so many, you have touched more lives than you really know. I'm honored to call you my friend, and I know why my friend Don fell so madly in love with you." – Maria Mantek, Texas.

My Husband is Not a Rainbow

"I am donating a full crib, car seat, and 5 boxes of infant and children's clothing and books to a local center for abused women and their children". – Stephanie Miller Morales, Texas

"I have been a volunteer with the Dunstable Summer Concerts for about 5 years now. Last year, we made a connection with someone that could get the RE/Max hot air balloon to come to one of our concerts. Their only request was that we donate all proceeds collected to a local cause, charity, or person in need. As the day got closer, I read about Pay it Forward, and suggested The Sharing Network Organ Donation as our cause. It was one of the largest turnouts that we have ever had, with over 300 people descending on the Common. We had signs letting people know what their donations would be going towards, and from there, over $400 was "raised". (That's a hot air balloon joke.)" – Laura Rothman, Massachusetts.

"I took a down on her luck friend out for lunch, and I also paid for an old woman's groceries in front of me, at Don's all-time favorite grocery store – PUBLIX! Her grocery items, you'll be happy to know, included Don's favorite Publix Sub." – Gin Malvita, Florida.

"Two acts of kindness on Don Day from me. Number One: Because I feel like I know Don personally through you, I paid a visit to New Jersey, to visit a friend who was having a lonely day. I took the NJ Transit to visit my friend, whom I love, and we did suburban things; mostly sat by the town pool for hours – BECAUSE THERE IS NOTHING TO DO IN THE SUBURBS!!! I love my friend and spending time with her is always a joy, but I was mindful the entire day about Don and what a good, good man he was. His love for you transplanted him to NJ, as my love

Kelley Lynn Shepherd

for my friend gets my ass on the train to spend a long day in the burbs. By the way; my friend, like Don, also thinks NJ is lame.

Number Two: I have a good friend in Los Angeles who is an animal lover, like Don. She rescues animals (literally goes out with a team when calls come in about abused or abandoned animals) and saves them. She also adopts those dogs and cats who are unadoptable because of age or illness. I made a donation to Elayne Boosler's "Tails of Joy" for her and sent her a tote bag so that she can spread the word out there about www.tailsofjoy.net. She is a woman whose husband died when he was only 46, and she was just 40. Like you. She is a writer/comedian, like you Kelley, so I thought she would be the perfect person to include in my thoughts about Don on this wonderful, new holiday." – Caitlin Kelly, New York.

"Today, in honor of my friend Kelley Lynn creating Pay It Forward for Don Day, on the one year anniversary of the sudden loss of her dear husband, Tails of Joy helped pay for 22 dogs to be transferred out of a Miami, Florida pound, and into a rescue that will heal them and find them new homes. We did the same thing for cats yesterday. Here is the message I left on the Chip In Board: "Thank you for all that you do. xoxo Elayne Boosler, Tails of Joy (in honor of Don Shepherd Pay it Forward Day)." – Elayne Boosler, California

"John and I stopped at the bank to get 50 one dollar bills. I typed up a short note that explained Don Day, and paper clipped to each dollar with the title: "Doling out Dollars at the Dollar Tree For Don's Day." My mom, dad, son Zane, and niece McKenna met me at the Dollar Tree to help me. I had 52 dollar bills and notes ready. We stood in front of the store and the kids gave the next 52 customers dollars, as I explained Don Day to each person. After several dollars, my son started sharing the

My Husband is Not a Rainbow

story too. Many were teary-eyed and wanted to hear more. Some were just thrilled to have an extra dollar, especially the kids. Several people said they wanted someone else to have their dollars, and they would pray for Kelley and Don instead. One man yelled: "There should be cameras here! This is the kind of thing that should be on the news! Thank you!" Four different people said they used their dollar to buy school supplies for needy children – already paying it forward. (The Dollar Tree was collecting donations for a charity inside the store.) Some shared their own stories and thought Kelley's idea was amazing and said they would tell others. When we passed out all of the money, we went inside to pick out some school supplies to donate in memory of Don. A little boy came running up to me to show me he had picked out a Thomas the Train puzzle. He was so thrilled, and his mom said he was telling everyone in the store what he was buying with his dollar. Who knew how much happiness a dollar could buy? I do know that we had a lot more than $52 worth of blessings, fun, conversation, smiles, and everything else, thanks to Kelley and Don. My son has decided that every July 13th we will be doling out Dollars for Don Day. This may be our best family tradition yet!" – Kelli Renee Williamson Fockler, London United Kingdom.

"My family and I are paying it forward in Don's honor by volunteering 30 hours at the 33rd Annual National Veteran Wheelchair Games. I am working with wheelchair-bound vets who are competing in various sporting events, much like the Paralympics. My family attended the opening ceremonies, where 600 veterans took part. It was a humbling experience. I know Don was in the Air Force, like myself, and I know he would be humbled by the courage, strength, and hope of these athletes, many of whom suffered injuries while in combat. So many heroes who exemplify the true meaning of "never leave a comrade behind." I am quite sure that Don would feel the same way."
- Alicia Gill Rossiter, FL.

Kelley Lynn Shepherd

"We put together an entire bedroom set from IKEA for an artist friend who just moved to NY and is having her own struggles. While this may seem lame, keep in mind there was no air-conditioning on the hottest day of the year, and you can imagine the annoyances of deciphering IKEA instructions for putting together an entire bed." – Andrew Block and Thom Christensen, NY.

"I was struggling to think of some way to pay it forward. It had to be special. I know it sounds crazy, but for some reason, sending you flowers from Don just came into my brain suddenly, as if he was asking me to do so. I think Don's spirit is really strong. I can't explain sending flowers to someone I've never even met! I hope this brings you some comfort." – 'Cindy' Shepherd (Don's sister, who I did finally meet in person, a couple years later.)

"Kelley, I was very happy and honored to do this for you and Don at our bands show. Our band, Rubber Soul / Beatles Tribute Band, put Don's guitar on display throughout our show at Legends Club in Fitchburg. At the beginning of set two, we played "Something", written by George Harrison, in dedication to Don. I know George was his favorite Beatle, and that was his favorite Beatles song. Your love for him will never die." - Ron DiNinno, MA

"The Gotham Comedy Foundation, GCF, is the nonprofit, charitable affiliate of The Gotham Comedy Club in NYC. The mission of GCF, is to bring humor to those who most need it, one laugh at a time. GCF sends stand-up comics to hospitals, nursing homes, senior centers, and social service agencies at no cost to these community partners, to bring laughter to the sick, aged, and lonely, as part of it's humor therapy program. As part of paying it forward, Kelley Lynn will be working with us on these programs, and performing as one of our stand-up comics, beginning this fall. Kelley Lynn is a member of GCF and take part in benefit performances at Gotham Comedy Club, as well as volunteer performances off-site." – Bill Drewes, Founder of GCF www.gothamcomedyfoundation.org)

"Today on the train home, a woman wanted a window seat so her niece with Downs Syndrome who is from back East, could have a view and see the ocean. I gave up my seat with a huge window view, to her. Hearing her excitement was so rewarding!" - Donna Cramer, CA

"My PIF was two-fold. I bought a raffle ticket for a project supporting our Vanderbilly/Guitar.com friend Davido, who suffered a stroke weeks ago. The $ raised will go to David and to help his recovery. Part 2 - if the ticket wins, I will donate the prize - a beautiful electric guitar - in Don's name, to our local high school's music program. RIP brother Don." - Larry Manch, TX

"I decided to dedicate my entire Saturday to Don. I even spoke of him when I helped prep the dinner at 'Not Bread Alone', the soup kitchen I volunteer at often. That afternoon, I visited a woman from our church who is unable to leave her apartment. I had Don's kindness on my mind all weekend long." - Aunt Debbie, MA

"Brought lunch for some unsuspecting EMS workers on Long Island. They got a surprise delivery of pasta salad, filet mignon sliders, and veggie slaw, all in Don's honor, from our 'Sage Bistro' restaurant. They were so grateful. I got the feeling that they don't get recognized or appreciated very much, which made it all the more rewarding for me." - Sarah Chamberlin, NY

Kelley Lynn Shepherd

"I got the reminder email Friday for PIF Day, and knew I'd be going to the Yankees game the next day, July 13th. My 1st thought was to put his name up on the big screen, so I start doing my research, and it says they need a weeks' notice. I call, no answer. I email them a request, and it's approved! Can you believe it? And all proceeds go to charity. While at the game, we took video and pictures of Don's name up there on the screen. They put him in the Anniversary category, as in "Angel-versary." There were 3 sets of names, and his name came up last. And while all the other names were shown for only a few quick seconds, Don's stayed up there, all alone, for a LOT longer. It was awesome. It felt wonderful to do that for Kelley, as I know Don LOVED the Yankees and it was something they loved together. She was so happy and crying at the same time. When I emailed her to let her know my plan, she was so sweet to say to do something in my family's name too, as I had lost my brother and father a few years ago. But I do many special remembrances for them, and today was Don's day. So, during the 5th inning - his name was displayed in Yankee Stadium. With the pictures, it will forever be in lights on his Anniversary, which I call his 'Angel Day.' My favorite pay it forward." - Laura Ameruso, NY

My Husband is Not a Rainbow

Pictured Above: Don's "Return" to Yankee Stadium.

Kelley Lynn Shepherd

Thank You

There are so many people who have helped me in so many ways, the past seven years, as I crawled through this tsunami. If I thanked everyone individually, it would take up a whole new book. Literally. So, I did my very best to make this list of thank yous specifically about book-related things. And a big, fat thank you to every person who has supported me in any way as I continue to move through life, in the aftermath of death. Thank you.

To mom and dad: For loving Don like a son and for never telling me to "get over it." For giving me the literal space to write this book and to tell my story. For always making me feel like, and know, that I am forever welcomed back home. I was able to complete this book, finally, because of you.

To my brother David: For showing up at mom and dad's place for weeks, almost every night, and working with dad to literally build me a bedroom/home office/writing space. For doing this after your own long work day, and for creating a room that feels inspiring, warm, and comfy. For loving Don like a brother and for being a loving brother to me.

To Misty: For gifting me your old laptop when mine died randomly, after my husband died randomly, and I had a meltdown over badly functioning technology. Your laptop was the one I used to type and write out the first half of the book. Thank you for your generosity and thoughtfulness.

To Casandra; For gifting me a gift card for Best Buy, where I purchased a brand new laptop a couple years ago, when the keyboard on Misty's started acting weird, and I began having a meltdown. I used this laptop to create a lot of the writing pieces and blog pieces that ended up in this book. I also want to thank you for being so incredibly generous, creative, and supportive during my book campaign. Your kindness floors me sometimes, and you are a really beautiful soul.

To Kevenn: For creating the perfect cover art in my book, and for taking people's rainbow pictures and creating gorgeous sketches for our "coloring book inside the book" concept. For being my editor, my friend, and the person I would go running to whenever I would have a meltdown about font size or uploading pictures or page size or any other boring tech thing that I hate. For putting up with my crazy. You are a talent beyond talents, and I'm so honored you are a part of this love project. www.kevenn.com

To Ray: For doing all of the lettering/style for the book cover title. Your work is beautiful; the same as your heart.

To the first Sarah I ever knew: For being my best friend through childhood and letting our friendship grow, develop, and change into adulthood. For the countless hours sitting in restaurants, dissecting apart life and death. For teaching me about a completely different kind of loss, that too often is overlooked or completely ignored. I truly wish you never had to teach me, or anyone. www.infertilityhonesty.com

To everyone at Adelphi University: Nick, Barbara, Maggie, Brian, Kerry, Michael. My friends and colleagues. For understanding why I needed to walk away from my job of sixteen years that I loved so I could finish this book and find my new path. For being there and helping me out during the early days of grief when I was totally overwhelmed.

To my acting and comedy students throughout the years: Thank you for inspiring me in all the ways that you do. Thank you for supporting my TEDx talk and sharing it through the internet with so many of your friends. Thank you for forcing me to be creative, when I often felt like I could barely function. Get out there and tell your stories!

To my "girls" over at Brides.com/Pearls and to Don's buddies over at Vanderbilly/Guitar.com: the two places where Don and I both met all of our "imaginary friends." The friendship, support, and generosity that has come from the members of both of these groups, often by people who have never even met Don or myself in person, is amazing. Thank you to Don's music friends for not forgetting him and for keeping him alive through music. He would absolutely love that.

To Michele, with one L: For writing your beautiful Foreword in my book. As always, your words are loving, thoughtful, and inspiring. For being one of my very favorite people in my life after loss. Mostly, for giving me a family, a place to inspire others through laughter, and a reason to believe in hope again. I honestly don't know what I would do without your beautiful friendship. www.soaringspirits.org

To Caitlin: Where do I even begin? I feel like you are deserving of your own book, because you have done so much for me, in so many different ways. For your Foreword in my book, which was wonderfully and poignantly written. For allowing me to share snippets of our dialogue/sessions in this book, and for always making SO MUCH DAMN SENSE! For telling me to "sit with it," when it came to me being impatient with my various grief struggles. For always taking my calls, my desperate emails. For helping me when it seemed like no-one else would. For showing me that I would be good at helping people process their own grief emotions. For going to the Christmas Tree with me all those times. You went above and beyond, and you mean the world to me.

My Husband is Not a Rainbow

To Armando: For taking charge of the "perks" section of my book campaign. It was incredibly helpful for me to not worry about the shipping and distributing of everything. For being a great friend and supporter of my writing in general, and for all the many ways you find to help me and to help me honor Don.

To Sarah: For putting together the moving and touching video "story" that appeared in my book campaign launch. I could have never created the beauty that you did with your talents. For inspiring me daily with your friendship, your strength, and your healing spirit. Mommy. www.streanor.com

To Kathryn: For your extreme generosity toward my book and for always sharing forward my writing pieces. For being a caring friend and for welcoming me into your in-person support groups for widows and widowers on Long Island, even though I lived in New Jersey. For being the first ray of light I felt on this widowed path, after meeting so many new friends at your group. If you're widowed and looking for support and friendship, Kathryn facilitates lots of various groups on Long Island and is one of the best people you could ever know. Go to www.widowednotalone.com

To Nick (my boss at my part-time job) at Pelletier Properties, Mark Kavanagh, and everyone at Keller-Williams North Central Office: For allowing me to use the office space in Westminster, during lots of weekends and after-hours, to write my book in a quiet, non-distracting place. And for allowing me to have such a flexible schedule so that I could spend so much time writing.

To everyone that knew Don and shared stories about him for the book or to help me remember. To my friend, who probably doesn't want to be named, who knew Don way back when: thank you from the bottom of my heart, for reading his autopsy report with me, word by word, until I understood that he did not suffer or feel any pain when he died. For years, I tortured myself about that, and after our talk, I felt instant peace. Thank you for giving me that.

To Susan and Vilma at Red Stocking: For giving me a chance with that directing gig, even though we all knew I had no clue what I was doing. For taking me to the ER (Vilma), instead of to rehearsal that one night. If you didn't have perfect timing showing up at my place, minutes after I passed out, who knows if I would have been okay or not. Thanks for being troopers during my moody, earlier grief days.
www.redstockingrevue.org

To the many, many people who gave one or more quotes to be scattered throughout the book and help tell the truth about love, grief, and loss. My original plan was to use song lyric quotes, but my editor informed me that we may run into copyright issues doing so. I was devastated, until I thought up the idea to use real quotes from all my many talented friends. The way your words have been woven into this book's story, like a tapestry, is so very profound and meaningful to me. Thank you for your collective and important words.

To my friends in the widowed community: My tribe. Thanks for getting it when nobody else does. For walking beside me and shining the light. For sharing my writings, sharing your stories of love and loss with me, and being a loving part of my life in the after. You are family to me.

To everyone at Sunstar Ambulance, Vanguard Healthcare, Hackensack Medical Center, and Petsmart/PAWS, and Petsmart Adoptions; especially Don's manager who found him collapsed, gave CPR, and called 911: Thank you for the comfort you all offered me after his death. Please know that he spoke of all of you with great fondness.

My Husband is Not a Rainbow

To Mary; for taking care of our kitties when I had to go and get out of the sad apartment. For telling me your rainbow story, which became the title for my play, my stand-up workshop, and this book. Who knew, that your story would create an endless, ongoing, loving, hilarious revolution???

To Mara, my Queens roomie and friend: For putting up with my weird writing schedule and my grief moods. And for buying Cookie Butter Sandwich cookies. You are evil!

To my love, Nick: For understanding how important this book is to me, sitting with me during my crazy emotions, and for supporting me 100%, the whole way through.

And to Don, for showing up AGAIN as a rainbow, on April 30th, 2018, the day I finished writing the book. Your timing was hilariously poignant. Knowing that you are proud of me, it means more than everything.

Kelley Lynn Shepherd

Contributor Thank You Wall

Once upon a time, a long time ago, back in 2014 or so, I did a little "crowdfunding" campaign in order to have the funds needed to be able to publish this book in the beautiful way I wanted. I knew I needed a community of people to help, and you all came running to support me. I will be forever grateful for all the many, many, many people who made the existence of this book possible. During the campaign, we had "perks" for specific donations. One of those was having your name listed as a contributor on the back pages of the book's thank you section. The following people named below are just a small percentage of the number of people who actually contributed to this love project. A good majority of people wished not to be listed in the book or chose to remain anonymous. Whether you are listed below, or one of the many who remain a mystery to the public, I thank you from the bottom of my heart, forever.

Jarlyn Philips, Bilal Mian, Jean Ann Garrish, Brett Alyse Clark, Kenny Altman, Annegret Eiermann, Barbara E. Jones, LaNita McLeod, The Revelant Family, Brenda L. Sieglitz, Stephanie Allen-Potupchik, Joshua Caldwell, Jon Fursh, Vera Bridges, Molly Fisher Foster, Kat Tamayo, Vicki Garcia, Jen Niemi, Dave Niemi, Beth Hensley, Dianne Bissonette, Iris Donitz, Patrick Burchill, Holly Soria, Roseann Kurdilla, Cynthia Boyd, Jamie Neally, Stacey Riggs, Ben and Rebecca Garrith, Aunt Debbie, Christine and David Niemi.

We Remember

During my book campaign, early on in the writing stages, I knew that I wanted to end the book with a big gigantic list of LOVE. I wanted to create pages and pages of all the many names that were loved, and continue to be loved, by just some of the many people who contributed to make this book happen. The names listed on the following pages are in no particular order, other than the order in which that supporter/contributor emailed me to give me the name of the person they wished to remember. These contributors chose the "We Remember" perk for their contribution - which was to have a deceased loved one's name listed at the end of the book. Seeing this many names, all together, one after another, doesn't make me sad. It represents what happens when we share love forward. It is powerful. This list is evidence of love being timeless and unstoppable in its power. Love grows love.

Mauna Lou Raymond
Walter Smith
August (John) Corrales
Timothy Hennessey
Mark Idzerda
Novice Stikeleather
Gary Campbell
Ken Rostkowski
Tony D'Alessandro
Al Zwicker
Jacob Thomas Milnes
Irene Morrison
Ray Cramer
Ken Gehle
Fred Mastromarino
Mary Moringiello
Denise Ryan

Ken Raymond
Margaret Smith
Trina Fischer
Karen Cameron
Sonja Hicks
Vincent Moore
Giovanni Pariente
Neal E. Shepherd
Ron Kim
Richard Levenson
Al Casey
Euclides Solivan
John Wilson
Gertrude and Arnold Beachum
Edna Mae Calkin
Annette Martino
Mike Derrickson

Kelley Lynn Shepherd

Ethan Chin-Kuchler	Gladys Zayas Ortiz
Mary Rivera Rodriguez	Robert Rivera
Olivia Bella Perez	Baby Rivera
Diona Parish	Bernie Capizzo
Christopher Picco	Papa Spinelli
Mel Olson	John Thuesen
Mildred Jackson	Dan Durocher
Robert Christian Lea	Jason Coombe
Jacquelyn Shaw	Frederick Shaw
Ed Litrenta	Grandma Rosemary Barbieri
Grandpa Placid Barbieri	Robert Raymond Fowler III
George Kehayas	Ann Marie Catlin
Roy Hjalmar Baken	Marc Straight
Steven M. Turner	Edward M. Robinson
Paul L. Belshe	David Johnston Stevenson
Thomas L. Sterner	Arlene Buckley
Grace Renode	Rex Wheeler
Nick Simone	Michael Johnston
Mike Johnston	Greg Shaw
Dana Nova	Chad Hendrix
Fr. Michael Lewis	Vern West
Lavern Alcock	William Alcock
Kevin Edward Boitson	Ron Knope
Wayne Price	Blanche Price Strunk
Tobias Looper	Simon Gilby
Eileen Foard	Sean Zeevy
Kenneth Hart	Nick Kay
Grandpa Joe Farquhar	Bruce Farquhar
Joseph Sporacio	Joseph Ross
Cheryl Darcy	Michael Ray Hensley
Beverly McNeil	John McNeil
Sean O'Connell	Christie LoPorto
Steve Norbeck	Thomas Phelan
Catherine Phelan	John Paccione
Evelyn Falcone	Grandma Mary
A.J. Moretti	Kevin Petersen

My Husband is Not a Rainbow

Kurt Boucek
Justin Kaan
Lewis Aronson
Michael E. Gaff
Rose Dauenhauer
J.W. Dyer
Carolyn Cawley Silvernale
Jessyca Lyn Katz
Annette Martino
Shirley Fisher
Mark C. Tremper, Sr.
Joseph Meechan
Harmon Heidt
Dan Braun
Tommy Owens
Arturo Burgos
George Izzo
Bill Hathaway
Steve Norbeck
Helen Branco
Frank "Chief Taofi" Fanene
Carlo Lanzillotti, Jr.
Joseph Branco
Joseph Ruzalski
Donna Scarpa
Bill Whelan
Claudia DeStefano
Anthony Lombardo
Jeanne McCotter
Joseph Alex Hath
Karen L. Wilson
Madison Delgado
Steven Ross
Ryan (Joe) Boduct
Mike Jennings
Saul Altman

Lois Stephens
Bella Schreiber-Bassoff
Margaret Lunn McGrath
Michael Kurdilla
Warren Dauenhauer, Sr.
Paul B. Silvernale, Jr.
Cary Pugh
Rose Marie Guardascione
Glenn Foster
Mort Fisher
Nancy Dello Russo
George Worner
David Z. Smith
Gregory Bruce Bjerg
Eric Sanguinetti
Pedro Sanchez
Mike Deighton
Kurt Boucek
Sean O'Connell
Yolanda Lanzillotti
Frank Fanene
Christopher Lanzillotti
Therese Henry
Kent Ownby
Dorothy Lasar
Robert Klein
Bill Hampl
Elizabeth Lombardo
Thomas Bermingham
James Louis Poulos
Melody Delgado
Leonardo Hernandez
Marion Tepper
Corey Rosentel
Marion Altman
Richard Valente

Kelley Lynn Shepherd

Al Valente
Rick Deggelman
Kay Monahan
Karen Cameron
Paul Cassidy
Dennis Murray
Rhoda Lally
Martha Hodge
Brett Douglas
RoseMarie Revelant
Finn Nobel
Darina Nolan
Geoff Clifford
Beloved Husband Mot
Amanda Ross

Nana (Frances) Vecchio
Fred Skillman
James (Jim) D. Eggers
Eva Kotovnikov
Robert Renode
Cathy Mucciarone
Jodi Shelton Godinez
Bill Tamburro
Greg Bjerg
Colby Diller
Rita Magnussen Hunt
Albert Dennis Raia
Terri Hammill
Brooks Cross
Arnel Andaya Pagaduan
Felix Hernandez
Evelyn Falcone
Bjarne Rasmussen
Glenn Hosler
Jessica Haggerty Harris

S-i-l Corey
Mary Lou Kenchelian
Sergio "Big Daddy" Villanueva
Eugene Kelly
Susan Reilly
Richard Murray
John Lally
Lawrence (Larry) Monaco
John O'Connell
Carsten Nobel
James D. Bishop
Kuth Williams
Adeline P. Kelly
Matthew Ross
Ralph G. Roman, Jr. Robert
Bernard Cullimore
Philip Hernandez
Jim Scott
Ernest Spencer
Chuck and Eve Wheeler
Christie LoPorto
Steve Duncan
Don Jones
Andrew (Drew) Ridge
Rob Lea
Poppa Fraser
Dustin May
Doug Ferguson
Melissa Killeen
Uncle Jack Burchill
Adrian Marcus Gutierrez
Joseph Rivera
Maria DeLecce
Barry David Oliver
Donald (Duke) Gregg
Wayne Fisler

My Husband is Not a Rainbow

Charles Anthony Caspio
Matthew Puleo
Cynthia Maxeiner
Eddie K. Smith Jr.
Verdie Katherine Smith

Josephine Virginia Caspio
Elena Prokay
Virginia Fredrickson
Marilyn Szalay
Theodore Francis Smoak

Sarah Chamberlin and Julio Valasquez's unborn children

My Extraordinary Denise Marie (Janikowski) Krewal

Kelley Lynn Shepherd

We Remember (Fur-baby Edition)

Clio Fuzz, and Angus (Gus)
Orion
Cleo, Caesar
Nissi
Wile E., Callie, Jerry
Kimba, Cha Cha, Lucy
Shadow, Daytona
Phoebe, Minnie, BoJo
Meatball

Dewey, Boy
Taz, Emmy
Rocky, Brandy, Sonny
Sparky, Tigger, Hansel and Gretel, Sadie, and Kiwi Branco
Ben, Sam
Motorhead, Woodstock
Guiness

Buster, Lola, Lily Fane Lally

Trixie, Gogo, Ratty
"Lucy the Lou" A.K.A. Wonderdog Raia
Pierre LeVuFrancais
Copper
Ammon
Carter Caspio-Smith

Simon, Sam, and Tigger

Sierra, Emily
Bud W., Draco, Girlie, Waggy
Ginger, Sasna, Lilly Coombe
Simon, Roscoe, Jag
Pebble, Lucky, Haberdasher
Oliver, Callie, Munchkin
Isabelle (Izzy), and Sweet Ginger Shepherd
Lucy, J.J., Max Petersen
Becky, R.J., Benny
Psandhix
Tuvok

Bill and Navajo Rupp
Jack and Blue Valente
Crabby Abby, Fearless Fred, Kitty Kennedy
Midnight, Sunshine, Digger, Wally
Mandy Bluebonnet
Sacha Gallo

Tiny
Donatello
Lucy Caspio-Smith

About the Author

Kelley Lynn is a writer, actor, speaker, comedian, and grief coach. This is her first book, which hit Number One for new Releases in the Grief and Loss category on Amazon.com in its first weekend and also Number Three in the Amazon Best Sellers for the Grief and Loss category. Her TEDx talk, "When Someone You Love Dies, There Is No Such Thing as Moving On," can be found on YouTube and has currently been viewed over half a million times. Kelley hopes to keep speaking and writing about living life in color after loss and to keep offering her one-on-one "from grief-to-life" coaching sessions. She would also very much like to be offered a role on "This Is Us," since she is obsessed with that show and has a lot of unwanted but personal knowledge on the topic of grief.

To book Kelley as a comic, speaker, or actor; or if you are interested in grief coaching sessions, you can find all information at her site: www.akelleylynnlife.com To see the real rainbow photographs that Kevenn T. Smith based his rainbow sketches on, go to the bottom of the About the Book page and check out the Rainbow Slideshow.

Kelley was born in Groton, Massachusetts, moved to NYC at age 18, and lived there for 26 years before relocating to Fitchburg, Massachusetts, where she currently resides in her parents' home with the two kitties that she and Don adopted years ago.

Kelley is a creator, a realist, and a widow. She hopes to move out of her parents' basement, and from there, begin to change the world.

Kelley Lynn Shepherd

This book ©Kelley Lynn Niemi 2018

Made in the USA
Coppell, TX
22 July 2020